THE
COLLEGE
PRESS
NIV
COMMENTARY

1 CORINTHIANS

THE COLLEGE PRESS NIV COMMENTARY

1 CORINTHIANS

RICHARD E. OSTER, Jr., Ph.D.

New Testament Series Co-Editors:

Jack Cottrell, Ph.D.
Cincinnati Bible Seminary

Tony Ash, Ph.D.
Abilene Christian University

COLLEGE PRESS
PUBLISHING COMPANY
Joplin, Missouri

Library of Congress Cataloging-in-Publication Data

Oster, Richard.
    1 Corinthians / Richard E. Oster, Jr.
       p.   cm. — (The College Press NIV commentary)
    Includes bibliographic references.
    ISBN 0-89900-633-7
    1. Bible. N.T. Corinthians, 1st—Commentaries. I. Title.
II. Series.
BS2675.3.O77 1995
227'.2077—dc20   95-35431
                                                         CIP

FOREWORD

Since the past few decades have seen an explosion in the number of books, articles, and commentaries on First Corinthians, a brief word to the readers might help them know what to expect or not to expect from this commentary. This commentary is intended for use by studious lay people, Bible teachers, and seminary students. Most scholars and specialists in the area of New Testament will probably find this commentary's treatment of 1 Corinthians and its problems too elementary. Because of the intended audience for this work and the constraints of length, the user should be aware of certain acknowledged limitations. There are at least four of these:

1. This commentary does not pretend to look at every problem, real or imaginary, which has caught the eye of previous scholarship.

2. The commentary does not attempt to cite continuously the interpretations of leading Christian thinkers as they have written on this Pauline letter.

3. Interpretations are given on individual passages without always citing the full evidence and without working through the attendant arguments, either for or against particular views.

4. Only a moderate number of footnotes have been used. In addition, the vast majority of the secondary literature cited will be English language and will, when possible, be in book form. The non-specialist for whom this commentary is intended has little interest in or access to technical materials, journal literature, or foreign language materials.

Those who wish to study this letter of Paul in more detail should look to some of the more technical commentaries (e.g., Gordon Fee, *The First Epistle to the Corinthians*).

I owe a special word of thanks to two individuals. My friend Gail Brady graciously typed the entire manuscript of this commentary for me. My friend and colleague Prof. Allen Black read the entire manuscript for me and saved me and my readers from more than one instance of an inappropriate choice of words as well as an occasional overstatement.

I dedicate this volume to my parents who shared with me over the years their own faith, hope, and love.

A WORD
FROM THE PUBLISHER

Years ago a movement was begun with the dream of uniting all Christians on the basis of a common purpose (world evangelism) under a common authority (the Word of God). The College Press NIV Commentary Series is a serious effort to join the scholarship of two branches of this unity movement so as to speak with one voice concerning the Word of God. Our desire is to provide a resource for your study of the New Testament that will benefit you whether you are preparing a Bible School lesson, a sermon, a college course, or your own personal devotions. Today as we survey the wreckage of a broken world, we must turn again to the Lord and his Word, unite under his banner and communicate the life-giving message to those who are in desperate need. This is our purpose.

ABBREVIATIONS

ABD . . . *Anchor Bible Dictionary*
AUSS . . . *Andrews University Seminary Studies*
BA . . . *Biblical Archaeology*
BAGD . . . *Bauer, Arndt, Gingrich, Danker*
BAR . . . *Biblical Archaeology Review*
BiblThecSac . . . *Bibliotheca Sacra*
BJRL . . . *Bulletin of the John Rylands Library*
BTr . . . *Bible Translator*
CMM . . . *Introduction to the New Testament by Carson, Moo, L. Morris*
ChrSt . . . *Christian Standard*
DPL . . . *Dictionary of Paul and His Letters*
ed. . . . *edited by*
EQ . . . *Evangelical Quarterly*
ExpT . . . *Expository Times*
HTR . . . *Harvard Theological Review*
JBL . . . *Journal of Biblical Literature*
JSNT . . . *Journal of Studies in the New Testament*
JETS . . . *Journal of the Evangelical Theological Society*
JTS . . . *Journal of Theological Studies*
n. . . . *note*
NovT . . . *Novum Testamentum*
NTS . . . *New Testament Studies*
RevEx . . . *Review and Expositor*
TB . . . *Tyndale Bulletin*
TDNT . . . *Theological Dictionary of the New Testament*
TS . . . *Theological Studies*
trans . . . *translated by*
WThJ . . . *Westminster Theological Journal*

INTRODUCTION

METHODOLOGY

The text of Scripture known as 1 Corinthians has provided a well from which believers have drunk for almost two millennia. This portion of Scripture has served the church as a resource for theology, for homiletical exposition, for pastoral issues, and more recently as a source for reconstructing social dimensions and dynamics of early Pauline Christianity. Whatever else one wants to say about 1 Corinthians, it cannot be doubted that it has had a significant impact on the Christian church.

Notwithstanding the necessity and value of this diversity of perspectives and interpretive methodologies which have come across the stage of Christian history, this present work is more narrowly focused in its approach. This work is primarily a historical-exegetical commentary, the goal of which is to understand and set forth the ideas, doctrines, and feelings Paul communicated in the letter of 1 Corinthians.[1] The phrase "ideas, doctrines, and feelings" is not intended to describe an "intellectual history" of the great Apostle. Rather, Paul's ideas, doctrines, and feelings, as recorded in 1 Corinthians, are engendered and evoked by a series of practices and beliefs, diverse in themselves, coming from individuals and groups in the church of God at Corinth.

A decision to write a historical-exegetical commentary brings with it several assumptions and commitments.

1. This means in the first instance that the feelings, doctrines, and ideas of Paul must, as far as possible, be understood in the historical framework, both in which he wrote them and in which

---

[1] In general see Gordon Fee, *New Testament Exegesis,* rev. ed. (Louisville: Westminster, 1993), p. 27; Douglas Stuart, "Exegesis," in the Anchor Bible Dictionary, eds. D.N. Freeman et al. (New York: Doubleday, 1992), vol. 2, pp. 682-688.

the first readers lived. A historical-exegetical approach has little in common with simplistic attempts to modernize Paul, to recreate him after the image of western Christianity. To be sure, every practicing believer knows firsthand the need to bring forward, with God's help and wisdom, the meaning of the ancient text into the modern world. How strange it appears, however, when those who wish to contextualize the Gospel in the modern setting have not invested the time and effort to first learn what it meant in its original context. Just as a good translation of Russian literature into French requires that one be familiar with both languages, so a good translation of the ideas of Paul's letter to the Corinthians into modern idiom requires a competent grasp of the original meaning of this letter as well as the modern world.

2. A commitment to a historical-exegetical methodology means that one must always recognize that Paul's letter to the Corinthians is an occasional document, arising in the first instance as direct responses to ad hoc issues and problems in the lives of believers living in a certain region of the Roman Empire, at a specific time, and under particular historical and cultural circumstances. Since the historical method infers that Paul's commands, arguments, and instructions were given in direct response to the issues raised by the lives and ideas of the Corinthians, one must openly acknowledge that 1 Corinthians may not address every issue that we, living two millennia later, hope it would. In fact, 1 Corinthians was not even adequate or appropriate for addressing the problem in all the Pauline churches. I am certain, for example, that the churches of Galatia would have been perplexed to receive 1 Corinthians as a solution to their specific problems. Indeed, even at Corinth it had to be supplemented by 2 Corinthians.

Not only does the historical method help restrain us from foisting our own agendas and ecclesiastical problems upon that small group of believers who lived at a particular time in Roman Achaia almost 2000 years ago, it also serves as a restraint for those who would twist the Scriptures and put forth their own ideology masquerading as exegesis. Time and again commentators have found a theology or doctrinal imprimatur in the text of 1 Corinthians which, even if generally true, has little in common with Paul's own intention and goals for this letter. Throughout the centuries preachers and theologians have strolled through the cafeteria of 1 Corinthians, appetite whetted, looking for some word, idea, or verse to place upon the plate from which they feed the church. At some point this kind of pragmatism in handling Scripture, which is driven by a variety of appetites, must be labeled as malpractice, and the student of Scripture needs to obey again the pastoral admonition to become "a workman who does not need to be ashamed and who correctly handles the word of truth" (2 Tim 2:15).

Even though a historical-exegetical method is the underpinning of this commentary, it is in no way the final task for the church in the interpretation of 1 Corinthians. Rather, the historical-exegetical approach should be the first step, and a necessary one, which is followed by many other steps taken by believers who, through the course of their journey, translate the manifold and variegated message of 1 Corinthians for the contemporary and global church of Jesus Christ. The individual tools and methods used in this process of contextualization would hopefully come from the guidance of God as well as study in the traditional theological disciplines of homiletics, systematic theology, pastoral theology, ethnotheology, and the like.

THE LETTER OF 1 CORINTHIANS[2]

DESTINATION

The letter of 1 Corinthians was sent by Paul and Sosthenes to the congregation of believers in the city of Corinth. This is in contrast to 2 Corinthians, which was written not only to believers in

---

[2]Compared to other letters within the collection of Paul's letters, there is not very much debate among scholars about the introductory matter (e.g., date, destination, authorship, etc.) of 1 Corinthians. This commentary will generally follow the conclusions reached by D.A. Carson, Douglas Moo, and Leon Morris, *Introduction to the New Testament* (Grand Rapids: Zondervan, 1992, henceforth CMM, *Introduction*) and W.G. Kümmel, *Introduction to the New Testament*, rev. ed., trans. H.C. Kee (Nashville: Abingdon, 1975), pp. 269-279.

Corinth but also to believers in the province of Achaia, of which Corinth was the capital (2 Cor 1:1). The content of 1 Cor 5:9 "I have written you in my letter not to associate with sexually immoral people" makes it evident that the letter of 1 Corinthians is not Paul's first written communication with the church at Corinth since he here refers to a previous letter he had already sent them and which they apparently misunderstood (5:9-11).

DATE

Even though the Acts of the Apostles was not written for the purpose of providing a historical framework for the Pauline Corpus, there are instances where Acts and facts from ancient historical records do supplement the letters of Paul.[3] One very important way in which Acts supplements the less specific material in the Pauline letters is in regard to chronology.[4] Without the chronological framework of Acts, it would be much harder to know how to arrange in sequence materials from Paul's letters and to assign dates to them. It is our good fortune to be able to assign dates to about five episodes mentioned in Acts, and thereby, assign relative dates to parts of Paul's correspondence.[5] One of these instances is the case of Acts 18 where Luke narrates the beginning of the Pauline mission in Corinth. At that point we have firm evidence for the date of the Christian mission based upon supplemental historical data. In particular, Acts indicates that Paul's work at Corinth took place while Gallio was the pro-

---

[3]Karl Donfried, "Chronology: New Testament" In *ABD* vol. 1, pp. 1011 & 1022.

[4]L.C.A. Alexander, "Chronology of Paul." In *Dictionary of Paul and His Letters*, eds. G.F. Hawthorne et al. (Downers Grove: InterVarsity, 1993), pp. 119-123.

[5]Donfried lists Edict of Claudius (Acts 18:2); Administration of Gallio (Acts 18:12); Reign of King Aretas (Acts 9:23-25; 2 Cor. 11:32-33); Famine under Claudius (Acts 11:28); Death of Herod Agrippa I (Acts 12:23); Proconsulship of Sergius Paulus (Acts 13:7); and Paul before Felix and Festus (Acts 23:23-24:27) "Chronology," pp. 1020-1021.

consul of Achaia (Acts 18:12).[6] This Roman official, who was the
brother of the Roman philosopher Seneca, is known from ancient
Roman literature as well as archaeological data. It is this latter
realm of evidence which helps specify the time of his career when
he was proconsul in Corinth.[7] This would put Paul's work at Corinth and his appearance before Gallio in the early 50s. Acts 18:11
indicates that Paul worked in Corinth for 18 months; this means
that Paul's correspondence in 1 Corinthians would have occurred
in approximately A.D. 55.[8] While some interpreters have attempted to get even more precise with the dating, it seems that
A.D. 55 is as specific as the evidence can support.

PROVENANCE

Paul was actually not far from Corinth when he wrote
1 Corinthians. First Corinthians 16:8 points decisively to a site on
the eastern side of the Aegean Sea, in Ephesus, on the western
coast of the Roman province of Asia. Travel between large port
cities such as Corinth and Ephesus was frequent and relatively
easy in the Roman world.[9] Consequently, it is no surprise to find
Corinthians visiting Paul, and Paul and his co-workers making
visits from Asia to Corinth.

---

[6]A helpful introduction to Gallio is given by Klaus Haacker, "Gallio." in
ABD vol. 2, pp. 901-903.

[7]Jerome Murphy-O'Connor. *St. Paul's Corinth*. Text and Archaeology.
Good News Studies, 6 (Wilmington: Michael Glazier, 1983).

[8]CMM, *Introduction*, pp. 264-265.

[9]The sea voyage from Athens to Ephesus took approximately two weeks
when Cicero traveled there in the summer of 51 B.C. Cicero, however,
wanted to spend the nights on land so each night his ship stopped at an
island. Normally, the boat trip from Athens to Ephesus lasted only four
to five days. Lionel Casson, *Travel in the Ancient World* (Toronto:
Hakkert, 1974), p. 151.

ROMAN CORINTH

The Greek city of Corinth had suffered defeat at the hands of the expanding Roman Republic in 146 B.C.[10] The archaeological evidence does not support, however, the idea that in the ensuing years all life and Greek influence vanished from this conquered and partially desolate site.[11] While the Greek Corinth was clearly defeated, it was not totally deserted in the decades following 146 B.C. When Julius Caesar, shortly before his assassination in 44 B.C., reestablished the city as a Roman colony, it would have quickly become a city which was dominantly, but not exclusively, Roman.[12] Consequently, any study of Paul's letter to the church of God at Corinth must take seriously the fact that Paul was addressing a city which had been, since 44 B.C., a Roman colony (*Colonia Laus Iulia Corinthiensis*).[13] Roman colonies were typically established as outposts for promoting Roman culture, religion, language, and political systems as well as providing lands for retired Roman soldiers. And even though Corinth was located geographically in Greece, there is no doubt that Roman mores and ideas impacted the local populace since, as Aulus Gellius noted (2nd cent. A.D.), Roman colonies "seemed to be miniatures, as it

---

[10]A general treatment of this can be found in Victor P. Furnish, "Corinth in Paul's Time — What Can Archaeology Tell Us?" *Biblical Archaeology Review* 15, 1988, 16-17.

[11]Many classical scholars and New Testament scholars have had a precritical attitude toward the ancient literary tradition that Corinth was totally destroyed in 146 B.C. and remained desolate until 44 B.C. The sources for this spurious literary tradition and the archaeological data that refutes it have been conveniently assembled by James Wiseman, "Corinth and Rome I:228 B.C.–A.D. 267," in *Aufstieg und Niedergang der römischen Welt* (henceforth ANRW). Edited by H. Temporini and W. Haase (Berlin: Walter de Gruyter, 1979) II.7.1: 491-496.

[12]The large percentage of Latin rather than Greek inscriptions from early imperial history in this direction; cf. the helpful observations by Ben Witherington, III, *Conflict and Community in Corinth: A Socio-Rhetorical Commentary on 1 & 2 Corinthians* (Grand Rapids:Eerdmans, 1995), pp. 7-8.

[13]Many interpreters have falsely concluded that the Greek culture of old Corinth was still dominate in the first century since Paul's letter to the Corinthians was written in Greek. If this were correct, how is one to understand that Paul's letter to the Romans was also written in Greek?

were, and in a way copies" of the Roman people.[14] Therefore, Corinth possessed all the appropriate Roman laws, magistrates and officials.[15]

Because of Corinth's mercantile character and important geographical location, it quickly attracted new residents from throughout the eastern Mediterranean. Consequently, by the time of Paul's arrival in Corinth, almost one century after its reestablishment as a city, the population would have included in not only Romans, but also Greeks, Jews, Egyptians, Syrians, etc.

ORIGIN, STRUCTURE AND CONTENT OF 1 CORINTHIANS

Even though there is not a consensus among interpreters regarding the exact nature and causes of the problems which Paul treats in 1 Corinthians, there is general agreement that the letter is organized around the cluster of problems which Paul is striving to remedy by his apostolic instruction.[16] The letter is basically a series of smaller units of thought, each of which seems to be directed to a particular aberration in the beliefs and/or practices of the Corinthians. Paul's style in the letter is to acknowledge the existence of a sin or problem, address the sin or problem, and then move on to the next one.

---

[14]Aulus Gellius, *Noctes Atticae* 16.13.9. *The Attic Nights of Aulus Gellius.* Loeb Classical Library (Cambridge: Harvard University Press, 1961) vol. 3, 181. "For they [i.e. colonies] did not come into citizenship from without, nor grow from roots of their own, but they are as it were transplanted from the State and have all the laws and institutions of the Roman people, not those of their own choice. This condition, although it is more exposed to control and less free, is nevertheless thought preferable and superior because of the greatness and majesty of the Roman people, of which those colonies seem to be miniatures, as it were, and in a way copies."

[15]A serious perusal of the inscriptions given by Allen B. West, *Corinth*, Vol. VIII, Pt. II, *Latin Inscriptions 1896-1926* (Cambridge: Harvard University Press, 1931) and John H. Kent, *Corinth*, Vol. VIII, Pt. III, *The Inscriptions 1926-1950* (Princeton: American School of Classical Studies at Athens, 1966) makes evident the Roman character of Corinth's civic and governmental institutions.

[16]John Hurd and CMM *Introduction.*

Paul's information about these various problems at Corinth did not come from firsthand knowledge of his own nor through inspiration. The majority, if not all, of Paul's information about the various issues with which he dealt in the letter came most likely from two distinct human sources.[17] The information and problems treated in 1 Cor 1-6 came from those from the house of Chloe. First Corinthians 1:11 states that "some from Chloe's household have *informed* me that there are quarrels among you," thereby identifying Paul's source of information for the problem he treats in 1 Cor 1-4. The wording of 1 Cor 5:1 "It is actually *reported*" points probably to additional information in 1 Cor 5-6 which was also supplied by those from Chloe's house. If this is not the case, then we have no idea who provided this report of immorality among the Corinthians.[18]

A second major source for Paul's information is mentioned in 1 Cor 7:1 when he wrote, "*Now* for the matters you wrote *about.*" Paul is expressly acknowledging here that the list of issues and problems that he is going to respond to came from a document authored and sent by Corinthian believers to him. Numerous modern interpreters believe, rightly so in my opinion, that this Corinthian document informed Paul not only about the issue discussed in 1 Cor 7:1ff, but also the matters discussed at 8:1ff (*Now about* food sacrificed to idols), 12:1ff (*Now about* spiritual gifts), and 16:1ff (*Now about* the collection for God's people).[19]

At least two points can be drawn from this information. The first is that the Corinthians themselves should receive credit for the broad outline of what was discussed and treated in 1 Corinthians. In addition, one ought not overlook the fact that Paul's treatment of the Corinthians' problems is a treatment of the problems as communicated to him through an unnamed informant of one of the women members of the congregation and through a letter (authors unknown) sent to Paul which already had, regardless of its tone, an agenda for which Paul was not re-

---

[17]S.J. Hafemann, "Corinthians, Letters to," *DPL*, pp. 164-167.

[18]CMM, *Introduction*, p. 260 raise the possibility that this report came from Stephanas, Fortunatus, and Achaicus (1 Cor 16:17).

[19]John C. Hurd, *The Origin of 1 Corinthians* (New York: Seabury Press, 1965); Fee, *First Epistle to the Corinthians*, pp. 266-267.

sponsible. It is obvious, then, that even though no one seriously doubts the Pauline authorship of 1 Corinthians, it is important for the interpreter to appreciate the complex role of the Corinthians in their contribution to the content and structure of the epistle.

PROBLEMS AT CORINTH

The task of identifying and reconstructing the multiple problems within the church of God at Corinth on the basis of Paul's letter to them is not a simple one. Writing decades ago on this very problem Prof. Kirsopp Lake commented,

> The difficulty which undoubtedly attends any attempt to understand the Epistles of St. Paul is largely due to the fact that they are letters; for the writer of letters assumes the knowledge of a whole series of facts, which are, as he is quite aware, equally familiar to his correspondent and to himself. But as time goes on this knowledge is gradually forgotten and what was originally quite plain becomes difficult and obscure; it has to be recovered from stray hints and from other documents by a process of laborious research, before it is possible for the letters to be read with anything approaching to the ease and intelligence possessed by those to whom they were originally sent. [20]

There are some scholars who wish to interpret most, if not all, of the problems in 1 Corinthians as arising from one group of individuals at Corinth. The evidence of 1 Corinthians does not, in my judgment, support such a theory. There are, admittedly, aspects of this approach which are attractive. Common traits, to be sure, can be found among some of the problems. For example, Paul refers to the sin of boasting as an ingredient in more than one of the problems within the Corinthians fellowship. Likewise, the terms "division" (σχίσμα, *schisma*) (1 Cor 1:10; 11:18) and "dissension" (also *schisma*) (1 Cor 12:25) are used by Paul in describing more than one problem situation among the letter's re-

---

[20] Kirsopp Lake, *The Earlier Epistles of St. Paul: Their Motive and Origin*, p. vii, cited by Hurd, *The Origin of 1 Corinthians*, p. 5.

cipients. This common denominator of *schisma* does not require
the conclusion that the problems of "party loyalty" in 1 Cor 1-4,
abuse of the Lord's Meal in 11:17-22, and misunderstanding and
misuse of spiritual gifts in 12-14 must all be traced back to a
common theological aberration, to the same social stratum in the
church, or to a particular house church in Corinth.

Since the goal in this commentary is to interpret 1 Corinthians
as Paul's coherent letter, we must respect Paul's own categorization of the issues at Corinth if we want to understand the intent of
his instruction and flow of thought as he responded and gave directions to the church of God at Corinth. If direct and explicit
social links between the organizational sub-units within
1 Corinthians can be isolated, so much the better for exegesis.
However, to this point in time many of the rhetorical, sociological
and anthropological reconstructions of the Christian commun-
ity(ies) at Corinth resemble, at times, a Procrustean Bed rather
than a picture put together on the basis of an exegetical-historical
model.[21]

Throughout the modern period of Pauline interpretation
scholars have regularly commented on the issue of Paul's opponents at Corinth.[22] In this interpretive context, the term opponent
has become almost synonymous with those who promoted or participated in the spiritual aberrations opposed by Paul in 1 Corinthians. More recently, however, other scholars have rightly attempted to both refine and redefine the term opponent.[23] From
this ongoing discussion two points are relevant to this study of 1
Corinthians. First, one must not automatically equate the personalities, groups and aberrations behind 2 Corinthians with those

---

[21]This should not be interpreted as a refusal to appreciate the insights
provided by various methodologies. The problem is that many times
these methods demand more of the text than it can, with a straightforward reading, supply.

[22]Some recent treatments are surveyed by Fee, *First Epistle*, pp. 4-15.

[23]P.W. Barnett, "Opponents of Paul." *DPL*, pp. 644-653; A more detailed
investigation is found in Jerry Sumney, *Identifying Paul's Opponents*, Journal for the Study of the New Testament Supplement 40 (Sheffield: JSOT,
1990).

behind 1 Corinthians.[24] There is no compelling reason to believe that the two letters were written to address the exact same problems. In fact, the internal evidence leads away from such a position.[25] (1) 1 Corinthians was written only to the church in Corinth, while 2 Corinthians was written not only to the church in Corinth but also to all believers in all the Roman province of Achaia, of which Corinth was the capital). (2) Most of the key terms and ideas of each letter are not found in the other. (3) The tenor and literary characteristics of each letter are distinctive.

The second observation from the contemporary discussion of Pauline opponents is the question of whether every spiritual aberration within a Pauline church should be interpreted as intentional and direct opposition to Paul himself. It is not a question of whether Paul ever had opponents (e.g., 2 Corinthians, Galatians), but whether the term opponent is the appropriate term for everyone who was guilty of spiritual perceptions and doctrines different than Paul's or whose lifestyle was not in harmony with Paul's ethical teachings. John Calvin touched on this point in his commentary on 1 Corinthians when he wrote, "Now, I have good reason for thinking that those worthless fellows, who had caused trouble in the Corinthian church, were not open enemies of the truth."[26] Calvin's point is well taken and his caution in using the term opponent will be followed in this work. More explicit and extended discussions on the topic of opponents will be found at the appropriate junctures in the commentary itself.

OUTLINE OF 1 CORINTHIANS

The recognition of literary units in 1 Corinthians is part and parcel of the task of exegesis. The opening and closing of units of thought are not merely arbitrary literary embellishments nor are

---

[24]CMM, *Introduction*, p. 279 write, "We must not read the situation of 2 Corinthians back into 1 Corinthians . . . ."

[25]Ralph Martin, *2 Corinthians*. Word Biblical Commentary, 40 (Waco: Word, 1986), pp. xxxii-xxxiii.

[26]J. Calvin, *The First Epistle of Paul the Apostle to the Corinthians*, trans. J. W. Fraser (Grand Rapids: Eerdmans, 1960), p. 8.

they just convenient ways to structure Paul's thought and feelings. These units put linguistic and semantic limits on the words and thoughts of Paul.[27] The recognition of these demarcations in 1 Corinthians is mandated, since it helps ensure that the flow of Paul's rhetorical argument remains within the limits set by the Apostle himself.[28] Moreover, a respect for the conceptual units and subunits of Paul's letter will greatly reduce the tendency to make his words mean more than he intended them to mean. This tendency to generalize Paul's thought and words beyond the immediate rhetorical setting comes at a high price, since it can only be maintained by denying the occasional nature of the Pauline correspondence as well as the universally recognized fact that meaning emerges from rhetorical and contextual usage.[29]

Introduction etc.		1:1-9
Issue 1	Disunity and Community Fragmentation	1:10-4:20
Issue 2	Reports of Immorality	5:1-6:20
Issue 3	Sexuality/Celibacy/Marriage	7:1-40
Issue 4	Foods Offered to Idols	8:1-11:1
Issue 5	Liturgical Aberrations	11:2-34
Issue 6	Misunderstanding of Spiritual Gifts	12:1-14:40
Issue 7	Misunderstanding of Believers' Resurrection	15:1-58
Issue 8	Instruction for the Collection	16:1-11
Concluding topics		16:12-24

---

[27]This issue is discussed in W.M. Klein, C.L. Blomberg, and R.L. Hubbard, *Introduction to Biblical Interpretation* (Dallas: Word, 1993), pp. 156-171.

[28]On the topic of Paul's use of rhetoric see G.W. Hansen, "Rhetorical Criticism," *DPL*, pp. 822-826.

[29]Regarding the use of rhetoric by Paul in his letters, one should remember the comment of D. Aune who observed, "By the first century B.C., rhetoric had come to exert a strong influence on the composition of letters, particularly among the educated. Their letters functioned not only as means of communication but also as sophisticated instruments of persuasion . . . ," *The New Testament in Its Literary Environment*. Library of Early Christianity (Philadelphia: Westminster, 1987), p. 160.

HISTORICAL MATRIX FOR THE CORINTHIAN PROBLEMS

Without going into the multifaceted issues about the historical evidence from Acts for Paul's churches and how this relates to the evidence for Paul and his churches from his own letters, it seems prudent to rely initially and primarily upon the evidence of 1 Corinthians itself rather than Luke's material in Acts to understand the nature and extent of the problems in the church at Corinth.[30] To be specific, one must not falsely conclude, on the basis of the Lukan picture of a predominant Jewish matrix of the church in Corinth, that Jewish beliefs and practices provide the matrix for most of the aberrations within the Corinthian church.[31] In this regard, Gordon Fee is correct when he points out that many of the problems at Corinth are explicitly traced by Paul to the converts' pagan heritage.[32] It can be argued, furthermore, that even those issues not explicitly traced to pagan heritage by Paul can be best understood by seeing them against the backdrop of Greco-Roman rather than Jewish mores and values.

The issues depicted in 1 Corinthians arose directly from the lives of that first generation Christian community, most of whom had been believers no more than 48 months. Since Paul nowhere implies in 1 Corinthians that the Corinthian problems were introduced by outsiders, the most reasonable course to follow in evaluating the origin of the Corinthian issues is to investigate the urban setting of Roman Corinth from which the converts came. This means that the religious and cultural perspectives which shaped the beliefs and practices of those whom Paul addressed in

---

[30]In general see Joseph A. Fitzmyer, S.J., *Paul and His Theology, A Brief Sketch*, 2nd ed. (Englewood Cliffs: Prentice Hall, 1989), pp. 3-21.

[31]Interpreters sometimes misuse the "Synagogue of the Hebrews" inscription discovered at Corinth. This inscriptional evidence is too fragmentary to date it precisely, but most scholars date this inscription and other Jewish archaeological evidence from Corinth at a date well after Paul's time there, Furnish, "Corinth in Paul's Time," p. 26; McRay, *Archaeology and the New Testament*, p. 319 seems to also accept the late date of this Jewish inscription.

[32]Fee, *First Epistle*, p. 14.

this letter provide the best circumstantial evidence and clues for the interpretation of 1 Corinthians.[33]

While the need to recognize the Greco-Roman matrix of the Corinthian problems might seem self-evident, the history of the interpretation of 1 Corinthians clearly reveals that not all interpreters have shared this methodological concern. In practice this approach to 1 Corinthians means that:

1. One must not attribute the Jewishness of Paul and the Scriptural basis of his own theology to those recent converts whom he was correcting. To extract texts and vocabulary from Jewish sources (e.g., Mishnah, Dead Sea Scrolls, Gospels, etc.) to understand the matrix of the Corinthians' problems is highly suspect. The fact that Paul often cites Scripture to remedy the problems at Corinth speaks more of his own Jewish heritage, his apostolic ministry, and his convictions that all Christians are to be guided by Scripture than it does that there was some significant Jewish background to the Corinthian problems.[34]

2. The mores, patterns of culture and specific religious institutions of Greco-Roman paganism must be seen as the soil in which the Corinthian problems were germinated and grew.

3. The specific condition of the Corinth of Paul's day should be taken as the immediate setting for the converts. One must exercise caution in using information about an earlier Greek Corinth which had been destroyed in the second century B.C. and no longer existed in Paul's day in order to describe the Corinth of Paul's day.[35]

4. One must recognize the multicultural nature of Corinth at Paul's time. It was geographically Greek, it was administratively and politically Roman, and its denizens came from throughout the central and eastern parts of the Mediterranean Basin. Conse-

---

[33] The evidence of Egyptian religions at Corinth has been collected and interpreted by D. Smith, "The Egyptian Cults at Corinth," *Harvard Theological Review* 70 1977, 201-231; A helpful survey is also found in Witherington, *Conflict and Community in Corinth*, pp. 12-19.

[34] Cf. 1 Cor 10:14 and notes there; in general cf. Rom 15:3-4; 2 Tim 3:14-17; a helpful overview and bibliography is given by M. Silva, "Old Testament in Paul," *DPL*, pp. 630-642.

[35] This issue is correctly noted by Witherington, *Conflict and Community in Corinth*, pp. 5-9.

quently, one must reckon with ethnic influences in Paul's Corinth which reflect Greek, Roman, Egyptian, Syrian, Jewish, and Anatolian influences.

5. Vague and anachronistic labels such as gnosticism should be avoided until appropriate historical evidence and documentation can be discovered and shown to be relevant to the issues at Corinth addressed by Paul.[36] A commitment to the notion of a gnostic background to 1 Corinthians still has advocates, though their numbers are surely down from that of the 19th and earlier part of the 20th century.[37] Quite recently, for example, Pheme Perkins argued that

. . . gnostic mythologizing does form part of the horizon within which the New Testament should be interpreted. Students of Christian origins have become accustomed to comparing the New Testament material with a wide variety of Jewish and Greco-Roman sources. The same efforts of analysis and comparison should be applied to the gnostic material.[38]

---

[36]The major difficulties with the traditional Gnosticism approach to the New Testament are spelled out in Edwin Yamauchi, *Pre-Christian Gnosticism: A Survey of the Proposed Evidences*, 2nd ed. (Grand Rapids: Baker, 1983); cf. also Richard E. Oster, Jr., "Christianity in Asia Minor," in *The Anchor Bible Dictionary*, 5 vols., eds. D.N. Freedman et al. (New York: Doubleday, 1992), vol. 1, 948-949.

[37]A Gnostic background for Paul and/or the Corinthians was assumed by many scholars in the last century and the first two-thirds of this century, e.g., Rudolf Bultmann, *Theology of the New Testament*, 2 vols. trans. by K. Grobel (New York: Scribners, 1951, 1955). A classic interpretation of 1 Corinthians from a perspective of Gnosticism is Walther Schmithals, *Gnosticism in Corinth*.

[38]Pheme Perkins, *Gnosticism and the New Testament* (Minneapolis: Fortress Press, 1993), pp. 4-5.

OUTLINE

BIBLIOGRAPHY

Alexander, L.C.A. "Chronology of Paul." In *Dictionary of Paul and His Letters*. Ed. G.F. Hawthorne et al. Downers Grove: Inter-Varsity Press, 1993, pp. 115-123.

Aune, David E. *The New Testament in Its Literary Environment*. Library of Early Christianity. Philadelphia: Westminster Press, 1987.

_____. *Prophecy in Early Christianity and the Ancient Mediterranean World*. Grand Rapids: Eerdmans, 1983.

Banks, R. "Church Order and Government." *DPL*, pp. 131-137.

Barnett, P.W. "Apostle." *DPL*, pp. 45-51.

_____. "Opponents of Paul." *DPL*, pp. 644-653.

_____. "Revolutionary Movements." *DPL*, pp. 812-819.

_____. "Tentmaking." *DPL*, pp. 925-927.

Barrett, C.K. *The First Epistle to the Corinthians*. New York: Harper, 1968.

Beasley-Murray, G.R. "Baptism." *DPL*, pp. 60-66.

Beker, J.C. *Paul the Apostle. The Triumph of God in Life and Thought*. Phliadelphia: Fortress, 1980.

Belleville, L.L. "Moses." *DPL*, pp. 620-21.

Black, M. "1 Cor. 11:2-16—A Re-investigation." *Essays on Women in Earliest Christianity*, Vol. 1. Ed. Carroll D. Osburn. Joplin, MO: College Press Publishing Co., 1993, pp. 191-218.

Blomberg, Craig L. *The Historical Reliability of the Gospels*. Downers Grove: InterVarsity Press, 1987.

Blue, B.B. "Food Offered to Idols and Jewish Food Laws." *DPL*, pp. 306-310.

_____ . "Apollos." *DPL*, pp. 37-39.

Bruce, F.F. *1 and 2 Corinthians.* London: Butler & Tanner Ltd., 1971.

Bultmann, Rudolf. *Theology of the New Testament.* 2 vols. Trans. by K. Grobel. New York: Charles Scribners, 1951, 1955.

Calvin, John. *The First Epistle of Paul the Apostle to the Corinthians.* Calvin's New Testament Commentaries. Trans. J.W. Fraser, Grand Rapids: Eerdmans, 1960.

Cantarella, Eva. *Pandora's Daughters. The Role and Status of Women in Greek and Roman Antiquity.* Trans. M.B. Fant; Foreword by M.R. Lefkowitz. Baltimore: Johns Hopkins University Press, 1987.

Carson, D.A. *Showing the Spirit. A Theological Exposition of I Corinthians 12-14.* Grand Rapids: Baker, 1987.

Carson, D.A., Douglas Moo, and Leon Morris. *Introduction to the New Testament.* Grand Rapids: Zondervan Publishing House, 1992.

Casson, Lionel. *Travel in the Ancient World.* Toronto: Hakkert, 1974.

Chamblin, J.K. "Freedom/Liberty." *DPL*, pp. 313-316.

Chrysostom, Dio. *The Eighth Discourse, on Virtue,* 9-10. Vol. 1. Trans. by J.W. Cohoon. Loeb Classical Library. Cambridge: Harvard University Press, 1949.

Clarke, Andrew D. *Secular & Christian Leadership in Corinth. A Socio-Historical & Exegetical Study of 1 Corinthians 1-6,* Vol. 18. Arbeiten zur Geshichte des Antiken Judentums & des Urchristentums. Leiden: E.J. Brill, 1993.

Comfort, P.W. "Idolatry." *DPL*, pp. 424-426.

Conzelmann, Hans. *I Corinthians.* Hermeneia. Philadelphia: Fortress Press, 1975.

Cottrell, Jack. *Feminism and the Bible: An Introduction to Feminism for Christians.* Joplin, MO: College Press Publishing Co.,1992.

——————— . *Gender Roles and the Bible: Creation, the Fall, and Redemption.* Joplin, MO: College Press Publishing Co.,1994.

de Lacey, D.R. "Holy Days." *DPL*, pp. 402-404.

Donfried, Karl. "Chronology: New Testament." In *Anchor Bible Dictionary.* Vol. 1. Ed. D.N. Freedman, et al. New York: Doubleday, 1992-1994, pp. 1011 & 1022.

Dover, K.J. "Classical Greek Attitudes to Sexual Behaviour." In *Women in the Ancient World. The Arethusa Papers.* Ed. John Peradotto and J.P. Sullivan. Albany: State University of New York Press, 1984.

Ellis, E.E. "Coworkers, Paul and His." *DPL*, pp. 183-189.

Engels, Donald. *Roman Corinth: An Alternative Model for the Classical City.* Chicago: The University of Chicago, 1990.

Everts, J.M. "Conversion and Call of Paul." *DPL*, pp. 156-160.

——————— . "Financial Support." *DPL*, pp. 295-300.

Fee, Gordon. *First Epistle to the Corinthians.* New International Commentary on the New Testament. Grand Rapids: Eerdmans, 1987.

——————— . *God's Empowering Presence.* Peabody, MA: Hendrickson Publishers, 1994.

——————— . "Gifts of the Spirit." *DPL*, pp. 339-347.

——————— . New Testament Exegesis. Rev. ed. Louisville: Westminster Press, 1993.

Ferguson, E. *Demonology of the Early Christian World.* Lewiston, NY: E. Mellin Press, 1984.

——————— . *Backgrounds of Early Christianity.* Second Edition. Grand Rapids: Eerdmans, 1993.

Fitzmyer, J. "A Feature of Qumran Angelology and the Angels of 1 Cor. xi.10." *New Testament Studies* 4 (1957-1958): 48-58.

_____ . "Another Look at ΚΕΦΑΛΗ in 1 Cor. 11.3." *NTS* 35 (1989): 503-511.

_____ . *Paul and His Theology. A Brief Sketch*. 2nd ed. Englewood Cliffs: Prentice Hall, 1989.

Fuller, R.M. "Rewards." *DPL*, pp. 819-820.

Fung, R.Y.K. "Body of Christ." *DPL*, pp. 76-82.

_____ . "Cursing, Accursed, Anathema." *DPL*, pp. 199-200.

Furnish, Victor P. "Corinth in Paul's Time — What Can Archaeology Tell Us?" *Biblical Archaeology Review* 15 (1988): 16-17.

_____ . *II Corinthians*. Anchor Bible. Vol. 32A. New York: Doubleday, 1984.

_____ . "Theology in First Corinthians." In *Pauline Theology*. Vol. II: 1 & 2 Corinthians. Ed. David M. Hay. Minneapolis: Fortress Press, 1991.

Gellius, Aulus. *Noctes Atticae* 16.13.9. *The Attic Nights of Aulus Gellius*. Vol. 3. Loeb Classical Library. Cambridge: Harvard University Press, 1961.

Gill, D.W.J. "The Importance of Roman Portraiture for Head-Coverings in 1 Corinthians 11:2-16." *Tyndale Bulletin* 41 (1990): 245-260.

Gillespie, Thomas W. *The First Theologians. A Study in Early Christian Prophecy*. Grand Rapids: Eerdmans, 1994.

Green, J.B. "Death of Christ." *DPL*, pp. 201-209.

Green, Michael. *I Believe in the Holy Spirit*. Grand Rapids: Eerdmans, 1975.

Guthrie, Donald and Ralph Martin. "God." *DPL*, pp. 354-369.

Gundry-Volf, Judith M. "Apostasy, Falling Away, Perserverance." *DPL*, pp. 42-43.

Haacker, Klaus. "Gallio." In *ABD*. Vol. 2, pp. 901-903.

Hafemann, S.J. "Corinthians, Letters to." *DPL*, pp. 164-179.

Hansen, G.W. "Rhetorical Criticism." *DPL*, pp. 822-826.

Hengel, Martin. *Crucifixion in the Ancient World.* Philadelphia: Fortress Press, 1977.

Hock, Ronald F. *The Social Context of Paul's Ministry. Tentmaking and Apostleship.* Philadelphia: Fortress Press, 1980.

Hodge, Charles. *An Exposition of the First Epistle to the Corinthians.* Grand Rapids: Eerdmans, 1965.

Holladay, Carl. *First Letter of Paul to the Corinthians.* Living Word Commentaries. Vol. 8. Austin, TX: Sweet Publishing Company, 1979.

Hooker, M.D. "Authority on Her Head: An Examination of 1 Cor. XI.10." *New Testament Studies.* Vol 10 (1963-1964): 410-416.

Horsley, G.H.R. "Invitation to the *Kline* of Sarapis." *New Documents Illustrating Early Christianity.* Vol.1, 1981, pp. 5-9.

Hurd, John C. *The Origin of 1 Corinthians.* New York: Seabury Press, 1965.

Keener, Craig S. *The IVP Bible Background Commentary. New Testament.* Downers Grove: InterVarsity Press, 1993.

Kent, John H. *Corinth.* Vol. VIII, Pt. III. *The Inscriptions 1926-1950.* Princeton: American School of Classical Studies at Athens, 1966.

Kim, S. "Jesus, Sayings of." *DPL*, pp. 474-492.

Kistemaker, Simon. *Exposition of the First Epistle to the Corinthians.* Grand Rapids: Baker, 1993.

Klein, W.M., C.L. Blomberg, and R.L. Hubbard. *Introduction to Biblical Interpretation.* Dallas: Word Publishing, 1993.

Kraemer, Ross S. "Non-literary Evidence for Jewish Women in Rome and Egypt." In *Rescuing Creusa. New Methodological Approaches to Women in Antiquity.* Ed. M. Skinner. Lubbock, TX: Texas Tech University Press, 1987.

Kümmel, W.G. *Introduction to the New Testament.* Rev. ed. Trans. H.C. Kee. Nashville: Abingdon, 1975.

Lake, Kirsopp. *The Earlier Epistles of St. Paul: Their Motive and Origin*, p. vii. Cited by John C. Hurd, *The Origin of 1 Corinthians*. New York: Seabury Press, 1965.

Luter, A. B., Jr. "Grace." *DPL*, pp. 372-374.

MacMullen, Ramsay. *Paganism in the Roman Empire*. New Haven: Yale University Press, 1981.

McKnight, S. "Collection for the Saints." *DPL*, pp. 143-147.

McRay, John. *Archaeology and the New Testament*. Grand Rapids: Baker, 1991.

Malherbe, A.J. *Moral Exhortation, A Greco-Roman Sourcebook*. Ed. W.A. Meeks. Philadelphia: Westminster Press, 1986.

Malick, D.E. "The Condemnation of Homosexuality in Romans 1:26-27." *Bibliotheca Sacra* 150 (1993) 327-340.

_____ . "The Condemnation of Homosexuality in 1 Corinthians 6:9." *Bibliotheca Sacra* 150 (1993): 479-492.

Marshall, I.H. "Lord's Supper." *DPL*, pp. 569-575.

Martin, Ralph P. *2 Corinthians*. Word Biblical Commentary, 40. Waco: Word, 1986.

_____ . *The Spirit and the Congregation*. Grand Rapids: Eerdmans, 1984.

Michaels, J.R. "Peter." *DPL*, pp. 701-703.

Mitchell, Margaret M. *Paul and the Rhetoric of Reconciliation. An Exegetical Investigation of the Language and Composition of 1 Corinthians*. Louisville: Westminster/John Knox Press, 1993.

Mohrlang, R. "Love." *DPL*, pp. 575-578.

Morris, Leon. "Sacrifice Offering." *DPL*, pp. 856-858.

_____ . "Faith." *DPL*, pp. 285-291.

Murphy-O'Connor, Jerome. *St. Paul's Corinth. Text and Archaeology*. Good News Studies, 6. Wilmington: Michael Glazier, 1983.

Nepos, Cornelius. *Great General of Foreign Nations.* Preface 4. Loeb Classical Library. Cambridge: Harvard University Press, 1960.

Nock, Arthur Darby. "The Vocabulary of the New Testament." *Journal of Biblical Literature* 52 (1933): 131-139.

Noll, S.F. "Qumran and Paul." *DPL*, pp. 777-783.

O'Brien, Peter T. "Church." *DPL*, pp. 123-131.

——————— . *Introductory Thanksgivings in the Letters of Paul.* Supplements to Novum Testamentum 49. Leiden: E.J. Brill. (1977): 107-137.

——————— . "Letters, Letter Form." *DPL*, pp. 550-553.

Osburn, Carroll D., Ed. "The Interpretation of 1 Cor 14:34-35." *Essays on Women in Earliest Christianity.* Vol. 1. Joplin, MO: College Press, 1993.

Oster, Richard E., Jr. "Christianity in Asia Minor." In *ABD.* Vol. 1. Ed. D.N. Freedman et al. New York: Doubleday, 1992, pp. 948-949.

——————— . "Use, Misuse and Neglect of Archaeological Evidence in Some Modern Works on 1 Corinthians." *Zeitschrift für die Neutestamentliche Wissenschaft* 83 (1992): 58-67.

——————— . "When Men Wore Veils to Worship." *New Testament Studies.* Vol. 34. (1988):481-505.

Osiek, Carolyn. "The Feminist and the Bible: Hermeneutical Alternatives." In *Feminist Perspectives on Biblical Scholarship.* Ed. Adela Y. Collins. Chino, CA: Scholars Press, 1985.

Perkins, Pheme. *Gnosticism and the New Testament.* Minneapolis: Fortress Press, 1993.

Plass, Ewald M., Ed. *What Luther Says: A Practical In-Home Anthology for the Active Christian.* St. Louis: Concordia, 1991.

Plautus. *Curculio* 37-38. Trans. by P. Nixon. Loeb Classical Library, 5 vols. Vol. 2. Cambridge: Harvard University Press, 1959.

Pliny the Elder. *Natural History* 28.2(3).10, 11. Translation taken from Jo-Ann Shelton, *As the Romans Did: A Source Book in Roman Social History.* New York: Oxford University Press, 1968.

Plutarch. *Bravery of Women* 249E. Cited by K.O. Wicker. *Plutarch's Ethical Writings and Early Christian Literature.* Leiden: E.J. Brill, 1978.

Pomeroy, S.B. *Women in Hellenistic Egypt from Alexander to Cleopatra.* Detroit: Wayne State University Press, 1990.

Porter, Stanley. "Holiness, Sanctification." *DPL*, pp. 397-402.

Reasoner, M. "Citizenship, Roman and Heavenly." *DPL*, pp. 139-141.

Reese, D.G. "Demons, New Testament." *ABD*. Vol. 2., 140-142.

Ridderbbos, Herman N. *Paul: An Outline of His Theology.* Grand Rapids: Eerdmans, 1975.

Robeck, C.M., Jr. "Tongues." *DPL*, pp. 939-943.

Robertson, Archibald and Alfred Plummer. *A Critical and Exegetical Commentary on the First Epistle of St. Paul to the Corinthians.* The International Critical Commentary. 2nd ed. Edinburgh: T. & T. Clark, 1914.

Sampley, J. Paul. *Walking Between the Times. Paul's Moral Reasoning.* Minneapolis: Fortress Press, 1991.

Sanders, E. P. *Judaism. Practice and Belief 63 BCE-66 CE.* Philadelphia: Trinity Press International, 1992.

Schmithals, Walther. *Gnosticism in Corinth; an investigation of the letters to the Corinthians.* Trans. J.E. Steely. Nashville: Abingdon, 1971.

Scroggs, Robin. *The New Testament and Homosexuality: Contextual Background for Contemporary Debate.* Philadelphia: Fortress Press, 1983.

_____ . "Paul and the Eschatological Women." *Journal of the American Academy of Religion* 40. Missoula, MT: Scholars Press (1972): 283-303.

Silva, M. "Old Testament in Paul." *DPL*, pp. 630-642.

Smith, D. "The Egyptian Cults at Corinth." *Harvard Theological Review* 70. Missoula, MT: Scholars Press (1977): 201-231.

South, James T. "A Critique of the 'Curse/Death' Interpretation of I Corinthians 5.1-8." *New Testament Studies*. 39 (1993): 539-561.

Spittler, R.P. *Testament of Job.* In *The Old Testament Pseudepigrapha.* Vol.1. Apocalyptic Literature and Testaments. Ed. J.H. Charlesworth. Garden City: Doubleday, 1983.

Stein, R.H. "Jerusalem." *DPL*, pp. 463-474.

Stuart, Douglas. "Exegesis." *ABD*. Ed. D.N. Freeman et al. New York: Doubleday, 1992.

Sumney, Jerry. *Identifying Paul's Opponents. Journal for the Study of the New Testament* Supplement 40. Sheffield: JSOT, 1990.

Theissen, G. *The Social Setting of Pauline Christianity.* Trans. H. Schütz. Philadelphia: Fortress Press, 1982.

Towner, P.H. "Household and Household Codes." *DPL*, pp. 417-419.

Trebilco, P. "Itineraries, Travel Plans, Journeys, Apostolic Parousia." *DPL*, pp. 446-456.

Vermes, G., Trans. *The Dead Sea Scrolls in English.* Baltimore: Penguin Books, 1968.

Walters, James. *Ethnic Issues in Paul's Letter to the Romans: Changing Self-definitions in Earliest Roman Christianity.* Valley Forge: Trinity Press International, 1993.

West, Allen B. *Corinth.* Vol. VIII. Pt. II. *Latin Inscriptions 1896-1926.* Cambridge: Harvard University Press, 1931.

Winter, Bruce. "Rhetoric." *DPL*, pp. 820-822.

Wiseman, James. "Corinth and Rome I:228 B.C.-A.D. 267." In *Aufstieg und Niedergang der römischen Welt.* Edited by H. Temporini and W. Haase. Berlin: Walter de Gruyter (1979) II.7.1: 491-496.

Witherington, Ben III. *Conflict and Community in Corinth. A Socio-Rhetorical Commentary on 1 and 2 Corinthians*. Grand Rapids: Eerdmans, 1995.

Yamauchi, Edwin. *Pre-Christian Gnosticism: A Survey of the Proposed Evidences*. 2nd ed. Grand Rapids: Baker, 1983.

1 CORINTHIANS 1

I. INTRODUCTION (1:1-9)

A. SALUTATION (1:1-3)

[1]Paul, called to be an apostle of Christ Jesus by the will of God, and our brother Sosthenes,

[2]To the church of God in Corinth, to those sanctified in Christ Jesus and called to be holy, together with all those everywhere who call on the name of our Lord Jesus Christ — their Lord and ours:

[3]Grace and peace to you from God our Father and the Lord Jesus Christ.

1:1 Paul, called to be an apostle of Christ Jesus by the will of God, and our brother Sosthenes.

Even though it is normal for Paul to use the self-designation "apostle" in his letters, the function and significance of the term apostle have deeper roots in 1 Corinthians than in most of Paul's other letters.[1] This concept plays an important role in the issue of division in chapters 1-4, a role in the Pauline directives regarding the treatment of the weak by the strong in chapters 8-10, a tangential role in the discussion of spiritual matters, chapters 12-14, and an important part of the argument for the resurrection in 1 Cor 15. It is noteworthy that 1 Corinthians is a good example of a letter in which ambiguity exists about the exact meaning of the Greek term ἀπόστολος, *apostolos*. While Paul obviously regards himself as an apostle, it is not always clear that he regarded himself as an Apostle in the same way as he regarded the Twelve (see 15:7, where "apostles" is used in a wider sense than the Twelve).

---

[1]On the general concept see P.W. Barnett, "Apostle," *DPL*, pp. 45-51.

First Corinthians makes it clear that the term "called" (κλητός, *klētos*) was not reserved for a select group of believers. While different believers were called to different tasks by God, all believers had received a call (1 Cor 1:2, 24). Quite naturally, Paul testified again and again in his letters that his call was by the will of God, an early hint that Paul's self-definition was rooted in a theocentric experience.[2]

The name Sosthenes is found only twice in the New Testament, here and at Acts 18:17. Since Sosthenes is depicted as the co-sender of the letter he must have been with Paul in Ephesus. There is no firm evidence that this was the same individual, a non-Christian synagogue leader in Corinth, mentioned in Acts 18:17. Homiletical needs have tended to identify the two individuals, but there is nothing in their respective circumstances or the text of Scripture which requires this identification. It is noteworthy that the place of Sosthenes in 1 Corinthians recedes markedly after 1:1.

1:2 To the church of God in Corinth, to those sanctified in Christ Jesus and called to be holy, together with all those everywhere who call on the name of our Lord Jesus Christ — their Lord and ours:

Evidence for the beginning of the church of God in Corinth is given in Acts 18. The closeness of the concepts sanctified (from ἁγιάζω, *hagiazō*) and holy (ἅγιος, *hagios*) is not as clear in English as it is in Greek, where the two words are cognates.[3]

The use of the phrase "church of God" for believers is one of several in the New Testament. This particular phrase reflects the Old Testament concept of the assembly of God. It is worth noting that many of the texts of 1 Corinthians that relate to what would be called Pauline ecclesiology reveal a distinctive theocentric perspective.[4]

---

[2] J.C. Beker, *Paul the Apostle. The Triumph of God in Life and Thought*, p. 355.

[3] In general see Stanley Porter, "Holiness, Sanctification," *DPL*, pp. 397-402.

[4] See Peter O'Brien, "Church," *DPL*, p. 126.

The term "everywhere" (Greek reads "in every place") need not be a reference to a public or formal assembly of believers. While the phrase "call on the name of the Lord" is often associated with initial salvation in the New Testament (Acts 2:21; 22:16; Rom 10:13) the text of 1 Cor 1:2, like 2 Tim 2:19 and numerous Old Testament texts (Gen 13:4; 21:33; 26:25; 1 Kings 18:24-25; 1 Chron 16:8; Ps 63:4; 99:6; 116:13, 17; Isa 12:4; Lam 3:55; Zeph 3:9), refers to those who are seeking God in prayer and pious devotion.

1:3 Grace and peace to you from God our Father and the Lord Jesus Christ.

The salutation of grace and peace is found in numerous Pauline letters (Rom 1:7; 2 Cor 1:2; Gal 1:3; Eph 1:2; Phil 1:2; Col 1:2; 1 Thess 1:1; 2 Thess 1:2; 1 Tim 1:2; 2 Tim 1:2; Titus 1:4; Phlm 1:3) and usually with the dual reference to God our Father and the Lord Jesus Christ.

B. THANKSGIVING (1:4-9)

[4]I always thank God for you because of his grace given you in Christ Jesus. [5]For in him you have been enriched in every way — in all your speaking and in all your knowledge — [6]because our testimony about Christ was confirmed in you. [7]Therefore you do not lack any spiritual gift as you eagerly wait for our Lord Jesus Christ to be revealed. [8]He will keep you strong to the end, so that you will be blameless on the day of our Lord Jesus Christ. [9]God, who has called you into fellowship with his Son Jesus Christ our Lord, is faithful.

1:4 I always thank God for you because of his grace given you in Christ Jesus.

As in many of his letters (Col 1:3; 1 Thess 1:2; 2 Thess 1:3; 2 Thess 2:13; Phlm 1:4), Paul here refers to his constant practice of thanking God in regard to his converts.[5] The spiritual realities expressed in this verse follow the normal Pauline pattern of theocentric piety by making God the object of praise and thanksgiving, while Christ is seen as the agency or locus in which God has acted. Paul's own piety, in stark contrast to many later Protestant pietists, was centered on the primacy of God the Father. Trinitarian piety with its adoration of the Spirit was the result of Catholic orthodoxy established in the needs of later Councils.[6] It is also important to observe, moreover, that Paul is not simply thanking God for the Corinthians, as though in spite of their many problems and sins, he was still patting them on the back. The NIV obfuscates what Paul made clear — his thanksgiving was *concerning* (περί, *peri*) the Corinthians, not *for* the Corinthians. As O'Brien rightly observed, "In this thanksgiving there was no attention paid to the achievements of the Corinthians — and with good reason!"[7]

What is clear throughout this thanksgiving summary is that Paul expresses thanks to God for what God has done and will do on behalf of the Corinthians. Verses 4-9 provide no evidence that Paul had in fact discovered some virtuous behavior among the Corinthians or that he was going to congratulate, to affirm, or to empower them on the basis of some ostensible goodness he found among their deeds. This summary of 1:4-9 is clearly focused on the actions of God the Father on behalf of the Corinthians, and it is God alone who is acknowledged as faithful (1:9).

In addition, there is a theme established in this summary which is not only an important perspective addressed to the Corinthians, but which is a frequent theme in the Pauline letters generally. This particular theme, highlighted by verbal links in Greek,

---

[5]A seminal study of this section is given by Peter T. O'Brien, *Introductory Thanksgivings in the Letters of Paul*. Supplements to *Novum Testamentum*, 49 (Leiden: E.J. Brill, 1977), pp. 107-137.

[6]For the issue of triune and trinitarian language in 1 Corinthians see notes on 1 Corinthians 12:4. Donald Guthrie and Ralph Martin state, "Of the Trinity there are many adumbrations in the NT, although it cannot be said that the doctrine is explicitly expounded in a formal way." "God," *DPL*, p. 366.

[7]O'Brien, *Introductory Thanksgivings*, p. 137.

is that gifts (χάρισμα, *charisma*) of God flow from the grace (χάρις, *charis*) of God.[8]

Some English translations obscure Paul's point by breaking down his one Greek sentence of 1:4-8 and making it into four English sentences. One of the effects of this translation decision is that it blurs the grammatical and theological relationship between the grace (*charis*) given in 1:4 and the gifts (*charisma*) mentioned in 1:8. The Greek word ὥστε (*hōste*, "therefore") in 1:7 begins a result clause and, in my judgment, is intended to highlight that the presence of gifts is a result of God's grace.

1:5 For in him you have been enriched in every way — in all your speaking and in all your knowledge —

The point Paul wants to make here is to express why he is so involved in always giving thanks to God (1:4); it is because (ὅτι, *hoti*) they have been enriched by God in all divine knowledge and in every proclamation. Interpreters vary in their judgment about whether Paul's intended focus in the reference to the enrichment of the Corinthians was the enrichment they experienced at the time of their conversion or later. Paul explicitly states that this enrichment took place "in him," which requires that it was at least available to the Corinthians since the time of their conversion to Christ. Moreover, the typical Pauline pattern in an epistolary thanksgiving section is have a present tense "I/we give thanks" statement followed by verbs and participles in the present tense indicating contemporaneous activity (e.g., Rom 1:8; Phil 1:3; Col 1:3; 1 Thess 1:2; 2 Thess 1:3). In this light, we should be more sensitive to the significance of the aorist tense used by Paul in 1:5 as we wrestle with the event Paul had in mind. The two terms "speaking" (λόγος, *logos*) and "knowledge" (γνῶσις, *gnōsis*) have a variety of meanings not only in the Pauline corpus, but even within 1 Corinthians. [9] The specific meaning Paul has for these two words in 1:5 will be found most likely by looking at 1:6 where he seems to continue his train of thought.

---

[8] A.B. Luter, Jr., "Grace," *DPL*, p. 373.
[9] *Logos*, 1:17, 18; 2:13; 4:20; 14:19; 15-54; *gnōsis* 1:5; 8:1; 13:2.

1:6 because our testimony about Christ was confirmed in you.

Paul clearly taught that the testimony about Christ preached by himself and others was verified and "confirmed" (from βεβαιόω, *bebaioō* and cognates, cf. Rom 4:16; 15:8; 1 Cor 1:6, 8; 2 Cor 1:21; Phil 1:7; Heb 2:3; 6:16; 13:9) in and among the Corinthians at Corinth. Paul here seems to be saying that the effect of this divine enrichment in Christ (Gr. aor. pass.) is similar to and especially evident in the past confirmation (Gr. aor. pass.) of the testimony about Christ among the Corinthians. Pentecostal and Charismatic interpreters, among others, tend to have the meaning of this verse supplemented by the reference to (spiritual) gifts in 1:7,[10] so that Paul is interpreted as teaching that the spiritual gifts, as presented most clearly in 12-14, are the source of enrichment and confirmation of the message of Christ. Other scholars infer a non-charismatic reading of 1:7 by looking more at the evidence regarding the confirmation of the testimony about Christ in: (1) the conversion stories from Corinth in Acts 18, (2) Pauline use of Scripture as confirmation, (3) Christian proclamation, and, (4) Paul's references to the Spirit of sonship as providing confirming testimony. Since it seems that 1:6-7 refer to the reasons (ὅτι, *hoti*) for Paul's thanksgiving in 1:4 and that 1:7 (ὥστε, *hōste*) refers to the intended results of receiving God's grace (1:4), I do not find convincing Fee's judgment that, "the clause (1:6) says that God himself confirmed Paul's witness to Christ among them by giving them these spiritual gifts, which is exactly what v. 7 will go on to reaffirm."[11]

1:7 Therefore you do not lack any spiritual gift as you eagerly wait for our Lord Jesus Christ to be revealed.

God's grace always supplies the needs (not to be confused with the wants) of the saints that are necessary for them to implement God's agenda. The occurrence of the English phrase "spiritual gift" in 1:7 is potentially misleading since it reflects an embellishment of the Greek of 1:7. While admittedly all translations require the addition of words that were not in the original Greek text, translations do sometimes promote a particular doctrinal perspec-

---

[10]Fee, *First Epistle*, p. 40.
[11]Ibid.

tive not evident in the Greek text.[12] With the charismatic domination of so much of contemporary Christian piety, it is important
to point out that the use of the phrase "spiritual gift(s)" here, as
often in 1 Corinthians, is not a translation of a corresponding
Greek phrase. The following chart displays the translation tendency of the NIV in comparison with the evidence of the Greek
text.

NIV		**Greek text**
1:7	any spiritual gift	gift *charisma* (lacks Greek word for spiritual)
12:1	about spiritual gifts	spiritual *pneumatikos* (lacks Greek word for gift)
14:1	desire spiritual gifts	spiritual *pneumatikos* (lacks Greek word for gift)
14:12	to have spiritual gifts	spirit *pneuma* (lacks Greek word for gift and spiritual)
14:37	spiritually gifted	spiritual *pneumatikos* (lacks Greek word for gift)

Verse 7 contains only the word gift (χάρισμα, *charisma*). Commentators such as John Calvin[13] and Gordon Fee[14] note that this
use of gift in 1:7 may refer to the gift(s) of God associated with our
salvation, rather than gifts as conventionally understood in chapters 12-14.

Situated on a spectrum of interpretations somewhere between
the popular charismatic interpretation of gifts and the redemptive
interpretation of gift, I would suggest that gift in 1:7 refers to gifts
given by God to his people to facilitate their calling, but that
Paul's definition, as demonstrated by his use of *charisma* in 1 Cor
7:7, would be broader than those stereotypical Pentecostal items
such as tongues.

Verse 7 concludes on an eschatological note, with expectant
language reminiscent of Rom 8:18-25; Phil 3:20; and Gal 5:5, and
makes it clear that the giftedness of the Corinthian church would
not cease prior to the return and revelation of the Lord Jesus
Christ. Paul can hardly be faulted for not knowing that the church

---

[12]G. Fee, "Gifts of the Spirit," *DPL*, p. 339 observes, "The term 'gift(s) of
the Spirit' does not occur in the Pauline corpus."

[13]Calvin, *First Epistle*, p. 22.

[14]Fee, *First Epistle*, p. 42.

of God at Corinth would itself cease to exist (along with its gifts) long before the return of Christ. The quintessential giftedness of the church expressed here fits with other statements of Paul about the church. The reference to Christ's return also anticipates the significant role played by eschatological perspectives in the close of this thanksgiving section (1:8-9) as well as in the remainder of 1 Corinthians. [15]

1:8 He will keep you strong to the end, so that you will be blameless on the day of our Lord Jesus Christ.

The same disposition of God that confirmed the testimony about Christ among the saints (1:6) will also confirm the blamelessness of the saints themselves until the time of Christ's return.

The phrase "to the end" is a clarion reference to the return of Jesus Christ and implies that some of the original readers would remain "until the end." The vitality and pervasiveness of such eschatological conviction flow naturally from the pen of one who prays "Maranatha" (1 Cor 16:22). The doctrine of the blamelessness of believers (cf. Col 1:22) arises from the forensic imagery of accusations in the courtroom of God's justice and the culpability of his saints. This doctrinal concept is evident in the scenes of the judgment of God's priest in Zech 3, in the accusation against the saints in Rev 12, and in the accusation theme depicted in the rhetorical questions of Rom 8:33-34.

1:9 God, who has called you into fellowship with his Son Jesus Christ our Lord, is faithful.

Paul concludes the thanksgiving with two affirmations about the character and work of God. The faithfulness of God, a frequent doctrine in the Old Testament as well as in the Pauline Corpus, (cf. 10:13) is mentioned here by Paul to undergird the prior statement about the blamelessness of the saints. Calvin may have been correct when he observed that "it was important for Paul to write this to prevent them from being dejected when they came face to face with all the faults, that he will reveal to them later on [in 1 Corinthians]."[16] In Paul's thinking the promise of the

---

[15]See notes on 1 Cor 7:29-31; 15:24-28, 50-55.

[16]John Calvin, *First Epistle*, p. 23.

eschatological blamelessness of the saints rests securely on the conviction of God's steadfast loyalty (2 Tim 2:12-13).

Second, Paul reminds them that it was God who called them and who was the author of their spiritual standing, described by Paul as fellowship with his son, the Lord Jesus Christ. The primary function of 1:9 in the literary unit of his thanksgiving was to underscore the foundation of their eschatological security. Paul may well have hoped, however, that this reference to God as the author of fellowship with Christ would have also reduced some of the boasting about human agents such as Cephas and Paul. Paul wanted to diminish the role attributed to them in facilitating the establishment of fellowship which the Corinthians had with the Lord Jesus Christ.

II. DISUNITY AND COMMUNITY FRAGMENTATION (1:10-4:20)

A. As we approach the first major problem at Corinth, 1:10-4:20, it is appropriate to summarize what the general issues are in this section and what may have been their source. Fragmentation and schism are the issues that Paul is addressing in this first major block of instruction. In particular, the point of strife seems to be group loyalties to various Christian leaders within the Corinthian fellowship.[17] It is anachronistic as well as counterproductive to the goals of exegesis to suggest that the division troubling the Corinthian church was similar to later ecclesiastical fragmentation which has characterized much of church history. Similarly, it is equally unfounded to impose a doctrinal framework of orthodoxy/heresy upon this division. All the evidence we have from the text suggests that the disunity is based upon a polarization of loyalties centering upon, but not necessarily engendered by, influential Christian leaders.

An attendant issue interwoven in these four chapters of the epistle is the matter of Corinthian disregard for Paul's own authority. Any interpretation of the first four chapters of

---

[17]Witherington, *Conflict and Community in Corinth*.

1 Corinthians must include this attendant issue. A natural consequence of party loyalties to Apollos and Cephas is that not everyone at Corinth will have an appropriate loyalty to Paul. Accordingly, a strategy that begins by attacking all party loyalty, even loyalty for Paul (1:12-16), shifts its focus first to an apology for Paul, then moves to a counterattack against Paul's detractors (4:1-13) and culminates with a demand for explicit loyalty to Paul over against other leaders at Corinth (4:14-21). This overview provides the best explanation for the fact that Paul employs the "I appeal" (παρακαλέω, parakaleō)[18] rhetorical device to address both divisions (1:10) and disloyalty to him (4:16). The recognition of this second facet of Paul's argument, namely its desire to solidify his apostolic authority rooted in God's calling rather than worldly preferences, clearly helps explain the dramatic shift in tone between 1:10-3:23 and 4:1-21.

B. The most natural explanation for the origin of this party loyalty problem comes directly from the urban context of Roman Corinth. Specifically, the fabric of Greco-Roman city life supplied the threads of strife and dissension woven into the life of the Corinthian church. Three realities of city life that could well have contributed are: (1) personal patronage — house churches, (2) philosopher-student loyalty, and (3) urban party loyalties. The social and economic infrastructure of this city, like all major Greco-Roman cities, was held together by a system of personal patronage and group loyalties. Every culture is based upon accepted social structures, group interaction and personal loyalties. Party spirit was a common fact of ancient city life and it was commented upon and lamented by more than one pagan author contemporary with early Christianity.

Thus, the phenomenon of divisions within the Christian community at Corinth arose quite organically from the social matrix of group interaction, social stratification, and urban alienation which existed in Corinth long before the arrival of the Gospel. The human soil from which the church of God at Corinth grew had been watered and cultivated for generations with party strife and loyalties.

---

[18]Peter O'Brien, "Letters, Letter Form," *DPL*, p. 552.

A. DIVISIONS IN THE CHURCH (1:10-17)

1. Report Received by Paul (1:10-12)

[10]I appeal to you, brothers, in the name of our Lord Jesus Christ, that all of you agree with one another so that there may be no divisions among you and that you may be perfectly united in mind and thought. [11]My brothers, some from Chloe's household have informed me that there are quarrels among you. [12]What I mean is this: One of you says, "I follow Paul"; another, "I follow Apollos"; another, "I follow Cephas[a]"; still another, "I follow Christ."

[a]*12* That is, Peter

1:10 I appeal to you, brothers, in the name of our Lord Jesus Christ, that all of you agree with one another so that there may be no divisions among you and that you may be perfectly united in mind and thought.

Paul's use of the term "appeal" (παρακαλέω, *parakaleō*) is striking for it was a term often used in ancient Greek documents to underscore the focal point and seriousness of a request.[19] Paul's urgent petition to the Corinthians contains three points:

1. all of you agree with one another
2. there be no divisions among you
3. you be united in the same mind and same thought.

The insertion of the phrase "so that" by the NIV translation at 1:10 sounds a bit more like modern ecumenism than Paul's Greek text reads. Paul urgently petitions for the three conditions listed above, but never directly states that any one of them is predicated upon the other. Paul's statement is taken by some interpreters to teach that unity (no divisions among you) stems from uniformity (agree with one another), but that view of intrachurch relations is not taught explicitly in this text. Furthermore, while Paul is no

---

[19]Fee, *First Epistle*, p. 53.

stranger to making a doctrinal plea on the basis of the universal practice of the church (1 Cor 4:17), that type of appeal is interestingly absent in this part of Paul's argumentation.

The wording of 1:10 is sufficiently vague, but it is reasonable to assume that the first readers of his letter would have known quite well what particular manifestations of strife Paul had in mind. Generally speaking it is clear that the issues of uniform thought, judgment and agreement must have pertained to the divisiveness and polarization mentioned in 1:11-17. It is unfortunate that the NIV chose to leave untranslated the Greek word "for" (γάρ, gar) which occurs in 1:11, since this would make the logical connection between the petition of 1:10 and the evidence of 1:11 patent. Accordingly, the specific doctrinal content concerning which Paul was arguing for sameness was the centrality of Christ. The uniformity for which Paul is so earnestly arguing is a common loyalty to Christ which brings with it a dissolution of intrachurch strife. Even though strife and division were culturally acceptable consequences of patronage and personal loyalties, they were unacceptable to Paul and his theology of the corporate fellowship which they had in the Lord Jesus Christ.

1:11 My brothers, some from Chloe's household have informed me that there are quarrels among you.

Paul identifies certain unnamed individuals from the household of Chloe as the source of his information concerning the quarrels and strife occurring among the Corinthian believers. Fee is of the opinion that Chloe and her household were Asian Christians and not members of the church in Corinth.[20] Given this reconstruction, Chloe (a Christian woman) had sent some of her financial agents on business to Corinth and when they were there they discovered this problem of division and reported it to Paul on their return home to Ephesus. While it is true that Stephanas, Fortunatus, and Achaicus were representatives from the Corinthian church (16:15-18), this need not preclude there being others from Corinth, who were not leaders, who traveled to Ephesus from Corinth on occasion and could report to Paul. The brevity

---

[20]Ibid., p. 54.

of the reference to Chloe suggests that all the Corinthian saints would have recognized sister Chloe, a more difficult scenario to imagine if she lived in Ephesus rather than Corinth.

1:12 What I mean is this: One of you says, "I follow Paul"; another, "I follow Apollos"; another, "I follow Cephas"; still another, "I follow Christ."

This one verse is as replete with exegetical and historical problems as any other single verse in 1 Corinthians. The following points, though admittedly not problem free, seem to rest upon the firmest evidence and most plausible historical reconstruction.

A. In light of the flow of Paul's argument which follows in 1:13-4:21 and the fact that this is a response to a secondhand summary, I regard it as clear that these believers were not intentionally choosing Paul or Apollos or Cephas as replacements for their devotion to God or Christ. Carnal decisions by Christians are rarely so self-evident. Rather, within the context of their intentional loyalty to God the Father and the Lord Jesus Christ, they were expressing personal loyalty to different leaders which, perhaps intentionally on their part, was leading to division and quarrels within the Christian fellowship at Corinth.

B. While the assumption of a fourth party at Corinth, namely a Christ party, has served well as fodder in anti-sectarian sermons, it seems historically unimaginable that any group at Corinth really thought that they, in contrast to the rest of the Corinthian brethren, gave their allegiance to Christ.[21] Moreover, if there were a Christ party, it is hard to explain why it drops from discussion after 1:12 since Paul continues with references to those who maintain loyalty to Paul (3:4-5, 22; 4:6) to Cephas (3:22) and to Apollos (3:4-5, 22; 4:6). I take the fourth slogan to represent Paul's own response and corrective to the first three slogans. It is hard to believe that Paul would belittle a slogan which pledged loyalty to Christ.

C. In light of the positive and supporting comments from Paul throughout the rest of 1 Corinthians it seems improbable that Paul regards Apollos or Cephas as supportive of these party loyal-

---

[21]Numerous interpreters do accept the fact that there was a Christ party at Corinth.

ists. There is no criticism in the letter, in either this sub-unit or elsewhere, of the practices of either Cephas or Apollos, but rather only of those who divide Christ because of misplaced loyalty to either Paul or Apollos or Cephas.[22]

D. In spite of recent trends reacting against previous scholarly excesses in describing these Corinthians parties,[23] it does seem that parties is still a useful term to describe the phenomenon Paul is combating in 1:10-4:21. To be sure, there were no parties whose central element was an elaborate theology. Paul is certainly not fighting, for example, against a Petrine school of theology. However, once it is recognized that in the Greco-Roman world one could have party advocacy which formed around leadership/ patronage as well as student/devotee loyalty to a teacher/ philosopher, then a similar situation among some new Christians in Corinth is not difficult to imagine.[24]

2. Christ Undivided (1:13-17)

[13]Is Christ divided? Was Paul crucified for you? Were you baptized into[a] the name of Paul? [14]I am thankful that I did not baptize any of you except Crispus and Gaius, [15]so no one can say that you were baptized into my name. [16] (Yes, I also baptized the household of Stephanas; beyond that, I don't remember if I baptized anyone else.) [17]For Christ did not send me to baptize, but to preach the gospel — not with words of human wisdom, lest the cross of Christ be emptied of its power.

[a]13 Or in; also in verse 15

---

[22]Other interpreters are not so positive in their analysis of Apollos's role. B.B. Blue thinks, "Apollos's ministry at Corinth precipitated a number of problems which Paul attempts to resolve in 1 and 2 Corinthians," "Apollos," *DPL*, p. 38.

[23]Fee, *First Epistle*, pp. 58-59.

[24]Carl Holladay, *First Letter of Paul to the Corinthians*, p. 29. "Nothing in the text permits an identification of different doctrinal positions held by the different parties."

1:13 Is Christ divided? Was Paul crucified for you? Were you baptized into the name of Paul?

All three of these questions anticipate a negative answer. The first questions calls upon the readers to reflect upon their beliefs about Christ, while the last two questions lead them to contemplate their understanding of Paul and his significance. Paul begins to use at this juncture a significant strategy which will run through 4:13. This strategy consists of destroying party loyalty by undermining the inflated significance attributed to the three personalities of Paul, Cephas, and Apollos. Sometimes this process involves a candid assessment of the various leaders, while at other times it includes denigration of himself and others. What better way for one of the principals in this issue to defuse the strife than by acknowledging his own insignificance and his personal ineptitude?

The fragmentation of unity which was epitomized by the slogans of 1:12 is challenged by Paul with the reference to the implied dividedness of Christ. If Christ is not divided, then how could his followers be? The linkage of crucifixion and baptism was already part and parcel of Paul's doctrinal teaching prior to this peculiar application in 1 Corinthians. In a few short months he will have employed this linkage in his letter to the church in Rome (Rom 6) and assumes that they, though not evangelized by him, are themselves familiar with it already. The passing reference to the vicarious nature (for you) of the crucifixion is noteworthy, though it will not be the dominant motif associated with crucifixion in this chapter.

As with the question of crucifixion, so with the issue of baptism, Paul expects the Corinthians to realize that the name of Christ, rather than Paul, belongs in the correct understanding of this act. Much has been written about the misunderstanding(s) of baptism held by at least some of the Corinthians (see comments on 10:1-5 and 15:29). I do not regard this verse as providing evidence for any bizarre theology of baptism held by the Corinthians any more than this verse supports the idea that there were Corinthians who literally believed in some bizarre way that Paul had undergone crucifixion for them. Verse 13 does attest that Paul's doctrine of baptism at Corinth and Ephesus included the idea of baptism "into the name of Christ" (cf. Rom 6), an idea also well attested in the Lukan picture of early Christianity (Acts 2:38; 8:16; 10:48; 19:5). Apparently the act of baptism was seen by some of those involved in factionalism as being so important that they thought that personal loyalty should be given to the baptizer. It is not difficult to imagine how this act of immersion, so essential to Christian conversion, would have been caught up and interpreted in a social world in which patron and client relationships were the norm and all benefactors, financial or spiritual, were the object of loyalty. Another part of the historical puzzle that helps us understand the origin of the baptism/personal loyalty pattern is that converts were often made by households.[25] The mixture of baptisms of households, the home as the locus of family loyalty as well as the architectural setting for patronage, and the matter of house assemblies readily engenders and exacerbates the Corinthian problem of loyalty on the basis of the one who performed the baptism.

1:14 I am thankful that I did not baptize any of you except Crispus and Gaius,

With some overstatement, Paul asserts that he baptized only Crispus and Gaius at Corinth; the conversion of a certain Crispus is known from Acts 18:8, while a Pauline co-worker Gaius who is mentioned in Acts 19:29 is called a Macedonian. The Gaius referred to in Rom 16:23 was probably the same individual as mentioned in 1 Cor 1:14. If the two individuals mentioned in this verse are identified with the converted synagogue ruler of Corinth in Acts 18:8 and the host of the entire church at Corinth mentioned in Rom 16:23, then it is obvious that Paul was personally responsible for the baptism and conversion of two of the socially elite and wealthy individuals within the church of God at Corinth. Paul apparently left the baptism of the Corinthians of lower social status, who would have comprised the majority of the church members, to co-workers.[26]

---

[25] In general see P.H. Towner, "Household and Household Codes," *DPL*, pp. 417-418.

[26] G. Theissen, *The Social Setting of Pauline Christianity: Essays on Corinth*, trans. by H. Schütz (Philadelphia: Fortress Press, 1982).

1:15 so no one can say that you were baptized into my name.

It is unclear whether Paul is, in hindsight, thankful that he baptized so few of the Corinthians, or whether he is writing that he intentionally did not baptize many of them so that the very problem that he is having to deal with would not occur. The idea in verse 15 of being baptized into Paul's name continues the issue raised about this in 1:13b. While we cannot know whether the Corinthians were explicitly stating, "I was baptized into the name of Paul," "I was baptized into the name of Apollos," etc., it is reasonable to conclude that it was not merely a matter of one following after Paul, Cephas, or Apollos, but one expressing loyalty on the basis of who performed (or perhaps authorized) the baptism.

1:16 (Yes, I also baptized the household of Stephanas; beyond that, I don't remember if I baptized anyone else.)

This verse clarifies that there were individuals besides Gaius and Crispus whom Paul baptized during his ministry at Corinth. In addition to acknowledging the baptism of Stephanas and his household (e.g., family members, slaves) Paul also confesses to a bit of amnesia in the matter of his baptizing activity in Corinth. It should not be overlooked that Stephanas probably shares with Crispus and Gaius the fact that he comes from the upper stratum of Corinthian city life, for not only did he have a household (rather than belonging to one), but he was also able to travel as one of the representatives of the Corinthian church to visit Paul in Ephesus (1 Cor 16:15-18). The use of parentheses at 1:16 in the NIV is somewhat misleading. Not only is 1:16 not disjointed or an afterthought in the argument of 1:14-17, it is conceptually and rhetorically connected to 1:17 by the linking word "for" (γάρ, *gar*) in 1:17a.

1:17 For Christ did not send me to baptize, but to preach the gospel — not with words of human wisdom, lest the cross of Christ be emptied of its power.

Paul begins this verse with an explanation of his comment about his faulty memory in the matter of the number of baptisms he performed at Corinth. He couldn't remember because (for, *gar*) God hadn't commissioned him to baptize, but to preach the gospel. Had he been commissioned to baptize, Paul would have remembered names and head count; since he wasn't, he didn't.

Paul's statement here serves both to conclude his argument about how one should view his apostolic ministry given by God and the rite of baptism, and to serve as a transition to the next component in this urgent appeal to the readers. This verse has been a favorite of those interpreters who have a view of religion that disdains ceremony. In his observations on this verse Gordon Fee noted, "Paul does not intend to minimize Christian baptism; his use of this imagery in Rom 6:3-7 would forever rule that out. The reason for expressing his own calling in this negative way has been dictated by the nature of the argument."[27] This is one of scores of examples in 1 Corinthians where it is imperative to interpret Paul's thoughts and words in the literary and rhetorical setting of a unit of thought.

It seems to me that Paul's statement here is no different in kind from Old Testament prophets who on occasion, for reasons of context and rhetorical effect, minimized God-ordained ceremonies and institutions (Isa 1:11-15; Jer 7:1-11) or Jesus who criticized pious acts such as prayer and fasting (Matt 6:1-18) or Paul who, in 1 Cor 13:1-3, denigrates for contextual reasons acts of piety which are normally admirable.

Paul knew that baptism had become one of the elements at the root of the quarreling in Corinth, and he wanted no part in leaving the Corinthians with the idea that he was supportive of their doctrine of a divisive baptism stemming from personal loyalty to the one who performed the baptism. The counterpoint to Paul's denial of the centrality of baptizing in his ministry is his affirmation that the focus of his commission by Christ was the proclamation of the gospel. This brief summary agrees completely with the picture of Paul's apostolic appointment as sketched in Acts and mentioned in his own letters.

---

[27]Fee, *First Epistle*, p. 63; on baptism in general see G.R. Beasley-Murray, "Baptism," *DPL*, pp. 60-66.

In its function to provide a transition to 1:18-31 this verse introduces central terms such as gospel, cross, and wisdom.[28] In order to understand the rhetoric and the flow of Paul's theological thought and reasoning in this literary unit of 1:10-4:21, it is imperative to acknowledge the single focus of this entire section. Even though there is an amazing variety in the rhetoric, in the illustrations, in the sub-arguments, and in the tenor of the material stretching from 1:18-4:21, one must not lose sight of the fact that all this is Paul's argument against the dissensions and quarreling mentioned in 1:10-12. The reason that this point must be made explicitly here is that sometimes interpreters use portions of Paul's arguments in this section as though they were directed to outsiders, to the lost of the world.

While admittedly 1:18-31 describes the unsaved world of Paul's day, both Jew and Greek, it is unacceptable to stop with that mere observation since it is clear that this section of Paul's argument was intended by Paul both to address and to ameliorate the problem of party strife among believers at Corinth. Proper interpretation of this section must discern the flow of Paul's thought by which he adapted this description of the attitudes of a world alienated from God into his argument designed to undermine the divisions among believers based upon personal loyalty.

To miss this point is to miss the Pauline intention behind all the variety in this section and it runs the great risk of misusing material from this section to make points and doctrinal affirmations which Paul had no intention of making. In light of the problem of a non-contextual reading of these verses, it is worthwhile to point out that there are two major internal textual indicators that the material set forth in 1:18-4:21 was written by Paul as a unified response to the congregational problem described in 1:10-17:

1. References to the slogans of party loyalty first mentioned in 1:12 are reintroduced later at 3:4-5, 3:21-22, and 4:6 by means of the names of Paul, Cephas and Apollos. This is the clearest proof that Paul is continuing to address the same problem.

---

[28]For example, of the twenty-eight occurrences of the word "wisdom" (σοφία, *sophia*) and its cognates in 1 Corinthians, twenty-six occur in the section 1:17-4:21. Although many English translations include the phrase "of its power" in 1:17, none of that wording is found in the Greek text.

2. The clustering of key terms associated with the division and quarrels at Corinth are evident throughout this epistolary section.

Word and cognates	Occurrences in Letter	Occurrences in 1:18-4:21
Wise/wisdom (σοφία, *sophia*)	28	26
Cross/crucified (σταυρός, *stauros*)	6	5
Fools/foolishness (μωρός, *mōros*)	10	10
World (κόσμος, *kosmos*)	17	10
Age/world (αἰών, *aiōn*)	8	6

Paul's statement at the end of 1:17 makes it clear that the cross of Christ and human wisdom are antithetical to one another. All attempts, Paul argues, to force the message of Christ crucified through the mold of human wisdom can only destroy the gospel he preaches. Even though the cross of Christ is central to Paul's gospel, it would be a mistake to reduce the multifaceted view Paul holds about the cross of Christ into a single oversimplified doctrine. Paul's utilization of his doctrine of the cross for the congregational problems he addressed throughout his letters reveals that this doctrine can be as diverse as the congregations themselves. When viewed in the setting of the congregational problems at Corinth, the point of irreconcilable difference between the cross and human wisdom in 1 Corinthians should not be viewed as Paul's desire to be obscure. Even more untenable is the view that Paul's disdain for human wisdom at Corinth was a result of his failure in his ostensible mishandling of human wisdom in Athens at the Areopagus (Acts 17). Finally, there is not sufficient internal evidence to demonstrate the existence of, let alone reconstruct, a "wisdom party" at Corinth. At times scholars have posited various wisdom emphases in the Corinthian church. It has even been suggested that Paul's pejorative use of wisdom terminology was directed against a single particular party, perhaps some group associated with the eloquent Apollos.[29] None of these attempts seem to fit explicit evidence of 1 Corinthians.

---

[29]For Apollos see notes on 1 Cor 1:12.

B. CHRIST THE WISDOM AND POWER OF GOD (1:18-2:5)

1. The Message of the Cross (1:18-19)

[18]**For the message of the cross is foolishness to those who are perishing, but to us who are being saved it is the power of God.** [19]**For it is written:**

"I will destroy the wisdom of the wise;

the intelligence of the intelligent I will frustrate."[a]

[a] *19* Isaiah 29:14

The only contextual explanation for Paul's broad attack, beginning in 1:17, upon wisdom is the issue of divisive personal loyalties which lead to a fragmented fellowship. There is simply no contextual or internal evidence that Paul is attacking some format of speculative wisdom or metaphysics being promoted by Gnostics, Hellenized Judaism, or Stoic-Cynic popular philosophy. As Margaret Mitchell noted in this regard, "The wisdom of the world is the set of values and norms which divide persons of higher and lower status into separate groups, a wisdom which prefers dissension to unity, superiority to cooperation."[30] It is in particular the societally accepted criteria for the evaluation of leaders and the direct impact that this worldly wisdom has on the disunity (is Christ divided? 1:13) of the church of God that leads Paul to construct this clear and stern antithesis.

It is really no secret why so many Corinthians would embrace this type of worldly wisdom. Plato's works[31] contain a dialogue in which an Athenian sets forth principles by which societies should rule themselves. The discussion includes the views that "the well-born have a title to rule the worse-born," that "the stronger should rule the weaker," and that "it is for the ignorant to follow and for the wise men to take over the lead and to rule."

---

[30]Margaret M. Mitchell, *Paul and the Rhetoric of Reconciliation: An Exegetical Investigation of the Language and Composition of 1 Corinthians* (Louisville: Westminster/John Knox Press, 1993), p. 211.

[31]*Laws* III.689e-690c.

1:18 For the message of the cross is foolishness to those who are perishing, but to us who are being saved it is the power of God.

Paul turns now directly to his strategy of bringing the believers to their spiritual senses by reminding them that the cross of Christ, on which their salvation rests, is disdained by the world. Paul is attempting to alienate the Corinthians' affections for worldly values and cultural acceptability, while at the same time rekindling their loyalty for the centrality of Christ crucified and the explicit foolishness attached thereto. There are many ways that Paul constructs his admonitions about unity among believers, both in this letter as well as in others. But at this juncture in 1 Corinthians other Pauline techniques and strategies for promoting unity and mutual acceptance (e.g., the one body theme) are neither germane nor effectual. At this point Paul must utilize some facet of fundamental Christian doctrine that will decimate the particular foundation upon which the divisions are erected and maintained. Given the origin of the struggle at hand, Paul's strategy requires a straightforward counter-culture argument. Accordingly, the cross aptly serves the theological needs of the moment, since it points to the bedrock of the Christian faith and also serves as a obvious point of disjuncture between the gospel on the one hand and urban respectability, status, and values of individualistic loyalty on the other.

1:19 For it is written: "I will destroy the wisdom of the wise; the intelligence of the intelligent I will frustrate."

Paul provides scriptural support for his observations in 1:18, highlighted by the phrase "for it is written," with a citation from Isa 29:14.[32] The linking term between the observations of 1:18 and the Scripture of 1:19 is the common Greek word ἀπόλλυμι (*apollumi*). It is not as evident in the English translation that a single Greek term is used in both verses since in the NIV the word is rendered *perishing* in 1:18 and *destroy* in 1:19. This text from Isaiah basically follows the LXX and is the first of numerous examples of

---

[32]Fee, *First Epistle*, pp. 69-70 believes that this verse from Isaiah is chosen because of the occurrence of the term wisdom in it.

Paul's pattern of addressing the problems and issues in this pagan setting by the citation of Scripture.[33]

2. Both Jews and Gentiles Offended (1:20-25)

[20]**Where is the wise man? Where is the scholar? Where is the philosopher of this age? Has not God made foolish the wisdom of the world?** [21]**For since in the wisdom of God the world through its wisdom did not know him, God was pleased through the foolishness of what was preached to save those who believe.** [22]**Jews demand miraculous signs and Greeks look for wisdom,** [23]**but we preach Christ crucified: a stumbling block to Jews and foolishness to Gentiles,** [24]**but to those whom God has called, both Jews and Greeks, Christ the power of God and the wisdom of God.** [25]**For the foolishness of God is wiser than man's wisdom, and the weakness of God is stronger than man's strength.**

1:20 Where is the wise man? Where is the scholar? Where is the philosopher of this age? Has not God made foolish the wisdom of the world?
The specific references in this rapid set of rhetorical questions has led to several interpretations. The general point of the questions is clear and there is little doubt about the function of these questions in the flow of Paul's argument. The major issue, and one for which there is not enough clear evidence, is, "do these three groups of people represent type of individuals from pagan Corinthian society or from ancient Judaism or from both?" Fee suggests that the wise man and philosopher would represent the pagan world while the scholar (γραμματεύς, *grammateus*) should be understood as a Jewish scribe, thereby anticipating the Jew and Gentile vocabulary of 1:22-23.[34]

There is a consensus among scholars that Paul's phrase "of this age" points to a widespread eschatological understanding among Jews which depicts history in terms of two dispensations, this age

---

[33]E.g., 1 Cor 1:19; 1:31; 2:9; 3:19; 9:9; 10:7; 14:21; 15:45.
[34]Fee, *First Epistle*, pp. 70-71.

and the age to come. This brief phrase serves as a window into Paul's eschatological thinking and reveals how naturally it flowed from his piety and theology into the various pastoral issues he dealt with among these Gentile converts. The notion of "this age" usually has pejorative connotations in an eschatological paradigm because it stands for contemporary history yet unredeemed and would have seemed to some of the Corinthians as "Paul's Dogmatic Imposition."[35] Paul declares that in fact God has looked upon the greatest wisdom and cultural acumen available in prosperous urban centers like Corinth and still regards it all as foolishness.

1:21 For since in the wisdom of God the world through its wisdom did not know him, God was pleased through the foolishness of what was preached to save those who believe.

In verse 21a the Apostle makes two points. The current situation (1:18-20), namely the world's inability to embrace God's wisdom, was set into place by God himself, in his own wisdom. Specifically, God so arranged matters that it would be impossible for humans to know God through and on the basis of their own wisdom. The Apostle's declaration that God did what pleased him finds its theological roots in the Old Testament idea of the sovereign will of God. Ps 115:3 and 135:6 contain the verbal antecedents of Paul's thoughts at this point in the affirmation that God does what pleases him. Even though Paul does not spell out here why God did it in this way, there are an abundant number of Scriptures which make clear God's disdain and hatred for boasting, pride and self-righteousness stemming from humanity's sense of self-determination and self-actualization,[36] all of which would eventuate had mankind through its wisdom come to know God. In Calvin's commentary he responds to those of his day who would disagree with Paul, and who argued that knowledge of God through philosophical inquiry was possible. Regarding philosophers Calvin wrote, "For you cannot find one of them who has not constantly fallen away from that principle of knowledge which

---

[35]J.C. Beker, *Paul the Apostle*, p. 170.
[36]Ps 5:5; 10:4; 12:3; 59:12; 75:4; Prov 8:13; 15:25; 16:18; 21:4; Isa 16:6; Jer 9:23.

I have already mentioned, to wanderings and misleading specula-
tions. They are mostly sillier than old wives!"[37]

It must be pointed out that Paul makes no mention here of
creation or general revelation of God in nature, and it would be
questionable to transfer the issues and arguments of Romans 1
into this Corinthian setting where the contingent setting of the
theological formulation is so distant from those of Jew-Gentile
ethnicity expressed in the letter to the Romans.[38]

Second, it was God's good pleasure to make the object of saving faith, Christ crucified, foolish by human standards. The meaning of the phrase "the foolishness of what was preached" can be
best appreciated only when one understands the shame, humiliation and sense of denigration associated with crucifixion in Roman antiquity.[39]

In verse 21b Paul makes reference to three items of Christian
doctrine which anticipate material found in his later letter to the
Romans:

1. The act of preaching is an essential component in the
   process of bringing individuals to faith.
2. Salvation is a unique act of God.
3. Active trust and faith is a precondition for salvation.

1:22 Jews demand miraculous signs and Greeks look for wisdom,

The assertion that "The Jewish mind was matter of fact and
crudely concrete" (while) "The Greek restlessly felt after something which could dazzle his ingenuous speculative turn, and he
passed by anything which failed to satisfy intellectual curiosity"[40]
is surely an overstatement. Admittedly the Greeks were well
known for, and wanted to be well known for, a love of wisdom,

---

[37]Calvin, *First Epistle*, pp. 40-41.

[38]James Walters, *Ethnic Issues in Paul's Letter to the Romans: Changing Self-
definitions in Earliest Roman Christianity* (Valley Forge: Trinity Press International, 1993).

[39]Martin Hengel, *Crucifixion in the Ancient World* is still the best treatment of this ancient form of execution and public humiliation.

[40]Archibald Robertson and Alfred Plummer, *A Critical and Exegetical
Commentary on the First Epistle of St. Paul to the Corinthians*, The International Critical Commentary, 2nd ed. (Edinburgh: T. & T. Clark, 1914),
p. 22.

philosophy. Paul's comments about the Jews probably contains an autobiographical element from his years of opposition to God's Anointed. It also reflects an outlook similar to early Christian Gospel traditions which focused on this characteristic of certain Jews (Matt 12:38–39; 16:1-4; 24:3, 24). The purpose of this Pauline generalization is to show that the entire cultural environment consisted of those who were at odds with God's wisdom.

1:23 but we preach Christ crucified: a stumbling block to Jews and foolishness to Gentiles,

Quite often God does not offer to individuals what they want, especially as incentives to faith. It is especially clear in the death of God's Anointed, that the desire to root faith in the soil of human understanding of how and when God should act has to be abandoned. Accordingly, Paul reaffirms that his message does not takes its cue from the religious passion of his contemporaries for signs and wisdom; rather, he offers a crucified Messiah. The Pauline gospel is a stumbling block (σκάνδαλον, *skandalon*) to the unbelieving Jews for the very reason that it fails, in their preconceived theology, to reflect an understanding of God and his kingdom that has any attraction to them. The Gentiles likewise regard the message of Paul as foolishness because it is so antithetical to the supposedly enlightened wisdom they have developed and taught for centuries.

1:24 but to those whom God has called, both Jews and Greeks, Christ the power of God and the wisdom of God.

Because of Paul's deeply rooted conviction about the sovereignty of God and the prevenient nature of grace, he may well have in mind an intentional contrast between lost mankind who "demand" and "look for" (1:22) and the saints who are called and can only respond to God's initiative. Paul was never bothered by retaining ethnic and cultural labels such as "Jews" and "Gentiles" for individuals, whether they were outsiders (cf. 9:20; 10:32; 12:13) or insiders. We see then in this verse that the saints at Corinth are still referred to by the terms appropriate for their culture and ethnicity.

In contrast to the foolishness ascribed by unbelievers to the crucified Christ, the saved at Corinth know God's Anointed as the wisdom and power of God. This verse makes it clear that Paul has no problem with Christians possessing wisdom, as long as their definition of wisdom flows from Golgotha rather than the agoras, temples, lecture halls, and offices of civic administration at Corinth.

It is difficult to know precisely what Paul meant by power in this context. The immediate temptation is to go to the ostensible parallel text of Rom 1:16 and affirm that Paul has in mind the power of God for salvation, primarily salvation from wrath and sin (cf. Rom 1:18; 3:9). However, Paul's use of the term "power" cannot be fully understood apart from his use of the term weakness in the following verse. The characteristics and ideas associated with these two terms "power" (δύναμις, *dynamis*) and "weakness" (ἀσθενές, *asthenes*) in the literary unit 1:10-4:21 provide important clues for determining the meaning of power in this issue of divisions in Corinth. These words occur in sub-units at 1:24-27; 2:3-5; 4:10. They highlight the fact that God's ways are not mankind's ways and that, in particular, God chose peoples and events that would be regarded as low status or substandard by the unsaved in contemporary Roman society. Thus, this term "weakness" interplays more with the socially derived matrix of the issue of church quarrels and divisions in Roman Corinth than it does with a soteriological affirmation about God's ability and method of saving lost sinners.

1:25 For the foolishness of God is wiser than man's wisdom, and the weakness of God is stronger than man's strength.

In this statement Paul takes the terms of derision (i.e., foolishness and weakness) which originate in the setting of the perishing world and shows how he can embrace them from his own cross-forged perspectives. Paul accomplishes this on the basis of the fundamental contrast between God and mankind. Paul is saying that while the cross may look foolish to mankind, even the most foolish thing God has done is wiser than any and all the wisdom of mankind. Granted that the cross may connote weakness to the perishing, but even the weakest act of God is stronger than the strongest act performed by mankind.

3. God's Choice of Foolish Things (1:26-31)

[26]Brothers, think of what you were when you were called. Not many of you were wise by human standards; not many were influential; not many were of noble birth. [27]But God chose the foolish things of the world to shame the wise; God chose the weak things of the world to shame the strong. [28]He chose the lowly things of this world and the despised things — and the things that are not — to nullify the things that are, [29]so that no one may boast before him. [30]It is because of him that you are in Christ Jesus, who has become for us wisdom from God — that is, our righteousness, holiness and redemption. [31]Therefore, as it is written: "Let him who boasts boast in the Lord."[a]

[a]*31* Jer. 9:24

1:26 Brothers, think of what you were when you were called. Not many of you were wise by human standards; not many were influential; not many were of noble birth.

Paul now moves his argument to the sphere of personal experience and social standing of the church at Corinth. The Corinthians are told to look at themselves and others in the church of God at Corinth and discern from that whether God works with and through the weak and foolish things of the world. By the term calling Paul here is referring to the status or station in life that characterizes the Corinthians. The phrase "not many" (οὐ πολλοί, *ou polloi*) is used three times to underscore the social standing of the majority of the Corinthian believers. Paul's statement, however, surely allows the modern reader to assume that there were at least *some* Corinthians who would be regarded by human standards as wise, influential, and of noble birth.[41] That there were

---

[41]On this whole question of "upperclass" members in the Corinthian church see the arguments, evidence, and bibliographies of G. Theissen,

certain Corinthian believers of high status, can also be demonstrated from other evidence in 1 Corinthians. Pauline congregations, like many religions of the Greco-Roman world whose membership was drawn from a Greco-Roman society with a negligible middle class, would have found most of their members in the lower classes.

One would be gravely mistaken to think that 1:26 contained the doctrinal seed needed to promote Christianity as a religion of the proletariat. All the evidence points to the fact that Paul's urban churches contained wealthy members. This Corinthian church contained people of wealth who served as host not only to Paul, but to the entire congregation (Rom 16), people who owned homes in which they could eat (1 Cor 11:22), and at least one of the influential members, namely Erastus (Rom 16:23), was an administrator in the Roman colony of Corinth.[42]

1:27 But God chose the foolish things of the world to shame the wise; God chose the weak things of the world to shame the strong.
The religious perspective of this verse is one which runs throughout the Scriptures, and Paul's choice of ideas here was influenced and inspired by the long history of God expressing his sovereign will through his choice of foolish and weak individuals to carry out his agenda. Whether one considers God's choice of Israel, or of Moses, or of Gideon, or of David, or of Mary the mother of Jesus, the Scripture is clear in its depiction of a God whose list of friends portrays a lot of foolishness and weakness by human standards.

Verses 27-28 are clearly linked together by the three occurrences of the phrase "God chose the _____ of the world in order to (ἵνα, hina) . . ." Each of these three phrases is a direct expansion upon the threefold reference to the social standing given in 1:26. The verbal and conceptual links between the threefold social references of 1:26 and the theology of 1:27-28 is somewhat obscured in English translations. The following chart of the

---

The Social Setting of Pauline Christianity, 1982 and more recently, Andrew D. Clarke, *Secular & Christian Leadership in Corinth: A Socio-Historical & Exegetical Study of 1 Corinthians 1-6* (Leiden: E.J. Brill, 1993).
[42]On the figure of Erastus see Furnish, "Corinth in Paul's Time," p. 20.

links will help make Paul's correlation of the ideas of 1:26 with 1:27-28 clearer.

Corinthian Status	God's Choice	God's Purpose
Not many wise (*sophos*)	Foolish things	To shame the wise (*sophos*)
Not many influential	Weak things	To shame the strong
Not many of noble birth (*eugenes*)	Lowly things (*agenes*)	To nullify existing things

The concept of God shaming the strong and boastful is a rich and pervasive theme of Scripture, typified by the verse which reads, "The Lord Almighty planned it, to bring low the pride of all glory and to humble all who are renowned on the earth" (Isa 23:9).

1:28 He chose the lowly things of this world and the despised things — and the things that are not — to nullify the things that are,
1:29 so that no one may boast before him.
This verse provides the results and rationale of God's queer choices throughout history. The upshot of Paul's point is that God's intention was to remove all possibility of mankind's boasting. The term boast is used here because it specifically represents one of the fundamental causes of the quarreling and division at Corinth. Unlike the sin of boasting that is referred to in other Scriptures and is rooted in ritual or moralistic self-righteousness, Paul here mentions a type of boasting that is rooted in party loyalty and worldly evaluation. In the presence of God and in light of the divine *modus operandi* highlighted in 1:27-28, every form of human boasting is precluded once for all, especially a boasting in human status (cf. 3:21).

1:30 It is because of him that you are in Christ Jesus, who has become for us wisdom from God — that is, our righteousness, holiness and redemption.
Paul has explicitly mentioned the term God thirteen times in the section 1:18-29 and has thereby maintained a visible theocentric focus. In verse 30 Paul gives attention to Christ, though still in the framework of a theocentric Godhead. This theocentricity is

evident in the phrase "it is because of him (God) that you are in Christ." This attention to the work of Christ, or rather God's work (from God) in Christ is intended to prepare the way for the Scripture quotation in 1:31 which clearly points to Christ. Paul reaffirms a Christ-centered focus for God's wisdom given to Christians. The Apostle then explains what God's wisdom consists of for those in Christ Jesus. The three concepts of righteousness (δικαιοσύνη, *dikaiosynē*), holiness (ἁγιασμός, *hagiasmos*) and redemption (ἀπολύτρωσις, *apolytrōsis*) are all well known doctrinal concepts in the Pauline corpus. Fee captures Paul's sense here in these words, "[God's] wisdom does not have to do with 'getting smart,' nor with status or rhetoric. God's wisdom — the real thing — has to do with salvation through Christ Jesus."[43]

1:31 Therefore, as it is written: "Let him who boasts boast in the Lord."

Because the Christian stands before God in Christ Jesus and because the benefits of righteousness, holiness, and redemption come through Christ, Christ is the only one in whom the believer should boast. To a church whose fragmentation arose as a result of boasting, Paul gives the exhortation that boasting is only acceptable if it is boasting in the Lord. It is only from the immediate context that one can identify the term Lord with Jesus Christ.

---

[43]Fee, *First Epistle*, p. 87.

1 CORINTHIANS 2

CHRIST THE WISDOM AND POWER OF GOD (1:18-2:5)

4. Paul's Message Not Based on Eloquence (2:1-5)

[1]When I came to you, brothers, I did not come with eloquence or superior wisdom as I proclaimed to you the testimony
about God.[a] [2]For I resolved to know nothing while I was with you
except Jesus Christ and him crucified. [3]I came to you in weakness
and fear, and with much trembling. [4]My message and my preaching were not with wise and persuasive words, but with a demonstration of the Spirit's power, [5]so that your faith might not rest on
men's wisdom, but on God's power.

[a]*1* Some manuscripts *as I proclaimed to you God's mystery*

**2:1 When I came to you, brothers, I did not come with eloquence
or superior wisdom as I proclaimed to you the testimony about
God.**
This is the second time Paul turns to autobiography (cf. 1:14-
17) to address the issue at hand. His purpose in this is to put distance between himself and any possible association with the strife
at Corinth stemming from human boasting and human wisdom.
In addition it allows Paul to remind them of the continuity, at
least implicit, between the circumstances of their initial faith and
acceptance of Paul and the perspectives which he is now advocating. On a later occasion Paul's detractors would agree with him
that his speech was unimpressive (2 Cor 10:9-10; 11:6).
There is much debate about the wording at 2:1 because of the
variant readings in the Greek papyri and Greek manuscripts at

that location.[1] One body of evidence supports the reading that Paul proclaimed the "mystery" (μυστήριον, *mystērion*) of God, while another equally important body of evidence supports the reading that Paul proclaimed the "testimony" (μαρτύριον, *martyrion*) of God. Those who favor "mystery of God" point to the use of the term mystery in 2:7, while those favoring "testimony of God" point back to the use of the term testimony in 1:6 and what they believe are the points of discontinuity between 2:1 and 2:7.

2:2 For I resolved to know nothing while I was with you except Jesus Christ and him crucified.

This verse cannot be taken at face value as though it were not part of a well crafted and contextually responsive argument filled with passion and rhetorical devices. The facts of the Gospel traditions (e.g., Mark 8:31), the evidence of the book of Acts (e.g., Acts 13:26-37), the explicit references in the Pauline Corpus (e.g., 1 Thess 1:9-10) to Pauline preaching, and the internal statements of 1 Corinthians regarding the essence of the gospel (15:3-5) all militate against a historical reconstruction which affirms that "Christ crucified" was the simple credo for the ministry of Paul. If the present focus on the ignominious death of the Christ were the simple and quintessential credo for Paul, it is difficult to explain why he withdrew it from his argumentation in the epistle after his treatment of strife and division.

Since the United States forbids, by law, the use of "cruel and unusual punishment" in its treatment of criminals, and since modern Western civilization has little firsthand experience with blood sacrifices, it has been possible for the Western Christian community to combine, perhaps unwittingly, two distinct emphases of the early church regarding the death of Jesus. One emphasis (which pervades Paul's writings) was the vicarious atonement brought about by the shedding of Jesus' blood at the time of his crucifixion.[2] A different emphasis, seen primarily in 1 Corinthians 1-4, is the counter cultureness of the cross due to the shame, bru-

---

[1] For the details of the debate, see Fee, *First Epistle*, p. 91.

[2] In general J. B. Green, "Death of Christ," *DPL*, pp. 201-209 and Leon Morris, "Sacrifice Offering," *DPL*, pp. 856-858.

tality, lower classness, and criminality associated with it, particularly in a Roman colony like Corinth.

2:3 I came to you in weakness and fear, and with much trembling.
The phrase rendered "I came to you" in the NIV can also be translated "I was with you." Since 2:1 points clearly to Paul's initial work with the church at Corinth, it seems preferable to understand 2:3 as a reference to his continuing work with them. Not only did Paul have an embarrassing message and an unimpressive delivery of that message when he came to the Roman capital of Achaia, but his 18 months with the Corinthians were also characterized by a less than impressive demeanor. Paul uses three prepositional phrases to describe his time with the Corinthians: (1) in weakness, (2) in fear, and (3) with much trembling. The exact meaning of all three of these is vague, and Fee rightly comments on the impossibility of knowing exactly what Paul had in mind.[3]

Regarding Paul being with the Corinthians in weakness, some interpreters have projected the narrative of Acts onto Paul's possible emotional condition at the time of Acts 18 when he arrived at Corinth. Archibald Robertson and Alfred Plummer, for example, give these comments in suggesting that Paul may have experienced

> shyness in venturing unaccompanied into strange surroundings (cf. Acts XVII.15, XVIII. 5), coupled with anxiety as to the tidings which Timothy and Silvanus might bring (cf. II Cor. XI.13. There was also the thought of the appalling wickedness of Corinth, of his poor success at Athens, and of the deadly hostility of the Jews to the infant Church of Thessalonica (Acts XVII.5, 13).[4]

Other writers have viewed this weakness as a reference to some illness, perhaps the enigmatic "thorn in the flesh" of 2 Cor 12:7.[5] While admittedly the reference to the "thorn in the flesh" is sur-

---

[3]Fee, *First Epistle*, p. 93.
[4]Robertson and Plummer, *First Epistle of St. Paul*, p. 31.
[5]See V. Furnish, *II Corinthians*. Anchor Bible, vol. 32A.

rounded by occurrences of the term weakness(es) (2 Cor 12:5, 9, 10), in my judgment 1 Cor 1-4 is a more logical place to begin the interpretive task of this obscure verse.

In the unified argument of 1:10-4:23 the word weak and its cognates occur four times (1:25, 27; 2:3; 4:10). In each of the other three cases the term is used to reflect the world's negative appraisal of God's work. It is because of the implementation of human standards that God's choice of the crucified Christ appeared as weakness (1:24-25), that God's choice of the low status Corinthian brethren indicated his proclivity for the weak (1:26-27), and that before the watching world the apostles, unlike the high status Christians at Corinth, have a job description characterized by weakness (4:9-10). In light of these facts, 2:3 seems to be Paul's affirmation that the nature of his ministry with the Corinthians fit snugly into the pattern of God's *modus operandi*, namely God's exercise of his sovereign power in spite of the surrounding culture's disdain and ridicule of his ways.

The terms fear and trembling, unfortunately separated by the NIV translation, belong together. Based upon the meaning of these two words in Phil 2:12 and Eph 6:5, Paul is pointing in 2:3 to his deeply rooted sense of responsibility and wholeheartedness, as well as the awesomeness of the task given him.

2:4a My message and my preaching were not with wise and persuasive words,

Paul's twofold concern with the idea of his message (λόγος, *logos*) and his preaching (κήρυγμα, *kērygma*) continues a distinction already highlighted in his argumentation. The Apostle had already argued for the cruciform nature of both the content of his message and the related issue of how it was communicated. Here Paul asserts that neither the content nor the style of the communication of his gospel had caved in to culturally accepted paradigms of persuasion.

Paul attacks in this verse (anticipating the wisdom of men in 2:5) persuasion based upon human wisdom.[6] Anyone familiar with the use of logic in Paul's own letters as well as the Lukan

---

[6]Witherington, *Conflict and Community at Corinth*, and Bruce Winter, "Rhetoric," *DPL*, pp. 820-822.

summary of Pauline preaching in Acts realizes that all of the extant testimony indicates that Paul was not opposed to human reasoning and logical thinking. Paul's theology and training as a Jew would have included an appreciation of the wisdom literature in Scripture, and he himself acknowledges the importance of wisdom in the individual and corporate lives of believers (cf. 1 Cor 12:8; Rom 11:33; Eph 1:8, 17; 3:10; Col 1:9, 28, 2:3; 4:5). Rather, Paul's concern is with believers being persuaded by a style and type of wisdom which does not originate with God.

2:4b but with a demonstration of the Spirit's power,

The cogency of Paul's message and preaching is manifested by the Spirit and God's power. Paul's thrust is to contrast the impotence of human wisdom to persuade people to embrace a crucified Christ with divine power which proves the veracity of the testimony of God proclaimed in the message and preaching of Paul.

1 Cor 2:4b bristles with grammatical, exegetical, and theological issues. In the matter of grammar one must wrestle with what to do with the two words, both in the dative case, Spirit and power. This is the first occurrence of the term Spirit or its cognates in 1 Corinthians, but it is a term which beginning at 2:4b is going to play an important role in the argument(s) of 2:6-3:4. The term power was first introduced at 1:18 and seems to have a conceptual life of its own. Since both of these concepts of Spirit(ual) and power have distinct functions to play in carrying the weight of Paul's argumentation in 1:10-4:23, it seems unwise to follow the NIV wording which blurs the Pauline phrasing when it reads "with a demonstration of the Spirit's power."

To be sure, all the exegetical questions about the phrases "in the Spirit" and "in power" at 2:4b cannot be fully settled in this space. It is important, nevertheless, to note what Paul does and does not say. Paul writes here, as he does in other places such as 1 Thess 1:5, that his apostolic proclamation of the gospel was attended by the working of God's Spirit and God's power. The two-pronged question this text leaves us with is, "Is Paul referring to the reception of the Holy Spirit at conversion" and "Does Paul refer to miracles with the term power?"

For the reasons listed below, it seems to me that Paul is refer-ring to the work of the Spirit in the conversion of the Corinthians and not to conversions "probably evidenced by spiritual gifts, es-pecially tongues" or conversions which "would automatically have recalled the visible evidences of the Spirit's presence."[7]

(1) There is no textual evidence in Acts in general or in Acts 18:1-18 in particular about Paul's mission that closely associates conversion with accompanying evidence of spiritual gifts, espe-cially tongues.

(2) There is no cogent textual evidence that necessarily equates the working of the Spirit in Christians with miracles. There are Pauline texts which portray the giving of the Spirit to Christians and the working of the Spirit in Christians as an activity distinct from God performing miracles in their lives (Gal 3:5; Rom 15:15-19). Accordingly one must exercise caution when attempting to correlate the two separate activities of God, namely God perform-ing miracles and God providing the Spirit to people.

(3) While all of the Corinthian believers had equally imbibed one Spirit and been immersed in one Spirit, not all of them spoke in tongues, or ever probably spoke in tongues (12:13, 30).

(4) While the doctrine of the working of the power of God as seen in the arguments of 1:10-4:23 would include spiritual experi-ences of the saved (1:18, 24; 4:20), this is quite different from Fee's statement that the proof of Paul's Gospel was in the accompany-ing *visible* evidence of the Spirit's power.[8]

2:5 so that your faith might not rest on men's wisdom, but on God's power.

In this verse Paul completes the sentence started in 2:4 by giv-ing a purpose clause (ἵνα, *hina*) in 2:5. As the Corinthian recipi-ents had learned by Paul's frequent use of purpose clauses (*hina*) in 1:18-2:5, the Apostle did not intend to leave the impression that God's choices were capricious. Not only were God's choices me-thodical, they were intended, according to the argument of 2:5, to establish and secure the Corinthian's faith in God's power rather than the thoughts, values, and wisdom of mankind. The function

---

[7]Fee, *First Epistle*, p. 95, fn. 33.
[8]Ibid., fn. 28.

of this point in the larger context is to underscore the solidarity of Paul's message and preaching with a faith in Christ crucified as the power of God. This meant contextually a repudiation of the enticements of cultural sophistries and the attendant boasting and pride that engendered party strife.

C. WISDOM AND SPIRITUAL MATURITY (2:6-3:4)

1. God's Secret Wisdom (2:6-9)

[6]We do, however, speak a message of wisdom among the mature, but not the wisdom of this age or of the rulers of this age, who are coming to nothing. [7]No, we speak of God's secret wisdom, a wisdom that has been hidden and that God destined for our glory before time began. [8]None of the rulers of this age understood it, for if they had, they would not have crucified the Lord of glory. [9]However, as it is written:

"No eye has seen, no ear has heard,
no mind has conceived
what God has prepared for those who love him"[a] —

[a]9 Isaiah 64:4

2:6 We do, however, speak a message of wisdom among the mature, but not the wisdom of this age or of the rulers of this age, who are coming to nothing.

This verse introduces a large block of thought which runs from 2:6-3:4. The understanding of this sub-unit is important since one's decision whether 2:6-3:4 forms one unit of thought or whether 2:6-16 forms one unit, with 3:1-4 functioning as a transition to a second unit of thought in 3:5-17, may well impact one's exegetical conclusions.[9]

The vocabulary and imagery of 2:5-3:4 refer to historically controversial issues such as mature Christians and baby Christians; the spiritual, natural, and fleshly man; spiritual revelation and the

---

[9]Fee, *First Epistle*, pp. 121-122.

deep things of God; and the rulers of this age. Fee rightly observed that these verses have "endured a most unfortunate history of application in the church."[10]

This section has seemed to some scholars to be a digression by Paul from his central concerns. There are others who never label it a digression, but, based upon the variety of doctrines they isolate in these verses, must either regard it as a doctrinal potpourri or are unconvinced that Paul's thought here is coherent.

It is clear that Paul believes that he is still focused on the same concern that he raised in 1:10ff. The presence in 3:4 of the slogans of strife and party loyalty found already at 1:12 seems to establish this beyond question. It follows then that the apostle will be attempting to address the same concerns he had in chapter 1, though of course with additional terms and images.

Even though 2:5 contained the pejorative idea of wisdom with its expression "men's wisdom," in 2:6 Paul reverts to a positive sense of wisdom which was used earlier at 1:21, 24, 30. The prepositional phrase "among the mature" has evoked varied, heated, and sometimes confused responses from later interpreters of Paul. One recent writer, for example, responded by stating, "First, New Testament writers present no evidence that distinguishes between two types of Christians: mature and immature, spiritual and natural, superior and inferior."[11] While few, if any, would try to find New Testament evidence for a doctrine of superior and inferior Christians, we cannot so quickly dismiss the possibility of a Pauline teaching about mature and immature Christians, since Paul himself introduces the word "mature" (τέλειος, teleios).

In an era of church life characterized by the ascendency of the "judge not" verse and equally afflicted with a severe case of spiritual entitlements syndrome, it is hard for some to conceive of the apostle Paul as judging, labeling and evaluating fellow Christians. The best approach is to seek an answer in Paul's own practices and recorded attitudes.

---

[10]Fee, *First Epistle*, p. 120.

[11]Simon Kistemaker, *Exposition of the First Epistle to the Corinthians* (Grand Rapids: Baker, 1993), p. 80.

The Apostle apparently had no reservations in labeling believers with discriminating and value-laden terms such as: weak and strong Christians, spiritual and transgressing Christians, Christians with and without God's approval, legitimate Christians and bastard Christians, brethren and false brethren, mature and immature Christians, and carnal Christians and spiritual Christians.[12] Admittedly the categorization of individuals among the people of God has been abused, but it is difficult to imagine a historical reading of Scripture that could totally miss this phenomenon since it is so prevalent in the Old Testament (e.g., Isa 1), the Gospels (e.g., Matt 23), and the remainder of the non-Pauline portions of the New Testament (e.g., Rev 1-3).

Paul's wisdom is neither derived from nor compatible with the mores and cultural values dominant in Roman Corinth. Paul is not, of course, revealing an obscurantist attitude or latent convictions about the need for believers to withdraw from Corinthian society. The Apostle will clarify this point in 5:9-10 and make clear that he does not want to be interpreted as fostering the concept of an insular Christian community.

In the context of 1:10-4:23, Paul is disavowing only those cultural perspectives that have engendered strife, promoted community fragmentation, and brought about disharmony in the church of God at Corinth. It is no coincidence that when Paul reverts to a positive use of the term wisdom, that he contrasts it with the worldview of a Roman colony. Notwithstanding Paul's own Roman citizenship,[13] the rhetorical and doctrinal function of Christ crucified in 1 Corinthians requires him to juxtapose God's wisdom in the cross with the blind and inexcusable ignorance of State authorities, the rulers of this age. The strategy behind this juxtaposition is to show the Corinthians that they, by implication, hold a wisdom similar to those who crucified Christ.

It would be only natural for some of the Corinthian believers, particularly high status ones, to have been seduced into a party loyalty mindset by the mores of their workplace. It may well have been the same believers who saw no conflict of interest or spiri-

---

[12]Passages from Paul's letters include Rom 14:1-15:13; Gal 2:4, 4:28-31, 6:1; 1 Cor 2:14-3:3, 14:37-38.

[13]M. Reasoner, "Citizenship, Roman and Heavenly," *DPL*, pp. 139-141.

tual problem with imposing the Roman court system on the issue of grievances among believers (cf. 6:1-8).

2:7 No, we speak of God's secret wisdom, a wisdom that has been hidden and that God destined for our glory before time began.

In stark contrast (ἀλλά, *alla*) to the ephemeral nature of the civic and political establishment, God's wisdom given through Paul was predestined before time began. This secret wisdom was not manifested in esoteric formulae or arcane philosophical speculation as one might find in pagan mystery cults or philosophic speculation. For the apostle Paul, God's secret wisdom was made known in the public execution of an ostensibly seditious Jewish teacher by the Roman occupation forces in Palestine at the behest of Jewish leaders.[14] In harmony with texts such as Acts 2:23; 4:27-28 and Eph 3:7-11, Paul tells the Corinthians that this action leading to Jesus' execution was predestined by God. While it is well known that Paul's theological perspectives were profoundly influenced by his doctrine of the last things, his eschatology, it is noteworthy in 2:7 that his doctrine of first things is also prominent. That is, to fully appreciate Paul's own perspective in 1 Corinthians, the interpreter needs to dwell not only on Paul's doctrine of God's activity at the ends of the ages (e.g., 10:11), but also God's activity before the outset of the ages.

By his use of the pregnant eschatological term "glory" (δόξα, *doxa*) (cf. 1 Cor 15:43; 2 Cor 4:16-5:10; Rom 8:18-30), Paul reveals to the Corinthians the importance of both first things and final things, the Alpha and the Omega, in his message of the cross.

2:8 None of the rulers of this age understood it, for if they had, they would not have crucified the Lord of glory.

The Apostle's castigation of Roman rulers, and perhaps other rulers under Roman sway, needs to be understood in the rhetorical and argumentative setting of 2:6-3:4. Keeping in mind, as Fee so persuasively argues, that these rulers are human individuals and not spiritual or demonic rulers, one should not over general-

---

[14]An overview of seditious Jewish groups in the first century is given by P.W. Barnett, "Revolutionary Movements," *DPL*, pp. 812-819.

ize Paul's statement about "none of the rulers of this age."[15] The life and execution of Jesus (as Corinthian believers would have known) took place within the administrative sphere of only a handful of the hundreds of Roman rulers and administrators who were in office during the early Julio-Claudian period. In 2:8 Paul makes it clear that he is only discussing those who, in some way, participated in the public execution of God's Christ and thereby manifested their human wisdom. Accordingly, one should not go down the interpretive path of S. Kistemaker when he concluded, "The Jewish and Gentile leaders who crucified Jesus are representative of all the rulers of the world. Whoever ignores the cause of Christ takes his place with the rulers who put Jesus to death."[16]

In 2:8 Paul inextricably links, it seems, the possession of God's wisdom with the acceptance of Christ. In 2:8b Paul uses a Greek construction known as a contrary-to-fact conditional sentence. The emphasis and purpose of this type of conditional sentence is to say "Had they only known (but they clearly didn't), they would not have crucified Christ."

As the original readers begin to digest Paul's point in 2:6-8, it is clear that they are being given a choice of self-determination. They can either align themselves with the Pauline message of Christ crucified as the wisdom of God (and the implications of that for their factious boasting and pride) or they can reject Paul's message and *ipso facto* embrace the wisdom of the current age that led to the rejection of the Lord of glory (and which continues to produce community fragmentation in the Corinthian congregation).

2:9 However, as it is written: "No eye has seen, no ear has heard, no mind has conceived what God has prepared for those who love him" —

The apostle Paul here brings forward a quotation to undergird his preceding ideas. Even though it is not clear which portion of Scripture Paul cites, the wording "as it is written" can hardly be anything other than a formulaic introduction to a Scripture quota-

---

[15]Fee, *First Epistle*, pp. 103-106.
[16]Kistemaker, *First Corinthians*, p. 83.

tion (cf. Rom 15:9).[17] The apostle's Scripture quotation appears to be primarily a combination of material from the Greek text of Isa 64:3 and 65:16 rather than a quotation from the lost *Apocalypse of Elijah*, a view first proposed by Origen but later refuted by Jerome.[18]

The wording of the quotation in Greek makes Paul's ideas relatively obvious, but regrettably the wording of the NIV obscures Paul's ideas and in one instance "misses the point altogether."[19] The intent of the citation is to highlight the radical dichotomy between the world's inability to grasp God's revelation and the church's privilege of receiving it. On the one hand Paul lists how the world forms its opinions: eyes, ears, mind. In Paul's phrase, "the mind (καρδία, *kardia*) of man," the term man (omitted by the NIV), is meant to be understood pejoratively, as it also is in 1:25; 2:5; 3:3,4, 21; 4:1.

The dominant epistemology of urban Roman culture cannot grasp, according to Paul, the very things that God has prepared for those who love him.

2. The Teaching of the Spirit (2:10-16)

[10]but God has revealed it to us by his Spirit.

The Spirit searches all things, even the deep things of God. [11]For who among men knows the thoughts of a man except the man's spirit within him? In the same way no one knows the thoughts of God except the Spirit of God. [12]We have not received the spirit of the world but the Spirit who is from God, that we may understand what God has freely given us. [13]This is what we speak, not in words taught us by human wisdom but in words taught by the Spirit, expressing spiritual truths in spiritual words.[a]

[a] *13 Or Spirit, interpreting spiritual truths to spiritual men*

---

[17]In general, see Robertson and Plummer, *First Epistle of St. Paul*, pp. lii-liv.

[18]Consult Robertson and Plummer, pp. 41-43.

[19]Fee, *First Epistle*, p. 107, fn. 39.

2:10 but God has revealed it to us by his Spirit. The Spirit searches all things, even the deep things of God.

If 2:9 is written to scripturally document the dichotomy mentioned in 2:6-8, then 2:10a is given to introduce the dichotomy in the epistemologies between those who receive the word of the cross and those who do not. As we begin this section, it is important to make three comments, one historical and two exegetical, about this and the following verses.

(1) Some interpreters have understood these verses in such a way that they become the basis for condemnations and harangues against secular culture in ancient Corinth.[20] Since it is sometimes necessary to state the obvious, we must point out that Roman Corinth was not secular. In fact, a majority of the problems Paul had to address in 1 Corinthians can only be explained by looking to the religiosity of the city.

(2) These verses have often played a central role in theologies of conversion and evangelism. Since the purpose of this section is fundamentally to redirect the thinking and behavior of members of the church of God at Corinth, Paul's teaching here is more germane to how the Spirit should be working in their lives than how it works in the process of evangelism and conversion.

(3) Commentators must wrestle with the issue in the verses of whom Paul includes in his use of the first person plural verbs and pronouns. One view is that the pronoun "we" includes only Paul and the apostles. Thus, this section is viewed as an apology for Paul's apostolic authority based on the teaching about the revelation and mind of Christ that he and the other Apostles have. In some camps of thought 2:13 is interpreted as supporting a very literalistic view of the inspiration of the words of the Apostles. Others view these verses as applying equally to all (mature) Christians. A third view, which seems the best interpretation of the evidence, regards the plural pronouns as references to the Corinthian readership (2:10, 12, 16) while the few occurrences of the Greek word λαλέω (*laleō*) (2:6, 7, 13 — "we speak"; 3:1 — "address") point to Paul's more distinctive work as an apostle. One of the strengths of this third view is that it preserves the significance of

---

[20]Kistemaker, *First Corinthians*, p. 85.

2:10ff for the Corinthian readership while also allowing Paul to begin to formulate an apology for this authority against judgmental detractors (see notes on 2:15).

Paul's doctrinal system as well as his personal piety were, in light of later ecclesiastical developments, astonishingly theocentric. God the Father was at the center of Paul's faith and preaching and vv. 2:6-3:4 is no exception. Notwithstanding the treatment of this section in modern piety, Paul's treatment of the Spirit in this section is primarily on the Spirit as the means or agent by which God gives revelation. The Spirit accomplishes this since (γάρ, *gar*) it knows the deep things of God. In light of the use of deep/depth imagery in Rev 2:24 (deep things of Satan) and Rom 11:33 (the depth of the riches, wisdom, and knowledge of God), Paul here teaches that the Spirit has full knowledge of God.

2:11 For who among men knows the thoughts of a man except the man's spirit within him? In the same way no one knows the thoughts of God except the Spirit of God.

Paul offers here an illustration, some would call it a proof, to show how the Spirit is the means through which (2:10) God is accessible. Paul sets forth an illustration of the working of the human spirit that all would agree upon and then transfers ("in the same way") the point of the illustration to the divine sphere. The force of this illustration within the contextual argument rests squarely upon Paul's use of the same word spirit (πνεῦμα, *pneuma*) in both the human and divine side of the illustration. Just as the human spirit serves as the window into a person's inner thoughts, convictions and values, so God's Spirit, and only God's Spirit, serves as a window into the deep and inner thoughts of God.

2:12 We have not received the spirit of the world but the Spirit who is from God, that we may understand what God has freely given us.

Having illustrated how God's Spirit alone knows the thoughts of God, Paul then declares that the Corinthian believers themselves have received this same Spirit from God. By this argument Paul is able to maintain both the otherness of God from the point

of view of epistemology, while at the same time affirming that believers can understand what God has freely given us.

In 2:11-12 Paul uses the Greek word *pneuma* (= spirit) three
times, each time with the Greek article τό (*to*). In 2:11 it referred to
a man's spirit, while in 2:12 it refers both to God's Spirit and to
the convictions and ethos of the contemporary fallen culture
(= wisdom of the world, 1:20). This is but one of many instances
in this letter where it is clear that the particular meaning of the
word "spirit" cannot be determined merely by the criterion of the
presence or absence of the Greek article.[21]

Paul has reminded the recipients that what they received (at
conversion from God) was not the prevailing worldview but access to God's wisdom. With ideas which sound quite similar to
Eph 1:17-19, Paul states that the purpose of this divine revelation
was to facilitate the believer's understanding of "what God has
freely given" to the believer. With this wording, Paul is making a
direct connection with the last part of 2:9 where he mentioned the
things which God had prepared for believers.

**2:13 This is what we speak, not in words taught us by human wis-
dom but in words taught by the Spirit, expressing spiritual truths
in spiritual words.**

The apostle is slowly but inexorably beginning to engage the
topic of his defense against detractors. In a two-pronged approach
Paul uses the material in 2:13 to enhance his apostolic authority.
It may not be as clear in the NIV as in Paul's Greek that the antecedent of "this is what we speak" is the closing idea of 2:12. With
this grammatical connection in mind, we see that Paul is correlating the things he speaks (2:13a) with the God-given pneumatic understanding of "what God has freely given us" (2:12b). The Apostle's strategy at this juncture is to make a correlation that begins to
solidify the authority of his teaching. To disagree with Paul's instruction would clearly set one in opposition to the Spirit of God,
an understanding clearly stated elsewhere in this epistle (e.g.,
14:37-38).

---

[21]An examination of the Greek text of Rom 8, 1 Cor 12-14, 2 Cor 3 or
Gal 5-6 makes this very evident.

The second prong of Paul's defensive strategy reflected in this verse is his explicit importation of the dichotomy "human wisdom against spiritual wisdom" into the issue of his own effort to correct the problem of party factions. This Pauline strategy was implicit from the outset. Paul's claim in 2:13 is clearly no longer a description of when he came to Corinth (2:1-5). The apostle now writes about the present time, as he has from 2:6ff, a time when "words taught by the Spirit" are directed to the church and not the outsider in Roman Corinth.

2:14 The man without the Spirit does not accept the things that come from the Spirit of God, for they are foolishness to him, and he cannot understand them, because they are spiritually discerned.

Since Paul is the agent through whom the Spirit of God speaks, the only explanation for Corinthian resistance to his apostolic teaching in this section is that these detractors are natural men (ψυχικὸς ἄνθρωπος, *psychikos anthrōpos*), men seemingly without the Spirit. To the degree that those who foster community faction follow the guiding light of Corinthian mores and cultural values, the admonitions and judgments of Paul will appear foolish (μωρία αὐτῷ, *mōria autō*).

There is an inevitability about the rejection of Paul's ideas by those without the Spirit. Paul writes that these types of people are unable to understand because (ὅτι, *hoti*) they lack the essential ability provided by the Spirit. Some of the apostle's Christian readership at Corinth are manifesting this problem to such an extent that he cannot address them as though they had the Spirit (esp. 3:1-3). Since he is dealing with a problem of carnality among the saints in this Roman city, it is misleading to suppose, as Kistemaker does, that the apostle is talking contextually about the "agnostic or atheist."[22]

---

[22]S. Kistemaker, *First Corinthians*, p. 92.

2:15 The spiritual man makes judgments about all things, but he himself is not subject to any man's judgment:

To follow Paul's point as closely as possible, the reader needs to be aware that the same Greek verb ἀνακρίνω (*anakrinō*) lies behind the translation "discerned" (2:14), "makes judgments" (2:15), and "subject to any man's judgments" (2:15). In the polemical rhetorical setting of chapters 1-4, Paul is teaching that he (and others) has the essential characteristic required for spiritual discernment (2:10, 12, 13). Consequently, he is enabled to make judgments about all things (πάντα, *panta*).

It is especially important not to remove 2:15b from its rhetorical context and exchange it into a broad generalization. Paul is obviously not teaching here that Spirit-filled people are granted some permanent immunity from the need for either self-examination or evaluation by fellow believers. Contextually he is asserting that the spiritual believer (πνευματικός, *pneumatikos*) is not subject to the perspectives and judgments of the ill-equipped fellow believer who operates from the sphere of the natural (*psychikos*) and fleshly (σαρκικός, *sarkikos*) individual (3:1-3). The term "any man's" in 2:15 should be read and interpreted in the light of the historical and contextual issues of this subsection of 1 Corinthians. When this is done, it seems unlikely that Paul is teaching that "the believer cannot be judged by the unbelievers."[23]

2:16 "For who has known the mind of the Lord that he may instruct him?" But we have the mind of Christ.

In this verse the apostle brings his immediate thoughts to a conclusion. This conclusion is based upon the correlation of the spiritual condition of Paul and a citation of Scripture (Isa 40:13, *LXX*; cf. Rom 11:34). The verbal link between the Scripture text from Isaiah and Paul's observation is the term "mind" (νοῦς, *nous*). The thrust of his argument here is to buttress the assertion of 2:15.

The reasons Paul's detractors cannot successfully scrutinize him and find fault is that, according to Scripture, the mind of the Lord (νοῦν κυρίου, *noun kyriou*) is in no need of examination and improvement, and Paul asserts that he indeed has the mind of

---

[23]Ibid., p. 93.

Christ (νοῦν Χριστοῦ, *noun Christou*). This, then, demonstrates why he and others who are spiritual cannot be subject to the human judgment of his detractors.

1 CORINTHIANS 3

C. WISDOM AND SPIRITUAL MATURITY (2:6-3:4)

3. Divisions a Sign of Worldliness (3:1-4)

¹Brothers, I could not address you as spiritual but as worldly — mere infants in Christ. ²I gave you milk, not solid food, for you were not yet ready for it. Indeed, you are still not ready. ³You are still worldly. For since there is jealousy and quarreling among you, are you not worldly? Are you not acting like mere men? ⁴For when one says, "I follow Paul," and another, "I follow Apollos," are you not mere men?

3:1 Brothers, I could not address you as spiritual but as worldly — mere infants in Christ.

In this section Paul is continuing the thoughts that he has expressed in the latter part of ch. 2. The dualistic concepts which Paul had spelled out at the end of 1 Cor 2 with his emphasis on the difference between spiritual thinking and worldly thinking, are carried forward in ch. 3. In 3:1 Paul lays out the dualistic categories of spiritual (πνευματικός, *pneumatikos*) versus fleshly (σάρκινος, *sarkinos*), or as the NIV reads, spiritual versus worldly. 3:1 is a stinging indictment against those Christians who are a part of the problem of fragmentation and party strife in the congregation at Corinth. While Paul wishes to address them as spiritual Christians, based on their behavior, he can only address them as carnal individuals. The last part of verse 1 makes it clear that these individuals, though they are acting in a worldly fashion are, nevertheless, in Christ. Paul specifically refers to them as babes in Christ.

3:2 I gave you milk, not solid food, for you were not yet ready for it. Indeed, you are still not ready.

Using nutritional metaphors, Paul indicates that the Corinthians not only received milk from him when he first preached to them, but that he in fact still can give them only milk. Paul explicitly acknowledges that there is solid food for the Christian to digest, but makes it clear that the Christians involved in this fragmentation at Corinth are not yet able to digest that material.

3:3 You are still worldly. For since there is jealousy and quarreling among you, are you not worldly? Are you not acting like mere men?

By use of the connecting word "for" (γάρ, gar), in 3:3 (omitted in the NIV translation), Paul makes it clear why the Corinthians are unable to receive and digest mature Christian teaching. Paul makes a direct connection between the worldly outlook of the readership and their inability to receive mature Christian teaching. In this verse Paul also makes it very clear what characteristics of worldly thinking he has in mind. Paul refers explicitly to the jealousy and quarreling found among segments of the Corinthian church. For the apostle these attitudes of jealousy and quarreling are clear hallmarks of the worldly thinking among the Corinthian Christians.

3:4 For when one says, "I follow Paul," and another, "I follow Apollos," are you not mere men?

This verse provides explicit testimony to the fact that Paul is treating the same problem that he introduced in 1:10. The slogans "I follow Paul," "I follow Apollos" found in 3:4, are virtually identical with the slogans Paul cited in 1:12. All of these share in common an attitude of party spirit and fragmentation. When Paul asks in 3:4, "are you not men," he is not asking a question concerning gender but rather is using the word "men" (ἄνθρωποι, anthrōpoi) as an antithesis to the divine perspective.

D. GOD THE MASTER BUILDER (3:5-23)

1. Paul and Apollos Merely Servants (3:5-9)

[5]What, after all, is Apollos? And what is Paul? Only servants, through whom you came to believe — as the Lord has assigned to each his task. [6]I planted the seed, Apollos watered it, but God made it grow. [7]So neither he who plants nor he who waters is anything, but only God, who makes things grow. [8]The man who plants and the man who waters have one purpose, and each will be rewarded according to his own labor. [9]For we are God's fellow workers; you are God's field, God's building.

3:5 What, after all, is Apollos? And what is Paul? Only servants, through whom you came to believe — as the Lord has assigned to each his task.

In this verse Paul gives us an important insight into his own strategy at destroying pride in human leaders. The first part of Paul's strategy is to point out that he and Apollos are merely servants (διάκονοι, *diakonoi*). The second part of Paul's strategy is to show that Apollos and Paul only played a role that had been assigned to them by the Lord in the process of the evangelization of individuals in Corinth. Even though the imagery and vocabulary will shift several times in the remainder of this chapter, in some ways the rest of this chapter is no more than a fuller answer to the question about the identity and significance of Apollos and Paul (cf. 3:22).

3:6 I planted the seed, Apollos watered it, but God made it grow.

Paul mentions here the specific ministry assigned to him and to Apollos by God in their respective ministries in the history of the church at Corinth. Since planting a seed precedes the need to water the seed, Paul is perhaps indicating that his ministry had chronological priority in God's work in the church in Corinth. Based on the narrative in Acts 18, it is very clear that Paul's work in Corinth began before that of Apollos, and that Apollos' ministry there had more to do with nurturing the gospel rather than planting the gospel. The function of Paul's statements in v. 6 is to highlight the autonomy and the sovereignty of God in the process of individuals coming to faith. Using the illustration of the growth of a seed, Paul points out that it is God himself who gives growth to the seed. That growth cannot be attributed to human agency.

3:7 So neither he who plants nor he who waters is anything, but only God, who makes things grow.

Paul makes it clear in this verse where he is trying to lead the Corinthians in their own thinking and their evaluation of who Paul and who Apollos are. Paul explicitly says that the one who plants the seed, namely Paul, as well as the one who waters, namely Apollos, are not anything. By contrast one should acknowledge that all of the spiritual growth that occurs in individuals or the church in Corinth must be attributed to God himself. The teaching of 3:7 is in harmony with the God-centeredness of Paul's teachings elsewhere. Throughout Paul's letters it is clear that God the Father is the only one to whom believers should give praise and thanks.

3:8 The man who plants and the man who waters have one purpose, and each will be rewarded according to his own labor.

Even though both Paul and Apollos have their own supporters among the believers at Corinth, Paul is not going to let congregational fragmentation detract from his own estimation of God's work through the ministry of Apollos. By the use of the phrase, "have one purpose" in 3:8, Paul expresses total solidarity with the ministry of Apollos and the harmony between the doctrine that Paul preaches and that which is associated with the ministry of Apollos.

In the second half of this verse Paul makes a statement which serves as a transition into the material that extends through 3:17. Some of this emphasis is not as clear in the translation of the NIV. In the Greek text of 3:8b Paul affirms that each one, namely himself and Apollos, will receive his "own reward" according to his "own labor."[1] This double emphasis on "own reward" and "own labor" is not reflected in the NIV translation. This latter part of

---

[1]See R. M. Fuller, "Rewards," *DPL*, pp. 819-820.

3:8 anticipates 3:10-17 both in terms of the idea of the compensation that the worker receives based on his effort and the occurrence of the word "reward" which is found in 3:8 and 3:14. Paul may be setting forth this particular teaching in self-defense against those who would detract from his own efforts in the gospel. This interpretation seems likely since the one other time in 1 Corinthians that Paul talks about this issue is in 9:17-18 (2 occurrences) where he is partially involved in a defense of his calling and ministry (cf. 9:3).

3:9 For we are God's fellow workers; you are God's field, God's building.

It would be a mistake to separate the ideas found in 3:9 from the affirmation that Paul makes at the end of 3:8. It seems likely that Paul's affirmation that he and Apollos are co-workers of God is intended to relate to the issue that they will be rewarded by God individually and based upon their own labor. This would also seem to explain why in this verse Paul affirms that he and Apollos are co-workers with God, in distinction from the Corinthians who themselves are described not as God's co-workers but as a field of God and a building of God.

In the section 3:9-17 Paul uses three metaphors to describe the people of God. They are the field of God, the building of God, and in v. 16 they are the temple of God. When Paul affirms in 3:9 that the Corinthian believers are God's field he is continuing the imagery that he introduced in v. 6 when he used agricultural metaphors to explain the ministry of himself and Apollos among the Christians. Imagery of planting and watering provides the background to the imagery that the converts are God's field. Paul's affirmation in 3:9, namely that the Corinthians are God's building, sets the stage for the imagery to be found in 3:10-16.

2. Building on the Foundation Laid by Paul (3:10-17)

[10]**By the grace God has given me, I laid a foundation as an expert builder, and someone else is building on it. But each one should be careful how he builds.** [11]**For no one can lay any foun-**

dation other than the one already laid, which is Jesus Christ. [12]If any man builds on this foundation using gold, silver, costly stones, wood, hay or straw, [13]his work will be shown for what it is, because the Day will bring it to light. It will be revealed with fire, and the fire will test the quality of each man's work. [14]If what he has built survives, he will receive his reward. [15]If it is burned up, he will suffer loss; he himself will be saved, but only as one escaping through the flames.

[16]Don't you know that you yourselves are God's temple and that God's Spirit lives in you? [17]If anyone destroys God's temple, God will destroy him; for God's temple is sacred, and you are that temple.

3:10 By the grace God has given me, I laid a foundation as an expert builder, and someone else is building on it. But each one should be careful how he builds.

1 Cor 3:10-16 has been a section that has produced many ideas about the relationship between works and salvation. It is important, however, to keep in mind the contextual function of Paul's ideas in these verses. These verses are an expansion of his affirmation that the Corinthians are God's building, which in turn is a response to the larger question about the role and significance of himself and Apollos in God's work. In the agricultural metaphors of 3:6, Paul wrote that he planted and Apollos watered. The same general point is being made in 3:10, where Paul says that he is the wise architect who laid the foundation of the Christian community upon which others built as they served God. As always, Paul acknowledges that his ministerial activities are a manifestation of the grace of God given to him. Regardless of what one's gift from God is, Paul always regards it as a manifestation of the grace of God in the life of that individual. In the Corinthian setting and in the particular context of 3:10-15, Paul describes his work as laying down a foundation as an expert builder. In the use of this architectural imagery, Paul is referring to his own work in planting the gospel and presenting the gospel to the Corinthians. Given the contextual reference to Apollos in this section (3:4, 5, 22) and the fact that Paul refers to someone else (in the singular), building

upon his own work, it is very likely that he has a follower of Apollos in mind here. Verse 10 ends with Paul's admonition that anyone who builds must be careful how he builds upon the foundation that Paul has already put in place. The background to Paul's thought here would go back to 3:8, where Paul says that each worker will receive his own reward according to his own labor. The reference to Apollos in this section does not necessarily mean that Apollos himself was in Corinth at that time and was involved in this activity. It is clear, however, from the context of chs. 1-4 that this may well include a person who claimed party loyalty to Apollos and that he needs to be careful how he is building upon the foundation that Paul has put down.

3:11 For no one can lay any foundation other than the one already laid, which is Jesus Christ.

As we have seen earlier in 1 Corinthians, Paul wants to make it very clear that he has special prerogatives in terms of the Corinthian work. By stating that there is no other foundation for the Christian community than the one that he himself has placed, Paul is highlighting his special role in the formation of the Christian community in Corinth. The purpose of Paul's affirmation in 3:11 is to preclude other Christian workers from claiming to be equal to Paul in his relationship with the church at Corinth.

3:12 If any man builds on this foundation using gold, silver, costly stones, wood, hay or straw,

Since Paul is an absent apostle, and since Paul knows that God will continue to be at work in the Corinthian church, he must deal with the fact that others will build upon the foundation that he has laid (e.g., Timothy). There is never a question in his mind whether others will be part of the ultimate growth of the church of God in Corinth.[2] Verse 12 is a clear acknowledgment that others will build upon Paul's work, but Paul is concerned about the nature of this work and the converts that follow from it.

---

[2]Paul obviously believes that those who are prophets, teachers, healers, etc. will be the instruments through whom God continues to bring edification and growth in Corinth.

As one interprets the words gold, silver, costly stones, wood, hay, or straw in 3:12, it is imperative that these are kept in the context of the metaphor in which Paul placed them. The larger contextual metaphor is that believers are a building.[3] This means then that the various building materials mentioned in 3:13 must be seen to be referring to converts themselves since the building is a people. Even though Paul gives six particular examples of building materials, it is very clear that these six readily divide into two groups, with gold, silver and costly stones being in one group, and with wood, hay and straw being in the second group. The exact significance of these two groups is only apparent when these images are taken in the context of the larger metaphor that Paul is using. It becomes apparent in 3:13 what significance Paul attributes to these two groups in light of the continuing imagery found there.

3:13 his work will be shown for what it is, because the Day will bring it to light. It will be revealed with fire, and the fire will test the quality of each man's work.

With the single reference to judgment day and the dual reference to fire found in 3:13, it becomes clear what Paul intends by his use of these two groups of building materials. The point of contrast between these two groups of materials that are used in buildings is how well they will stand up against the heat of fire. In order to understand Paul correctly in this section, it is very important to comment on Paul's use of the word "work" (ἔργον, *ergon*) in this particular metaphor. Because of Paul's use of the term "works" in his discussion of faith and works in other parts of the New Testament, many interpreters have thought that he is referring to that in this section. However, it is very clear that his use of the singular term "work" in this illustration in 3:10-15 has little to do with his discussion of faith and works in other epistles. Paul's use of the term "work" here has much more in common with his

---

[3]Similar metaphorical useage is found in other Pauline letters, 1 Peter, and in the Jewish documents discovered by archaeologists at Qumran. This point is not adequately treated in S.F. Noll, "Qumran and Paul," *DPL*, p. 783.

use of that term in 9:11, where he asks the Corinthians, "are you not my work in the Lord?"

This means then that Paul's comment about one's work has not so much to do with the totality of one's activity for God, but rather the fate and duration of the converts who are represented by the various building materials. It is for the very reason that not all of the converts in the Corinthian church will stand up as well against God's eschatological fire, that Paul affirmed in 3:10 that each of those who works among the converts should be very careful how he builds upon the foundation of the gospel. Paul realized full well that metaphorically speaking the building materials in God's spiritual house varied from convert to convert. This eschatological warning in 3:13 plays a very important role in Paul's effort to deal with the attitudes of pride and boasting which lie behind the congregational fragmentation. Paul is basically saying that individuals should not be too proud too soon, since no one knows the real quality of the converts until all of them stand before God's judgment and his refining fire on judgment day. It is at that point, according to 3:13, that God will test the quality of each man's work (not works). In this setting of 1 Corinthians, each man's work probably refers to those efforts by Paul, Apollos, and others. That would surely make sense in light of the reference to party slogans for Paul and Apollos found in 1 Cor 3, 4, 5 on the one hand and in the repetition of those names in 3:22.

3:14 If what he has built survives, he will receive his reward.

The wording of 3:14 makes it very clear that Paul recognizes the fact that all or part of one's efforts in the kingdom of God may not survive.[4] It is Paul's conviction that clearly some of the converts will survive. These would be represented by the images of gold, silver, and costly stones. The second half of 3:14 affirms what Paul had already mentioned in 3:8, namely that he and Apollos will receive a reward from God for their efforts. In neither of these cases does Paul make clear what the reward is. Christians have often speculated about degrees of reward and punish-

---

[4]Paul's speech to the Ephesian (Acts 20) manifestly demonstrates that he even believed that some of the shepherds of God's flock, whom he converted, could fall away from the Gospel.

ment from God at judgment day, but there is no specific information in either of these verses to indicate what the reward is. Some have suggested that it is the satisfaction of seeing one's converts receive eternal life. Others have suggested that it is the satisfaction of seeing one's work for God withstand the judgment day. One thing that is very clear in this context is that Paul's idea of reward here has nothing to do with financial remuneration. Paul is not concerned here with making affirmations about physical blessings or compensation that comes with success in God's work.

3:15 If it is burned up, he will suffer loss; he himself will be saved, but only as one escaping through the flames.

Paul begins this verse by acknowledging that the work, namely some of the converts of Christian workers, may be burned up in God's eschatological fire.[5] When this happens, Paul says, the worker himself will not be lost because his converts are lost. Even though it is very clear that Paul affirms that the Christian worker will be saved, it is not as easy to understand his idea when he says, "only as one escaping through the flames." This phrase has received various interpretations throughout church history. As early as the third century A.D., this text was understood to be scriptural proof for the concept of purgatory.[6] Others have understood this imagery to be saying that even though one's life and doctrine have been unacceptable to God, these impurities will all be burned away at judgment day. This view is represented, for example, by John Calvin in his commentary where he deals with this verse. Calvin says,

> there is no doubt that Paul is speaking of those who, while always retaining the foundation, mix hay with gold, stubble with silver, wood with precious stones. In other words, they

---

[5]It is easy to find strong denials of the possibility of the loss of salvation among Paul's interpreters. After a rather tortured interpretation of several Pauline texts, Judith M. Gundry-Volf concluded, "Traditionally some Pauline texts have been seen to show the possibility of forfeiting salvation. . . . But a re-reading of these texts suggests that for Paul unethical behavior . . . does not result in the actual loss of salvation," *DPL*, p. 43.

[6]Evidence in Fee, *First Epistle*, p. 144.

build on Christ, but because of the weakness of the flesh, they give way to some human viewpoint, or through ignorance they turn aside to some extent from the strict purity of the Word of God. . . . Paul says that men like that can be saved but on this condition. If the Lord wipes off their ignorance and purifies them from all uncleanness. And that is what the phrase "as if by fire" means.[7]

After giving his interpretation of this issue Calvin comments, "I am sure that my interpretation will satisfy all of sound judgment." Even though the position of the Roman Catholic church (which advocates purgatory) as well as the position advocated by John Calvin has had many supporters, neither of these seems to take as seriously as they should the immediate context and metaphorical imagery of chapter 3.

Perhaps the best interpretation of this admittedly difficult phrase is that found in the *Greek Lexicon of the New Testament and Other Early Christian Literature* by Walter Bauer.[8] In his lexical notes on the Greek word for fire (πῦρ, *pyr*), he makes the following comments about this verse. "Of the Christian worker who has built poorly in the congregation, it is said, he will be saved as through the fire, that is, like a person who must pass through a wall of fire to escape from a burning house." Bauer goes on to give examples of this prepositional phrase "through the fire" from ancient Greek literature, both pagan and Jewish. If this is correct, then the following would be Paul's point in this highly symbolic and metaphorical affirmation. Paul would be saying that there is no doubt about the salvation of the Christian worker himself and that the best way to explain the salvation of the Christian worker, given the limitations of the metaphorical language which Paul has already established, is to say that he will come out of this burning building as one breaking through a building that is on fire.

---

[7]Fee, *First Epistle*, p. 77-78.
[8]BAGD *Greek Lexicon* s.v. πῦρ.

3:16 Don't you know that you yourselves are God's temple and that God's Spirit lives in you?

Paul shifts now to the third metaphor that he uses regarding God's people in this context. The third metaphor is that the congregation at Corinth is the temple (ναός, *naos*) of God. Even though Paul will use similar metaphors to depict his understanding of the Christian's personal body as the temple of God in 1 Cor 6, it is important that we do not confuse the two distinct ideas being presented in 3:16-17 and that presented in chapter 6. The theological idea that the community of God could be understood metaphorically as God's temple was an idea already found within Judaism prior to Paul.[9] In addition, this idea is also found in other early Christian literature, such as 1 Peter and the Apocalypse. Since the collective people are the temple of God, then it follows quite naturally that God's spirit would dwell within them as his temple. The notion of God's presence dwelling in his temple is an idea that had been within Judaism and its Zionistic theology for centuries prior to the advent of Christianity.[10] The language as well as the theology found here is similar to that which Paul expresses in the epistle to the Eph 2:20-22. The contextual function of 3:16 regarding the people being the temple of God is not so much to stress the need for corporate purity, but to set in place the images necessary to warn them about the consequences of promoting congregational fragmentation.

3:17 If anyone destroys God's temple, God will destroy him; for God's temple is sacred, and you are that temple.

Having established that the community is in fact the temple of God in which God's spirit dwells, Paul now explicitly discusses the consequences of destroying that temple. In the context of 1 Cor 1-4, reference to the destruction of the temple of God means nothing other than promoting strife, jealousy, and fragmentation in the Christian community at Corinth. These are in fact the hallmarks of the very problem Paul is addressing as he had reminded the Corinthians in 3:3-5. The affirmation of 3:17 is in sharp contrast to some of the points made in the preceding

---

[9]*Dead Sea Scrolls.*
[10]In the Ark of the Covenant and thereby the Temple.

metaphor of 3:10-15. Paul has a strong message for Christian workers who promote fragmentation. 3:17 makes it very clear that those who promote fragmentation among the Christians, who encourage party loyalties, will in fact be destroyed by God.

While these detractors of Paul may not be preaching another gospel as they were in the churches of Galatia and while they would have agreed with many aspects of Paul's own theology, he nevertheless consigns them to destruction if they participate and encourage strife, jealousy, and division in the church of God at Corinth. 3:17b makes it very clear why there are such dire consequences which result from promoting church strife. By his use of the word "for" (γάρ, gar) Paul makes it clear that the consequences of division are so strong because what is being destroyed is God's sacred temple. Those at Corinth of the Pauline Party were assuredly shocked to hear Paul consigning to destruction those who were promoting Paul himself.

For people who were only a few years from their pagan heritage in which the term "temple of God" typically referred to a pagan sanctuary, it is important for Paul to remind them of the fact that they, as a people, are God's temple in Corinth. Since in 3:17 Paul does not associate the idea of sacred temple or God's temple with the Christian's personal body, it would be contextually inappropriate to draw inferences from 3:17 about God's destruction of the Christian in attempt to relate that to the issue of one's misuse of his own body as a Christian. Specifically, this verse says nothing about the consequences that come from the Christian's destruction of his body through suicide or sexual abuse.

3. God's View of Wisdom (3:18-23)

[18]Do not deceive yourselves. If any one of you thinks he is wise by the standards of this age, he should become a "fool" so that he may become wise. [19]For the wisdom of this world is foolishness in God's sight. As it is written: "He catches the wise in their craftiness"[a] ; [20]and again, "The Lord knows that the thoughts of the wise are futile."[b] [21]So then, no more boasting about men! All things are yours, [22]whether Paul or Apollos or Cephas[c] or the

world or life or death or the present or the future — all are yours,
²³and you are of Christ, and Christ is of God.

ᵃ*19* Job 5:13   ᵇ*20* Psalm 94:11   ᶜ*22* That is, Peter

**3:18 Do not deceive yourselves. If any one of you thinks he is
wise by the standards of this age, he should become a "fool" so
that he may become wise.**

Spiritual and doctrinal deception are constant threats to the
Christian community. Consequently, Paul refers to this problem
several times in his letters, including the Corinthian correspondence. In this verse Paul warns the Corinthians in particular
about self-deception. Paul reintroduces in 3:18b the pejorative use
of the word "wise" (σοφός, *sophos*). Even though in 3:10 Paul had
used the word "wise" of himself in the positive sense, in 3:18 he
uses it in a negative sense, much in the same way that he did in
1:18. When Paul uses the phrase "wise by the standards of this
age," he is once again employing the term "age" (αἰών, *aiōn*) in a
pejorative sense. Age in this context refers to a worldly perspective, an outlook which Paul had presented early in 2:6. For Paul,
becoming a fool, as he advocates in 3:18, means abandoning
worldly standards on the basis of which the misevaluation of himself and Apollos and other leaders is based. It is only after one
has become a fool by the standards of this age that he can become, given God's criteria, a person of true wisdom.

**3:19 For the wisdom of this world is foolishness in God's sight. As
it is written: "He catches the wise in their craftiness";**

In this section Paul explains why the Corinthians must embrace foolishness by worldly standards and jettison human wisdom. In the first instance he says God is unimpressed by the wisdom of this world. In fact, it is foolishness in God's sight. Paul
then establishes his point on the basis of a Scripture citation. With
a citation from Job 5:13, part of the Old Testament wisdom literature, Paul says that the wise will be captured by God in their own
craftiness (πανουργία, *panourgia*).

3:20 and again, "The Lord knows that the thoughts of the wise are futile."

Paul continues his argumentation in this verse by a second citation from the Old Testament. This time Paul chooses to cite Scripture from Ps 94:11. The key term in this citation from the Old Testament, just as in the preceding citation from the Old Testament, is the word "wise" (*sophos*). Paul has chosen both of these Old Testament citations because of the negative attitude they express toward those who claim to have the wisdom, but are nevertheless insignificant in the sight of God. The affirmation of Ps 94:11 is that God in fact knows the faults of the wise, and he knows the fact that these are futile. All of this is designed by Paul to be a commentary on those leaders and trend setters among the Corinthian church, who because of their own seduction by Corinthian standards are contributing to the fragmentation and division in the church of God there.

3:21 So then, no more boasting about men! All things are yours,

The point of both Scripture citations according to Paul in 3:21 is to lead the Corinthians to cease boasting on human standards. Not only have the Corinthians been boasting on the basis of human standards, but their object of boasting had been human personalities. It is clear from the following verse in 3:22 that Paul specifically has in mind party loyalty to himself, to Apollos, to Peter, and perhaps to others. It is regrettable that the NIV did not translate all of the concluding thoughts of 3:21. The Greek text includes the word "for" (γάρ, *gar*), thereby showing a connection in the thought of 3:21a and 3:21b. The reason that the Corinthians should no longer boast in human leaders is because all that they need to have they already have. Some of those addressed in this part of 1 Corinthians apparently thought their prestige or spirituality was being enhanced by these party loyalties. Paul makes it clear that this boasting in humans is unnecessary because all things are already in their possession, because of their relationship to God.

3:22 whether Paul or Apollos or Cephas or the world or life or death or the present or the future — all are yours,

In this verse Paul gives a rapid series of eight items, the first three of which refer to personalities in the religious fragmentation in Corinth. Paul, Apollos, and Cephas are mentioned, thereby recapping the parties and the party slogans found in 1:12 where Paul mentioned loyalties to Paul, Apollos, and Cephas.

The last five items in the series in 3:22 relate not specifically to individuals but to the certainty that indeed all things are ours. This last part of 3:22 manifests Paul's use of extravagant polarities. In this regard it is similar to other instances in Paul's letters where he uses polarities to underscore a theological truth he has expressed. For example, in Rom 8:37 Paul affirms that Christians are more than conquerors in Christ who has loved them. Then in Rom 8:38-39 he gives a list, in some way similar to the list in 1 Corinthians. The point of the list in Rom 8:38-39 is to establish, by means of a series of polarities, the certainty of the claim he has made. Just as Paul's use of the terms "life or death or things present or things to come," etc. in Rom 8:38 is designed to confirm the certainty of God's promises in terms of his ever abiding love, so likewise in 1 Cor 3 Paul uses items such as life, death, the present age or the age to come to underscore the certainty that Christians can have that all things belong to them. In light of this understanding of the rhetorical function of Paul's use of polarities in 3:22, one need not be as pessimistic as C.K. Barrett when he observes on this passage that "at this point Paul expresses ideas that do not immediately seem strictly coherent within the context."[11]

3:23 and you are of Christ, and Christ is of God.

The reason that the readers of 1 Corinthians are in possession of so many things is not on the basis of their own worldly wisdom. Their right to these kinds of possessions does not arise from human wisdom or their accommodation to the values present in a first-century Roman colony. The position of the Corinthians as possessors lies rather in their relationship to God. In v. 23a Paul affirms that the Corinthians belong to Christ, and then secondar-

---

[11]C.K. Barrett, *The First Epistle to the Corinthians* (New York: Harper, 1968), p. 95.

ily he affirms that Christ belongs to God. By setting forth his spiritual understanding in these terms, Paul makes it very clear once again that his own religious spiritual understanding is very theocentric. Moreover, as is evident in other places in 1 Corinthians, Paul's understanding of the relationship between Christ and God is one of a hierarchy. Paul understands God's reign to be that of a monarchy in which even Christ is subject to God, much as Christians in turn are subject to Christ (15:24-28).

1 CORINTHIANS 4

E. APOSTLES OF CHRIST (4:1-21)

1. The Apostles as Servants of Christ (4:1-5)

[1]So then, men ought to regard us as servants of Christ and as those entrusted with the secret things of God. [2]Now it is required that those who have been given a trust must prove faithful. [3]I care very little if I am judged by you or by any human court; indeed, I do not even judge myself. [4]My conscience is clear, but that does not make me innocent. It is the Lord who judges me. [5]Therefore judge nothing before the appointed time; wait till the Lord comes. He will bring to light what is hidden in darkness and will expose the motives of men's hearts. At that time each will receive his praise from God.

4:1 So then, men ought to regard us as servants of Christ and as those entrusted with the secret things of God.
C.K. Barrett is correct in his comments on these opening verses of 1 Cor 4 when he observes "in the new paragraph Paul winds up his treatment of the arrogant and divided Corinthian church so far as its troubles arise out of and are reflected in its relations with its apostolic leaders."[1] By his use of the two words "men" and "regard" in 4:1, Paul makes it clear that he is still involved in an apologetic response to those who would be his detractors as well as to those who have an incorrect evaluation of the Christian leaders. In many ways this verse is a restatement of the topic he introduced in 3:5.

---

[1]Barrett, *First Epistle*, pp. 98-99.

The English word in 4:1, "regard," is a translation of a Greek term (λογίζομαι, *logizomai*)which is most familiar to students of Paul for its use in the book of Romans (4:4), where Paul uses this term to talk about God reckoning righteousness to people on the basis of faith. However, in the Corinthian context this word takes on a clearly different meaning. Paul's use of this Greek word in 4:1 is very similar to his use of this term several times in the polemical sections of 2 Corinthians (2 Cor 10:2; 11:5; 12:6).

The fact that 4:1 occurs in an apologetic setting is made clear on the basis of the occurrence of several words in this section of 1 Corinthians. In particular, the occurrence of the words "judged" (ἀνακρίνω, *anakrinō*) and "judge" (κρίνω, *krinō*) in 1 Cor 4:3, 4, and 5 make this apologetic context evident. The use of the word "us" in 4:1 can only refer in this context to Paul and Apollos. This is made clear by contextual references such as 3:5, 22, and 4:6. While what Paul says in 4:1 can be generally applied to a larger setting, we must not lose sight of the contextual application of this principle in 4:1 that Paul has in mind. The Greek word translated "servants" in 4:1 (ὑπηρέτας, *hypēretas*) is found only here in the letters of Paul, but is paralleled to the concept of servants found in 3:5, where Paul uses his more frequent and familiar Greek word for servants (διάκονοι, *diakonoi*). Lying behind the English phrase of 4:1, "those entrusted with," is a single Greek word (οἰκονόμους, oikonomous) whose meaning ranges from the idea of manager or administrator to that of a religious official in pagan religions.[2] There is no evidence in the New Testament that this term was ever used in regard to a specific church office, though it can be used in reference to a bishop (Titus 1:7), as well as to Christians at large.

There is understandably some difference of opinion about what the apostle Paul had in mind when he referred to the secret things of God. Part of the confusion and disagreement arises from the fact that Paul used the plural, "secret things" (μυστήρια, *mystēria*) of God. Because of Paul's use of the plural here, some interpreters have thought that Paul's use was perhaps influenced by the plural term "mysteries," a term found in contemporary pa-

---

[2]BAGD, s.v. οἰκονόμος.

gan religions. In particular in earlier generations it was suggested that Paul's use of ideas such as "mysteries" or "secret things" derived from his borrowing of terminology of pagan cults and philosophies. "Many curious imaginations have flitted across the minds of men as they have sought to reconstruct the past, but there can have been few more curious," wrote Arthur D. Nock against such ideas, "than the picture of Paul listening attentively to Stoic lectures at Tarsus or making enquiries about Mithraism and later enriching Christianity from these stories."[3]

Though it is a complicated exegetical question, Gordon Fee points in the right direction in his following comments

> most likely, as in 2:7, it reflects again Paul's own semantic usage, in which he, as one who has the spirit, has been given to understand God's plan of salvation long hidden to human minds but now revealed in Christ. Thus, the mysteries of God means the revelation of the gospel now known through the spirit and especially entrusted to the apostles to proclaim.[4]

4:2 Now it is required that those who have been given a trust must prove faithful.

Paul's point in this verse is very clear. He emphatically states that God expects faithfulness of those whom he has entrusted with a task. It would be very inconsistent if at this point Paul wrote that God demanded that his followers always be successful. Paul had made it very clear in 3:5 that both he and Apollos did nothing on their own. They were merely servants used by God, and it was God who gave the increase in their ministries.

4:3 I care very little if I am judged by you or by any human court; indeed, I do not even judge myself.

Since Paul and Apollos are servants of the mysteries of God, it is only God's judgment that they need to be concerned with. This is why at times Paul can have almost an apathetic posture toward

---

[3]Arthur Darby Nock, "The Vocabulary of the New Testament." *Journal of Biblical Literature* 52, 1933, p. 39.

[4]Fee, *First Epistle*, p. 160.

his human detractors. In the most profound sense, it is irrelevant whether Paul's ministry receives condemnation or applause from human beings, since he was not commissioned by humans. The occurrence of the prepositional phrase, "by you" in 4:3, makes it explicit that Paul does have detractors among the recipients of the Corinthian correspondents.

Paul's reference in 4:3 to the human court has no direct bearing on his later pejorative understanding of the Roman court system which he expresses in 1 Cor 6. The word translated "court" in 4:3 is simply the typical Greek word for "day" (ἡμέρα, *hēmera*); thus, in 4:3 when Paul makes reference to the human "day," he does so as a contrast to the day of the Lord, which he referred to in 3:13 and alludes to in 4:5. The apostle is willing to plant his feet very firmly on the idea of the centrality of God's judgment on the Lord's day, but puts no confidence in any human judgments expressed prior to that time. God's own faithfulness is what allows us to have confidence in the certainty of our blamelessness on the day of our Lord Jesus Christ (cf. 1:8) and to reject attempts at premature judgment and human judgment. Paul is so convinced about the theocentric foundation of judgment that he acknowledges in 4:3 that he is not even capable of rendering a meaningful judgment against himself. There is no support either in early church history or in the evidence from the Corinthian letters to support the suggestion that the term "human court" meant an ecclesiastical court that was convened to test Paul's apostleship."[5]

4:4 My conscience is clear, but that does not make me innocent. It is the Lord who judges me.

Paul's wording in this verse makes it very clear that the human conscience is not the last court of appeal in determining human guilt or innocence in the sight of God. Paul's ultimate justification, or being made innocent (from δικαιόω, *dikaioō*), as he so eloquently depicts in other letters, rests solely in God's hands. Even when one's heart or one's conscience is at its very best, it is still human and fragile in the presence of God. In the context of 1 Corinthians 4:4, in Paul's problem with detractors, the apostle

---

[5]Kistemaker, *First Corinthians*, p. 130.

COLLEGE PRESS NIV COMMENTARY

here is emphasizing that the final evaluation of his own apostolic stewardship rests in the sovereign judgment of God.

4:5 Therefore judge nothing before the appointed time; wait till the Lord comes. He will bring to light what is hidden in darkness and will expose the motives of men's hearts. At that time each will receive his praise from God.

For those Corinthians who would judge either Apollos' or Paul's stewardship and their ministries, Paul tells them that not only is human judgment inappropriate, but that any judgment before the second coming of Christ is premature. There is no point in time in human history when all the evidence will be available. There is no time in the ministries of Paul and Apollos when all the hidden things will be known prior to the return of Jesus. As Jeremiah had pointed out centuries earlier, no one is capable of knowing the depth of the human heart (Jer 17:9). The apostle Paul agrees with the point and proclaims that the motives of human beings, including himself and Apollos, will never be fully known until they are examined in the pure light that comes from the glory of God. It is only at the time of Christ's return that individuals will truly receive complete praise from God for the ministries in which they have been involved.

2. Overcoming Human Pride (4:6-7)

[6]Now, brothers, I have applied these things to myself and Apollos for your benefit, so that you may learn from us the meaning of the saying, "Do not go beyond what is written." Then you will not take pride in one man over against another. [7]For who makes you different from anyone else? What do you have that you did not receive? And if you did receive it, why do you boast as though you did not?

4:6 Now, brothers, I have applied these things to myself and Apollos for your benefit, so that you may learn from us the meaning of the saying, "Do not go beyond what is written." Then you will not take pride in one man over against another.

Paul encourages the Corinthians to take himself and Apollos as human examples. As the Corinthians look at the lives of Paul and Apollos, they should see in them a pattern, which if they were to follow, would undermine and destroy the strife and self-aggrandizement which has so plagued the Corinthian fellowship. One of the specific things Paul tells the Corinthians they should learn from him and Apollos is not to go beyond the things which have been written. While there are several interpretations of what Paul has in mind with this phrase, it seems that the clearest interpretation is one that sees this as a reference to Old Testament citations which he has been using in the Corinthian correspondence.[6] Even a casual reader of the book of Acts knows that Apollos was well known as a student and expounder of scripture. Even the casual reader of 1 Corinthians knows that the apostle Paul goes again and again into the Old Testament to find Scripture texts and themes to oppose immaturity and sinfulness in the Corinthian fellowship. One has only to retrace Paul's use of the Old Testament in the first three chapters of 1 Corinthians or to look forward to his use, for example in 1 Cor 10, of the Old Testament, to understand what Paul had in mind when he said, "so that you may learn from us." It comes as no surprise in v. 6 that the specific sin Paul is hoping the Corinthians can overcome, by using himself and Apollos as examples, is the sin of human pride and boasting, one against the other.

4:7 For who makes you different from anyone else? What do you have that you did not receive? And if you did receive it, why do you boast as though you did not?

This verse contains three rhetorical questions whose goal is to help the Corinthians reevaluate themselves. As a set, these rhetorical questions are designed to move the Corinthians beyond the pride to which Paul referred in the preceding verse. Paul's use

---

[6]See notes on 1 Cor 10:11.

of the Greek word "for" (γάρ, gar) indicates clearly that v. 7 follows up on the idea found at the end of v. 6. The exact meaning of the first rhetorical question in 4:7 is not clear. The NIV translation of the Greek word διακρίνω (diakrinō) by the English phrase "makes you different" from anyone else represents one school of interpretation. This interpretive approach takes its cue from the end of v. 6 when Paul referred to the fact that the Corinthians were being puffed up against one another. Paul's question then would be, "what makes any of you any better than or distinguished from anyone else?"

A different interpretation of this verse places its emphasis more on the Corinthians viewing of themselves as different over against Paul. Gordon Fee summarizes this second interpretive approach with these words, "the English equivalent to such rhetoric would be, who in the world do you think you are anyway, what kind of self-delusion is it that allows you to put yourself in a position to judge another person's servant."[7] Since the verb that Paul uses in 4:7 is a cognate of the Greek verb that means to judge (ἀνακρίνω, anakrinō), and which he had used previously in this chapter (4:4), he may be asking them to think about the fact that the God who judges them is no different from the God who will judge others.

The meaning of the second and third rhetorical questions is somewhat easier. Paul's intent is clearly to engender a new awareness of humility on the part of the readers. If the Corinthians can be successfully reminded that all that they have came from beyond themselves, then it is Paul's hope that this will undermine the boasting which has so characterized their interaction.

3. Honor and Dishonor (4:8-13)

[8]Already you have all you want! Already you have become rich! You have become kings — and that without us! How I wish that you really had become kings so that we might be kings with you! [9]For it seems to me that God has put us apostles on display at the end of the procession, like men condemned to die in the

---

[7]Fee, *First Epistle*, p. 171.

arena. We have been made a spectacle to the whole universe, to angels as well as to men. [10]We are fools for Christ, but you are so wise in Christ! We are weak, but you are strong! You are honored, we are dishonored! [11]To this very hour we go hungry and thirsty, we are in rags, we are brutally treated, we are homeless. [12]We work hard with our own hands. When we are cursed, we bless; when we are persecuted, we endure it; [13]when we are slandered, we answer kindly. Up to this moment we have become the scum of the earth, the refuse of the world.

4:8 Already you have all you want! Already you have become rich! You have become kings — and that without us! How I wish that you really had become kings so that we might be kings with you!

While most interpreters correctly understand that 4:8a reflects sharp sarcasm by Paul, some have mislabeled the exact issues that Paul is addressing here through his phrases "you have all you want" "you have become rich," and "you have become kings." Specifically, scholars who tend to view Paul's Corinthian readers with the lens of "over realized eschatology" have created an interpretive approach that is flawed in two ways.

First, there are grave problems with labeling the position of Paul's antagonists as eschatological just because Paul himself responds to an issue out of his own eschatology. This technique of reconstructing the theology of Paul's antagonists by "mirror reading" his response has never been able to be applied consistently or accurately. Accordingly, just because Paul addresses a problem with an eschatological solution does not necessarily mean that the problem with the antagonists was that they were espousing an aberrant eschatology. The pervasiveness that Fee, among others, attributes to the problem of "spiritualized eschatology"[8] among Paul's detractors at Corinth more accurately characterise spiritual idiosyncracies in later eras of church history and dogma.

Second, and more to the point of 4:8a, one can show how naturally the remarks of Paul fit into the broader issues of chapters 1-4, which have essentially nothing to do with eschatology. As

---

[8]Fee, *First Epistle*, p. 12.

Witherington and others have demonstrated, Paul has been arguing long and hard since 1 Cor 1:10ff that Corinthian-style rhetoric
and wisdom is at odds with the message of the cross.   The catch-
words of eschatology are not significantly manifest in the rhetorical setting of 1 Cor 1-4. The issues Paul attacks, namely, "I'm sufficient, I'm wealthy, I rule," are all known to be part-and-parcel of
men-of-wisdom ideology in Greco-Roman and Hellenistic Jewish
writings. The Greek satirist Lucian gives the stereo typically un-
sympathetic view of one of these "wise men" trained in the philosophy of the period.   This arrogant man is portrayed as pro-
claiming (in a metaphorical sense as Paul does) "there will be
nothing to stop me being the only rich (Greek *plousios*) man and
the only king (Greek *basileus*)."[9] The ancient writer Diogenes Laer-
tius[10] summarizes these views of "wise-men" when he writes,
"Moreover, according to them not only are the wise (*hoi sophoi*)
free, they are also kings (*basileis*)." Similar metaphors are in the
writings of the Roman slave Epictetus,[11] the Hellenistic Jewish
author Philo and the Roman poet Horace[12] who comments that
the sage is only lower than the god Jove and "is rich, free, hon-
oured, beautiful, nay a king of kings." The intellectual and cultural values reflected in the above quotations provide a much
more obvious background to Paul's rejoinders written to an urban Greco-Roman congregation than do vague allusions to
"eschatology."

**4:9 For it seems to me that God has put us apostles on display at
the end of the procession, like men condemned to die in the
arena. We have been made a spectacle to the whole universe, to
angels as well as to men.**
    The apostle here continues his comments on the general issue
of 4:1 (how people should regard us) and specifically addresses
the problem of "taking pride in one man over against another"
(4:6). Paul clearly wants to illustrate his previous assertion that he

---

[9]Hermotimus 81.
[10]*Lives of Eminent Philosophers* 7.122.
[11]*Discourses* 3.63,79.
[12]*Epistles* 1.1.106-08.

strives to model the paradigm of humility in the life and ministry of himself and Apollos (4:6).

The imagery about being at the end of the procession may stem from the staging of the "Roman triumph, in which a conquering general staged a splendid parade [where] at the very 'end of the procession' were those captives who had been 'condemned to die in the arena.'"[13] The adaptation of this Roman cultural practice functions to underscore the despicable state in which apostles such as Paul and Apollos stand according to the prevailing urban values.

4:10 We are fools for Christ, but you are so wise in Christ! We are weak, but you are strong! You are honored, we are dishonored!

Next Paul chooses three sets of antitheses to contrast the radical difference between the humble status of the apostles and the elevated status of certain of the Corinthians. The power of these is manifest in Paul's terse irony and sarcasm. The terms he employs for the carnal minded are "wise" (φρόνιμοι, *phronimoi*), "strong" (ἰσχυροί, *ischyroi*), and "honored" (ἔνδοξοι, *endoxoi*). All three of these terms appeal to the status-seeking nature of certain believers. This particular nature is promoted by self-aggrandizement and covered with a thin veneer of Christianity.

The self-directed epithets of "weak" (ἀσθενεῖς, *astheneis*), "fools" (μωροί, *mōroi*), and "dishonored" (ἄτιμοι, *atimoi*) are nurtured and transformed on the other hand by the word of the cross in the life and experiences of Paul.

4:11 To this very hour we go hungry and thirsty, we are in rags, we are brutally treated, we are homeless.

In light of the occupational hazards of travel and preaching unpopular religious and moral messages, it is no shock to read of Paul's catalogue of hardships here (cf. 2 Cor 11:23-29). The modern reader should be aware that similar lists can be located both in the autobiographical accounts and in the biographical reports about the hardships faced by non-Christian preachers and missionary-minded moralists of the Greco-Roman world. As Mal-

---

[13]Fee, *First Epistle*, p. 174; cf. 2 Cor 2:14.

herbe noted, "Moral philosophers, especially Stoics and Cynics, made extensive use of lists of hardships or unfavorable circumstances in describing themselves or their heroes."[14] A helpful example of the type of hardships experienced in the Roman world of Paul comes from a comment in one of the sermons of the pagan moralist Dio Chrysostom. He mentions "grappling with hunger and cold, withstanding thirst," the need to "endure the lash or give his body to be cut or burned" (cf. 1 Cor 13:3), and "hunger, exile, loss of reputation, and the like."[15]

4:12 We work hard with our own hands. When we are cursed, we bless; when we are persecuted, we endure it;

In Paul's catalogue he includes reference to manual labor since this was a clear point of contention between himself and some of the Corinthians (cf. ch. 9; see also Acts 20:33-35). Paul was himself cursed and persecuted in many instances according to both the record of Acts and his own letters (Acts 14:22; 20:19; 2 Cor 11:23-29). The ethical response of blessing (εὐλογοῦμεν, *eulogoumen*) those who curse you shows up in Rom 12:14-20, was manifested forcefully in the cross of Christ, and was rooted, according to Rom 12:19-20, in the Old Testament Scriptures.

4:13 when we are slandered, we answer kindly. Up to this moment we have become the scum of the earth, the refuse of the world.

Fee rightly observes that the apostle ends this line of thought and autobiographical reflection "with the most unflattering of metaphors, indicating the world's reaction to this way of living."[16] The phrases "scum of the earth" and "refuse of the world" are chosen by Paul to present the starkest reminder to those who pledge party loyalty to various apostles (1:12; 3:4; 4:6) how absurd this is. This forceful analysis is given by Paul as a final answer to the issue of 4:1. He intends to obliterate the ill-placed pride in apostles as well as warn (4:14; through irony and sarcasm) some of

---

[14] A.J. Malherbe, *Moral Exhortation: A Greco-Roman Sourcebook*, ed. by W.A. Meeks (Philadelphia: Westminster, 1986), pp. 141-142.

[15] *Oration* 8.9-16 cited from Malherbe, *Moral Exhortation*, no. 2, p. 27.

[16] Fee, *First Epistle*, p. 180.

the Corinthians who had imbibed too deeply at the wells of Greco-Roman wisdom and culture.

4. Paul's Warning as Father (4:14-17)

¹⁴I am not writing this to shame you, but to warn you, as my dear children. ¹⁵Even though you have ten thousand guardians in Christ, you do not have many fathers, for in Christ Jesus I became your father through the gospel. ¹⁶Therefore I urge you to imitate me. ¹⁷For this reason I am sending to you Timothy, my son whom I love, who is faithful in the Lord. He will remind you of my way of life in Christ Jesus, which agrees with what I teach everywhere in every church.

4:14 I am not writing this to shame you, but to warn you, as my dear children.

In the section 4:14-21 Paul brings to a conclusion the major block of material which he began in 1:10. This section serves then as the climax to his various arguments and appeals against the problem of strife and fragmentation in the church of God at Corinth. Two ideas are very prominent in this verse and they gives us some insight into this entire concluding section. The first is Paul's use of the term "my dear children" (τέκνα μου ἀγαπητά, *tekna mou agapēta*). Paul's use of family imagery in this verse sets the stage for his later use of the word "father" in v. 15 and the word "whip" in v. 21. A second interesting concept in this verse is seen in Paul's use of the term "warn" (νουθετέω, *noutheteō*). This is the same concept he uses in Eph 6:4 when he talks about fathers bringing up their children in the admonition of the Lord. It is the same concept found in Col 1:28 when he speaks about the fact that he tries to warn all men of God's truth and in Col 3:16 when he exhorts Christians to admonish and warn one another (cf. 1 Thess 5:12, 14; 2 Thess 3:15; Titus 3:10). By his use of these two important phrases in 4:14, Paul is clearly setting up his spiritual authority over them in the matters that he is addressing.

4:15 Even though you have ten thousand guardians in Christ, you do not have many fathers, for in Christ Jesus I became your father through the gospel.

Even though Paul argued at length against party strife and party loyalties throughout the first four chapters, he nevertheless believes that he has special prerogatives among the Corinthian believers. He does not want anyone to say "I am of Paul" in the same way that someone else might say "I am of Cephas," but he nevertheless expects and demands absolute loyalty from all the Corinthian believers. The illustration and imagery of 4:15 make this clear. He acknowledges that the Corinthians may have many guardians in Christ, many spiritual leaders, but he emphatically asserts that he alone has the right to be seen as their father in the gospel. Paul's claim to fatherhood in this verse does not rest upon ideas of spiritual maturity or special theological insight. Rather this special role as father is predicated on the fact that he is the one who brought them to faith in Christ (from γεννάω, *gennaō*). Paul's letters are filled with other examples of family metaphors, such as calling fellow Christians "brothers." This, however, is one of the few places where Paul exerts his authority over entire congregations by the use of father/son spiritual authority language. In addition to establishing his own authority among the Corinthians based on the imagery of 4:15, Paul has also disarmed the claims of those who would appeal to the spiritual influence of workers such as Cephas or Apollos.

4:16 Therefore I urge you to imitate me.

In this verse Paul pushes even harder to undergird his unique relationship with the church of God at Corinth and to reestablish his dwindling influence among certain of the members in that fellowship. This is seen by the fact that he urges them to become imitators of Paul. In 4:6 he had pointed out that both he himself and Apollos had served as examples for the Corinthians, but here he goes one step farther and urges them to follow in his footsteps. Paul's use of the word "therefore" (οὖν, *oun*) makes it very clear that this appeal for the Corinthians to imitate him arises from the spiritual relationship he has established with them through his work in bringing them to faith. Paul makes a similar appeal in 11:1.

4:17 For this reason I am sending to you Timothy, my son whom I love, who is faithful in the Lord. He will remind you of my way of life in Christ Jesus, which agrees with what I teach everywhere in every church.

Paul's technique for facilitating the Corinthians' imitation of himself is that he will send Timothy to the Corinthians to remind them of Paul's life in Christ. It is no accident in 4:17 that Paul refers to Timothy as "my son" (τέκνον, *teknon*) when this is read in the light of the fact that in 4:14 he referred to the Corinthians in general as his children. The same Greek word is used in both verses even though that is not shown in the NIV translation.

Not only will Timothy remind the Corinthians of Paul's ways in the Lord, but these will be ways in the Lord which Paul teaches in all of his congregations. In light of Paul's use of the word "teach" (διδάσκω, *didaskō*) at the end of 4:17, the reference to "my ways" would include not only Paul's lifestyle, but also his doctrinal perspectives. Accordingly, 4:17 ends with a reference to the fact that what Paul is trying to inculcate into the Corinthians is the same thing that he teaches everywhere in every church. This appeal to the similarity of what Paul teaches the Corinthians with what he teaches everywhere else is found several times in the first letter to the Corinthians. We cannot be certain why this particular type of appeal was so needed in the Corinthian correspondence, but it is noteworthy that it shows up with much greater frequency in 1 Corinthians than any other of the Pauline letters.

5. Arrogance to Be Confronted (4:18-21)

[18]Some of you have become arrogant, as if I were not coming to you. [19]But I will come to you very soon, if the Lord is willing, and then I will find out not only how these arrogant people are talking, but what power they have. [20]For the kingdom of God is not a matter of talk but of power. [21]What do you prefer? Shall I come to you with a whip, or in love and with a gentle spirit?

4:18 Some of you have become arrogant, as if I were not coming to you.

Paul's accusation against his detractors in this verse is that they are arrogant (from φυσιόω, *physioō*). Paul used the same Greek word in v. 6 when he spoke about Corinthians having pride over against one another. Here Paul clearly has in mind those among the Corinthians who will not accept his paternal authority over them as beloved children. These detractors do not believe that Paul will return to Jerusalem and use this opportunity to jettison any submission they might have had to Paul's leadership.

4:19 But I will come to you very soon, if the Lord is willing, and then I will find out not only how these arrogant people are talking, but what power they have.

Paul indicates in this verse that he is anticipating an imminent visit to the city of Corinth. He acknowledges that all of his plans in this matter are predicated upon the will of God (as in Acts 18:21; Rom 1:10; 15:32; Phil 1:19). Verse 19 is clearly Paul's effort to throw down the gauntlet in the face of his detractors to see if they have any conviction that lies behind their words against Paul.

4:20 For the kingdom of God is not a matter of talk but of power.

Paul takes the contrast he gave in 4:19 between talk and power and utilizes that in 4:20 to threaten his detractors and any Corinthians who might be wavering in their loyalty to him. Paul has little to fear from the talk of these detractors, since the kingdom of God is not based upon human discourse and talk but rather upon the power (δύναμις, *dynamis*) of God.

4:21 What do you prefer? Shall I come to you with a whip, or in love and with a gentle spirit?

Paul concludes the sub-unit of 4:14-21 and, therefore, the larger unit of 1 Cor 1:10-4:21, with a clear threat. The imagery and impact Paul intends for the Corinthians to receive comes from the material set forth in 4:14 and 15. Anyone familiar with the Old Testament and later Jewish teachings about the discipline of the Lord knows that it was not intended to be pleasant. The God of Scripture is clearly presented as a God who is slow to anger and who abounds in steadfast love. Nevertheless, the writers of Scripture never present him as a permissive parent with undisciplined children. Paul is of course aware of Greco-Roman practice as well as Jewish teachings about the importance of corporal punishment for disobedient and rebellious children. This is the thought world from which the apostle draws his point in 4:21. He is, spiritually speaking, threatening the disobedient Corinthians with a whipping if they do not accept his parental authority over them in the Lord. On the other hand, if they do express compliance and acknowledge Paul's authority, then Paul says he can come to them with a gentle spirit. It is noteworthy that this section ends in a question, for Paul has put the choice before the Corinthians and allows them to participate in what kind of response Paul will have to them when he comes to Corinth.

1 CORINTHIANS 5

III. REPORTS OF IMMORALITY (5:1-6:20)

A. DISCIPLINE FOR THE IMMORAL BROTHER (5:1-13)

1. The Corinthians' Pride in Tolerance (5:1-5)

¹It is actually reported that there is sexual immorality among you, and of a kind that does not occur even among pagans: A man has his father's wife. ²And you are proud! Shouldn't you rather have been filled with grief and have put out of your fellowship the man who did this? ³Even though I am not physically present, I am with you in spirit. And I have already passed judgment on the one who did this, just as if I were present. ⁴When you are assembled in the name of our Lord Jesus and I am with you in spirit, and the power of our Lord Jesus is present, ⁵hand this man over to Satan, so that the sinful nature[a] may be destroyed and his spirit saved on the day of the Lord.

[a] 5 Or *that his body*; or *that the flesh*

5:1 It is actually reported that there is sexual immorality among you, and of a kind that does not occur even among pagans: A man has his father's wife.

Paul begins here a two-chapter section that focuses on sexual immorality among believers at Corinth. Paul's information about these several problems laid out in chapters 5-6 are based upon secondhand information, perhaps from those of Chloe's household. The term translated immorality here is the Greek term πορνεία (*porneia*), a term whose cognates are found several times in 5:1-6:20.

Part of the apostle's strategy is to shame the readers by stating (with obvious exaggeration) that such a sin is found nowhere among pagans. Of course both Paul and the Corinthians knew that such immorality did occur among pagans. In fact, had it not been taking place among pagans in Corinth, it would not have been taking place in the church at Corinth. Interpreters who do not fully appreciate Paul's use of rhetoric have interpreted the apostle here as "meaning not that no Gentile had ever committed it [i.e., incest], but that the Gentiles themselves condemned it."[1] Admittedly there were Roman authors who condemned incest[2] (e.g., Cicero) but it was both practiced and advocated from time to time in the pagan world.[3] Indeed, the Roman author Cornelius Nepos, who wrote at about the same time Corinth was refounded as a Roman colony in the first century B.C., tells us Greeks and Romans did not agree in their attitudes toward incest.[4]

The final clause of 5:1 makes it clear that incest is the manifestation of immorality that Paul has in mind. To have one's father's wife was strictly forbidden by Mosaic legislation (Lev 18:8; Deut 22:30; 27:20), a fact which in itself probably points to advocacy of this immorality by the pagan nations which surrounded Israel. The details of this heinous relationship of immorality are not spelled out by Paul, since the readership would surely have been familiar with the details (e.g., was the father dead, or alive, or divorced?). It is noteworthy that the apostle believed, in light of his reliance on Leviticus and Deuteronomy here and in 5:13, that this body of scriptural legislation from the Mosaic Law "still applied to Christians" in the church of God at Corinth.[5]

---

[1]Barrett, *First Epistle*, p. 121.
[2]Cicero, *Pro Cluentio* 5.12-6.16; Apuleius, *Metamorphoses* 10.2-12.
[3]Clarke, *Secular and Christian Leadership*, pp. 73-88 is very helpful in surveying the primary sources.
[4]Cornelius Nepos, *Great General of Foreign Nations*, Preface 4.
[5]Witherington, *Conflict and Community in Corinth*, p. 156.

5:2 And you are proud! Shouldn't you rather have been filled with grief and have put out of your fellowship the man who did this?

Paul is almost as shocked by the Corinthians' toleration of this immorality as he is by the immorality itself. Paul regards this acceptance of this immorality as a direct challenge to his own authority. The word translated "you are proud" in 5:2 (φυσιόω, *physioō*) is a term used elsewhere to describe Corinthian arrogance and opposition to Paul (e.g., 4:6, 18). Since Paul had already written the Corinthians to disassociate themselves from immoral church members (1 Cor 5:9f), Paul sees this toleration of incest as a defiance to the previous letters he had written them.

The reference to feelings of grief and lamentation in response to sin and its fruit is well attested in Scripture. This is readily apparent in Jeremiah's petition in Jer 9:1-2:

Oh, that my head were a spring of water and my eyes a fountain of tears! I would weep day and night for the slain of my people. Oh, that I had in the desert a lodging place for travelers, so that I might leave my people and go away from them; for they are all adulterers, a crowd of unfaithful people.

Most religious communities, both ancient and modern, have boundary markers which help define membership and reinforce acceptable behavior. The same was true of the early Jesus movement as well as the later Pauline mission. In large part due to modern pluralism, many have construed early Christianity to be a highly inclusive movement. This, however, is revisionistic and cannot be supported by a straightforward reading of the documents of the New Testament. Although the grounds and context for community expulsion were not always identical in Paul's letters, it is clear that it was a recurring part of his apostolic and pastoral strategy. Sometimes Paul rejected inclusivity and was directed by the need to enforce boundaries. He did this in light of both doctrinal aberration (Gal 4:28-31) and behavioral aberration (Rom 16:17-20). In the case of incest, Paul's policy of exclusion was triggered by moral aberration (cf. 1 Cor 5:13).

5:3 Even though I am not physically present, I am with you in spirit. And I have already passed judgment on the one who did this, just as if I were present.

Paul's strategy for correcting the Corinthians had to acknowledge the problems of enforcement caused by his absence (cf. 4:17-21). This is not the only example where Paul affirms his apostolic presence and authority in absentia (cf. Col 2:5). Paul's statement regarding his prior judgment could refer to:

1. the letter he has already sent (5:9) on this issue

2. his resolution to condemn this moral perversion through Timothy (4:17), or

3. this present letter.

The apostle also wants to make it clear that the decision about how to respond to this sin is not open to plea bargaining or the consensus of the majority (cf. 2 Cor 2:6). For Paul, it is a settled matter.

5:4 When you are assembled in the name of our Lord Jesus and I am with you in spirit, and the power of our Lord Jesus is present,

Even though most of the contemporary discussion about Christian assemblies in the latter part of the 20th century has focused on worship experiences, Paul knew that one of the purposes of Christian assemblies was to reinforce Christian boundary markers for the community. Judgment and grieving were appropriate in the assembly of the church of God at Corinth when it was confronted with egregious immorality in its membership. With the double reference "in the name of our Lord Jesus" and in "the power of our Lord Jesus" Paul anchors this assembly and its purpose and authority in the bedrock of the church's life and identity. If the congregation is not acting in response to the clear teaching of God, it has no business censuring its members, but if it has clear teaching from God, it has no choice but to censure a member.

5:5 hand this man over to Satan, so that the sinful nature may be destroyed and his spirit saved on the day of the Lord.

In this verse Paul describes the spiritual realities involved in the process of putting this believer "out of your fellowship" (5:2).

The immoral individual is to be handed over to Satan (cf. 1 Tim 1:20). This meant that this Christian "was to be thrust back into that [sphere] in which Satan still exercised authority,"[6] namely the world. Because the phrase in Greek "for the destruction of the flesh" (εἰς ὄλεθρον τῆς σαρκός, *eis olethron tēs sarkos*) has often incorrectly been interpreted to mean physical death,[7] the NIV renders the Greek "so that the sinful nature may be destroyed." While both the Old Testament and New Testament testify to punitive miracles at the Lord's hand, this verse does not point in the direction of physical death. How could Paul have hoped that this Christian might be saved at the time of Christ's return if he drops dead at the time the congregation hands him over to Satan?

The last half of 5:5 sheds light on Paul's understanding here of church discipline. First of all, this man's sin, grave though it was, did not permanently move him beyond the reach of God's forgiveness. Moreover, one of the purposes for this expulsion was to lead this believer to salvation through repentance of his transgression. The phrase "day of the Lord" clearly refers to the return of Christ (cf. 1:8; 4:5).

2. Getting Rid of the Old Yeast (5:6-8)

[6]**Your boasting is not good. Don't you know that a little yeast works through the whole batch of dough?** [7]**Get rid of the old yeast that you may be a new batch without yeast — as you really are. For Christ, our Passover lamb, has been sacrificed.** [8]**Therefore let us keep the Festival, not with the old yeast, the yeast of malice and wickedness, but with bread without yeast, the bread of sincerity and truth.**

---

[6]Barrett, *First Epistle*, p. 126.

[7]One should consult the very informative article by James T. South, "A Critique of the 'Curse/Death' Interpretation of I Corinthians 5.1-8," *New Testament Studies* 39 (1993): 539-561.

5:6 Your boasting is not good. Don't you know that a little yeast works through the whole batch of dough?

The Corinthian problem with boasting is put in its proper light by Paul. How could they, Paul asks, continue to boast when they both tolerate such sin and are themselves susceptible to being infected by such a grievous display of immorality?

Not only does Paul use Mosaic moral instruction as his guide in this matter of incest, but even the metaphors and illustrations he employs to teach the Corinthians about the need for church discipline come from the Mosaic Law. The leaven (yeast) and dough illustration stems clearly from the unleavened bread (Exod 13) and the Passover (Exod 12) feasts. The principle of a little yeast affecting the whole batch is intended by Paul to illustrate how a single case of immorality will, if not removed, affect the whole church at Corinth. By means of this rhetorical question the apostle hopes to get the Corinthians to realize how dangerous this single case can be for them all (cf. Gal 5:9).

5:7 Get rid of the old yeast that you may be a new batch without yeast — as you really are. For Christ, our Passover lamb, has been sacrificed.

The logic of Paul's reasoning in 5:7a is "become what you are." In reality, because of the work of Christ, you are a batch without yeast — therefore, act like it by getting rid of any old yeast. The affirmations of the spiritual condition of the Corinthians are based upon God's prior work in Christ. Paul's use of the term "for" (γάρ, *gar*) connects the reality of the believers' status with the sacrifice of Christ. It is crucial to remind ourselves that the status of being a new batch without yeast did not come about because all the old leaven was removed by human effort and perfectionism. The purity of the people of God is always rooted in the redemptive work of God and never in the people's success in driving out the immoral members.

It should not be overlooked that Paul's explicit Christological formulation here, to a predominantly Gentile group, arose from explicitly and uniquely Jewish categories and experiences. This verse also provides an interesting example of the apostle's correlation of the blood-sacrifice of the Messiah with Christian lifestyle and ethics, a far cry from how the typical philosophers of that age formulated their ethics.

5:8 Therefore let us keep the Festival, not with the old yeast, the yeast of malice and wickedness, but with bread without yeast, the bread of sincerity and truth.

The festival which Paul refers to here is of course the Passover Feast. He has spiritualized this Jewish feast in such a way that he can now refer, based upon a typological interpretation, this to the Christian life. There is no indication that Paul has the Lord's Supper in mind when he refers to the feast. Having identified Jesus with the Passover lamb, he then completes the adaptation of this redemptive event for the church at Corinth. Paul specifically identifies the elements of the old yeast which must be cleaned out and thrown away: these are the characteristics of malice and wickedness. The purity of the "yeast free" celebration of the redemptive act of God in the Passover lamb commemorated by Jews typifies the sincerity and truth of the Christian lifestyle.

3. Separating From Evil (5:9-13)

[9]I have written you in my letter not to associate with sexually immoral people — [10]not at all meaning the people of this world who are immoral, or the greedy and swindlers, or idolaters. In that case you would have to leave this world. [11]But now I am writing you that you must not associate with anyone who calls himself a brother but is sexually immoral or greedy, an idolater or a slanderer, a drunkard or a swindler. With such a man do not even eat.

[12]What business is it of mine to judge those outside the church? Are you not to judge those inside? [13]God will judge those outside. "Expel the wicked man from among you." [a]

[a]*13* Deut. 17:7; 19:19; 21:21; 22:21,24; 24:7

5:9 I have written you in my letter not to associate with sexually immoral people —

This reference to a previous letter is important for several reasons:

1. It reminds the Corinthian readers that this is not the first time that Paul has written them about the issue of immorality.

2. It allows Paul the opportunity to clarify any misconceptions or misinterpretations of this previous letter regarding judgment against the immoral.

3. It allows Paul the chance to anticipate some of the moral aberrations with which he must deal in the remainder of 1 Corinthians.

The practice and theory of religious non-association was well known in Paul's Jewish background. Jewish communities such as those at Qumran as well as Pharisaic communities practiced non-association against aberrant behavior. The same was true of some pagan cults and religious associations. The Greek term translated "not to associate" (μὴ συναναμίγνυσθαι, *mē synanamignysthai*) is the same found in 5:11 and in a similar context in 2 Thess 3:14. The community boundary markers in this context are clearly not doctrinal, in the technical sense, but ethical.

5:10 not at all meaning the people of this world who are immoral, or the greedy and swindlers, or idolaters. In that case you would have to leave this world.

The apostle feels the need to clarify lest some Corinthians incorrectly believed, either on their own or by misreading Paul, that they should withdraw from contact with pagan immorality. There could never have been a Pauline mission had Paul advocated non-association with the pagan world. The pre-Cornelius position that "it is against our law for a Jew to associate with a Gentile or visit him" (Acts 10:28) was clearly at loggerheads with Paul's consistent practice of rubbing shoulders with the non-Jewish world.

The three terms "greedy," "swindlers," and "idolaters" all fit the culture of a Roman colony with a dynamic economy based upon propitiously located ports. With a realism that few who are at home in the Judeo-Christian West can appreciate, Paul acknowledges that it would be impossible even to live in a city such as Corinth and not have social intercourse with idolaters, the greedy, and swindlers. This acceptance of the necessity for association between believers and immoral people fits well in the life of one who had friends among pagan Asiarchs at Ephesus (Acts 19:31) and whose gospel presented a God who had already reconciled a sinful world to himself (2 Cor 5:16-19).

5:11 But now I am writing you that you must not associate with anyone who calls himself a brother but is sexually immoral or greedy, an idolater or a slanderer, a drunkard or a swindler. With such a man do not even eat.

This verse makes it clear that the apostle has a different criterion for non-association with believers than with non-believers. When someone regards himself as a believer he puts himself under the discipline and judgment of the community of faith. Isolated and unchurched believers were unknown to Paul, and the whole idea was doctrinally incompatible with his own understanding of the Christian life (cf. 1 Cor 12). Paul assumed that to be a believer meant to be a believer in the context of the community of believers.

Paul's list of sins includes six items, four of which are taken from the list in 5:10. Interpreters have discussed and argued about the reasons for Paul's choice of these particular six sins and this choice viewed in the light of the larger issue of the catalogues of virtues and vices found in Paul's letters.[8]

It seems unreasonable to imagine that this list is merely arbitrary and unrelated to the issues Paul addressed in his previous letter (5:9) as well as in the remainder of 1 Corinthians. My own understanding of the contextual nature of this list leads me to see these six items as very germane to the issues at Corinth that disturb Paul, some of which had to be readdressed in 2 Corinthians.

Sexually immoral (πόρνος, *pornos*)

Greedy (πλεονέκτης, *pleonektēs*)

Idolater (εἰδωλολάτρης, *eidōlolatrēs*)

Slanderer (λοίδορος, *loidoros*)

---

[8]A helpful overview is given by Fee, *First Epistle*, pp. 220-226.

Drunkard (μέθυσος, *methysos*)

Swindler (ἅρπαξ, *harpax*)

The non-association demanded by Paul includes the issue traditionally called "table-fellowship." It is well known that this form of censure was practiced by Pharisaic and Essenes Jews of the first century. Those regarded as unclean were not allowed to share in meals (e.g., Luke 15:2). This type of Pharisaic attitude was carried over in the early church by "some of the believers who belonged to the party of the Pharisees" (Acts 15:5) and who persecuted believers who wished "to eat with the Gentiles" (Gal 2:11-13). Paul's commandment about the denial of table fellowship would have included both the Lord's Supper as well as other social and communal meals among the Corinthian believers.

5:12 What business is it of mine to judge those outside the church? Are you not to judge those inside?

In 5:12a Paul resumes the thought of 5:10a, namely that the believer is not required to practice non-association against unbelievers. This avoidance of unbelievers would manifest a judgment against those outside the church. Paul is manifestly not against all forms of judging and censure. As the last half of 5:12 makes clear, believers are exhorted to judge fellow believers.

Although it is in vogue at the present to repudiate the idea of Christians judging one another, there is hardly any section in the entirety of Scripture that does not advocate, either by injunction or example, God's people holding one another accountable to the community's standards of faithfulness. The apparent fact that the statement "Do not judge" (Matt 7:1) is the most popular verse among American Evangelicals stems from American individualism and pluralism rather than from any profound insight from the Scriptures.

5:13 God will judge those outside. "Expel the wicked man from among you."

Paul does not reject the doctrine of the judgment of nonbelievers, but only teaches that this is not within the purview of the church. This future tense could refer either to the future judgment of the unbeliever at the time of Christ's return or to ongoing judgment of God against unbelievers. Since Paul does not have criminals in mind in 5:12-13, it does not seem likely that this judgment refers to God's use of the Roman State to punish unbelievers (cf. Rom 13:1-6).

While the interpreter is left hanging about the nature and extent of God's judgment of those outside, Paul is very clear in regard to the action he expects from the church. Based upon the multiple occurrences of the phrase and idea of expulsion in Deuteronomy (17:7; 19:19; 22:21, 24; 24:7), Paul has abundant scriptural authority to order the church at Corinth to expel the incestuous man from its midst.

1 CORINTHIANS 6

B. LAWSUITS AMONG BELIEVERS (6:1-11)

1. Settling Disputes in the Church (6:1-8)

¹If any of you has a dispute with another, dare he take it before the ungodly for judgment instead of before the saints? ²Do you not know that the saints will judge the world? And if you are to judge the world, are you not competent to judge trivial cases? ³Do you not know that we will judge angels? How much more the things of this life! ⁴Therefore, if you have disputes about such matters, appoint as judges even men of little account in the church!ᵃ ⁵I say this to shame you. Is it possible that there is nobody among you wise enough to judge a dispute between believers? ⁶But instead, one brother goes to law against another — and this in front of unbelievers!

⁷The very fact that you have lawsuits among you means you have been completely defeated already. Why not rather be wronged? Why not rather be cheated? ⁸Instead, you yourselves cheat and do wrong, and you do this to your brothers.

ᵃ*4 Or matters, do you appoint as judges men of little account in the church?*

6:1 If any of you has a dispute with another, dare he take it before the ungodly for judgment instead of before the saints?
Many interpreters rightly detect that the link between 5:9-13 and 6:1-8 is supplied by the word judge (κρίνω, *krinō*), a term whose occurrences are very concentrated in chapters 5-6. Fee nicely describes the logical connection between the end of 5 and the beginning of 6 in these words:

Paul concludes the previous argument by insisting that the church is not to judge those "outside" but must judge those "inside." That had to do first of all with the expulsion of the incestuous man; but it also has to do with another kind of "judgment" that must take place within the Christian community, namely in matters of everyday life where one member has a grievance against another. [1]

Paul begins his instruction by faulting not litigation but litigation before the pagan and ungodly courts of Roman Corinth.

6:2 Do you not know that the saints will judge the world? And if you are to judge the world, are you not competent to judge trivial cases?

Since litigation in the presence of saints rather than sinners is so right and obvious to Paul, he was surely amazed that Roman believers had not yet grasped this idea. Accordingly, Paul walks the readers step-by-step through his own assumptions and reasoning.[2] The notion of the saints' eschatological judgment of the world was apparently rooted in the Greek version (LXX) of Daniel 7:22 and was appropriated by late Jewish and early Christian writers.

If in fact the members of the church of God at Corinth will participate in the future judgment of the world (κόσμος, *kosmos*), how is it, Paul asks, that they cannot judge trivial cases among themselves in the city of Corinth? There is an ironic similarity between Paul's advice here that the religious community should not have to go outisde to get help with internal matters and the pronouncement of the Roman governor Gallio in Acts 18:14-16. When unbelieving Jews in Corinth brought their fellow-Jew Paul before the court of Gallio, he told them to "settle the matter yourselves. I will not be a judge of such things" (Acts 18:15).

Even though Paul never directly mentions the issue at stake in the litigation, he clearly regards it as trivial. It is not totally clear whether he means trivial by normal standards or trivial in light of

---

[1]Fee, *First Epistle*, p. 228.

[2]The phrase "Do you not know" is used with unusual frequency by Paul in this chapter, 6:2,3,9,15,16,19.

judging the entire world, though I believe the former is the most natural reading. As far as one can discern, Paul does not have in mind here major criminal or capital offenses.

6:3 Do you not know that we will judge angels? How much more the things of this life!

Using a similar rhetorical strategy to the one he employed in 6:2, the apostle affirms that believers will serve as judges in the final judgment. If God allows believers to judge angels, how much more would he not expect them to adjudicate in temporal and everyday affairs?

6:4 Therefore, if you have disputes about such matters, appoint as judges even men of little account in the church!

The direct verbal link between 6:3 and 6:4 is lost in the NIV. The Greek word βιωτικά (biōtika) rendered "things of this life" at the end of 6:3 is the very first word in 6:4, but is strangely translated "about such matters." In 6:4a Paul implies that such conditions will arise and the congregation will need to address litigation about everyday matters.

The correct translation and exact meaning of 6:4b is problematic. Simon Kistemaker correctly noted, "No translation or interpretation is free from difficulties."[3] Some translations take 6:4b as a question while others regard it as an imperative. Some understand the "men of little account" to be Christians, while others take them to be pagan judges. Some (the majority) translate ἐκκλησία (ekklēsia) as church while others believe that "It is more likely that the ekklēsia in this verse is the secular assembly, not the Christian congregation."[4]

6:5 I say this to shame you. Is it possible that there is nobody among you wise enough to judge a dispute between believers?

The apostle is certainly not above using shame to admonish and modify the behavior of the Christians at Corinth (cf. 4:14; 15:34!). The reference to shame probably points backward to the arguments Paul made in 6:2-4. Mild sarcasm is the style of argu-

---

[3]Kistemaker, *First Corinthians*, p. 182.
[4]Witherington, *Conflict and Community in Corinth*, p. 165.

mentation used by Paul in the latter part of this verse. Given the preoccupation with wisdom among certain Corinthians in the church (e.g., 3:18) Paul queries why none of these (worldly) wise believers have come forward and settled this case of litigation and dispute between believers.

6:6 But instead, one brother goes to law against another — and this in front of unbelievers!

Paul brings to a conclusion the point he has been making since 6:1 about the unacceptability of the saints going before the ungodly (ἄδικος, *adikos*) for litigation. The apostle uses the term "unbelievers" here (ἄπιστοι, *apistoi*), but his point is the same. The New Testament does sporadically reveal the existence of believers who hold "public office" in the pagan world (e.g., Erastus, director of the city's public works, Rom 16:23), who serve in the Roman military (Cornelius, Acts 10) or even serve on a city's judicial board (Dionysius, a member of the Areopagus, Acts 17:34), but first century believers would have no reason, on a regular basis, to expect anyone but unbelievers among the judges and juries of their day.

The Christians in Roman Corinth were not the only followers of a deity to be told that they should not take one another before public courts. The followers of the god Bacchus frequently formed themselves into Bacchic societies. Archaeologists discovered a Greek inscription which contains lengthy rules to regulate a particular Bacchic society and the relationships between its members (known as *Iobacchi*). A portion of this inscriptions reads:

> And if anyone come to blows, he who has been struck shall lodge a written statement with the priest or the vice-priest, and he shall without fail convene a general meeting, and the Iobacchi shall decide the question by vote under the presidency of the priest, and the penalty shall be exclusion for a period to be determined and a fine not exceeding twenty-five silver denarii. And the same punishment shall be imposed also on one who, having been struck, fails to seek

redress with the priest or the arch-bacchus but *has brought a charge before public courts.*[5]

6:7 The very fact that you have lawsuits among you means you have been completely defeated already. Why not rather be wronged? Why not rather be cheated?

Paul now presses down hard on another reason why he is opposed to brother against brother litigation. In a litigious urban culture[6] lawsuits are a sign of power and success, but Paul regards them as hallmarks of defeat in the community of believers. In addition to the issue of going before the ungodly and unbelievers, he now points out that suffering injustice and being wronged is more desirable than winning litigation since the latter is proof of total defeat of the church's life together.

Commentators have rightly asked whether Paul here is reflecting earlier ideas of Jesus. On this issue Gordon Fee writes,

> This is another sure instance of the influence of the teaching of Jesus on Paul (cf. 4:16-17). Paul regularly enjoins that one not return evil for evil (I Thess. 5:15; Rom. 12:17), a direct reflection of the teaching and example of Jesus (see on 4:12-13).[7]

6:8 Instead, you yourselves cheat and do wrong, and you do this to your brothers.

The two passive ideas of "be wronged" and "be cheated" in 6:7 are now turned into active accusations in 6:8. The apostle now addresses those against whom the litigation had been brought.

---

[5]This English translation is taken from E. Ferguson, *Backgrounds of Early Christianity* (Lewiston, NY: E. Mellen Press, 1984), which contains the entire inscription.

[6]The imperial period rhetorician and philosopher Dio Chrysostom complains about "the lawyers innumerable perverting justice" who were at Corinth, *The Eighth Discourse, on Virtue,* 9-10, trans. by J.W. Cohoon, Loeb Classical Library (Cambridge, MA: Harvard University Press, 1949), vol. 1, p. 381.

[7]Fee, *First Epistle,* p. 241.

Apparently in Paul's judgment, they were guilty of cheating and doing wrong against fellow believers. Insult is added to injury by the fact that these believers not only act immorally, but that they do so against their own brothers.

We have no way of knowing what particular legal and moral transgressions these Corinthian believers had committed. We have seen, however, Paul's attitude toward the effects. While Paul's own response to this situation reflected his apostolic wisdom and revelation, it is not as "generally irrelevant" as Fee suggests [8] to point out that several ancient philosophers, as far back as Socrates, taught that it was always better to be wronged than to do wrong.

2. The Inheritance of the Wicked (6:9-11)

[9]Do you not know that the wicked will not inherit the kingdom of God? Do not be deceived: Neither the sexually immoral nor idolaters nor adulterers nor male prostitutes nor homosexual offenders [10]nor thieves nor the greedy nor drunkards nor slanderers nor swindlers will inherit the kingdom of God. [11]And that is what some of you were. But you were washed, you were sanctified, you were justified in the name of the Lord Jesus Christ and by the Spirit of our God.

6:9 Do you not know that the wicked will not inherit the kingdom of God? Do not be deceived: Neither the sexually immoral nor idolaters nor adulterers nor male prostitutes nor homosexual offenders

A. Robertson and A. Plummer correctly observed that 1 Cor 6:9-11 "conclude the subject of vv. 1-8 by an appeal to wider principles, and thus prepare the way" for Paul's treatment of immorality in 6:12-20. [9] It is unfortunate that virtually no English translation maintains the verbal linkage between 6:8 and 6:9 that is so evident in the Greek text. The phrase in 6:8 "you yourselves do

---

[8]Fee, *First Epistle*, p. 241, note 11.
[9]Robertson and Plummer, *First Epistle of St. Paul*, p. 117.

wrong" (ἀδίκεισθε, *adikeisthe*) is clearly linked to the term "wicked" (ἄδικοι, *adikoi*) in 6:9, the former being the verbal form while the latter is the noun. This means that Paul's words of warning in 6:9-11 at least begins with a warning to the brother addressed in 6:8.

As we read through the warning of 6:9 and the catalogue of sins, it is important to keep before us the function of the material in this section of the letter. Because of the connection between 6:8 and 6:9-11, because of the warning against self-deception, and because of the preceding (5:1-13) and subsequent (6:12-20) treatment of sexual immorality being committed by believers, it must be the case that Paul is warning believers that their sinful behavior will disqualify them from inheriting God's kingdom.[10]

The partial listing in 6:9 is an expansion of the terms given in 5:10 and 5:11. All those particular sins listed in 6:9-10 are manifestations of the lifestyle of the wicked. Interpreters have struggled to explain exactly why he includes some sins in this list but omits others. If it were not for the term idolaters, all the items in 6:9 would relate to sexual aberrations. Given the frequent associations of sexual immorality with pagan temples in Jewish and pagan writings, Paul is perhaps appropriating this common association. If pagan temples and the ideas sometimes associated with them do not provide the satisfactory setting for Paul's list in 6:9, then one might look at the ubiquitous social institution of Roman and Greek paganism known as the banquet. Pagan meals and banquets were above all else characterized by frequent opportunities for every sin mentioned in 6:9.

Due to political and cultural changes in Europe and North America in the past three decades there has been a significant increase in the discussion about homosexual or homoerotic orientation and activity. Since the ancient attitudes toward homoerotic activity as well as the terminology of 1 Cor 6:9 are at the center of these discussions, a few historical and philological comments are in order at this point.

In antiquity homoerotic acts were often practiced and generally accepted. Since most of the extant evidence comes from the aristocratic, the well educated (philosophers and rhetoricians),

---

[10]See comments on 1 Cor 10:1-13.

and the male representatives of society, we obviously know much more about homosexuality among these groups.

Generally speaking pederasty was a widespread phenomenon in Greek and later Roman society. These sexual experiences were a typical part of a young boy's education and were practiced by leading thinkers such as Plato as well as later by many Emperors of the Roman Empire.[11] Even though this type of relationship had both pedagogical and emotional facets, it would be exceedingly anachronistic to think that these homoerotic relationship and experiences with boys were based upon "Platonic love." The classical scholar K.J. Dover makes this very point in a candid observation when he remarked,

> It was taken for granted in the Classical period that a man was sexually attracted by a good-looking younger male, and no Greek who said that he was 'in love' would have taken it amiss if his hearers assumed without further enquiry that he was in love with a boy and that he desired more than anything to ejaculate in or on the boy's body. I put the matter in these coarse and clinical terms to preclude any misapprehension arising from modern application of the expression 'Platonic love' or from Greek euphemism. [12]

Paul's condemnation of homosexual activity naturally included, but was not limited to, pederasty. Scholars who advocate the acceptability of contemporary homoerotic activity for Christians sometimes base their appeal on the point that since pederasty was the major manifestation of homosexuality, this is the only

---

[11]Suetonius, *Lives of the Twelve Caesars* Gaius 41.

[12]K.J. Dover, "Classical Greek Attitudes to Sexual Behaviour," in *Women in the Ancient World: The Arethusa Papers*, eds. John Peradotto and J.P. Sullivan (Albany: State University of New York Press, 1984), p. 149. With the same candor Dover summarizes the extant visual portrayal of pederasty in the archaeological evidence of Greek vase paintings. He states, "The vase-painters very frequently depict the giving of presents by men to boys and the 'courting' of boys (a mild term for an approach which includes putting a hand on the boy's genitals), but their pursuit of the subject to the stage of erection, let alone penetration, in a variety of positions, is commonplace," p. 151.

kind Paul opposed.[13] This view has at least three weaknesses from a historical and exegetical perspective:

1. The historical record is quite clear that homoerotic activity was not confined only to pederasty in the classical world. Homosexual practices also took place between adult men and between adult women.

2. To focus Paul's concern on the sole issue of pederasty reflects, I suspect, modern convictions about the abhorrence of sexual activity (of any kind) with minors. It is very improbable that Paul would have had any theological or cultural problems with sex between adults and minors within the context of marital heterosexuality. Generally speaking, Greek, Roman, and Jewish (first) marriages in Paul's day involved marriage between an adult male and a pubescent girl, usually half the age of her husband. The concept of lawful sex with minors was not the oxymoron that it is perceived to be in modern Western culture.

3. Paul's argumentation against homoeroticism elsewhere makes it clear that it is homoerotic behavior itself, and not just some form of it, that is contrary to nature.

The two Greek terms translated "male prostitutes" and "homosexual offenders" are rather graphic terms and clearly refer to sexual acts and not sexual orientation or sexual preference. The first term (μαλακοί, malakoi) generally means "soft" and when applied to a sexual setting can mean "effeminate" or refer to the passive individual (of any age) in a homoerotic activity. The second Greek term (ἀρσενοκοῖται, arsenokoitoi) is very rare in ancient Greek literature and is apparently a compound Greek word of Jewish origin which stemmed from the wording of Lev 18:22 and 20:13 in the LXX.[14] Since both of these Scripture texts explicitly mention general homosexual activity, this provides the most obvious conceptual background to the apostle's condemnation of this practice in 1 Cor 6:9.

---

[13]E.g., Robin Scroggs, *The New Testament and Homosexuality: Contextual Background for Contemporary Debate* (Philadelphia: Fortress Press, 1983).

[14]For this philological evidence and argumentation see D. E. Malick, "The Condemnation of Homosexuality in Romans 1:26-27." *Bibliotheca Sacra* 150 (1993) 327-340 and especially "The Condemnation of Homosexuality in 1 Corinthians 6:9," *Bibliotheca Sacra* 150 (1993) 479-492.

6:10 nor thieves nor the greedy nor drunkards nor slanderers nor swindlers will inherit the kingdom of God.

Except for the reference to thieves, all the sins mentioned in this verse are found in the list of 1 Cor 5:11 (cf. comments on 5:11 for the contextual relevance of this list). This is not the only verse in the New Testament that categorizes theft as a serious sin. This type of behavior is prohibited in other Pauline (Rom 2:21; 13:9; Eph 4:28) as well as Petrine (1 Pet 4:15) letters. Jesus' conversation recorded in Mark 10:19 would seem to support Paul's notion that this issue of theft impinged on one's ability to have eternal life and an inheritance in God's kingdom.

The inextricable connection between one's lifestyle and one's fellowship with God, both in the present age and the age to come, is a connection rooted in the Law, the Prophets, and the Wisdom literature of the Apostle Paul's Scripture. The Corinthians were no different from the Galatians in their need to hear repeatedly this inextricable connection (Gal 5:19-21).

6:11 And that is what some of you were. But you were washed, you were sanctified, you were justified in the name of the Lord Jesus Christ and by the Spirit of our God.

The apostle resorts here to his "before-and-after" illustration, this time to highlight the contrast between their prior exclusion from God's inheritance and their current state of purity, holiness, and justification. This analysis of the Corinthians' pre-Christian lives is in many ways a statement of the obvious. The sensational aura given to this analysis could only arise among people with roots in Judeo-Christian culture. What else would one expect from a first generation urban church with pagan converts but that some of them would have been living lives commensurate with paganism?

The true sensationalism of 6:11 is found in the threefold use of the strong adversative word "but" (ἀλλά, *alla*) to introduce each of the three aorist verbs. Even though by all human and divine standards these people have no right to a relationship with God, they, in fact, are now washed, sanctified and justified. At least two doctrinal issues are often discussed in relationship to 6:11. The first regards the meaning of "washed" and its relationship to the words "sanctified" and "justified." The most cogent interpretation relates washed to the believer's participation in water baptism. This view builds upon the frequent association of water baptism with imagery of washing in the New Testament (Acts 22:16; Eph 5:26; Heb 10:22). An additional fact, usually denied or ignored by commentators and translations, is that the Greek word translated "washed" is a middle voice (ἀπελούσασθε, *apelousasthe*) and not a passive voice verb like the Greek words translated "sanctified" (ἡγιάσθητε, *hēgiasthēte*) and "justified" (ἐδικαιώθητε, *edikaiōthēte*). Since all three verbs are not in the same Greek voice, and since the meaning of this particular verb (ἀπολούω, *apolouō*) in the middle voice is "you have washed yourselves," the assertion that, "the three verbs [of 6:11b] refer to the same rarity, and . . . each of them has 'God' as the implied subject" is exceedingly problematic.[15] If, however, one interprets washed as a reference to believer's baptism, where the Corinthians "entered the water as voluntary agents, just as St. Paul did,[16] "then one is not compelled to advance specious grammatical arguments."

"Sanctified" (and its cognates) is a pervasive term in Paul's writings and is clearly a work of God, through his Spirit, in the life of the believer. Just as baptism was a demarcation between the "before" and "after" phases in the life of the Corinthian believer, so too was the sanctifying work of God's Holy Spirit. The lifestyle of the wicked is no longer acceptable for those upon whom God has begun his spiritual work.

C. SEXUAL IMMORALITY (6:12-20)

1. The Body As a Member of Christ (6:12-17)

[12]"Everything is permissible for me" — but not everything is beneficial. "Everything is permissible for me" — but I will not be mastered by anything. [13]"Food for the stomach and the stomach for food" — but God will destroy them both. The body is not

---

[15]Fee, *First Epistle*, p. 246
[16]Robertson and Plummer, *First Epistle of St. Paul*, p. 119.

meant for sexual immorality, but for the Lord, and the Lord for the body. [14]By his power God raised the Lord from the dead, and he will raise us also. [15]Do you not know that your bodies are members of Christ himself? Shall I then take the members of Christ and unite them with a prostitute? Never! [16]Do you not know that he who unites himself with a prostitute is one with her in body? For it is said, "The two will become one flesh."[a] [17]But he who unites himself with the Lord is one with him in spirit.

[a]*16 Gen. 2:24

6:12 "Everything is permissible for me" — but not everything is beneficial. "Everything is permissible for me" — but I will not be mastered by anything.

In this section 6:12-20 Paul returns to the general issues of sexual immorality begun in 5:1. The issue under discussion in 6:12-20 is prostitution. Houses of prostitution were widespread in the Greco-Roman world and were generally looked upon as a social necessity. The venerable Roman leader Cato was supposed to have congratulated a young man he saw departing from a brothel. When your sexual passions are strong, he told the young man, it is better to have sex with a prostitute than another man's wife.[17]

Commentators usually attempt to interface this issue with the city's widespread reputation for sexual promiscuity and immorality. The first piece of evidence usually cited includes the philological evidence that the Greek verb meaning "to be a Corinthian" (κορινθιάζεσθαι, korinthiazesthai) meant to fornicate or to be sexually immoral.[18] The principal evidence for this, however, comes from authors living during the time of the Greek city of Corinth, not the Roman city (See Introduction).[19]

---

[17]This story is recounted in the works of the Roman poet Horace, *Satires* 1.2.28-36.

[18]According to J. Murphy-O'Connor, *St. Paul's Corinth*, p. 56, the Greek author Aristophanes (c. 450-385 B.C.) created this verbal connection.

[19]The list of authors from the period of the Greek Corinth include: Philetaerus (4th century), Poliochus (4th century), Antiphanes (4th century) and Plato (4th century) according to J. Murphy-O'Connor, *St. Paul's Corinth*, p. 56.

A second point of Corinthian culture that earlier commentators related, incorrectly I believe, to this text is the account of
Corinth's temple to Aphrodite (goddess of sexual pleasure) in
which 1,000 sacred prostitutes worked. The historical reference to
this temple is found in the works of the Greek author Strabo who
writes,

> And the temple of Aphrodite was so rich that it owned
> more than a thousand temple-slaves, prostitutes, whom
> both men and women had dedicated to the goddess. And
> therefore it was also on account of these women that the
> city was crowded with people and grew rich. [20]

Since Strabo himself discusses this temple in the context of the
old city of Corinth (destroyed in the second century B.C.), it is
unlikely that it was still standing or in use in the Roman city of
Corinth.[21] Even if this temple of 1,000 sacred prostitutes were op-
erational in the mid-first century A.D., it is important to notice
that there is no evidence in 1 Corinthians that Paul has this or any
other temple's prostitutes in mind.

It can be concluded that the church of God at Corinth had no
special monopoly on the problems of sexual sins, and many times
the city of Corinth has borne a reputation for being a superlative
"sin city" that exceeds the historical evidence.[22] Contemporary
scholarly thought is best reflected in J. Murphy-O'Connor's judgment in this matter that, "It is doubtful that the situation at Corinth was any worse than in other port-cities of the eastern Mediterranean."[23]

---

[20]Strabo *Geography* 8.6.20c, cited from J. Murphy-O'Connor, *St. Paul's Corinth*, p. 55.

[21]There are scholars still convinced by Strabo's report, including most recently John McRay, *Archaeology and the New Testament*, (Grand Rapids: Baker, 1991), p. 316. There is certainly no clear literary or archaeological testimony for such a temple in the Roman era.

[22]Donald Engels, *Roman Corinth: An Alternative Model for the Classical City* (Chicago: The University of Chicago, 1990), pp. 97-99 also refutes the older interpretations and judgments of New Testament and classical scholars about Corinthian Aphrodite and the supposed moral degrada-tion of Roman Corinth.

[23]J. Murphy-O'Connor, *St. Paul's Corinth*, p. 56.

Turning now to the wording of 6:12, this verse is usually regarded as beginning with quoted slogans from those believers who participated in, or at least condoned, sexual immorality. From this perspective the supporters of sexual immorality are promoting a kind of libertinism. Paul retorts to their libertine slogan by asserting that permissibility is not the final issue. Paul places his accent upon what is beneficial, much as he does in 10:23. The apostle repeats the slogan and retorts with an emphasis upon self-control. Those given over to carnal indulgence and a libertine lifestyle are characterized by Paul as being mastered or ruled by it (cf. Rom 6:16-20).

6:13 "Food for the stomach and the stomach for food" — but God will destroy them both. The body is not meant for sexual immorality, but for the Lord, and the Lord for the body.

This verse likewise begins with a hedonistic slogan that places emphasis upon the satisfaction of human appetites. The particular placement of quotations marks (which the ancient Greeks did not use), in the NIV translation marks the phrase "but God will destroy them both" as Paul's retort. Some scholars argue, however, that the entire first sentence ("Food . . . both") should be viewed as the hedonistic slogan and 6:13b ("The body . . . the body") should be viewed as Paul's response.[24] If this interpretation is correct, then the phrase "but God will destroy them both" would reflect the libertine view that since God will destroy both food and stomach, he obviously cares little about mankind's physical nature and appetites. Therefore, the argument runs, God is not that concerned about bodily appetites and does not care about how and with whom one's sexual appetites are satisfied.

The apostle's affirmations in 6:13b about the body and the Lord were radically out of step with the cultural values and ethical mores indigenous to a pagan urban setting. Like much of 20th century paganism that affirms that men's and women's sexual activity should be based upon personal choice and inalienable rights and that argues that their bodies are their own private property, so also most ancient pagans did not correlate the satis-

---

[24]Gordon Fee, *First Epistle*; this view is also accepted by Witherington, *Conflict and Community in Corinth*, p. 168.

faction of bodily sexual appetites with a view of divine ownership of their bodies. For the most part neither ancient religions nor ancient philosophies affirmed anything like the Biblical view that the divine creation of mankind (with its sensual appetites) placed mankind's sexual expressions and activities under divine authority and legislation. The Biblical view simply stated is that mankind is, was, and will always be creation and will never evolve into the status of the Creator. As such, the creations of God are subject to God's laws and his divine odering of creation. Humans are never wise enough or holy enough to guide their own steps.

As is often the case, the "free love" attitudes found among some in the Roman world involved a double standard. Immoral sex was tolerated much more if committed by men than by women, and of course there were certain societal norms which were suppose to be observed. As is recorded in the works of one Roman author, "Provided you keep away from married women, virgins, young innocents, and children of respectable families, love anyone you want."[25]

In the matter of prostitutes, the prevailing cultural views which were brought into the church of God by pagan converts and against which Paul is arguing in this section are capsulated in a statement by a leading Roman politician and philosopher of the first century B.C. Cicero wrote:

> Mind you, if there is anyone who thinks that young men ought not to visit prostitutes, he is certainly narrow-minded (no doubt about it), and completely out of step with our present liberal thinking. In fact, he has nothing in common with the customs and behaviour of previous generations, who were quite broadminded on the subject. [26]

---

[25]Plautus, *Curculio* 37-38, trans. by P. Nixon, Loeb Classical Library, 5 vols (Cambridge, MA: Harvard University Press, 1959), vol. 2, pp. 191-193.
[26]Cicero, *Pro Caelio* 48.

6:14 By his power God raised the Lord from the dead, and he will raise us also.

This verse functions as a refutation of the hedonistic affirmation of 6:13a. It is not correct, Paul writes, to argue from a belief that God will destroy the body (=the stomach). Rather, just as God raised the Lord, so too he will raise up believers from the dead. The belief expressed here fits into Paul's overall eschatological picture where believers are raised, stand before the judgment throne of God, and will be judged on the basis of what they have done in and with their bodies (2 Cor 5:10).

While there is insufficient evidence to be dogmatic about it, there is the real possibility that the apostle's need to affirm the future resurrection of believers in the context of his treatment of sexual immorality is related to his treatment of these issues in 1 Cor 15:12-58. Even though the discussion and argumentation in 1 Cor 15 is clearly focused upon the reality of the future resurrection, the case for the connection with 6:14 is made stronger when one observes that Paul's argument in 1 Cor 15 contains explicit attacks against hedonistic slogans (15:32) and sinful activities (15:33-34).

6:15 Do you not know that your bodies are members of Christ himself? Shall I then take the members of Christ and unite them with a prostitute? Never!

This verse is structured around two questions and an imperative. This is the first of three uses of the "do you not know" phrase in this section (cf. 6:16, 19). The term "bodies" (σώματα, *sōmata*) connects this question to the prior affirmations about the body expressed in 6:13. This relational illustration about being members of Christ anticipates similar relational statements which make up Paul's comprehensive doctrine of the Body of Christ (cf. 1 Cor 10:16; 12:12-27; Rom 12:5; Eph 1:22-23; 4:11-16; 5:23; Col 1:18).

In this context it is clear that Paul is referring to the personal human bodies of believers when he writes that they are members of Christ. Since their personal bodies are connected with Christ, when a Corinthian believer had sexual relationship with a prostitute, he established a union between Christ and the prostitute through the medium of the believer's body. This sinful situation is never acceptable for a Christian.

Paul's declaration that sexual immorality is unacceptable was addressed to those who had a choice about the matter. It must be kept in mind that large numbers of boys and girls and men and women, especially slaves, had little choice about their sexual involvement. The Roman author Seneca the Elder once commented that:

"Losing sexual purity was a crime if you were a freeborn."
"Losing sexual purity was a necessity if you were a slave."
"Losing sexual purity was a duty if you were a freedman."

6:16 Do you not know that he who unites himself with a prostitute is one with her in body? For it is said, "The two will become one flesh."

Paul's teaching in 6:15 was probably very opaque to believers recently converted from a pagan worldview and lifestyle. In 6:16 Paul invokes the teaching of Scripture to demonstrate the reality of the union presented in 6:15. The phrase "one with her in body" anticipates the "one with him [i.e., the Lord] in spirit" of the following verse. Paul reaches back to Gen 2:24 to find the language of "oneness" related to sexual intercourse. The function of the "one flesh" doctrine here in the context of prostitution is obviously not to address the issue of the permanency of marriage, but rather to highlight the oneness that occurs during and only during sexual intercourse.

Given the sexual promiscuity that characterized large segments of pagan society, Paul wanted to emphasize that more takes place during sexual intercourse than the mere fulfillment of animal urges and concupiscent impulses. There is a temporary oneness that occurs that has profound implications for the believer's relationship with the Lord.

6:17 But he who unites himself with the Lord is one with him in spirit.

Paul uses the same word for "unites" (κολλώμενος, *kollōmenos*) with the Lord as he did for "unites" with the prostitute in 6:16. The oneness with the Lord takes place, however, in the realm of

Spirit (ἕν πνεῦμα, *hen pneuma*). Nevertheless there is a bodily connection with the Lord since the believers' bodies are now members of Christ (6:15) As Sampley noted in this matter, "The human options are sketched boldly by Paul: either immorality (*porneia*) or the Lord; either the Lord or a prostitute. If one is genuinely bonded to the Lord, then *porneia* is out of the question and must be shunned."[27]

2. The Body As the Temple of the Holy Spirit (6:18-20)

[18]Flee from sexual immorality. All other sins a man commits are outside his body, but he who sins sexually sins against his own body. [19]Do you not know that your body is a temple of the Holy Spirit, who is in you, whom you have received from God? You are not your own; [20]you were bought at a price. Therefore honor God with your body.

6:18 Flee from sexual immorality. All other sins a man commits are outside his body, but he who sins sexually sins against his own body.

It is no accident that the imperative form of the verb "flee" (φεύγω, *pheugō*) is used once in 1 Corinthians with sexual immorality and once with idolatry (10:14). Idolatry and sexual immorality were the two most frequent sins that characterized the pagan world from the viewpoint of Jewish thinking and Scripture.

Paul's next comment (all other sins . . . his own body) has engendered much discussion and the creation of hypotheses by scholars. On the face of it, Paul's affirmation seems incorrect since drunkenness or suicide, the argument runs, also do harm to (i.e., sin against) one's body. Some have even suggested that the clause "all other sins . . ." was a slogan from Corinthian opponents and the final words "but he who sins . . ." was Paul's response.[28] Those who view this verse as a mixture of a hedonistic

---

[27]J.P. Sampley, *Walking Between the Times, Paul's Moral Reasoning* (Philadelphia: Fortress Press, 1991), pp. 104-105.

[28]Fee, *First Epistle*, pp. 260-263, cites numerous options.

Corinthian slogan and Paul's response are drawing upon fanciful hypotheses which are not really necessary.

Both the veracity and logic of Paul's assertion are contextually evident when 6:18 is interpreted in light of the Scripture quotation given in 6:16. None of the other sins that Paul has mentioned elsewhere in 1 Corinthians (e.g., 5:11) actually create a bodily union with a prostitute. To be sure, drunkenness can exclude one from the kingdom of God (6:10) and can cause physical harm to one's body. Nevertheless, even those sins which can physically harm the body do not, as it were, contaminate the body by a unification with immorality. It is exactly this unique nature and capacity of the body to be both united with Christ and with a prostitute that is illuminated by the Scripture citation of Genesis. Furthermore, it is exactly because of the truth that sins of sexual immorality are uniquely inimical to the body that it is in this setting that Paul stated that, "The body is not meant for sexual immorality, but for the Lord, and the Lord for the body" (1 Cor 6:13).

6:19 Do you not know that your body is a temple of the Holy Spirit, who is in you, whom you have received from God? You are not your own;

The apostle moves his argument forward at this juncture by shifting to an argument based upon the dichotomy of the sacred and profane. Even though Gentile believers could no longer worship at a temple with approval, both they and Jewish believers knew the concept of the sacredness of temples. Paul here teaches that the individual personal body of each believer is the dwelling place (ναός, *naos*) of the Holy Spirit which each and every believer at Corinth received from God.

The force of Paul's imagery was so obvious to his readers that he did not even have to draw out the implication that the holiness of the believer's body is incompatible with impurity and fornication. The apostle may have needed to teach them that their bodies were the abode of the Holy Spirit, but they already knew that sacred dwellings were not to be contaminated with unclean and impure objects and people. Jewish believers of course knew the same thing from their training in laws of Levitical holiness.

The last phrase of this verse belongs thematically with 6:20. Paul here rejects the notion of ethical self-determination. The believer cannot make choices about sexual behavior on the basis of his or her own preferences. That notion of the autonomy of ethical decisions regarding sexual acts is essentially incompatible with Christian existence and redemption.

6:20 you were bought at a price. Therefore honor God with your body.

The NIV fails to translate Paul's word γάρ (*gar*) which means "for" and which shows the conceptual connection between verses 19 and 20. The reason that the believer, according to Paul, can no longer claim free choices is that he is now the personal property of another. The imagery of "bought at a price" probably derives from the slave auctions so well known in the ancient world. Its emphasis, therefore, is not on having a ransom paid that leads to freedom, but rather on a change of ownership.[29]

Since the believer, including his body, is the personal possession of God, Paul believes that the saint must bring glory to God "in the concrete circumstances in which the physical members operate."[30] There was for Paul no stronger antidote against sexual promiscuity and prostitution than claiming the believer's body, and not just his soul and spirit, as the location for the glorification of God.

---

[29]Robertson and Plummer, *First Epistle of St. Paul*, p. 129 and Sampley, *Walking Between the Times*, p. 105.
[30]Barrett, *First Epistle*, p. 153.

1 CORINTHIANS 7

IV. SEXUALITY, CELIBACY, AND MARRIAGE (7:1-40)

It is not easy to discover the Corinthian situation and issues that lie behind Paul's words in 1 Corinthians 7. Nevertheless, since Paul acknowledges that his judgments and directives in these matters are a direct response to Corinthian communication with him, the interpreter is obligated to propose a framework at Corinth that best corresponds to the statements and logic of this chapter. There is a new interpretation which has been widely disseminated through the publications of Gordon Fee on 1 Corinthians. Fee advances the theory that the problems related to matters of sexuality and abstinence in 7:1-7 should be traced to women who fit a paradigm which he calls the "eschatological woman."[1] Since Fee's views of this eschatological woman animates his exegetical treatment of other texts in 1 Corinthians which deal with women (e.g., 11:2-16) and serves as a pillar in his feminist reading of Paul, it is important to investigate this hypothesis. He gives the following description:

> What would seem to lie behind this position is once again their present pneumatic existence, which has Hellenistic dualism at its roots and their own brand of 'spiritualized eschatology' as its repeated expression. As those who are 'spiritual' they are above the merely earthly existence of others; marriage belongs to this age that is passing away. One wonders further whether we do not have here the first evidence for the so-called 'eschatological women' in Cor-

---

[1] This phrase was first emphasized in New Testament scholarship by Robin Scroggs, "Paul and the Eschatological Women," *Journal of the American Academy of Religion* 40 (1972), 283-303.

inth, who think of themselves as having already realized the 'resurrection from the dead' by being in spirit and thus already as the angels (cf. 11:2-16; 13:1), neither marrying nor giving in marriage (cf. Luke 20:35). [2]

There seem to be three major problems with the utilization of the eschatological woman paradigm to interpret the issue of sexual abstinence in marriage as discussed by Paul in 1 Cor 7:1-7.

1. The text and structure of 1 Cor 7 make it clear that Paul is addressing the issue to believers of both genders.[3] The following display makes this plain:

7:2 each *man* should have his own *wife*, and each *woman* her own *husband*.

7:3 The *husband* should fulfill his marital duty to his *wife*, and likewise the *wife* to her *husband*.

7:4 The *wife's* body does not belong to her alone but also to her *husband*. In the same way, the *husband's* body does not belong to him alone but also to his *wife*.

Based upon Paul's own treatment of the issue, we would have to also include an "eschatological man," an ingredient which would nullify Fee's hypothesis and his feminist interpretation.

2. The eschatological woman notion relies heavily upon information within the Synoptic Gospels, particularly Matt 22:30; Mark 12:25, and Luke 20:35, about the belief that in the resurrection the saints will be like angels and not be married. It is not only far from certain that new Corinthian converts would have known these particular teachings of Jesus by A.D. 50-55, but it is even more uncertain that they would have transmuted it into something which resembled Fee's eschatological woman.

The background of Jesus' teaching regarding no sex in heaven can be traced directly to well known Jewish laws about the impurity and uncleanness attached to the menstruation of women (Lev 12:2-5; 18:19), the ejaculation of men (Lev 15:16-32; 22:4) and the

---

[2]Fee, *First Epistle*, p. 269; the same view is advocated in his more recent work *God's Empowering Presence*, p. 145.

[3]Cf. my remarks in "Use, Misuse and Neglect of Archaeological Evidence in Some Modern Works on 1 Corinthians," *Zeitschrift für die Neutestamentliche Wissenschaft* 83 (1992), pp. 58-64.

event of childbirth (Lev 12:1-8). These are the clear reasons why there will be no marriage (=sex and procreation) in heaven — it violates fundamental principles of Scriptural holiness taught in Leviticus. The Essenes may have gone too far with the idea, but they were on the same wavelength as the Mosaic Law when they legislated that members of their community could not have sexual relations while in the Holy City Jerusalem.[4] Until further evidence is presented, it is exceedingly difficult to find any statements in the text of 1 Corinthians which point to a group of believers who would have the Jewish concerns necessary to worry about either Mosaic purity laws or Sadducean debates over the relationship between the Old Testament Levirite marriage law and marriage in heaven.

3. The "eschatological woman" hypothesis fails to reckon seriously with the similarities between the issues Paul treats in 1 Cor 7:1-7 and current practices of sacred celibacy in Greco-Roman pagan piety.[5] Specifically, certain pagan cults, both at Corinth and other locations, emphasized the need for its members to abstain from all sexual relations for periods of time, even within marriage. The Latin satirist Juvenal, for example, pictures a scene in which wives had to receive forgiveness of sins from their goddess Isis because they had had sexual intercourse with their husbands during a period of time supposedly devoted to sacral celibacy.[6] It seems to me that the most natural place to look for the antecedents to this issue among believers in the church of God is within their pre-Christian marriage and sexual practices. When that is done, it is clear that the cult of Isis, as well as other religions, sheds important light upon this problem of celibacy within marriage that Paul is handling in 1 Cor 7:1-7.

---

[4]The Damascus Rule 12.1 states, "No man shall lie with a woman in the city of the Sanctuary, to defile the city of the Sanctuary with their uncleanness." *The Dead Sea Scrolls in English*, trans. by G. Vermes (Baltimore: Penguin Books, 1968), p. 113. Helpful insights can also be gained by following this discussion in E. P. Sanders, *Judaism. Practice and Belief 63 BCE-66 Œ* (Philadelphia: Trinity Press International, 1992), pp. 219-220; 353.

[5]Oster, "Use, Misuse and Neglect of Archaeological Evidence," pp. 58-64.

[6]Juvenal, *Satires* 6.535-537.

A. GODLY USE OF SEXUALITY (7:1-7)

[1]Now for the matters you wrote about: It is good for a man not to marry.[a] [2]But since there is so much immorality, each man should have his own wife, and each woman her own husband. [3]The husband should fulfill his marital duty to his wife, and likewise the wife to her husband. [4]The wife's body does not belong to her alone but also to her husband. In the same way, the husband's body does not belong to him alone but also to his wife. [5]Do not deprive each other except by mutual consent and for a time, so that you may devote yourselves to prayer. Then come together again so that Satan will not tempt you because of your lack of self-control. [6]I say this as a concession, not as a command. [7]I wish that all men were as I am. But each man has his own gift from God; one has this gift, another has that.

[a] *1 Or "It is good for a man not to have sexual relations with a woman."*

7:1 Now for the matters you wrote about: It is good for a man not to marry.

Scholars continue to debate whether the pro-celibacy statement of 7:1 comes from the Corinthian document Paul is responding to or whether it is Paul's own affirmation. It should be noted that there is nothing unpauline about either the wording or the theology of 7:1. His pro-celibacy views are introduced with the same phrase, "it is good for a person" in 7:26. While the instructions of ch. 7 obviously flow from Paul's own theology of marriage, morality, and ministry, we do Paul's response to the Corinthians' statement an injustice if we fail to see the prominent (though not exclusive) role given to the libido and sex in this chapter.

One indication of the difference in the starting point that most North American Christians have with sex is that for us sex, lewdness, and pornography are far more culturally, and at times legally, controlled and repressed than in a city like Roman Corinth or classical Athens. One authority on ancient sexuality and eroticism noted,

That most pagans were in many ways less inhibited than most Christians is undeniable. Not only had they a goddess specifically concerned with sexual pleasure; their other deities were portrayed in legend as enjoying fornication, adultery and sodomy. A pillar surmounted by the head of Hermes and adorned with an erect penis stood at every Athenian front-door; great models of the erect penis were borne in procession at festivals of Dionysus. [7]

It is inappropriate, then, to see this as only a generalized chapter on pastoral advice about whether to marry. Moreover, if one is uncomfortable with the close correlation in this chapter between marriage and the satisfaction of sexual urges, one might do better to complain against the Corinthians who formulated the issue rather than Paul.

7:2 But since there is so much immorality, each man should have his own wife, and each woman her own husband.

Paul's advice here, as in other places, is not unconditional. While celibacy is desirable, an absence of fornication is more desirable. A life of fornication, whether with prostitutes, slaves, concubines, etc., is unacceptable to Paul. Accordingly, Paul strongly encourages those susceptible to the lures of fornication to do the very thing he discouraged in 7:1. In 7:2 Paul encourages those Corinthians to have their own husbands and wives. There is diversity of opinion about the precise nuance of the word "have" in 7:2. In light of the meaning of the same terms "have a wife" and "have a husband" in 1 Cor 7:12, it seems that Paul is referring to the state of marriage and not "having sex" in marriage, the latter idea being discussed in 7:3-5. To put it in plain terms, 7:2 affirms marriage as an acceptable relationship in which to disregard the pro-celibacy instructions of 7:1.

---

[7]K.J. Dover, "Classical Greek Attitudes to Sexual Behaviour," in *Women in the Ancient World*, 144.

7:3 The husband should fulfill his marital duty to his wife, and likewise the wife to her husband.

This brief verse reveals several aspects about Paul's views of sexual intimacy in marriage. First, it is obvious that Paul's views are not male-centered. That is, Paul is even-handed in the parallel structure evident in his instructions. Eva Cantarella's point on this verse is worth noting. She judged that early Christian teaching like that expressed in this verse "disturbed the Romans" since it taught that "men and women had equal dignity in marriage."[8]

Second, by his use of the term duty (ὀφειλή, *opheilē*), Paul highlights the importance attributed to sexual intimacy within Biblical Theology. Lamentably, Christians have often failed, or simply refused, to respond to the sexual implications of the creation account of Genesis or the Song of Solomon.

7:4 The wife's body does not belong to her alone but also to her husband. In the same way, the husband's body does not belong to him alone but also to his wife.

In this verse Paul broadens the framework for understanding both the idea of duty as well as the even-handedness of his teaching with regard to both genders. In matters of conjugal rights, each spouse has an authority over the body of the other. Paul is clearly teaching in this context of sexual intimacy that there is no place for either spouse to claim prerogatives of personal preferences or rights. Martin Luther saw the crucial importance of sexual intimacy within marriage when he commented on a spouse's continual refusal to give conjugal rights. Whether one agrees with Luther's views on remarriage in this section, it seems that he has surely caught Paul's seriousness about this topic and Paul's assessment of the gravity of this type of situation when he wrote,

> One spouse may rob and withdraw himself or herself from the other and refuse to grant the conjugal due or to associate with the other. One may find a woman so stubborn and

---

[8]Eva Cantarella, *Pandora's Daughters. The Role and Status of Women in Greek and Roman Antiquity*, trans. M.B. Fant; Foreword by M.R. Lefkowitz (Baltimore: Johns Hopkins University Press, 1987), p. 157.

thickheaded that it means nothing to her though her husband fall into unchasteness ten times. Then it is time for the man to say: If you are not willing, another woman is; if the wife is not willing, bring on the maid. But this only after the husband has told his wife once or twice, warned her, and let it be known to other people that her stubborn refusal may be publicly known and rebuked before the congregation. If she still does not want to comply, then dismiss her; let an Esther be given you and allow Vashti to go, as did King Ahasuerus (Esther 2:17). [9]

7:5 Do not deprive each other except by mutual consent and for a time, so that you may devote yourselves to prayer. Then come together again so that Satan will not tempt you because of your lack of self-control.

In this verse Paul employs the second person plural and commands those at Corinth not to refuse to fulfill this marital duty. Since Paul uses the reciprocal pronoun "each other" (ἀλλήλους *allēlous*) it seems clear that both spouses are included in the imperative "Do not deprive."

Having given an imperative, Paul then proceeds to state the exceptions to his own imperative. This self-imposed celibacy can only receive Paul's consent, he tells the Corinthians, if it is based upon mutual agreement, if it is short lived, if it is a celibacy undertaken in conjunction with periods of intense prayerfulness, and if the husband and wife resume sexual relationships again.

Paul concludes this sentence with a purpose clause. The reason they are commanded not to deprive each other of sexual satisfaction is in order that Satan not tempt them. The phrase "because of your lack of self-control" is parallel to the earlier phrase "because of fornications" (7.2).

7:6 I say this as a concession, not as a command.

This verse has two trouble spots in it. The first regards the demonstrative pronoun "this" (τοῦτο, *touto*). Is Paul referring to

---

[9] Ewald M. Plass, ed., *What Luther Says: A Practical In-Home Anthology for the Active Christian*, (St. Louis: Concordia, 1991), paragraph 2811.

preceding or following material? Either is grammatically possible. I interpret 1 Corinthians 7:6 as referring to 7:7. Thus, the antithesis between Paul's concession and God's command in 7:6 is reflected respectively by the antithesis in 7:7 of "I wish" and "but each has his own gift from God."

The issue of Paul's judgment as distinct from God's command has raised various issues for later Christians. It seems clear that Paul's self-understanding, set forth succinctly in 1 Cor 1:1, is that he was a divinely chosen apostle. Paul was called by God to plant and nurture churches among the Gentiles. In regard to the Corinthians, he had unparalleled authority over them (1 Cor 4:14-21) and claims that his instructions to the Corinthians are from the Lord (14:37). It seems that the same perspective that believes Paul when he writes that "what I am writing to you is the Lord's command" would believe Paul when he writes "I say this ...   not according to a command" (7:6) or "I have no command from the Lord, but I give a judgment" (7.25).

7:7 I wish that all men were as I am. But each man has his own gift from God; one has this gift, another has that.

Paul's pro-celibacy theology is as clarion in 7:1a as anywhere. The word for "men" (ἄνθρωπος *anthrōpos*) in 7:1 is generic in this instance and would include both men and women. Since Paul understands that his own spiritual authority and wisdom is not equal to God's, he can contrast (but, ἀλλά, *alla*) his wishes with God's sovereign gift to individuals. Paul uses the term "gift" (χάρισμα, *charisma*) here, and demonstrates thereby that he does not limit God's gifts to liturgical expressions and charismatic spiritual experiences. In this setting in chapter 7, *charisma* must refer to one's calling from God to either marriage or to a life of celibacy. As we learn later in this very letter, Paul acknowledges that members of the Twelve, Jesus' own family and many other apostles were, in fact, married (1 Cor 9:5).

B. CELIBACY VS. MARRIAGE (7:8-11)

[8]Now to the unmarried and the widows I say: It is good for them to stay unmarried, as I am. [9]But if they cannot control themselves, they should marry, for it is better to marry than to burn with passion.

[10]To the married I give this command (not I, but the Lord): A wife must not separate from her husband. [11]But if she does, she must remain unmarried or else be reconciled to her husband. And a husband must not divorce his wife.

7:8 Now to the unmarried and the widows I say: It is good for them to stay unmarried, as I am.

There is some difficulty in this particular rhetorical context in knowing whether Paul's statements here reflect his judgment or the Lord's instruction. The following chart makes clear why scholars cannnot agree on this matter. Paul shifts more than once in this chapter between giving his advice and giving the Lord's teaching, but he unfortunately does not always signal the shift.

Given the fact that he addresses the married in 7:10 and the never married in 7:25, the material in 7:8-9 would most naturally be understood as instructions for the "single again." Paul uses his phrase "it is good" to advocate his pro-celibacy position as in 7:1 and likewise presents himself as a paradigm for this calling in life (cf. 7:6).

7:9 But if they cannot control themselves, they should marry, for it is better to marry than to burn with passion.

This is Paul's third reference (cf. 7:1, 5) to the problems for a believer who has an uncontrollable libido. In this reference he invokes the imagery of burning sexual passion and argues that marriage is far better than a life of celibacy or attempted celibacy compromised by a lack of sexual self-control. The phrase "to burn" (πυροῦσθαι, *pyrousthai*) most naturally fits the contextual imagery of sexual passions aflame; moreover, Paul, unlike Jesus, is not known for referring to the flames of hell. As seen already in this chapter (7:1-7; cf. 7:11, 14-15) Paul gives advice only to qualify it or allow exceptions. He does the same here with the phrase introduced by the words "it is better" (κρεῖττόν ἐστιν, *kreitton estin*).

7:10 To the married I give this command (not I, but the Lord): A wife must not separate from her husband.

In this section Paul addresses those who are married and instructs them that the Lord forbids them to divorce. Since the case of a Christian married to a non-Christian is brought up specifically in 1 Cor 7:12f, 7:10 probably refers to a marriage where both parties are believers. Verse 10 should dispell older and unfounded ideas that only men could initiate divorce in Greco-Roman society. There are an adequate number of examples from ancient Mediterranean societies to demonstrate that women could terminate marriages to their husbands.[10] The Roman satirist Juvenal was lamenting the conditions of the Roman capital rather than a Roman colony, but he complained about the proclivity of Roman women to ruin their marriages and seek divorces from their husbands.[11] Clearly the upshot of Paul's concern in 7:10-11 is with Christian women who might initiate a divorce from a Christian husband.

Even though translations often render the Greek word χωρίζομαι (*chōrizomai*) as "separate" (which it clearly can mean), in Greek literature and legal documents it also existed as a technical term for divorce. One must be careful not to impose a modern legal understanding of marriage and separation onto Greco-Roman jurisprudence. This Greek word *chōrizomai* is also used of the dissolution of the marriage between a believer and non-believer when the non-believer wants to end the marriage (7:15).

---

[10]Testimony for this within a Jewish setting is found in Mark 10:12 and within Jewish papyri discovered in Egypt dating from the late first century B.C. For the Egyptian situation and evidence one can consult Ross S. Kraemer, "Non-literary Evidence for Jewish Women in Rome and Egypt." In *Rescuing Creusa: New Methodological Approaches to Women in Antiquity*, ed. M. Skinner, Special Issue of *Helios* n.s. 13(2) 1987, 95 who cites the *Corpus Papyrorum Judaicarum* no. 144. The broader context is set by S.B. Pomeroy, *Women in Hellenistic Egypt from Alexander to Cleopatra* (Detroit: Wayne State University Press, 1990), 83-124.

[11]Juvenal, *Satires* 6.229-391.

Moreover, Paul refers to the marital status of the women who initiated the action of *chōrizomai* in 7:10 as "unmarried" (ἄγαμος, *agamos*).

7:11 But if she does, she must remain unmarried or else be reconciled to her husband. And a husband must not divorce his wife.

Long before Jesus' acknowledgment in Matthew 19:8 that God allowed exceptions because of mankind's rebellious nature, the student of the Old Testament marriage laws knew that God did not always coerce obedience to his rules of marriage. The Israelite law of Levirite marriage (Deut 25:5-10; cf. Matt 22:23-24) clearly stated God's will (a widow must marry the brother of her former husband and bear a child by him) and then included how to handle exceptions and disobedience to God's will in this matter ("However, if a man does not want to marry his brother's wife . . . .")

For the Christian woman who disobeys the instruction of 7:10 (don't divorce your Christian husband) Paul allows only two alternatives. This Christian woman can either remain unmarried or she can return to her Christian husband and be reconciled to him.

Paul ends 7:11 with a commandment for Christian men likewise not to divorce their Christian wives. For Paul, God's plan called for monogamy (1 Cor 7:2) and permanence in marriage (Rom 7:2-3). And God's plan was the obligation of both the husband and the wife.

C. DIVORCE AND SEPARATION (7:12-16)

[12]**To the rest I say this (I, not the Lord): If any brother has a wife who is not a believer and she is willing to live with him, he must not divorce her. [13]And if a woman has a husband who is not a believer and he is willing to live with her, she must not divorce him. [14]For the unbelieving husband has been sanctified through his wife, and the unbelieving wife has been sanctified through her**

believing husband. Otherwise your children would be unclean, but as it is, they are holy.

¹⁵But if the unbeliever leaves, let him do so. A believing man or woman is not bound in such circumstances; God has called us to live in peace. ¹⁶How do you know, wife, whether you will save your husband? Or, how do you know, husband, whether you will save your wife?

7:12 To the rest I say this (I, not the Lord): If any brother has a wife who is not a believer and she is willing to live with him, he must not divorce her.

Paul disclaims any personal revelation from the Lord on the topic under consideration in 7:12ff. The interpreter must not forget that many of those early believers who received 1 Corinthians had been believers less than 48 months when Paul writes this letter. Many of the Christian recipients of this first generation church would have entered marriage as pagans only to find themselves now believers who had non-believing, probably pagan, spouses. We can only conjecture what was leading some of these believers to seek a divorce from unbelieving mates. At least three different views should be mentioned:

1. Some interpreters look to the situation depicted in the writings of later Christian Apologists (e.g., Justin Martyr) who knew of the personal trials and tribulations believers faced from their unbelieving and hostile spouses. It may be anachronistic, however, to impose the situation of 50-100 years later upon this early situation in light of the significant changes that evolved in the period between the Corinthian letters and the later Apologists. In this period there were many significant changes in matter of church and state, the church and the Jewish community, and the hostility between believers and their Greco-Roman environment.

2. Another possible source of the desire to abandon marriages to pagans was the partial misreading of Paul's first letter to the Corinthians. 1 Cor 5:9ff makes it clear that some of the believers at Corinth incorrectly thought that Paul had advocated a total separation of believers from pagans. Accordingly, they were seeking further clarification from Paul regarding how this instruction

should impact their marriages to the immoral idolaters to whom they were married.

3. Another possible scenario is that some of the believers were confused by the implications of Paul's teaching about the "union" that occurs during sexual intimacy. It is easy to see how a believer, especially a relatively new convert from paganism, could be perplexed or misguided by a certain interpretation of 1 Cor 6:15-20. If our bodies are members of Christ and if we join Christ to whomever we have sex with, as Paul reasons, would it not be inappropriate — to say the least — to join Christ to an idolater? If a Corinthian believer is joined to and becomes one body with an idolatrous spouse (cf. 1 Cor 6:16), then should not the believer flee such a situation which offers nothing more than a series of sexual encounters which continually defile the temple of God, which is the Christian's body?

Even though we might sympathize with the plight, whatever it was, of the believer married to the unbeliever, Paul forbids a believer to divorce an unbeliever, if the latter wishes to remain in the marriage.

7:13 And if a woman has a husband who is not a believer and he is willing to live with her, she must not divorce him.

This verse complements 7:12 in acknowledging that this scenario can arise regardless of whether the believer is a man or a woman. And Paul surely does not have a double standard based upon gender in his instructions on this topic.

7:14 For the unbelieving husband has been sanctified through his wife, and the unbelieving wife has been sanctified through her believing husband. Otherwise your children would be unclean, but as it is, they are holy.

Many different solutions have been given to interpret this somewhat enigmatic teaching. The occurrence of the word "for" (γάρ, gar) makes it clear that this is Paul's rationale for why the believer should not divorce his happily married pagan spouse. Irrespective of how one understands the details of 7:14, it is clear that Paul counsels the permanence of the marriage with a cooperative pagan because of the benefits it will bring in the life of the pagan spouse and the offspring of that marriage. Most interpreters regard the benefits received by the unbelieving spouse and children to be the sanctifying influence of the godly spouse, leading ultimately to their future salvation. This interpretation is strengthed by the fact of Paul's later use of the idea of salvation in this regard (7:16; cf. 1 Pet 3:1-6).

7:15 But if the unbeliever leaves, let him do so. A believing man or woman is not bound in such circumstances; God has called us to live in peace.

Having established a case in 7:14 for remaining married to an unbeliever, Paul now acknowledges the exceptions. Beginning in this verse, Paul teaches that his instructions are completely different if the unbelieving spouse is not happily married. That is, if the pagan mate wants to stay married to a Christian, the Christian cannot divorce him or her, but if the pagan mate wants out of the marriage, so be it!

The very perspectives and divine rules which would keep a Christian married to another Christian (7:10-11) or a Christian married to a happily married pagan (7:12-14) are revoked in the case of a believer married to an unhappily married pagan. Let them have their divorce, Paul writes. In such circumstances the Christian brother or sister need not operate under the same constraints as given in earlier situations. The reason that the Christian is not bound in these situations of inevitable divorce from an uncooperative pagan is that the foundation and principles of a godly marriage are not present. Marriages can be held together by loyalty to God or they can be held together by self-interest, but nothing godly is accomplished by trying to keep a non-believer in a marriage where there is no peace. Peaceful relationships are a two-way matter (cf. Rom 12:18), and Paul excused the Corinthian believers from any need to coerce non-believing mates into staying in the marriage.

7:16 How do you know, wife, whether you will save your husband? Or, how do you know, husband, whether you will save your wife?

Paul uses 7:16 to give his practical rationale ("for," *gar*, is omitted in the NIV) for letting the pagan spouse depart. Paul turns his previous counsel, in the different context of 7:14, on its head. When the unbeliever was cooperative Paul argued on the basis of the sanctification of the unbeliever. When the unbeliever is recalcitrant Paul expresses grave doubt about the possibility of the future sanctification of the unbeliever. This very realistic advice is designed to motivate the Christian to cooperate in the departure of the unbelieving spouse and to overcome a misuse of Paul's own advice given only a few verses earlier.

D. REMAINING AS YOU WERE CALLED (7:17-28)

[17]Nevertheless, each one should retain the place in life that the Lord assigned to him and to which God has called him. This is the rule I lay down in all the churches. [18]Was a man already circumcised when he was called? He should not become uncircumcised. Was a man uncircumcised when he was called? He should not be circumcised. [19]Circumcision is nothing and uncircumcision is nothing. Keeping God's commands is what counts. [20]Each one should remain in the situation which he was in when God called him. [21]Were you a slave when you were called? Don't let it trouble you — although if you can gain your freedom, do so. [22]For he who was a slave when he was called by the Lord is the Lord's freedman; similarly, he who was a free man when he was called is Christ's slave. [23]You were bought at a price; do not become slaves of men. [24]Brothers, each man, as responsible to God, should remain in the situation God called him to.

[25]Now about virgins: I have no command from the Lord, but I give a judgment as one who by the Lord's mercy is trustworthy. [26]Because of the present crisis, I think that it is good for you to remain as you are. [27]Are you married? Do not seek a divorce. Are you unmarried? Do not look for a wife. [28]But if you do marry,

you have not sinned; and if a virgin marries, she has not sinned. But those who marry will face many troubles in this life, and I want to spare you this.

7:17 Nevertheless, each one should retain the place in life that the Lord assigned to him and to which God has called him. This is the rule I lay down in all the churches.

Most interpreters have rightly observed that the content of 1 Cor 7:17-24 is initially surprising, but that Paul's intent in these verses fits well into the overall purposes of ch. 7. The initial surprise arises because Paul temporarily shifts to a discussion of circumcision and slavery. The contextual coherence of this section is evident in the apostle's use of the linking term "called." In no other place in Paul's letters does one encounter such a frequency of the term "called" (ἐκαλήθη, *ekalēthē*), occurring as it does seven times in 7:17-24 in the verb form (usually the aorist passive of κα-λέω, *kaleō*). That Paul intends the principles from this section 7:17-24 to be applied to marriage is clear from the introduction of this term at 7:15.

As Calvin correctly observed at this juncture, "Paul takes the opportunity, as he often does, to make a short digression from a particular aspect, to a general exhortation about 'calling.' At the same time he confirms, with different examples, what he had said about marriage."[12]

The place in life to which Paul refers is primarily one's marital status. Since the two issues broached in 7:17-24, i.e., circumcision and slavery, have only little significance in other parts of 1 Corinthians (compared to other Pauline letters,) it is unlikely that these two issues are as problematic or controversial at Corinth as other topics addressed more directly by Paul. Irrespective of one's thought about the significance of "circumcision" and "slavery" issues in the Corinthian congregations, the rhetorical function of these topics in 1 Cor 7 is anchored to the admonition expressed in the terms "remain" and "called."

What the apostle has in mind by the term "called" seems to be one's situation at the point of one's conversion to the gospel, a

---

[12]Calvin, *First Epistle*, p. 152.

perspective supported by the use of "called" for the Corinthian believers at 1:2, 9, 24. The sharpness of Paul's conflict with some of the Corinthian saints over the issue of hopping out of marriages is made evident by his appeal to the universality of his judgment in all the churches. In light of the adversarial relationship between Paul and some of his Corinthian children (cf. 4:14-17), he informs them on this issue "that theirs is the theology that is off track, not his."[13]

7:18 Was a man already circumcised when he was called? He should not become uncircumcised. Was a man uncircumcised when he was called? He should not be circumcised.

Although there is no strong evidence that a Jew-Gentile struggle was occurring at Corinth, Paul, perhaps for this very reason, refers to a man already circumcised. The picture of a man attempting to eradicate the indications of circumcision most probably points to a Jewish individual rather than a Gentile proselyte. There is a well known passage in 1 Maccabees which recounts an episode where Jews who were assimilated to Hellenism "removed the marks of circumcision" (1 Macc 1:14-15), thereby jettisoning their inheritance in God's covenant.[14]

What was true for the Jewish believer is also true for the Gentile. An uncircumcised (Gentile) believer should not seek to become circumcised now that he is a believer.

7:19 Circumcision is nothing and uncircumcision is nothing. Keeping God's commands is what counts.

Paul here presents the theological rationale behind the imperatives of the preceding verse. Both circumcision and uncircumcision are (in this particular setting at Corinth) matters of indifference (cf. the language of Gal 5:6; 6:15). It is not that Paul believes every issue is one of indifference. On the contrary, God's commandments are of fundamental significance, but God has no word on the necessity of either condition. When and where God's commands exist, the keeping of them is of profound importance (cf. Rom 2:27; 1 Tim 6:14).

---

[13]Fee, *First Epistle*, p. 311.
[14]Cf. Josephus *Antiq*. 12.241 and Assumption of Moses 8:3.

7:20 Each one should remain in the situation which he was in when God called him.

See notes on 7:17.

7:21 Were you a slave when you were called? Don't let it trouble you — although if you can gain your freedom, do so.

The apostle now switches from the topic of circumcision to that of slavery. Given the large number of slaves in the Roman world one can only assume that a high percentage of those early believers would be or would have been slaves at some point in time. It is regrettable that many North American interpreters of Paul and Pauline ethics have assumed that Paul's attitudes toward ancient slavery could be smoothly transposed into the American practice of slavery in previous centuries.[15] We certainly cannot anticipate what a person such as Paul would have thought about this issue of American slavery since he himself was a Roman citizen and lived in a period of time when no one imagined democracy in the sense that it is understood in this century in America. Since ancient slave systems, both in Hebrew Scripture and Graeco-Roman society, were not identical in important ways to the American system, one ought to look suspiciously upon a naive hermeneutical logic which reasons:

(1) Paul condoned slavery in his social ethics

(2) American Christians rightfully disown America's slavery and racism therefore

(3) We can disown Paul's social ethics since they do not conform to the most recently affirmed implications of the American Constitution.

Scholarship has not been able to reach a consensus about the intent of Paul's thought in 7:21b. In addition to the ambiguities in the meaning of the Greek words themselves, the contextual rhetorical arguments of 7:17-24 have led different interpreters to different conclusions. One scholar noted concerning these difficulties, the history of the interpretation of this verse for almost 2,000 years, and the conclusions of the modern exegete that,

---

[15]Some general remarks about these differences can be found in Witherington, *Conflict and Community in Corinth*, pp. 181-185.

. . . as he mulls over these problems, his understanding of Paul's theology, of the theology of the Corinthians and of the social and legal circumstances of the first century A.D. will play significant roles in his thinking.[16]

If one goes with the translation choice of the NIV then Paul is saying that one should not be troubled by being a slave. The apostle goes on to qualify his remarks, as he has done on more than one occasion in this chapter, by encouraging believers to welcome manumission when granted to them. There were recognized legal means (there were few slave revolts in Paul's Roman world) by which a slave could be freed from the legal status of slavery in the Roman setting. It is in light of these legal options well known to Paul and his readership, that Paul acknowledges the preference to manumission.

7:22 For he who was a slave when he was called by the Lord is the Lord's freedman; similarly, he who was a free man when he was called is Christ's slave.

At this point Paul gives his reasons ("for," γάρ, *gar*) and perspectives which underlie 7:21a. C.K. Barrett rightly observes that "Particularly important is the *for* (γάρ),"[17] since it highlights the shared nomenclature among all believers. A saint who is a slave within the Roman system is, nevertheless, a freedman of the Lord's. Conversely, the individual who was not a slave at the time of his conversion became one in Christ. To his readers whose social/legal standing included slavery he writes,

Since the liberty of the spirit is far preferable to the liberty of the body, he suggests that slaves ought to be able to put up with the bitterness of their situation if only they would reflect upon that inestimable gift which had been bestowed upon them.[18]

---

[16]S.S. Bartchy, *First-Century Slavery and 1 Corinthians 7:21*. SBL Dissertation Series II, p. 10.
[17]Barrett, *First Epistle*, p. 171.
[18]Calvin, *First Epistle*, p. 154.

7:23 You were bought at a price; do not become slaves of men.

Writing at this point within the metaphorical world of slavery/ freedman imagery, Paul now utilizes the concept of the manumission price. This wording closely resembles that of 6:20 (see notes there). While divine ownership is assumed here (cf. 7:22), the exact meaning of 7:23b is contested. Some interpreters view it as Paul's continuing admonition about not altering one's social/ interpersonal status. Accordingly, he would be prohibiting one's sale of oneself into legal slavery, for whatever reason. A second interpretive approach regards "slaves of men" as a spiritual concept. From this point of view, Paul's statement means don't be enslaved by the values, mores, and spiritual perspectives of other humans.

7:24 Brothers, each man, as responsible to God, should remain in the situation God called him to.

With these thoughts he brings to an end his repeated affirmations about remaining in the circumstance one was in when called by God, all of which function to encourage believers in remaining in their respective marital situations.

7:25 Now about virgins: I have no command from the Lord, but I give a judgment as one who by the Lord's mercy is trustworthy.

Paul here resumes his previous line of thought by directing his attention to those who have never been married (περὶ δὲ τῶν παρ- θένων, *peri de tōn parthenōn*). The apostle's focus on this particular issue is evident in the section 7:25-38 by his repeated use of the term "virgin" (7:25, 28, 34, 36, 37, 38), a frequency found no where else in the New Testament. The apostle acknowledges that this instruction is not based upon revelation from the Lord. Rather, Paul confesses that this counsel stems from his own personal judgment, but a judgment that is better informed than most. Since Paul cannot argue this point on the basis of divine revelation, he attempts to persuade the Corinthians on the basis of the force and character of his own spiritual trustworthiness which comes from God. The personal origin of Paul's advice is evident in this section by his use of the cluster of terms "I think" (7:26); "I mean"

(7:29); "I would like" (7:32); "I am saying" (7:35); and "I think" (7:40).

7:26 Because of the present crisis, I think that it is good for you to remain as you are.

Paul's advocacy for celibacy is consistent with what one finds earlier in this chapter. The reader finds again Paul's phrase "it is good" used to introduce his pro-celibacy position. What is new here, however, is the fact that Paul gives a reason ("because," διά, *dia* + accusative) for his pro-celibacy instruction. Paul states that the advisability of his teaching is based upon the existence of a imminent crisis. Since Paul does not, at least in this verse, interpret or explain what the present crisis is, interpreters have never been inhibited in putting forward numerous suggestions and explanations of this phrase, some obviously more plausable than others. Any hope of discovering Paul's original meaning here must take into account what he also wrote and meant on this topic in the same context, specifically in 7:29 and 31. Taking into account the tenor of 7:29 (the time is short) and 31 (this world . . . is passing away) as well as the heightened eschatological spirituality Paul himself conveys at other places in 1 Corinthians (e.g., 1:7-8; 4:5; 16:22), it seems best to understand the words "present crisis" in an eschatological sense.

The concepts associated with Paul's spirituality and theology of the last things are diverse and sophisticated. When stating that Paul held and taught a heightened eschatological spirituality, I do not mean that he necessarily thought the world would end in 48 hours and that believers should abandon society in order to prepare for their departure from the world. Indeed, Paul's eschatology had little in common with classic Christian millennarianism and even less in common with 20th century premillennial dispensationalism. Paul's eschatological piety was in no way in conflict with his ability and concerns to make long-range missionary plans to continue his work in areas such as Italy and Spain (Rom 1:8-13, 15:23-24).

We see, then, that Paul admonishes the readers to retain their virginity and singleness because of an eschatological crisis which is part and parcel of the imminent day of the Lord.

7:27 Are you married? Do not seek a divorce. Are you unmarried? Do not look for a wife.

There is probably no verse in this chapter of 1 Corinthians which has been so clearly misinterpreted because of poor translations as this verse. Even though Paul explicitly states that he is dealing with virgins in 7:25ff, many translations and interpreters have Paul abandon his stated topic and begin to discuss the issue of divorce and remarriage. The two brief questions and answers stated in 7:27 deal with the issues and decisions facing those never before married, not those who are single again (or hoping to be single again).

Paul's first question, in Greek, is "Are you obligated to a woman"? Paul's answer is, "Do not seek [your] freedom." The apostle's second question is "Are you free from a woman?" Paul's answer is, "Do not seek a wife." Paul is writing to those who are obligated by engagement to a woman. He is not requiring that they terminate this relationship. "Are you free from a woman" refers to being free from a relationship of engagement. To those at present unengaged, Paul counsels them not to enter such a relationship with a woman.

By means of these brief questions and answers, Paul sets forth his trustworthy judgment regarding the proper decisions virgin men should make.

7:28 But if you do marry, you have not sinned; and if a virgin marries, she has not sinned. But those who marry will face many troubles in this life, and I want to spare you this.

Based upon Paul's style earlier in this chapter, the reader is not surprised that the apostle immediately grants exceptions to his own imperatives in this matter. That is, if the readers ignore the imperatives of 7:28, Paul states that they have not, thereby, committed sin against the law of God. Thus, if a virgin (man) marries, he has not sinned, according to Paul. In addition, Paul states, if a virgin (woman) marries, she likewise has not sinned.

While Paul makes it clear that it is not a sin to ignore or to disobey his own judgments, he is very concerned about the troubles that the married will face. This verse makes is abundantly clear that Paul's pro-celibacy views, unlike the views of a true ascetic, arise from concerns about troubles which attend the married life and not from a dualistic and negative attitude toward the body and human sexuality.

E. FREEDOM FROM CONCERN (7:29-40)

[29]What I mean, brothers, is that the time is short. From now on those who have wives should live as if they had none; [30]those who mourn, as if they did not; those who are happy, as if they were not; those who buy something, as if it were not theirs to keep; [31]those who use the things of the world, as if not engrossed in them. For this world in its present form is passing away.

[32]I would like you to be free from concern. An unmarried man is concerned about the Lord's affairs — how he can please the Lord. [33]But a married man is concerned about the affairs of this world — how he can please his wife — [34]and his interests are divided. An unmarried woman or virgin is concerned about the Lord's affairs: Her aim is to be devoted to the Lord in both body and spirit. But a married woman is concerned about the affairs of this world — how she can please her husband. [35]I am saying this for your own good, not to restrict you, but that you may live in a right way in undivided devotion to the Lord.

[36]If anyone thinks he is acting improperly toward the virgin he is engaged to, and if she is getting along in years and he feels he ought to marry, he should do as he wants. He is not sinning. They should get married. [37]But the man who has settled the matter in his own mind, who is under no compulsion but has control over his own will, and who has made up his mind not to marry the virgin — this man also does the right thing. [38]So then, he who marries the virgin does right, but he who does not marry her does even better.[a]

³⁹A woman is bound to her husband as long as he lives. But if her husband dies, she is free to marry anyone she wishes, but he must belong to the Lord. ⁴⁰In my judgment, she is happier if she stays as she is — and I think that I too have the Spirit of God.

ᵃ *36-38* Or ³⁶*If anyone thinks he is not treating his daughter properly, and if she is getting along in years, and he feels she ought to marry, he should do as he wants. He is not sinning. He should let her get married.* ³⁷*But the man who has settled the matter in his own mind, who is under no compulsion but has control over his own will, and who has made up his mind to keep the virgin unmarried – this man also does the right thing.* ³⁸*So then, he who gives his virgin in marriage does right, but he who does not give her in marriage does even better.*

7:29 What I mean, brothers, is that the time is short. From now on those who have wives should live as if they had none;

The reference to the shortness of time fits best within an eschatological framework (cf. 1 John 2:18; James 5:7; 1 Peter 4:7; Rev 1:3). Unlike some leaders in ancient as well as modern apocalyptic cults, Paul's view here is not an alarmist view about the approaching Armageddon. Even though the time was short, Paul continued to talk to the Corinthians about his own future plans to visit them (4:19; 11:34; 16:5-8) and the need for them to make and execute plans for a donation to aid in relief work among churches in Judea (1 Cor 16:1-4; cf. 2 Cor 8-9), plans whose consummation was two or three years in the future.

Once we realize that Paul's eschatology is not the same as an apocalypticist's, then we can better appreciate the way Paul's eschatological piety shapes his pro-celibacy judgment. Paul's recurring phrase in 7:29-31 is "as if," and he means by this phrase that in light of the realities of God's kingdom and the ever present nearness of history's consummation, the believer should never plant his roots firmly in the soil of this passing world and its relationships. Without even leaving 1 Corinthians and going to other Pauline letters, it should be obvious that Paul's "as if" perspective does not vitiate prime directives about the believer's loyalty to love (1 Cor 13) or the married believer's obligation to conjugal rights (1 Cor 7:1-5).

Even though the rhetorical setting has shifted when Paul writes 2 Corinthians, this eschatological piety of 1 Cor 7 is clearly seen in more detail in 2 Cor 4:16-5:10. The believer's truest self is in-

vested in the realities and values of an unseen world, since that
world is the only one which is eternal and in which what is mortal
will be swallowed up by life (2 Cor 5:4).

In making a pejorative statement about the ultimate shortcomings of marriage, Paul is aligning himself with Jesus' own devalua-
tion of marital and familial loyalties in comparison with the
higher calling of God's Kingdom. In addition, the reader should
observe that Paul does not have a double standard on this issue of
the ephemeral nature of marital relationships. He does not dis-
courage marriage for the virgins on the basis of a theology which
can be jettisoned after entering into marriage. Those who are already married stand under the same eschatological dictum as
those who are still virgins and merely considering marriage.

**7:30 those who mourn, as if they did not; those who are happy, as
if they were not; those who buy something, as if it were not theirs
to keep;**

In this verse Paul makes reference to activities which are part
of the everyday world of humans. The mention of mourning and
being happy refer to those experiences of this world which are
engendered by contact with transitory events and relationships.
In light of the numerous positive depictions of mourning and re-
joicing found in the New Testament, one should not miss the rhetorical hyperbole of this Pauline counsel.

Since Paul himself was an artisan, a merchant, and a consumer, he can hardly be advocating the lifestyle of the mendicant
sage who owns no possessions. Even though Calvin missed the
eschatological underpinnings of Paul's idea here, he was correct
about the apostle's views on consumer purchases in his observation that,

> All the things which make for the enriching of this present
> life are sacred gifts of God, but we spoil them by our mis-
> use of them. If we want to know the reason why, it is be-
> cause we are always entertaining the delusion that we will
> go on for ever in this world. The result is that the very

things which ought to be of assistance to us in our pilgrimage through life, become chains which bind us.[19]

7:31 those who use the things of the world, as if not engrossed in them. For this world in its present form is passing away.

The first part of this verse gives the fifth and final item in the list of things conditioned by "as if not." This reference to the things of the world (κόσμον, *kosmon*) is the most comprehensive concept to be found in this list of five experiences. This means that Paul's eschatological perspective is germane not only to every believer at Corinth, but also to every believer in every aspect of life. One cannot exempt his own life from this Pauline counsel just because he does not happen to have a wife or be a consumer. Sampley summarizes Paul's point here by stating that "there are possessions and goods in the world that one can deal with, use, and even enjoy as long as one's involvement with them is an eschatological engagement."[20]

This leads to the final point the apostle states in this verse, namely the eschatological foundation for the preceding ethic. By his use of the term "for" (γάρ, *gar*) Paul is giving the theological grounds for his perspective. This world in its present form has already begun to collapse. The specific meaning of this multifaceted word "world" (κόσμος, *kosmos*) is determined here by its meaning in the first part of this verse and its implications in its remaining uses in 7:33-34. When Paul uses the term *kosmos* in this section he does not mean the mere physical universe or the literal planet upon which the Corinthians lived; neither is he referring to the world in its rebellious and sinful state in the sight of God. Rather, *kosmos* refers to the totality of those experiences which the believer has in typical human existence which are necessary but essentially ephemeral. Paul both anticipates and accepts that all believers will use the things of the world. His admonition to not be engrossed in them is not founded upon the essential evilness of the things of this world, but rather upon their transitory

---

[19]Calvin, *First Epistle*, p. 159.
[20]J. Paul Sampley, *Walking Between the Times: Paul's Moral Reasoning*, p. 29.

(παράγει, *paragei*) character, their Achilles heel in light of the impending and eternal reign of God.

7:32 I would like you to be free from concern. An unmarried man is concerned about the Lord's affairs — how he can please the Lord.

This may well be Paul's expansion on his previous reference in 7:28 to the many troubles in this life that the married will encounter. He wants both the male and female virgins in the congregation(s) to be free from concern (ἀμερίμνους, *amerimnous*). The unmarried (ἄγαμος, *agamos*) believer can be focused in his concern (μεριμνᾳ, *merimna*) with the issues and concerns of the Lord. The only agenda before him will be the Lord's and his only aim will be to please the Lord.

7:33 But a married man is concerned about the affairs of this world — how he can please his wife —

If this unmarried believer decides to marry (γαμήσας, *gamēsas*), then the natural focus of his concerns and his agenda will surely shift to matters and concerns of this world. The principal contextual manifestation of the believer's new concern with human relationships of this world will be his concern to please his wife.

7:34 and his interests are divided. An unmarried woman or virgin is concerned about the Lord's affairs: Her aim is to be devoted to the Lord in both body and spirit. But a married woman is concerned about the affairs of this world — how she can please her husband.

With the advent of the new entangling marital relationship the previously unmarried believer who was undivided in his focus and concerns (7:32) is now married, has an additional focus and concern (7:33), and is thereby characterized by a divided (μεμέρισται, *memeristai*) concern and agenda for his life (7:34).

Paul is not guilty of having a double standard which believes only women are the cause of divided concerns and agendas in the lives of believers. Even though the Greek text at this juncture is exceptionally diverse in its various manuscript readings,[21] it seems that Paul now turns to the example of a female virgin believer (ἡ γυνὴ ἡ ἄγαμος καὶ ἡ παρθένος, *hē gynē hē agamos kai hē parthenos*) who is likewise derailed in her service to the Lord by her participation in a marriage relationship. Since Paul's terminology has shifted from virgin to unmarried following verse 28, he may have felt the need to qualify the phrase "the unmarried woman" by the addition "or virgin" to clarify that he was still dealing particularly with teaching related to virgins (esp. 7:25, "now about virgins").

This celibate woman is characterized by Paul as having a concern about the affairs of the Lord (μεριμνᾷ τὰ τοῦ κυρίου, *merimna ta tou kyriou*).

7:35 I am saying this for your own good, not to restrict you, but that you may live in a right way in undivided devotion to the Lord.

Having concluded his advocacy of female celibacy among believers, Paul affirms that he has argued this for their own good (πρὸς τὸ σύμφορον, *pros to symphoron*). The apostle has no interest in restricting the free choice of these women. Paul's Greek terms for "restrict" (βρόχον ἐπιβάλω, *brochon epibalō*) are quite graphic. The word βρόχος (*brochos*) "is a halter or lasso . . . [and Paul] has no wish to curtail their freedom, as one throws a rope over an animal that is loose, or a person that is to be arrested."[22]

There is not a consensus among interpreters regarding Paul's thought in the last half of 7:35 because of the ambiguities in the Greek text. Fee states that Paul's idea "is less than clear,"[23] and Barrett concludes that "close translation is scarcely possible."[24] Given the immediate context of Paul's argumentation as well as his forceful advocacy for celibacy, Barrett's view, rather than Fee's, is correct when he states that Paul is saying, "if you avoid marriage you avoid encumbrances, and you can devote yourself

[21]See the issues and evidence in Fee, *First Epistle*, pp. 345-346.
[22]Robertson and Plummer, *First Epistle of St. Paul*, p. 158.
[23]Fee, *First Epistle*, p. 347.
[24]Barrett, *First Epistle*, p. 182.

to the Lord's work without incurring problems, difficulties, and anxieties, which married people incur."[25]

7:36 If anyone thinks he is acting improperly toward the virgin he is engaged to, and if she is getting along in years and he feels he ought to marry, he should do as he wants. He is not sinning. They should get married.

Paul now directs his focus to male believers who are single but engaged to a virgin (τὴν παρθένον, *tēn parthenon*, cf. 7:25).[26] In particular Paul is addressing those men who are already engaged and who are acting improperly (ἀσχημονεῖν, *aschēmonein*). While Paul does not specify the exact impropriety he has in mind, the immediate context as well as the opening words of chapter seven point decidedly toward sexual impropriety.

The next clause of 7:36 which contains the NIV translation "she is getting along in years" is subject to much debate. The debate arises from the fact that Paul uses a Greek term here (ὑπέρακμος, *hyperakmos*) that grammatically could describe either the man or his virgin, and which is found nowhere else in the Greek New Testament. If one takes it to modify the virgin, then it connotes the idea that she is almost beyond the typical years for marriage. If it modifies the man, then it means that he has strong sexual passions. C.K. Barrett takes it as referring to the male and translates it as "oversexed."[27]

Contrary to the NIV perspective, it seems to me that Paul is talking about the man's condition. Accordingly, the apostle is saying that if a believing man is acting sexually in an inappropriate way toward his fiancée and it is because of the strength of his sexual passions, then he should do as he wishes and they should marry (γαμείτωσαν, *gameitōsan*). In accordance with his "it is better to marry than to burn (with sexual passion)" outlook already expressed at 7:9, Paul writes that to marry one's fiancée is not a sin

---

[25]Ibid.

[26]One school of thought believes that Paul is addressing fathers about their virgin daughters whom they will give in marriage. The commentaries by Barrett, *First Epistle*, pp. 182-184 and Fee, *First Epistle*, pp. 349-352, rightly prefer the view that it is a man and his fiancée.

[27]Barrett, *First Epistle*, p. 182.

when strong passion (*hyperakmos*) and improper behavior are present.

Unlike some of the pagan philosophers of his day, Paul was not ashamed to acknowledge the role of strong sexual passion in the believer's decision to enter marriage. In contrast to certain philosophers of the Greek and Roman world who could justify sexual pleasure only for the sake of procreation,[28] the apostle Paul does not even mention procreation but rather affirms that sexuality and its sensual manifestations in the state of marriage are in harmony with God's will.

7:37 But the man who has settled the matter in his own mind, who is under no compulsion but has control over his own will, and who has made up his mind not to marry the virgin — this man also does the right thing.

Even though Paul allowed the believing man to abandon his celibacy in 7:36, he now turns to continue his advocacy of the celibate life. For the saint who is resolute about his celibacy, who is not guided by sexual compulsion, and who is able to make a free choice, this man should keep his fiancée as a fiancée.

Many suggestions have been made about Paul's rather long qualifying statement in 7:37. It may reflect the seriousness of the decision to remain engaged with no commitment to marriage, or the fact that not everyone (e.g., slaves) had control over his own will, or that some did not have a true assessment of the force of their own sexual drive, or other numerous social pressures which fostered marriage.

In any case, if a man could evaluate his choice for celibacy in light of the criteria given here by Paul and still prefer celibacy, then Paul congratulates him for a good choice.

7:38 So then, he who marries the virgin does right, but he who does not marry her does even better.

In this verse Paul gives a summary restatement of his preceding counsel. Since marriage is not a sin, the man who marries his

---

[28]See Musonius Rufus Fragment 12 cited in A.J. Malherbe, *Moral Exhortation*, pp. 152-154.

fiancée does well, but the one who decides not to marry her will do even better.

7:39 A woman is bound to her husband as long as he lives. But if her husband dies, she is free to marry anyone she wishes, but he must belong to the Lord.

Gordon Fee is correct in his evaluation of 7:30 that, "This final word to the women comes as something of a surprise."[29] In this concluding two verse section Paul writes specifically about the various situations of believing women who are no longer virgins. Concerning believing women who have husbands, they are to remain married as long as their husbands are alive. The freedom (ἐλευθέρα, *eleuthera*) that the believing widow has to remarry is not unconditional. She is limited in her choices to a man who is "in the Lord" (ἐν κυρίῳ, *en kyriō*), that is, who is a saint.

7:40 In my judgment, she is happier if she stays as she is — and I think that I too have the Spirit of God.

Even though Paul has summarized the nature and issues of remarriage for a widow, he hopes no widow will follow through on them. Paul apparently cannot end this chapter of thought without a final appeal for celibacy. It is Paul's Spirit-guided judgment that any widow would be happier if she would remain celibate following the death of her husband.

---

[29]Fee, *First Epistle*, p. 355.

1 CORINTHIANS 8

V. DEALING WITH IDOLATRY (8:1-11:1)

A. FOOD SACRIFICED TO IDOLS (8:1-13)

1. The General Principle (8:1-3)

¹Now about food sacrificed to idols: We know that we all possess knowledge.ᵃ Knowledge puffs up, but love builds up. ²The man who thinks he knows something does not yet know as he ought to know. ³But the man who loves God is known by God.

ᵃ1 Or "We all possess knowledge," as you say

8:1 Now about food sacrificed to idols: We know that we all possess knowledge. Knowledge puffs up, but love builds up.

As we begin this section of chapter 8, it is important to notice that this is the beginning of a three-chapter section that extends from 8:1-11:1. Because of the occurrence of the phrase "now about" (περὶ δέ, *peri de*) in 8:1, scholars believe that Paul is responding to one of the issues that the Corinthians had asked Paul about (see notes in Introduction). Although there is no consensus regarding the correct understanding of these three chapters and the relationship of the separate units within them, many scholars believe that these chapters address themselves to three separate scenarios related to the consumption of food sacrificed to idols. The details of the first scenario can be reconstructed on the basis of 8:1-13, the second scenario can be constructed on the basis of the verses in 9:24-10:22, and the third scenario can be constructed based on the information in 10:23-11:1. In order to correctly understand Paul's response to the issue of scenario number 1, it is important to make two observations about Paul's use of the word "knowledge" (γνῶσις, gnōsis) in this section. First, just because Paul uses the word knowledge one need not assume that he is alluding to a problem of Gnosticism in the Corinthian church (see notes in Introduction). In fact, the reader will learn in a few verses what the content of this knowledge is, and it becomes readily apparent that it has nothing to do with classical forms and teachings of Gnosticism. The second thing to notice is that Paul uses the term knowledge in a pejorative sense. The rhetoric of 8:1 makes this very clear by Paul's stark contrast between the characteristics of knowledge and those of love.

This contrast between knowledge and love sets the stage for Paul's treatment of the issue of deference to the believer with a weak conscience in this chapter. Since Paul contrasts knowledge and its fruit of "puffed-up-ness" with love and its fruit of encouragement and edification (οἰκοδομέω, oikodomeō), this clues the reader to the fact that Paul is focused on the proper treatment of one's fellow Christian.

8:2 The man who thinks he knows something does not yet know as he ought to know.

Paul continues to dwell on the theme of knowledge in this verse and does so in a way to highlight the weaknesses of believers at Corinth who think that they possess the right kind of knowledge on the issue of food offered to idols. It is important to note that Paul himself possesses the same knowledge that these Corinthians possess ("we all know," πάντες, pantes). The difference, however, between Paul and these Corinthians is that he knows the difference between possessing knowledge and being possessed by it.

8:3 But the man who loves God is known by God.

When there is a conflict between love and knowledge Paul always prefers love. In fact, the apostle says that loving God is the prerequisite for being known by him. Fee correctly summarized Paul's point in this verse when he stated, "Christian behavior is not predicated on the way of knowledge, which leads to pride and destroys others, but on the way of love, which is in fact the true way of knowledge. . . . In Christian ethics knowledge must always lead to love."[1]

2. The Non-reality of Idols (8:4-6)

[4]So then, about eating food sacrificed to idols: We know that an idol is nothing at all in the world and that there is no God but one. [5]For even if there are so-called gods, whether in heaven or on earth (as indeed there are many "gods" and many "lords"), [6]yet for us there is but one God, the Father, from whom all things came and for whom we live; and there is but one Lord, Jesus Christ, through whom all things came and through whom we live.

8:4 So then, about eating food sacrificed to idols: We know that an idol is nothing at all in the world and that there is no God but one.

It is in this verse that Paul reveals the specific content of the knowledge that is under discussion. The specific doctrinal knowledge that Paul has reference to by his several uses of the words "know" and "knowledge" is the doctrine of Christian monotheism. This point is made very clearly by Paul in 8:4 when he says we know that an idol is nothing and that there is no God but one. The ideas expressed in 8:4b clearly reflect Paul's Jewish monotheistic background. The Jewish prohibition against worshiping idols is well known throughout the Old Testament Scriptures, both in the law and in the prophets. The concept of the oneness of God is likewise known in central Jewish affirmations such as those found in Deut 6:4, which reads "Hear O Israel: the Lord our God, the Lord is one." In light of the information given by Paul in 1 Cor 8:4, it is noteworthy, then, that the specific knowledge which puffs up is the knowledge of Christian monotheism.

Most of the pictures of Paul's preaching in the book Acts are in the context of his sermons to Jewish audiences. We do know, however, that when he preached to pagan audiences, he preached

---

[1]Fee, *First Epistle*, pp. 368-369.

against their idolatry (Acts 17 — Athens; Acts 19 — Ephesus).[2] The idea that the conversion of Gentiles regularly required a forsaking of their pagan idols is also testified to in Paul's letter of 1 Thessalonians where he wrote, "therefore we do not need to say anything about it, for they themselves report what kind of reception you gave us. They tell how you turned to God from idols to serve the living and true God" (1 Thess 1:8-9). One can well anticipate the consternation of these readers at Corinth whose behavior, based upon the implications of accurate doctrinal affirmations (i.e., Christian monotheism), is being challenged by a fellow monotheist.

8:5 For even if there are so-called gods, whether in heaven or on earth (as indeed there are many "gods" and many "lords"),

Paul's affirmation about the oneness of God is given in the context of an animistic and polytheistic world. Accordingly, he must acknowledge the fact that believers do live in a world populated by so-called gods (λεγόμενοι θεοί, *legomenoi theoi*). One could not walk through the streets of Roman Corinth and deny the reality of the presence of idols. Ancient literary descriptions of Corinth as well as the archeological evidence that has been excavated there all point to an urban setting that was replete with statues, altars, idols, and temples to pagan gods and goddesses. Paul's phrase "in heaven" or "on earth" refers to the abode of these pagan deities as reflected in the theology of polytheistic religion. In the polytheistic world of Paul's day, the gods of Greece and Rome populated the heaven as well as the earth.

Some scholars have been perplexed by the last portion of 8:5 since it superficially seems to concede that in fact there are many other gods (θεοὶ πολλοί, *theoi polloi*) and lords (κύριοι πολλοί, *kyrioi polloi*) whom Paul recognizes. The NIV translation attempts to circumvent this problem by placing this troublesome phrase in parentheses. One solution offered for this problem is to infer that Paul still has in mind the notion of "so-called" which he used earlier in this verse. Given this approach, Paul would merely be acknowledging that there were indeed many so-called gods and

---

[2]On idolatry in Paul's world and his response to it, including 1 Corinthians, see P. W. Comfort, "Idolatry," *DPL*, pp. 424-426.

many so-called lords. Another approach to this interpretive problem rests its solution upon some concepts found in Old Testament texts which seem, at least rhetorically, to acknowledge the existence of other gods. While this is an issue far too complex to investigate at this point, it seems that the Old Testament sometimes accommodates the notion of the existence of other deities, but proclaims the supremacy of Yahweh over them. Deut 10:17, for example, reads, "for the Lord your God is God of gods and Lord of lords, the great God mighty and awesome who shows no partiality and accepts no bribes." In addition, the first of the ten commandments reads "you shall have no other gods before me" (Deut 5:7), which may well imply that Moses is acknowledging the existence of other deities, at least in the minds of the surrounding cultures. Another Old Testament text cited for this perspective would be Ps 82:1, which states, "God presides in the great assembly; he gives judgment among the gods."

In light of the fact that Paul has stated his explicit monotheistic beliefs in 8:4, Fee's assessment of the meaning of 8:5 is helpful when he states,

> Paul also recognizes the existential reality of pagan worship, and he knows that some within the Corinthian community are going to be affected by that reality. Thus, he interprets the concession with the affirmation "as indeed there are many gods and many lords." He does not intend by this that the gods exist objectively. Rather, as verse 7 indicates, they exist subjectively in the sense that they are believed in.[3]

8:6 yet for us there is but one God, the Father, from whom all things came and for whom we live; and there is but one Lord, Jesus Christ, through whom all things came and through whom we live.

Notwithstanding the plethora of idolatrous altars, idols, and temples in a city like Corinth, Paul declares that for believers there is only one God. As one would expect in Paul's own theology, God the Father is at the pinnacle of any reference to mono-

---

[3]Fee, *First Epistle*, pp. 372-373.

theism. God the father, for the apostle Paul, was not only the ultimate source of all reality (ἐξ οὗ τὰ πάντα, *ex hou ta panta*), but was also the ultimate goal of all creation and reality (εἰς αὐτόν, *eis auton*). If God the Father is the ultimate source and destination for all things, how then is one to understand the Lord Jesus Christ? In a very typical Pauline manner the apostle emphasizes the role that the Lord Jesus plays as agent through whom (δι᾽ οὗ, *di' hou*) God acts. Paul affirms that there is also one Lord and he is the one through whom all things came and continue to exist. Though clearly in a different setting, the reference to one God and one Lord in some ways anticipates the later Pauline references in Eph 4:5-6, where Paul refers to one Lord and one God and Father of all.

3. The Weak Brother's Dilemma (8:7-8)

⁷But not everyone knows this. Some people are still so accustomed to idols that when they eat such food they think of it as having been sacrificed to an idol, and since their conscience is weak, it is defiled. ⁸But food does not bring us near to God; we are no worse if we do not eat, and no better if we do.

8:7 But not everyone knows this. Some people are still so accustomed to idols that when they eat such food they think of it as having been sacrificed to an idol, and since their conscience is weak, it is defiled.
It is at this juncture that the reader is made aware how there could be such a significant conflict between love (*agapē*) and monotheistic knowledge in the church in Corinth. By his statement here that not everyone knows this, Paul is making it explicit that not all the believers in the church of God at Corinth totally accepted the Christian monotheistic position that he and certain other believers embraced.

While it may sound surprising at first to hear Paul acknowledging that there are believers in Corinth who do not embrace monotheism fully, this should really come as no surprise to the modern interpreter. As has been pointed out before, many of those Christians at Corinth who received this letter had been Christians less than forty-eight months. It is not surprising, therefore, that certain ones from a pagan idolatrous background would in some cases continue to have pagan polytheistic baggage with them in their Christian walk.

Some modern (Western World) interpreters find it hard to conceive that certain believers could truly still be having difficulty with tensions concerning idols and monotheistic convictions. Simon Kistemaker, for example, asserts that Paul's reference to idols does not mean the gods of paganism but rather "refers to the pagan environment of which the believers recently had come."[4] Part of Kistemaker's argument is based upon a peculiar philological understanding of the word "idol" in this verse. Even though the NIV has the wording "accustomed to idols," the Greek text refers to idol (τοῦ εἰδώλου, tou eidōlou) in the singular. Kistemaker argues that since Paul used the singular and not the plural, he could not be referring to pagan deities. This attempt to make a radical distinction in the meaning of the word based on whether it occurs in the singular or the plural falls apart when one sees Paul's use of the singular form of the same Greek word in 10:19 where eidōlon clearly refers to a pagan deity and not to general pagan cultural influence. Gordon Fee, likewise, does not want any of these weak Corinthian believers to still embrace polytheism.[5] To be certain, Paul is not accusing these believers of being guilty of blatant and cavalier idolatry. Nevertheless, since the issues discussed in this chapter are in terms of what individual believers "know" or "do not know," it does seem to be the case that this issue of monotheism versus polytheism is at the center.

Paul affirms that these believers are still accustomed to some of their pagan ways. In particular, Paul refers to situations when these believers who are weak in conscience (συνείδησις, syneidēsis) eat food that has been offered to an idol. Their defilement is a result of the fact that they do not with full spiritual conviction possess monotheistic loyalty to the one God. Consequently, because of their lack of a robust monotheism and because they are still partially caught in the web of polytheism, their conscience is

---

[4]Kistemaker, *First Corinthians*, pp. 269-270.
[5]Fee, *First Epistle*, p. 379.

defiled. C.K. Barrett's analysis of the situation assumed by and depicted in this verse is better than most when he writes,

> there are in Corinth men who have eaten sacrificed food all their lives and have always thought of it as sacrificed to an idol having real existence, and thus bearing real spiritual significance and force. In becoming Christians, they have not ceased to believe in the reality of the spiritual beings behind idols and have accordingly not ceased to think of the food itself as having religious meaning.[6]

8:8 But food does not bring us near to God; we are no worse if we do not eat, and no better if we do.

If v. 7 contains Paul's description of those "weak in conscience" Christian polytheists, then v. 8 is directed toward those who hold to the monotheistic doctrine that Paul likewise believes in. Since food and the eating of food is at the center of the issue, Paul must remind the offending monotheists that food does not bring one near to God. Since Paul has already characterized these believers who bear his own monotheistic convictions as puffed up (8:1), it is easy to imagine that they would have made the issue of food an important one. Paul's point is to show that dietary matters or questions of freedom of diet are spiritually speaking matters of indifference (cf. Rom 14:1-15:13).

4. The Proper Use of Freedom (8:9-13)

[9]**Be careful, however, that the exercise of your freedom does not become a stumbling block to the weak. **[10]**For if anyone with a weak conscience sees you who have this knowledge eating in an idol's temple, won't he be emboldened to eat what has been sacrificed to idols? **[11]**So this weak brother, for whom Christ died, is destroyed by your knowledge. **[12]**When you sin against your brothers in this way and wound their weak conscience, you sin against**

---

[6]Barrett, *First Epistle*, p. 194.

Christ. [13]Therefore, if what I eat causes my brother to fall into sin, I will never eat meat again, so that I will not cause him to fall.

8:9 Be careful, however, that the exercise of your freedom does not become a stumbling block to the weak.

Since Paul has already expressed his convictions about the superiority of love over knowledge, it is not surprising that he focuses the argument in this verse on how one treats his fellow Christian. For Paul, the correct use of one's freedom in Christ will be based more upon what is the loving thing to do rather than solely upon the criterion of who has the most correct information. This is apparently true for Paul even when the correct information is something as fundamental as Christian monotheism.

The Greek word ἐξουσία (*exousia*) translated here as "freedom" is a very important concept throughout this three-chapter block of material related to food offered to idols. Although this term is typically translated by the word "right(s)" in chapter 9, rather than by the word freedom, for Paul's rhetorical argument it is important to see that this is a linking term between the two chapters. The idea of stumbling block is introduced by Paul in 8:9. Robertson and Plummer give this insight into Paul's idea of the stumbling block when they write, "it is that against which the man with weak sight stumbles; it is no obstacle to the man who sees his way; but the weak sighted must be considered."[7] Because of the frequent abuse of the idea of stumbling block to the weak, it should be pointed out that stumbling block does not refer to any practice or belief that happens to offend another believer. It is clear by v. 11 that becoming a stumbling block to the weak is tantamount to destroying (ἀπόλλυται, *apollytai*) or contributing to the destruction of that person's relationship with God. Verse 13 makes it equally clear by describing this situation as one in which "my brother falls into sin."

---

[7]Robertson and Plummer, *First Epistle of St. Paul*, p. 171.

8:10 For if anyone with a weak conscience sees you who have this knowledge eating in an idol's temple, won't he be emboldened to eat what has been sacrificed to idols?

Since interpreters have sometimes hastily drawn a parallel between Paul's teaching here with that in Rom 14:1-15:13, some important differences between these two texts should be noted. Particularly, it should be pointed out that there is a significant difference between the issues in 1 Cor 8 and the issues of strong and weak believers in Rom 14, 15. Unlike 1 Cor 8, the strong and weak in Rom 14, 15 seem to be divided based upon the Jew/Gentile background of each. That is, ethnicity is a central factor in the situation at Rome.[8] Moreover, in Romans 14 and 15 the strong and weak brothers disagree with one another and are involved in either looking down upon or judging one another. In contrast to the situation we find in Romans where fellow believers strongly disagree over dining customs, the issue in 1 Cor 8 does not assume that the brothers disagree with one another. In fact, the problem is that the weak brother of 1 Cor 8 wishes to emulate the dining customs of the robustly monotheistic fellow believer. Finally, the terminology of weak and strong is not nearly as pronounced in 1 Corinthians as in Romans. In fact, the term "strong" is actually not used in this setting in 1 Corinthians. Accordingly, I have tried to avoid it in my comments since it basically imports issues and ideas not attested in 1 Corinthians.

It is in this verse that we learn the specific occurrence in which the weaker brother is led into sinful behavior on the basis of the exercise of the freedom of the monotheistic fellow believer. A plausible reconstruction based upon 8:10 goes something like this. A firmly convinced monotheistic Christian is invited to a meal in a dining hall at a pagan temple. Since this believer knows that the many gods and goddesses worshiped at these temples and whose names are invoked at the meals in these temples are nothing, this monotheistic Christian is not harmed by the surrounding polytheistic environment.

---

[8]See especially James Walters, *Ethnic Issues in Paul's Letter to the Romans: Changing Self-definitions in Earliest Roman Christianity* (Valley Forge: Trinity Press International, 1993).

It appears that Paul has no problem with a monotheistic Christian accepting an invitation to go to a meal in a banquet hall at a pagan temple. The problem arises, however, when a Christian with a weak conscience, who has not fully embraced monotheism, sees these actions of a confident Christian and attempts to copy them. The weak Christian will be emboldened to eat what has been sacrificed to idols, and thereby, because of his weakness in conscience, will in fact participate in an idolatrous activity.

Numerous scholars have questioned whether Paul's permissive attitude toward "eating in an idol's temple" is not in total contradiction to teaching given later in these three chapters.[9] Some interpreters of 1 Corinthians are still unconvinced that the picture the chapter 8 allows monotheistic believers to eat in an idol's temple if there are no weak in conscience believers around. Certainly there was no concept of "non-religious" meals in pagan temples. It must be remembered, however, that temples often had dining halls attached or associated with them and that these were also used for ceremonies other than the official worship of the deity. The apostle Paul can envision attendance there by saints which would not involve idolatry. In light of Paul's encouragement to Christians to associate with pagan idolaters (1 Cor 5:9-10, 12), it takes little imagination to see believers being invited by pagan friends to banquets. Consequently, these monotheistic brothers could have attended numerous social and cultural events (e.g., meals, birthday parties)[10] associated with temple sites. Even though some New Testament interpreters have been hesitant to read 1 Corinthians in the way advocated here, classical scholars and archaeologists have followed similar lines of thought. Prof. Ramsay MacMullen, for example, noted

> St. Paul provides the most familiar evidence for our subject
> in Greece. He speaks to the Christian community in Cor-
> inth about its members, or about people who are at least

---

[9]Much of the following material is taken from R.E. Oster, "Use, Misuse, and Neglect of Archaeological Evidence in Some Modern Works on 1 Corinthians" *Zeitschrift für die Neutestamentliche Wissenschaft* 83 (1992), pp. 64-67.

[10]In general see G.H.R. Horsley, "Invitation to the *Kline* of Sarapis," *New Documents Illustrating Early Christianity* vol.1 (1981) , pp. 5-9.

not devotees of some given pagan deity, joining the real
devotees in that deity's temple grounds to share in the eating of sacrificial meat. His rather offhand reference to the
scene as something quite everyday fits with the frequent
epigraphic mention of dining rooms opening off the stoas
that ran around sacral areas. [11]

**8:11 So this weak brother, for whom Christ died, is destroyed by
your knowledge.**

Even though it might seem very peculiar and ironic to modern
readers, this verse shows how incorrect actions predicated upon
correct knowledge, used by those who are guided by knowledge
alone rather than love, can cause the destruction of a fellow
Christian. The idea of the destruction of a Christian brother is a
sober thought for the apostle Paul. Fee correctly noted in this regard that

> in saying that the brother is destroyed, Paul most likely is
> referring to eternal loss, not simply some internal falling
> apart because one is behaving contrary to the dictates of
> conscience. The latter idea is altogether too modern; and
> elsewhere in Paul this word invariably refers to eternal
> ruin.[12]

The apostle has painted in this verse the grim scene of the consequences of the use of spiritually correct information without the
moral compass of love for guidance.

**8:12 When you sin against your brothers in this way and wound
their weak conscience, you sin against Christ.**

Paul states explicitly that this kind of blatant disregard for the
spiritual condition of a fellow believers is tantamount to sin
against them (ἁμαρτάνοντες εἰς τοὺς ἀδελφούς, *hamartanontes eis tous
adelphous*). The monotheistic believer would probably like to argue with Paul and claim that he is not responsible for the weak

---

[11]Ramsay MacMullen, *Paganism in the Roman Empire* (New Haven: Yale
University Press, 1981), p. 37.
[12]Fee, *First Epistle*, p. 387.

conscience of his fellow believer. Paul, however, will have none of that. Paul knows that one believer's actions and attitudes do in fact impact those of other believers. Because the thoughtless behavior of certain monotheists has led the weak into sin, Paul says that this is sin against Christ himself (εἰς Χριστὸν ἁμαρτάνετε, *eis Christon hamartanete*).

8:13 Therefore, if what I eat causes my brother to fall into sin, I will never eat meat again, so that I will not cause him to fall.

By the use of the connecting word "therefore" (διόπερ, *dioper*) at the beginning of this verse and his shift to the first person singular, Paul reveals how concerned he is not to be guilty himself of sinning against Christ. Since the litmus test of true love is concern for one's fellow believer and his edification (8:1), Paul is willing to radically alter his own lifestyle in order to build up saints. In a particularly emphatic Greek idiom Paul says that he will never ("not at all . . . forever," οὐ μὴ . . . εἰς τὸν αἰῶνα, *ou mē . . . eis ton aiōna*) eat meat again if by that self-limitation he can keep one brother from falling into idolatry because of the weak conscience. Paul's vow to never eat meat again must of course be kept in the historical and rhetorical context of chapter 8, which specifically relates to a spiritually threatened brother who is led into sinful behavior by an attempt to emulate the monotheistic believer's freedom to eat food that had been offered to idols.[13]

---

[13]On this issue see B. B. Blue, "Food Offered to Idols and Jewish Food Laws," *DPL*, pp. 309-310.

1 CORINTHIANS 9

B. THE RIGHTS OF AN APOSTLE (9:1-27)

1. Paul's Rights as Apostle (9:1-6)

[1]Am I not free? Am I not an apostle? Have I not seen Jesus our Lord? Are you not the result of my work in the Lord? [2]Even though I may not be an apostle to others, surely I am to you! For you are the seal of my apostleship in the Lord.

[3]This is my defense to those who sit in judgment on me. [4]Don't we have the right to food and drink? [5]Don't we have the right to take a believing wife along with us, as do the other apostles and the Lord's brothers and Cephas[a]? [6]Or is it only I and Barnabas who must work for a living?

[a]5 That is, Peter

9:1 Am I not free? Am I not an apostle? Have I not seen Jesus our Lord? Are you not the result of my work in the Lord?

Even though the issue of eating food that had been offered to idols is not explicitly mentioned in chapter 9, this chapter nevertheless follows quite logically upon these very issues mentioned in the preceding chapter. After having instructed those knowledge-abusers among the Corinthian believers to defer to their weaker brothers, Paul realizes it will be necessary for him to demonstrate this principle of deference to others in his own life. Calvin makes a similar observation in commenting on the opening words of 9:1. Calvin writes,

> he [Paul] confirms from actual fact what he had just been saying, that he would never taste meat all his life, rather than cause a brother to stumble. At the same time he makes

203

it plain that he cannot demand anything from them which he himself had not put into practice. There is no doubt that natural justice requires that anybody who imposes some obligation on others, should observe it himself. But a Christian teacher, above all, should discipline himself in this way, so that men may always see teaching backed up by the example of his life.[1]

The issue of freedom (ἐλεύθερος, *eleutheros*) that Paul brings up in 9:1 is conceptually related to the issue of rights which is addressed throughout this chapter.[2] In order to highlight the magnitude of the freedom which Paul is willing to forsake in his life, he introduces the fact that he is an apostle. Having mentioned his apostolic calling (see notes on 1:1), Paul then mentions two of the criteria that establish his credentials as an apostle. The first is his experience of the risen Lord.[3] Even though Paul could never have been qualified to be in the inner circle of the Twelve, he was, based upon his experience of the risen Lord, an apostle in the service of God. (On the relationship between apostolic calling and experience of the risen Lord, see notes on 15:7-8.) Since the concept of apostolic calling related directly to the issue of establishing and nurturing churches, it was quite natural for Paul to mention his work among the Corinthians themselves as a second proof of his apostolic calling. This is specifically what Paul has in mind by the question, "are you not the result of my work in the Lord?" As C.K. Barrett noted in this regard, "the existence of the church authenticates, as nothing else could do, the apostolic ministry of its founder."[4]

9:2 Even though I may not be an apostle to others, surely I am to you! For you are the seal of my apostleship in the Lord.

The content of this verse leads the interpreter into a second issue which Paul wants to address in this chapter. The second issue

---

[1]Calvin, *First Epistle*, p. 182.

[2]On this issue in 1 Corinthians see J.K. Chamblin, "Freedom/Liberty," *DPL*, pp. 315-316.

[3]The evidence for this is collected by J.M. Everts, "Conversion and Call of Paul," *DPL*, pp. 157-160.

[4]Barrett, *First Epistle*, p. 201.

that is woven throughout this chapter is that of Paul's need to make a defense of his apostolic ministry and practice. The defensive nature of Paul in this section is evident in the fact that he acknowledges that not everybody regards him as an apostle. When Paul writes that he may not be an apostle to others, this is not just a historical observation that he did not found all the Christian congregations in the first century. Rather, he is calling upon the loyalty of the Corinthians so that they will stand behind his apostolic authority against detractors. Because of the tight connection between these two issues which Paul addresses in chapter 9, many scholars rightly believe that the saints whom Paul is criticizing are in fact some of the very ones more prone to challenge his apostolic authority. It is probably correct then to see these two issues going together hand in hand not only in the rhetoric of this chapter but also in the historical realities of the church at Corinth at this time.

Not all scholars, however, would agree with this reconstruction. Witherington states, for example, that, "there is no hint here that Paul thinks that his apostolic office is seriously doubted by any significant number of people."[5] Granted, we cannot know whether the detractors consisted of "any significant number of people." It is clear, however, from other places in 1 Corinthians that Paul was aware of saints in Corinth who did not express a loyalty to him. (1:10ff and ch. 4). By his use of the metaphor "seal" (σφραγίς, *sphragis*) in 9:2, Paul points toward the idea that the Corinthians themselves are the attestation of his apostleship in the Lord. This argument reminds the Corinthians that if he were not an apostle then they would not be believers, and since they are, then he is.

9:3 This is my defense to those who sit in judgment on me.

Notwithstanding the fact that some interpreters do not believe that Paul is involved in an apology for his apostleship in this chapter, the occurrence of the phrase "my defense" (ἐμὴ ἀπολογία, *emē apologia*) here militates against this understanding. Certainly the entire chapter is not a defense of his apostolic calling. Fee

---

[5]Witherington, *Conflict and Community in Corinth*, p. 203.

points in the right direction about the nature of the issue that Paul is dealing with in chapter 9 when he writes, "since a crisis of authority lies behind much of this letter (cf. 4:1-5; 5-6; 14:36-37), Paul takes this occasion, which arose directly from their letter, to hit it head on."[6] Since Paul acknowledges in 9:3 that some believers were sitting in judgment of him, the question arises for the interpreter about what points they were judging him on.

9:4 Don't we have the right to food and drink?

The reference to "the right" (ἐξουσία, *exousia*) to food and drink in this verse has engendered two major interpretive traditions. One school of thought relates the food and drink back to the preceding chapter. This would indicate that Paul is affirming that he has the right to participate at banquets in temple dining halls. C.K. Barrett, for example, is sympathetic with this view when he writes "it appears that there is also much weight in the view that Paul is claiming here the right to eat and drink without regard to the idolatrous or other origin of his food."[7]

A second line of interpretation sees the reference to food and drink in the context of the other issue mentioned in verses 4-6. In particular, according to this second perspective, Paul would be referring to food and drink as one of the normal components of life, much like having a wife (9:5) and working for a living (9:6). This second school of interpretation seems to be the one that has more evidence in its favor.

This means then that some of Paul's detractors who sit in judgment of him are complaining about issues related to his method of support and his apostolic lifestyle.[8] At this juncture it is important to give an overview of the cultural values and assumptions some of Paul's detractors may have participated in which would have led them to be critical of Paul in these matters. It is important for the modern interpreter of Paul to understand that there was a significant debate in the ancient world regarding the methods and ways in which men like Paul received remuneration

---

[6]Fee, *First Epistle*, p. 393.

[7]Barrett, *First Epistle*, p. 202.

[8]See the helpful article by J.M. Everts, "Financial Support," *DPL*, pp. 295-300.

for their efforts. Cities of the ancient world were filled with both stationary and itinerant moral philosophers as well as religious preachers. Long before the advent of the gospel and long before the widespread presence of Jews in Greek and Roman cities, wandering pagan philosophers would travel from town to town, collect disciples, and propagate their individual messages. But how were these activities financed?

There were apparently four major ways that these ancient moral philosophers and religious teachers found support for their individual services.[9] The first way of support was by charging fees for their teaching. The second was by entering the household of a wealthy and influential individual, thereby gaining a patron. The third was through begging, and the fourth was by working.[10] Each of these four methods of acquiring support had its advocates and critics in the ancient world. While we cannot know with certainty, it was probably the case in Corinth that some of those believers whose practices Paul challenged in chapter 8 were the very ones who were critical of Paul in the matter of his financial base and support.

This reconstruction is very plausible in light of prior evidence that is seen in chapter 4. In 4:10-12 Paul contrasts his own socioeconomic and cultural status with those of some of his detractors at Corinth who are much higher in their social standing than he is. It is important to notice that these contrasts are not solely doctrinal but socioeconomic differences. Thus, in 4:11 he points out that he goes hungry and thirsty, is dressed in rags, and is homeless. In addition he points out in 4:12 that he, unlike his detractors, works hard with his own hands.[11] It is highly probable then that Paul is having to defend his means of income in 9:4 because of the attacks against him and the disdain that some of the Corinthian converts feel toward him because of the menial nature of his

---

[9]The ancient evidence for this has been collected and analyzed by, among others, Ronald F. Hock in a work entitled, *The Social Context of Paul's Ministry. Tentmaking and Apostleship.* Hock points out that pagan teachers and preachers could support themselves through one of four ways.

[10]Hock, *Social Context*, pp. 52-59.

[11]On Paul's manual labor as a "tentmaker" see P.W. Barnett, "Tentmaking," *DPL*, pp. 925-927.

profession. As Hock noted, "in the social world of a city like Corinth, Paul would have been a weak figure, without power, prestige, and privilege. . . . to those of wealth and power, the appearance of the artisan was that befitting a slave."[12]

9:5 Don't we have the right to take a believing wife along with us, as do the other apostles and the Lord's brothers and Cephas?

Paul now raises the issue of his right to be married. The phrase that the NIV translates as "believing wife" is based upon Greek words which mean a sister as a wife (ἀδελφὴν γυναῖκα, *adelphēn gynaika*). Most commentators rightly take the word sister there in its metaphorical sense, whereby Paul is pointing to a woman fellow believer. It is hard to picture the apostle Paul allowing a believer to take an unbeliever as a spouse (cf. 1 Cor 7:39).

In this verse he also acknowledges that other apostles have wives. We cannot be certain which group the apostle Paul is referring to by his use of the term the other apostles. (See notes on the word "apostle" at 15:7). The expression the "brothers of the Lord" would most naturally refer to Jesus' biological siblings which are mentioned in the gospels as well as the book of Acts, and perhaps in the reference to James in 1 Cor 15:7. The word Cephas in 9:5 refers to the apostle Peter, whose name played an important role in the issue of division and strife in 1 Cor 1-4.[13] The fact that Cephas was married is attested also by Mark 1:30, where the evangelist refers to the illness of Peter's mother-in-law.

The historic Roman Catholic position that the apostle Peter and his later successors as popes were not married had great difficulty with the content of this verse. Calvin's commentary testifies to the intensity of this debate during the period of the early Protestant reformation. Calvin notes,

> but here the papists evade the issue by a fine piece of cunning reason, of their own devising. For they say that the apostles refrained from intercourse, but took their wives about with them, so that they might get the fruits of the gospel, in other words their maintenance at other people's

---

[12]Hock, *Social Context*, p. 60.
[13]In general see J. R. Michaels, "Peter," *DPL*, pp. 701-703.

expense. As if, indeed, they could not be supported by the churches unless they wandered from place to place! And, also as if one could believe that those wives ran all over the place of their own free will, and when there was no need to do so, simply to live in idleness at public expense! Ambrose's explanation that the reference is to other men's wives, who were eagerly following the apostles to hear what they had to teach, is far-fetched indeed.[14]

9:6 Or is it only I and Barnabas who must work for a living?

In harmony with the intent of questions in the preceding verses, Paul here wants to demonstrate that he and Barnabas have given up rights that they have. It is regrettable that the NIV's translation has obscured the punch line in Paul's question in this verse. In the Greek text of verses 4, 5, and 6 Paul repeats the same phrase, "do we not have the right" (οὐκ ἔχομεν ἐξουσίαν, *ouk echomen exousian*). It is unfortunate that the NIV translated this phrase consistently in verse 4 and 5 but failed to render it consistently in verse 6. The interpreter, however, needs to be aware of the fact that Paul is raising the same fundamental issue in verse 6 that he has raised in 9:4-5.

Paul's point in 9:6 is to ask the Corinthians whether or not he and Barnabas in fact have the right not to work for a living in their Christian service. Paul's point is that he in fact does have the right to receive remuneration from the Corinthians, thereby excluding the need for himself and Barnabas to have to work (ἐργάζεσθαι, *ergazesthai*) with their own hands. Having established the fact that he has a right not to work, he will then proceed to demonstrate that he has surrendered this right to receive support from the Corinthians.

At one level Paul's strategy in 9:6 is to exploit the cultural prejudices of his detractors to justify his decision to neither do manual labor or to be "patronized" by them. By his phrase "work for a living" Paul is referring to manual labor. As Robertson and Plummer noted in this regard, "here again Greek sentiment would be against the apostle's practice. That a teacher who claimed to

---

[14]Calvin, *First Epistle*, p. 186.

lead and to rule could work with his hands for a living would be thought most unbecoming: nothing but the direst necessity excused labor in a free citizen (Aristotle *Politics* 3.5)"[15]

2. General Principle Stated (9:7-14)

[7]Who serves as a soldier at his own expense? Who plants a vineyard and does not eat of its grapes? Who tends a flock and does not drink of the milk? [8]Do I say this merely from a human point of view? Doesn't the Law say the same thing? [9]For it is written in the Law of Moses: "Do not muzzle an ox while it is treading out the grain."ᵃ Is it about oxen that God is concerned? [10]Surely he says this for us, doesn't he? Yes, this was written for us, because when the plowman plows and the thresher threshes, they ought to do so in the hope of sharing in the harvest. [11]If we have sown spiritual seed among you, is it too much if we reap a material harvest from you? [12]If others have this right of support from you, shouldn't we have it all the more?

But we did not use this right. On the contrary, we put up with anything rather than hinder the gospel of Christ. [13]Don't you know that those who work in the temple get their food from the temple, and those who serve at the altar share in what is offered on the altar? [14]In the same way, the Lord has commanded that those who preach the gospel should receive their living from the gospel.

ᵃ*9* Deut. 25:4

9:7 Who serves as a soldier at his own expense? Who plants a vineyard and does not eat of its grapes? Who tends a flock and does not drink of the milk?

As Kistemaker has observed,[16] 9:3-6 lists three rhetorical questions that anticipate an affirmative answer while 9:7 gives three questions which call for a negative response. Each of these three

---

[15]Robertson and Plummer, *First Epistle of St. Paul*, p. 182.
[16]Kistemaker, *First Corinthians*, p. 291.

questions is designed to show the right that an individual has for some form of remuneration based upon labor. These are designed by Paul to undergird again the strength of his position which asserts his rights but shows his willingness to surrender his rights and freedoms. The point of the illustration here is not to indicate that a Christian is a soldier in God's army but to make an appeal to a well-known economic reality. All of Paul's readers understood that soldiers were paid by others. Paul's second illustration, this one from agriculture, points to the fact that one who labors in the vineyard receives a form of compensation, namely the right to eat of its grapes. The third illustration is that of a shepherd who tends a flock. The apostle's point is that this individual has the right to drink of the milk.

9:8 Do I say this merely from a human point of view? Doesn't the Law say the same thing?

Paul now moves to undergird his point in these three illustrations with a Scripture quotation. When Paul uses the phrase "human point of view" (κατὰ ἄνθρωπον, *kata anthrōpon*) he is referring to mere human wisdom and observation of life. The apostle realizes his need to anchor his point within the teaching of Scripture. Accordingly, he will cite Old Testament materials which concur with the point of the three illustrations found in 9:7. (For Paul's other uses of the Old Testament citations, see notes at 10:11; 14:21, 34).[17]

9:9 For it is written in the Law of Moses: "Do not muzzle an ox while it is treading out the grain." Is it about oxen that God is concerned?

Paul's citation here of the law of Moses comes from Deut 25:4, which is obviously written in an agricultural context. In the quoted verse Moses is saying that an ox that is being used in the harvesting of a crop must be allowed to enjoy the benefits of that harvest. Since the ox is not muzzled, it is able to enjoy the grain. Just as the ox is entitled by God to enjoy the material benefits which come from its labor intensive activity, so the Christian

---

[17]In general consult M. Silva, "Old Testament in Paul," *DPL*, pp. 630-642.

worker is entitled by God to enjoy material benefits from his work in God's service (in God's field, cf. imagery in 1 Cor 3:9). In order to validate the process of taking an illustration from Deut 25 and applying it to the context of a church in a Roman colony, Paul ends verse 9 with a question. The point of the question is to affirm the fact that there are principles involved in this legislation about the ox which go beyond God's concern only for oxen.

9:10 Surely he says this for us, doesn't he? Yes, this was written for us, because when the plowman plows and the thresher threshes, they ought to do so in the hope of sharing in the harvest.

By his twofold use of the phrase "for us" (δι' ἡμᾶς, *di' hēmas*) in this verse, Paul reveals his deep belief that all Scripture is designed by God for use in instructing the people of God (2 Tim 3:16-17). The apostle Paul obviously would not deny that Deut 25:4 was also concerned about the practice of how the Israelites treated their oxen in the Old Testament, but it is very clear that Paul wants to affirm that it does have abiding significance for members of the church of God in the Roman colony of Corinth. (On this use of the Old Testament by Paul, see the notes at 1 Cor 10:11).

Paul continues in v. 10 with an expansion of the illustration of the harvest of crops and the ox. Paul moves the illustration beyond the ox by inserting the expectations of the laborers who are involved in such a harvest. Both the one who plows and the one who threshes do so, Paul affirms, in the hope of reaping the material benefit from their tasks. This verse allows the apostle to expand the illustration and metaphors beyond the bare elements found in Deut 25:4 in order to make a more pointed application in the next verse.

9:11 If we have sown spiritual seed among you, is it too much if we reap a material harvest from you?

Just as verse 10 enlarged the illustration from the preceding verse, so also in 9:11 Paul enlarges the elements of the illustration beyond that of the preceding verse. In all probability Paul embellished this cluster of metaphors to include the sowing of seed in

order to make a more direct connection to a metaphor which depicted his own apostolic ministry. While we cannot know with
certainty whether Paul knew of Jesus' parable of the seed and
sower (Matt 13), we do know from 1 Cor 3:6 that Paul regarded his
ministry at Corinth as one of planting seed in God's field. The
paradigm of spiritual seed (πνευματικὰ ἐσπείραμεν, *pneumatika espei-
ramen*) and material harvest (σαρκικὰ θερίσομεν, *sarkika therisomen*)
is closely analogous to Paul's paradigm of spiritual blessings and
material blessings which he addressed a few months later to the
church in Rome (Rom 15:27).

**9:12 If others have this right of support from you, shouldn't we
have it all the more? But we did not use this right. On the contrary, we put up with anything rather than hinder the gospel of
Christ.**
    In this verse Paul's argumentation and rhetoric takes an unex-
pected turn. As Witherington observed,

> one would expect the next line to be a request by Paul for
> his rights to material support to be honored. But in fact in
> the period 12b, Paul turns around and says that he also has
> the right not to make use of such support, sustenance, or
> patronage. Paul sees the receiving of ongoing support and
> patronage as a possible hindrance to the preaching of the
> gospel.[18]

Paul uses this important term "right" (ἐξουσία, *exousia*) two times in
this verse. Paul insists that he and others have the "right" to receive support from the Corinthians, but then acknowledges that
he does not use this right. By this acknowledgment, Paul is setting
himself forward as an example to the Corinthians to encourage
them to surrender rights and freedoms that they have in the gospel, but which have counterproductive consequences among the
believers at Corinth. If the apostle can put up with anything rather
than hinder the gospel, it is his hope that the readership at Corinth will endure their loss of privileges rather than hindering the
gospel among those who are weak in terms of food offered to

---

[18]Witherington, *Conflict and Community in Corinth*, p. 208.

idols. Accordingly, we see that for Paul an unloving act which
caused a weaker brother to be ruined, even if predicated on doctrinal monotheism, is tantamount to the hindrance of the gospel.

**9:13 Don't you know that those who work in the temple get their
food from the temple, and those who serve at the altar share in
what is offered on the altar?**

In this verse Paul shifts again to another cluster of images used
to underscore the point that those who "sow the seed of the gospel" have every right to be compensated for this effort. Although
it would not make much difference in the point of Paul's argument here, there is a debate among scholars whether Paul has
reference here to the converts' awareness of practices in pagan
temples or a possible awareness they might have about the practices of the temple in Jerusalem. Paul's point is true in either case.
Interpreters who believe that Paul must be referring to Old Testament Levitical practices include Simon Kistemaker,[19] and John
Calvin who noted, "an argument derived from the custom of the
heathen, would certainly have been a poor one, for the revenues
of the priests were not devoted to necessities like food and clothing, but to costly furnishings, regal splendor and extravagant lux-
ury."[20] C.K. Barrett, on the other hand,[21] states that Paul may be
making a reference to practices in idolatrous temples. It seems
best to conclude that the evidence from 9:13 is insufficient for one
to be dogmatic about this question.

We can say with certainty though that Calvin's interpretation is
flawed when he says that pagan temples did not have the practice
of their priests eating from the food that had been offered. There
is far too much ancient literary and archaeological evidence that
proves just the opposite. Fee correctly points out that Paul's point
in 9:13 is abundantly clear whether one assumes a Jewish or pagan
background for the imagery of working in the temple and serving
at the altar. He also observes that the Greek word for "serve"
(παρεδρεύω, *paredreuō*) in 9:13b is found no other place in the New

---

[19]Kistemaker, *First Corinthians*, p. 297.
[20]Calvin, *First Epistle*, p. 190.
[21]Barrett, *First Epistle*, p. 207.

Testament nor in the Greek Old Testament, and is typically found in pagan authors who are referring to the work of pagan priests.[22]

9:14 In the same way, the Lord has commanded that those who preach the gospel should receive their living from the gospel.

By his use of the phrase "in the same way," Paul makes clear that he wants to take the imagery and practices found in first century cultic activity and apply those metaphorically to those who work and serve in the planting and reaping of the gospel. The majority of New Testament scholars recognize the fact that the texts of the New Testament cannot be used to justify the modern clergy/laity distinction.[23] Nevertheless, in 9:14 Paul does indicate that the apostles, i.e., those who preach the gospel, have been commanded by God to receive remuneration for their gift and ministry. It would be extremely difficult to demonstrate that Paul believed every other Christian ministry was designated by God as one worthy of financial compensation.[24] In light of Paul's theology of gifts (see especially 1 Cor 12:28-30), it is hard to imagine that he would have used a phrase like "those who preach the gospel" (τοῖς τὸ εὐαγγέλιον καταγγέλλουσιν, *tois to evangelion katangellousin*) to describe the Christian activity of countless other believers in the ancient church. The only thing that probably would have seemed as foreign to Paul as the later clergy/laity distinction is an idea that every believer is a missionary. But for apostles, Paul argues in this context, God has commanded that they have the right to receive payment for their work in the proclamation of the gospel.

3. Paul's Deferment of Rights (9:15-18)

[15]**But I have not used any of these rights. And I am not writing this in the hope that you will do such things for me. I would rather die than have anyone deprive me of this boast.** [16]**Yet when**

---

[22]Fee, *First Epistle*, p. 412.

[23]R. Banks, "Ordination, as we know it, does not appear in the Pauline letters," in "Church Order and Government," *DPL*, p. 135.

[24]Ibid.

I preach the gospel, I cannot boast, for I am compelled to preach. Woe to me if I do not preach the gospel! [17]If I preach voluntarily, I have a reward; if not voluntarily, I am simply discharging the trust committed to me. [18]What then is my reward? Just this: that in preaching the gospel I may offer it free of charge, and so not make use of my rights in preaching it.

9:15 But I have not used any of these rights. And I am not writing this in the hope that you will do such things for me. I would rather die than have anyone deprive me of this boast.

Even though the Greek text does not contain the word "rights," Fee is correct in arguing that this is surely the point Paul is making at this juncture.[25] The apostle is apparently undisturbed by the fact that he refuses to go along with that which God, according to 9:14, had commanded. Just as Paul had been able in 8:1-3 to exalt the virtues of love over the virtues of correct doctrine misused, so also in 9:15. Paul is able to arrive at a decision which allows him to decline the normal method for compensation in order to achieve a higher good.

Paul was certainly not against receiving compensation in certain situations and he was surely not beyond receiving gifts from fellow believers.[26] Nevertheless, in the historical and cultural realities of the Corinthian setting Paul realized that to accept compensation from them would be, in the words of 9:12, a hindrance to the gospel of Christ. The sensitivity of this issue in the context of Paul's ministry among the Corinthians is made apparent by the continuing references to it in 2 Cor 10-13.

In this verse Paul denies that he is trying to either shame or manipulate his readers into now beginning to give him compensation; quite the contrary. He states in fact that he would rather die than have anyone deprive him of his grounds for boasting (καύχημα, kauchēma). The details of Paul's argumentation in 9:15b have often struck commentators as quite difficult to follow. Not only are there abnormalities in the Greek text, but there are points at which Paul's reasoning takes the reader by surprise.

---

[25]Fee, *First Epistle*, p. 416, fn. 12.
[26]J. M. Everts, "Financial Support," *DPL*, pp. 296-297.

Paul's introduction of the term "boast" at the end of 9:15 is very significant. In fact, it is this concept of boasting which serves as a catalyst for what Paul will express in the following verses.

9:16 Yet when I preach the gospel, I cannot boast, for I am compelled to preach. Woe to me if I do not preach the gospel!

In this verse Paul clarifies what the grounds of his boasting are. He states explicitly that preaching the gospel is not grounds of his boasting. The reason that preaching is disqualified as a reason to boast is because he must preach out of necessity. Paul's reasoning says that there is nothing virtuous in performing the ministry received from God because that was what he was commanded to do. Moreover, Paul is so convinced about the divine mandate that lies behind his apostolic preaching that he pronounces a woe upon himself (οὐαὶ γάρ μοί ἐστιν, *ouai gar moi estin*) if he were to fail to follow God's commandment in this matter.

9:17 If I preach voluntarily, I have a reward; if not voluntarily, I am simply discharging the trust committed to me.

At this point Paul drops the terminology of boast and pursues the conceptually related term "reward" (μισθόν, *misthon*). Paul uses two brief logical arguments in 9:17 to help the Corinthians understand his distinction between preaching with compensation and preaching without compensation. In the first case Paul refers to voluntary preaching, which he himself does not do since, according to 9:16, he is compelled to preach and would be punished by God if he did not. In such an instance when one preaches voluntarily Paul acknowledges that there is a reward. This individual, using earlier terminology, would be able to boast of his preaching activity. In the second instance Paul refers to someone whose preaching is not voluntary. This illustration would point to Paul's own situation. When one's life of preaching is not voluntary, then that person has no reward but is discharging the duty given to him by God.

9:18 What then is my reward? Just this: that in preaching the gospel I may offer it free of charge, and so not make use of my rights in preaching it.

The logical conclusion of the two examples mentioned in 9:17 is that Paul does not have a reward. This leads then to the question at the opening of 9:18, what then is the reward that Paul has since he preaches involuntarily? The *reward* that the apostle Paul has (=the *boast* that the apostle Paul has) is namely that he preaches the gospel without remuneration from the Corinthians.

Paul brings his reasoning and argumentation in the preceding several verses to its culmination by his use of the word "my rights" in 9:18. Gordon Fee rightly points out that part of Paul's emphasis at the end of 9:18 is missed by the unfortunate translation made by the NIV.[27] The NIV phrase "make use of my rights in preaching it" would be more accurately rendered "make use of my right in the gospel." Paul's wording is in fact much more appropriate to the contextual situation. Those puffed up believers whose behavior Paul criticizes in chapter 8 were claiming their "right" in the gospel, not their rights in preaching it. Consequently Paul's argumentation needs to demonstrate that he himself has been willing to jettison "his right in the gospel" and not his right in preaching it. Those believers whose correct monotheistic doctrine had led them to be puffed up rather than be concerned about edifying the weaker brother would surely have claimed that their "right" to act in this way existed because of the truth of the monotheistic gospel. Accordingly, it is at this very point in the examination of one's right(s) in the gospel that Paul needed to respond to them.

4. To the Jew as a Jew (9:19-23)

[19]**Though I am free and belong to no man, I make myself a slave to everyone, to win as many as possible. **[20]**To the Jews I became like a Jew, to win the Jews. To those under the law I became like one under the law (though I myself am not under the law), so as to win those under the law. **[21]**To those not having the law I be-**

---

[27]Fee, *First Epistle*, p. 421, fn. 43.

came like one not having the law (though I am not free from
God's law but am under Christ's law), so as to win those not having the law. ²²To the weak I became weak, to win the weak. I have
become all things to all men so that by all possible means I might
save some. ²³I do all this for the sake of the gospel, that I may
share in its blessings.

**9:19 Though I am free and belong to no man, I make myself a
slave to everyone, to win as many as possible.**
This verse introduces the very important section of 9:19-23. At
the outset it must be noticed that this section has sometimes been
misused to justify a variety of ill-conceived and theologically
flawed missiological perspectives and decisions. Anyone who believes that these verses prove that the apostle Paul's strategy and
style make him resemble a chameleon has failed to see the rhetorical and occasional nature of this material. Even a superficial
reading of the first Corinthian letter makes it abundantly clear that
Paul is no chameleon. It is interesting to notice, for example, that
in this list of groups to whom he is willing to accommodate himself in verses 20-22 one does not find a reference to those who
have knowledge.
There are an adequate number of examples in this very letter
to demonstrate that Paul could be anything but accommodating
in specific instances where he had fundamental disagreements
with either the aberrant lifestyle or unacceptable doctrine of fellow believers. If one takes this section out of its rhetorical setting
in which Paul is defensively attempting to rescue falling believers
(1 Cor 8:13), one derives a picture of Paul that can stand up neither to the evidence in the Pauline letters nor to the evidence
concerning Paul's methods portrayed in the book of Acts.
With this affirmation of his own personal freedom Paul recon-
nects with the terminology he used at the beginning of this chapter in 9:1. The strength of Paul's affirmation in 9:19 comes from
his use of radical dichotomies. On the one hand he is free and
belongs to no one, while on the other hand he chooses to enslave
himself to everyone. Paul is very clear when he states the goal or
purpose of this self-enslavement. The agenda that leads to this
lifestyle comes from his vision and commitment to his apostolic

calling. His desire is to win as many as possible. Because of the importance of the term "win" in the section 9:19-23, it is necessary to make a brief comment on the meaning of this term (κερδαίνω, *kerdainō*). Even though this term *kerdainō* carries with it the general idea of "gain" or "win," the most contextually insightful evidence comes from the parallelism between this verb and the verb save in 9:22. Because of this parallelism between the verb to save (σώζω, *sōzō*) and the verb to win, it is best to understand to win in the sense of to facilitate or encourage the salvation of someone else.

9:20 To the Jews I became like a Jew, to win the Jews. To those under the law I became like one under the law (though I myself am not under the law), so as to win those under the law.

Keeping in mind the situation and context of this chapter, we remember that Paul's underlying concern is to rescue the saints who are weak in conscience so that their relationship to God and Christ will not be destroyed. (See notes on 8:11-13). Accordingly, as Paul makes his way in verse 20 through a list of various groups whom he attempts to evangelize, such as Jews, those under the law, and those outside the law, we must not lose sight of the fact that the goal of this argumentation is to lead the reader to 9:22 where Paul mentions individuals who are weak. Contextually Paul can have no one else in mind by his reference to the weak other than the threatened brothers under discussion throughout 1 Cor 8.

There have been many attempts by interpreters of Paul to find specific instances, particularly in the book of Acts, which would demonstrate Paul's ability to become a Jew in order to win the Jews. One must be careful, however, not to assume that the Corinthian readership would have known about all the examples in the book of Acts which the modern reader of the New Testament knows about, obviously including those events in Acts which had not even occurred by the time of Paul's writing this letter to the Corinthians.

The historical question that arises immediately from 9:20 is how does someone who is already a Jew like Paul become a Jew in order to win the Jews? Fee is clearly correct when he answers this question in these words, "the obvious answer is, in matters that have to do with Jewish religious peculiarities that Paul as a Christian had long ago given up as essential to a right relationship with God."[28]

Numerous interpreters agree that Paul's reference to those under the law in 9:20 is especially enigmatic. The major difficulty is to determine what group Paul has in mind by this phrase. There would be no problem if Paul referred either to the Jews or to those under the law, but the question arises because he refers to both. How does Paul distinguish between these two groups? None of the traditional explanations for this enigma are problem free. What the apostle probably has in mind is the fact that ancient Judaism was composed of Jews who were more law conscious than other Jews were. From this perspective the term Jew might have more racial or national characteristics associated with it, while the phrase "those under the law" would point to Jews whose zeal for the law was far more rigid. In this regard it is noteworthy that in Paul's autobiographical descriptions of his life before Christ in Judaism he acknowledges that not all Jews had the same level of interest and intense zeal for the law (Phil 3:6; Gal 1:14).

It is very helpful to the modern interpreter of Paul to read Paul's acknowledgment that he himself is no longer under the law (ὑπὸ νόμον, hypo nomon). This does not mean, of course, that Paul did not believe in the authority and the normative character of the Old Testament Scriptures (cf. 2 Tim 3:16; Rom 15:4). This latter fact is abundantly clear throughout the book of Corinthians (see notes on 1 Cor 10:11).

9:21 To those not having the law I became like one not having the law (though I am not free from God's law but am under Christ's law), so as to win those not having the law.

The phrase "those not having the law" (τοῖς ἀνόμοις, tois anomois) surely refers to the Gentile mission. Even though there were ways in which Paul would accommodate himself to the Gentile mission, he is quick to point out that he did not live lawlessly as a servant of Christ. In fact, even though Paul was not, according to

---

[28]Fee, *First Epistle*, p. 428.

v. 20, under the law, v. 21 makes   it clear that he is not free from
Christ's law. It would be a great travesty for someone to imagine
that Paul's gospel was a lawless gospel. Clearly Paul was not interested in imposing aspects of Mosaic *ceremonial* legislation upon
Gentile believers (e.g., Galatians, Romans, Philippians), but his
letters, including 1 Corinthians, make it very clear that Paul is
committed to a people of God who stand under the regulations
and laws of Christ. The purpose of this accommodation to the
Gentiles, Paul says, is to win those who have had no history of
association with the historic people of God.

**9:22 To the weak I became weak, to win the weak. I have become
all things to all men so that by all possible means I might save
some.**

Those Corinthian Jews and Gentiles who were now saved because of Paul's ability "to become all things to all people" will
have to face the consequences of that Pauline strategy in terms of
Paul's present loyalty to the weak (τοῖς ἀσθενέσιν, *tois asthenesin*). It
is one thing for a Jew or Gentile convert at Corinth to applaud
Paul's commitment to adaptability in winning new converts, but it
is quite another to continue this applause as this principle requires the surrender of rights and freedoms in their new relationship to Christ.

It is no accident then that Paul's accommodation to the weak
is found at the end of this presentation, with the very missionary
principles which led to the success of the Pauline mission in cities
like Corinth now being brought to bear on internal problems
among members of the church. When Paul says he became weak
to the weak he is obviously referring to the weak believers mentioned in chapter 8. A concrete example of this accommodation
to the weak was already established by Paul in 8:13 when he says
that he would never eat meat again if it would cause a weak Christian to lose his salvation.

This verse ends with a comprehensive statement of the principle that has guided Paul in the specific actions mentioned in 9:19-
22. The apostle states in very unguarded terminology his adaptability to all people in all circumstances so that some might experience salvation. Since it is the very salvation of the weak that

concerns Paul, it is appropriate that he refers to the goal of salvation in the context of the weak.

9:23 I do all this for the sake of the gospel, that I may share in its blessings.

The gospel is the only legitimate foundation for Paul's encouragement for others to defer to the weak. He states here that all the abdication of personal rights and prerogatives mentioned in the preceding verses are to be understood as part of his response to the gospel (διὰ τὸ εὐαγγέλιον, *dia to euangelion*). Kistemaker commented on this verse in these words:

> We would expect Paul to be the loser when he announced his intention to be a servant of all those who wanted to listen to the gospel. Paul is not the loser but the beneficiary of the blessings that accompany the preaching of the good news.[29]

5. Looking Forward to the Prize (9:24-27)

[24]Do you not know that in a race all the runners run, but only one gets the prize? Run in such a way as to get the prize. [25]Everyone who competes in the games goes into strict training. They do it to get a crown that will not last; but we do it to get a crown that will last forever. [26]Therefore I do not run like a man running aimlessly; I do not fight like a man beating the air. [27]No, I beat my body and make it my slave so that after I have preached to others, I myself will not be disqualified for the prize.

9:24 Do you not know that in a race all the runners run, but only one gets the prize? Run in such a way as to get the prize.

Interpreters of 1 Corinthians have not been of one mind in their understanding about the relationship between 9:24-27 to the verses that precede it, as well as its relationship to the section

---

[29]Kistemaker, *First Corinthians*, p. 310.

found in 10:1-22. In light of the athletic metaphors which dominate in 9:24-27 and the fact that 10:1ff is focused on the disqualification that some of the Corinthian believers may experience, it seems to be a judicious conclusion to interpret 9:24-27 as an introduction to the thoughts found in 10:1ff.

As we have seen in other sections of 1 Corinthians when Paul has stern comments to make to his readers, he often inserts illustrations in the first person singular, so that he speaks autobiographically. A similar phenomenon can be seen in the section 9:24-27. Paul is not unique in his use of athletic imagery to encourage those whom he mentors to struggle and persevere in a life of excellence and faithfulness. Similar illustrations can be found in Jewish writers of the period as well as in several Stoic or Cynic popular philosophers of the early Roman empire. It should be obvious that the point of the illustration in 9:24 is not to affirm that only one individual will receive the prize of eternal life. Rather, Paul's intention is to point out the obvious fact that mere participation in the race is not the same as receiving the prize that goes to the victor. Accordingly, Paul challenges his readership to participate in the race in a way that will insure that they will receive the prize.

The obvious implication of this section is that Paul recognizes, and in fact fears, the possibility that certain Corinthian believers may run in such a way that they will not receive the prize. Since this rather straightforward meaning of the text has caused difficulty to certain theological systems, Fee raises the question whether Paul could actually be teaching what it sounds like he is teaching. Fee states that some interpreters cannot believe that Paul is teaching that believers could fail to obtain the prize. He then observes that they usually come to this conclusion "because of prior theological commitment, not because of what the text itself says."[30]

---

[30]Fee, *First Epistle*, p. 440.

9:25 Everyone who competes in the games goes into strict training. They do it to get a crown that will not last; but we do it to get a crown that will last forever.

A key phrase in the first half of 9:25 is the phrase "goes into strict training" (ἐγκρατεύεται, *enkrateuetai*). This phrase is one of the indications that this section is conceptually linked to the issues Paul will attempt to deal with in 10:1ff, namely, the lack of spiritually robust training in the life of some of the Corinthian believers. One observes again and again in the life of Paul that he never places requirements upon his converts which he himself does not fulfill. Accordingly, after acknowledging the necessity of strict training, he demonstrates how his own life is characterized by this strict training.

While crowns were not the only form of reward received by victors in ancient athletic competition, they were a very common form of prize that signified one's victory. While some victorious athletes of antiquity received crowns of gold, many times victorious competitors received wreaths made of various parts of trees and vegetation. These crowns clearly would not last forever. It is at this juncture that Paul makes a contrast between the crown that human athletes receive, which is short-lived, and the crown the believer wins that lasts forever.

Paul's words in the last part of 9:25 contain a purpose clause (ἵνα, *hina*) which makes a clear connection between the disciplined life that Paul both leads and encourages others to lead and his desire for a crown that will last forever. The apostle Paul's motivation to persevere in the calling he had received from God was certainly a multi-sided motivation. Paul obviously did not rely on any single perspective or motivation. What we see in this context, however, is a clear reference to a motivation that is rooted in his anticipation of receiving an eternal reward from God, spoken of metaphorically here as crown that is imperishable.

9:26 Therefore I do not run like a man running aimlessly; I do not fight like a man beating the air.

Because the apostle has fixed his vision steadfastly upon receiving this imperishable crown, he does not take his strict training lightheartedly. Even though runners in ancient athletic competition would obviously not be characterized as running aimlessly, Paul is aware that this image fits well the life of some of his readers. As this illustration pointedly underscores, aimless running has never led to a crown. Therefore, the apostle refuses to conduct himself in any way that would disqualify him from this imperishable crown. He then shifts the metaphor from that of a runner to a metaphor of a boxer. There has been more than one interpretation of the point of Paul's metaphor of a man beating the air. Perhaps the best interpretation is that given by Witherington.[31] He points out that this image of a shadow boxer was used in antiquity to negatively describe one's philosophic opponents. The first-century Greek-Jewish author Philo, for example, calls some of the sophists of his day shadow boxers. The imagery of a boxer merely throwing punches in the air is certainly analogous to the other image of a runner running aimlessly.

9:27 No, I beat my body and make it my slave so that after I have preached to others, I myself will not be disqualified for the prize.
In this verse it is imperative to understand that Paul is still speaking metaphorically. The apostle's choice of the words "I beat my body" is best explained by the fact that he is continuing to use metaphors that depict rigor in athletic competition. During the centuries-long history of Christianity, there have been schools of interpretation which took Paul's words at face value and attempted to emulate what they believed he was encouraging others to do. John Calvin noted in this regard, "the monks of long ago, wanting to comply with this direction, thought out many disciplinary exercises; for they used to sleep on benches; they forced themselves to keep unduly long night vigils; and, in their way of life, kept clear of all luxuries."[32] The apostle's point is to affirm the fact that in his own life he strives hard to make sure that he practices self-control and makes himself a slave. Even though the words of 9:27 express the idea that Paul recognizes the possibility that he himself might be disqualified for the prize, some interpreters have found this impossible to believe. It is important for the modern interpreter of 9:27 to keep in mind the literary func-

---

[31]Witherington, *Conflict and Community in Corinth*, p. 214.
[32]Calvin, *First Epistle*, p. 199.

tion of Paul's autobiographical comments in this verse. He is offering himself as a model to the Corinthian readership. He can hardly expect them to take seriously this need for a life of strict training and the possibility of disqualification if he does not subject himself to those same truths and realities. As Witherington noted in his observations about Paul's point here, "it is quite clear that Paul considers it possible for him and his audience to lose the crown if they do not follow the law of Christ."[33]

---

[33]Witherington, *Conflict and Community in Corinth*, p. 214.

1 CORINTHIANS 10

C. WARNINGS FROM ISRAEL'S HISTORY (10:1-13)

1. Wandering in the Desert (10:1-5)

¹For I do not want you to be ignorant of the fact, brothers, that our forefathers were all under the cloud and that they all passed through the sea. ²They were all baptized into Moses in the cloud and in the sea. ³They all ate the same spiritual food ⁴and drank the same spiritual drink; for they drank from the spiritual rock that accompanied them, and that rock was Christ. ⁵Nevertheless, God was not pleased with most of them; their bodies were scattered over the desert.

10:1 For I do not want you to be ignorant of the fact, brothers, that our forefathers were all under the cloud and that they all passed through the sea.

In light of the fact that 9:27 ended on the note of possible disqualification in receiving the imperishable crown, one would do well to note the connection between this theme and the point Paul makes in 10:1ff. In fact, this connection is secured with Paul's use of the word "for" (γάρ, *gar*) in 10:1. The apostle is moving from the common athletic illustrations and metaphors of everyday life to the authority of Scripture to demonstrate and anchor the truth of his point. The strategy we recognize at this juncture in 9:24-10:1 is one of moving from human illustrations to scriptural attestation, which we also observed in Paul's argument in 9:7-10.

It is important for the interpreter to keep in mind that Paul is still within the larger three-chapter section dealing with issues related to the consumption of food offered to idols. This point will be made explicit by him in the following verses when he actually begins to use the terms idols and idolaters.

The apostle is clearly concerned in 10:1 about the ignorance of these Corinthian brothers. (On theme of ignorance, cf. 12:1). If one knows Paul's own theology and writings it comes as no surprise that he would regard Gentile believers at Corinth as spiritual kinfolk of the Old Testament Israelites. This is certainly what Paul has in mind when he refers to them as "our forefathers who were all under the cloud." Calling ancient Hebrews of the second millennium B.C. the forefathers of believers in the church at Roman Corinth, is cut from the same cloth as when Paul instructed them regarding their participation in the spiritual Passover and feast of the unleavened bread (1 Cor 5:6-8). The reference to cloud and sea points to the Exodus narrative found in the Pentateuch.

10:2 They were all baptized into Moses in the cloud and in the sea.

Beginning in this verse Paul employs a hermeneutical method in interpreting the Old Testament which has often been called typology. One reason this terminology is applied to this illustration is because of the apostle's use of the word τύποι (typoi) (10:6), which is translated in the NIV as "examples." With this method of interpretation it is clear that Paul is working with the specific realities of the Corinthians' spiritual situation and going backward into the Mosaic materials to find points of correlation.[1] This is what the apostle is doing when he writes that all of the forefathers were baptized into Moses (from βαπτίζω, baptizō) in the cloud and in the sea. The reference to baptism here can only be intelligible and meaningful if we understand it typologically. That is, Paul wants to observe and comment on a point of correspondence between the spiritual realities in the church at Corinth and the spiritual realities at the time of Moses. Paul probably chose the verb "baptized" because of possible misunderstandings about its efficacy in the church at Corinth. While this suggestion has not been accepted by all, some scholars believe that the reference to the

---

[1]On Paul's use of the figure of Moses see L.L. Belleville, "Moses," *DPL*, pp. 620-621.

cloud and the sea in 10:2 are typological references to the Holy
Spirit and the water of baptism.[2]

10:3 They all ate the same spiritual food

Another point of correspondence between the Corinthian believers and their Hebrew spiritual forefathers is that both groups
consumed a spiritual (πνευματικός, *pneumatikos*) food. Paul clearly
has in mind here God's provision of manna to the Israelites (Exod
16:4ff). The typological correspondence with the saints in Corinth
would obviously be the bread which they ate at the Lord's Supper
(cf. 10:16-17).

10:4 and drank the same spiritual drink; for they drank from the spiritual rock that accompanied them, and that rock was Christ.

Next Paul refers to a spiritual drink (πνευματικὸν πόμα, *pneumatikon poma*) that the Israelites imbibed, a drink which corresponded to the Christian participation in the fruit of the vine (cf.
10:15-16; 11:25-26). Paul next identifies the source of the spiritual
drink which the Israelites drank. He continues his typological interpretation with a reference to the spiritual rock that accompanied the Israelites in their wilderness wanderings. Here the apostle
refers to the account found in Exod 17:6 and Num 20. The refreshment that came from this rock was remembered centuries
later in Israelite hymnody. Ps 78:15-16 reads, "He split the rocks in
the desert and gave them water as abundant as the seas; he
brought streams out of a rocky crag and made water flow down
like rivers." Next the apostle Paul correlates that rock with the
presence of Christ, again a point of correlation between the Corinthian experience of Christ and the Israelite experience.

10:5 Nevertheless, God was not pleased with most of them; their bodies were scattered over the desert.

This verse makes explicit what Paul's point in all this typology
is. His point is that notwithstanding the central spiritual experiences of baptism, of a spiritual meal, and of the presence of
Christ, God's people are not thereby irrevocably protected from

---

[2]On Paul's views about baptism, see G.R. Beasley-Murray, "Baptism,"
DPL, pp. 60-66.

the destruction and wrath of God.[3] Witherington's summary of
the apostle's point is helpful when he states that Paul,

> is not arguing that the Red Sea crossing was a sacrament,
> since actually the Israelites went across on dry ground and
> did not get wet. Nor is he suggesting that the manna was in
> some sense a sacramental food just like the Lord's Supper.
> His point is the Israelites had the same sort of benefits as
> Christians do, even benefits from Christ himself, and even
> this did not secure them against perishing in the desert and
> losing out on God's final and greatest blessing.[4]

While Paul's confrontational and judgmental message at this
juncture does not fit comfortably with all interpreters' views of
Paul, it is very clear that his message is in harmony with other
ideas expressed in 1 Corinthians. Of course one must not forget
that Paul's harsh lesson in 10:1ff is directed against saints at Corinth who are involved in overt idolatry. It should be remembered,
furthermore, that in Paul's previous letter to the Corinthians (see
notes at 5:9ff) the apostle advocated withdrawal from fellow
Christians who practiced idolatry. In 5:11ff Paul emphatically
makes the same point again and states that idolatrous believers
are not even to share in the fellowship of a meal with fellow Christians. And finally, in 6:9, Paul clearly states that idolaters will not
inherit the kingdom of God. This judgmental illustration based
upon the wilderness wandering narratives should not come as a
surprise to readers who had been following the tone of Paul's
ethical concerns in previous chapters.

2. Punishment for Sins (10:6-10)

**[6]Now these things occurred as examples[a] to keep us from set-
ting our hearts on evil things as they did. [7]Do not be idolaters, as**

---

[3]Because of her commitments to "perseverance of the saints," Judith M.
Gundry-Volf believes that the text of 1 Cor 10 "may actually have in view
false profession of faith in Christ," rather than the "actual loss of salvation," in "Apostasy, Falling Away, Perserverance," *DPL*, pp. 42-43.
[4]Witherington, *Conflict and Community in Corinth*, p. 219.

some of them were; as it is written: "The people sat down to eat and drink and got up to indulge in pagan revelry."[b] [8]We should not commit sexual immorality, as some of them did — and in one day twenty-three thousand of them died. [9]We should not test the Lord, as some of them did — and were killed by snakes. [10]And do not grumble, as some of them did — and were killed by the destroying angel.

[a]6 Or *types*; also in verse 11　　[b]7 Exodus 32:6

10:6 Now these things occurred as examples to keep us from setting our hearts on evil things as they did.

Paul has used an interpretive principle which allows him to argue about the way that God will treat sinful Christians on the basis of how God treated sinful Israelites. His use of this hermeneutical technique reveals that he would have no sympathy for depicting the "God of the Old Testament" as being radically different from the "God of the New Testament," particularly in the matter of God's destruction of his covenant people when they abandon loyalty to him. The apostle would have no sympathy for a glib presentation which treats the God of the Old Testament as a God of anger and the God of the New Testament as a God of love and forgiveness. Not only do the Old Testament Scriptures teach on several occasions that "God is slow to anger and abounds in steadfast love" (e.g., Exod 34:6; Ps 103:8; Jonah 4:2; cf. Deut 4:31), but New Testament Scriptures make it equally plain that the gospel includes a word about the wrath of God. The purpose of this Old Testament example, Paul explains, is to inhibit the believers at Corinth from being involved in the same kind of evil that those Israelites were.

10:7 Do not be idolaters, as some of them were; as it is written: "The people sat down to eat and drink and got up to indulge in pagan revelry."

By the occurrence of the word "idolaters" in 10:7 Paul explicitly states what his concern is. Even though there are more occurrences of the word "idol" and its cognates in 1 Corinthians than the entirety of Paul's other letters together, scholars are still not in agreement regarding the exact nature of Paul's concern in chapter 10 in comparison to his concern expressed in chapter 8. While chapter 8 seemed to be more concerned about the situation of a weak Christian being seduced into idolatry, chapter 10 seems to be focusing more on overt and explicit acts of idolatry. Given the pervasiveness of idolatry in Greco-Roman antiquity, the fact that the church in Corinth was a first-generation church, and the fact that there would be tremendous social pressure to participate in acts of idolatry, one is not surprised to learn that some of these saints have succumbed to this significant temptation.

To remind his readers of the details of the immorality practiced by the idolatrous Israelites, the apostle Paul quotes from Exod 32:6. In light of Paul's comments in 10:14-22 and everyone's awareness in antiquity that idolatrous meals included eating and drinking, it is not surprising that Paul would cite a verse which referred to the sinful Israelites sitting down to eat and drink in their own idolatrous rebellion. Since pagan temples and pagan feasts were sometimes associated with debauchery and immorality in the Greco-Roman period, the apostle is trying to warn the Corinthian believers to avoid indulgence in pagan revelry by his citation of Exod 32:6.

10:8 We should not commit sexual immorality, as some of them did — and in one day twenty-three thousand of them died.

That Paul would refer to the problem of sexual immorality in the same breath that he would mention idolatry comes as no surprise. Rom 1 and Jewish texts from the ancient world make it clear the Jews viewed idolatry and sexual immorality as different sides of the same coin. In chapter 10:8 the apostle is referring to a story found in Num 25 in order to underscore the fact that God will destroy his covenant people who participate in sexual debauchery and immorality. It is clear that Paul points to a scene in which Israelite men "began to indulge in sexual immorality with Moabite women who invited them to the sacrifices to their gods. The people ate and bowed down before these gods. So Israel joined in worshiping the Baal of Peor. And the LORD's anger burned against them" (Num 25:1-3). Once again the apostle has used a typological correspondence between the contemporary sins and problems of the Corinthians and those of their forefathers in the Old Testament.

10:9 We should not test the Lord, as some of them did — and were killed by snakes.

Having dealt with idolatry in v. 7 and sexual immorality in v. 8, Paul now turns in this verse to the theme of testing the Lord. Because Paul mentions here the role of snakes in God's punishment of the Israelites, we are able to relate this story to the Old Testament episode mentioned in Num 21:4-9. Paul may be drawing upon this particular Old Testament vignette because in this place the Israelites are complaining about the rules God had set in place which controlled their menu. Since Paul has already shown some interest in 10:6 in the concept of eating and drinking, it should come as no surprise to find the Israelites in Num 21:5 saying against God "we detest this miserable food."

10:10 And do not grumble, as some of them did — and were killed by the destroying angel.

A straightforward reading of Num 21:4ff indicates that one of the problems with the Israelite attitude was their grumbling against God. This leads then to theme of grumbling in 1 Cor 10:10 and the serious consequences of this in the life of the people of God. Usually two Pentateuchal texts are suggested as the probable background to the grumbling motif Paul alludes to here. Typically interpreters refer to Num 14 and 16, the former a story of the general rebellion against Moses' leadership and the latter the better known story of the rebellion of Korah, Dathan, and Abiram. Paul's point is not only that the Corinthians should not grumble against the will of God, but in all probability also that they should not murmur against Paul himself and the instructions he has given them.[5]

---

[5]Robertson and Plummer, *First Epistle of St. Paul*, p. 206.

3. Examples for Us (10:11-13)

[11]**These things happened to them as examples and were written down as warnings for us, on whom the fulfillment of the ages has come. [12]So, if you think you are standing firm, be careful that you don't fall! [13]No temptation has seized you except what is common to man. And God is faithful; he will not let you be tempted beyond what you can bear. But when you are tempted, he will also provide a way out so that you can stand up under it.**

10:11 These things happened to them as examples and were written down as warnings for us, on whom the fulfillment of the ages has come.

Paul mentions again that these punitive actions taken by God were to serve as examples for Christian believers. In fact, Paul continues, these were recorded in Scripture to provide warnings for Corinthian saints. While Scripture clearly has a manifold purpose for the people of God, one of those purposes is to contain warnings so that God's people do not continue to make the same mistakes that their spiritual ancestors made at an earlier time (2 Tim 3:16-17). The term "warnings" (νουθεσία, *nouthesia* and cognates) was a favorite of Paul's. In fact Paul saw warning as a very important part of his apostolic ministry and the ministry that believers had with one another. (See use of this Greek term in Rom 15:14; 1 Cor 4:14; Col 1:28; 3:16; 1 Thess 5:12, 14; 2 Thess 3:15; and Titus 3:10). Paul ends this verse with a very important reference of eschatological significance to his readership. The apostle's phrase "ends of the ages" (translated by the NIV as "the fulfillment of the ages") clearly reflects his eschatological perspective. When Paul uses the term "ages" he is reflecting the Jewish apocalyptic notion of this age and of the coming age (cf. Eph 1:21; 2:7). The apostle has already used the phrase "this age" in 1 Cor 1:20; 2:6, 8; 3:18 in a pejorative sense. Because of Christ's resurrection and current reign at the right hand of God, Paul affirms that Christians live in the final period of human history, a period whose boundaries are set by the resurrection and ascension of Christ at one end and by Christ's second coming at the other end. Since all of God's prior dealings with mankind, both through his general revelation as well as his revelation through his elect people, pointed toward the age characterized by the reign of Christ, Paul affirms all prior Scriptures have as their ultimate goal instruction and teaching for those who live in the era of the Messiah. This is why Paul so naturally embraces the concept that everything which occurred in past generations and everything recorded in sacred Scripture is meaningful for God's people who live in the last days of God's dispensation.[6]

10:12 So, if you think you are standing firm, be careful that you don't fall!

Because of the surrounding contextual injunctions against idolatry as well as Paul's threats to the Corinthians about possible destruction by God, there is little doubt what Paul intends to communicate here. This verse is written to persuade idolatrous Corinthian believers that they can have too much confidence about their security with God. Within the rhetorical context of 1 Cor 10 Paul's reference to standing firm refers to a misplaced confidence that certain believers have that they can continue to participate in immorality and idolatry and never be punished by God.

Even though these saints had Corinth had been baptized, had partaken of the Lord's Supper and had a relationship with Christ, none of these insulated them from the need to be told "be careful that you don't fall." John Calvin's interpretation which says that Paul does not want them to "be afraid that there is doubt about their salvation"[7] can only be maintained by removing this verse from its clear exegetical setting which is characterized by threats of destruction from God because of idolatry, immorality, the testing of God, and open rebellion.

The Christian's assurance of blamelessness based upon the work of God in Christ (1:7-9) was not meant to negate or undermine the teaching found in ch. 10. In fact, as Paul will point out in v. 13, his acknowledgment of the possibility of destruction from God is not predicated on the issue of the faithfulness of God.

---

[6]On Paul's use of the Old Testament consult M. Silva, "Old Testament on Paul," DPL, pp. 630-642.

[7]Calvin, First Epistle, p. 213.

10:13 No temptation has seized you except what is common to man. And God is faithful; he will not let you be tempted beyond what you can bear. But when you are tempted, he will also provide a way out so that you can stand up under it.

In light of the possibility of falling and being destroyed by God, Paul wants to remind the Corinthians that they cannot justifiably excuse themselves from bearing responsibility in their own sinful behavior. In the Greco-Roman world temptations of immorality, idolatry, etc. were commonplace. This means that the Corinthians cannot excuse themselves on the basis of special pleading regarding their unique circumstances in their temptations.

Next the apostle affirms the faithfulness of God, though it is not a faithfulness which will preclude the possibility of the Corinthians sinning and falling. Rather the faithfulness of God is manifested in the fact that he will support them spiritually and prevent them from being overwhelmed by an unbearable temptation. Kistemaker rightly noted in this regard "God's faithfulness to his people is perfect, even though man's faithfulness to him is imperfect. Scripture proves that not God but man is a covenant breaker."[8] Since the faithfulness of God is likewise a doctrinal affirmation of the Old Testament, there is no way that Paul would have assumed the affirmation of the faithfulness of God would excuse God's covenant people from owning moral responsibility.

Nor would the faithfulness of God, as the previous Old Testament illustrations demonstrate, preclude God's severe punishment of his covenant people. Having spoken a word about the character of God ("God is faithful") and a word about the action of God ("he will not let you be tempted"), Paul now shifts to the second person plural and tells the Corinthians about their responsibilities. He instructs them with the words, "you can bear," thereby jerking them out of any misconceived notions of passivity on the part of a believer in moral choices. Paul next affirms that as temptations occur in the context of temptations to immorality and idolatry, God will provide an exit. As the concluding phrase of v. 13 make evident, though, the way out which God provides is

---

[8]Kistemaker, *First Corinthians*, p. 336.

that the believer endures the temptation. C.K. Barrett's analysis of these concluding thoughts and their connection to the following unit of thought in chapter 10 are quite helpful. The Christian

> . . . must resist, and he must not put his trust in false securities; this would be to court and insure disaster. The way out is for those who seek it, not for those who (like the Corinthians) are, where idolatry is concerned, looking for the way in. The connection with the next paragraph makes this clear.[9]

D. IDOL FEASTS AND THE LORD'S SUPPER (10:14-22)

1. The Lord's Supper a Participation (10:14-17)

[14]Therefore, my dear friends, flee from idolatry. [15]I speak to sensible people; judge for yourselves what I say. [16]Is not the cup of thanksgiving for which we give thanks a participation in the blood of Christ? And is not the bread that we break a participation in the body of Christ? [17]Because there is one loaf, we, who are many, are one body, for we all partake of the one loaf.

10:14 Therefore, my dear friends, flee from idolatry.
Because of the occurrence of the word "therefore," (διόπερ, *dioper*) commentators have rightly noted that this is Paul's interpretation of how Christians can endure the temptation. They are, namely, to flee from idolatry. When the Corinthian believer is faced with entrapment in idolatrous or immoral activities, Paul does not expect the believer to wait for some *deus ex machina* to snatch the believer from the jaws of sin. Because of the profound and disastrous results of a saint's participation in idolatry, Paul can think of no better imperative than the word "flee."[10]

---

[9]Barrett, *First Epistle*, p. 229.
[10]See P.W. Comfort, "Idolatry," *DPL*, pp. 424-426.

10:15 I speak to sensible people; judge for yourselves what I say.

Since the apostle has no way to coerce cooperation and obedience from the readers at Corinth, he asks them to consider for themselves the nature of their present behavior. He hopes to win them over by persuasion, part of which includes their own self-evaluation. While it is true that Paul's letters are filled with imperatives, it would be much more accurate to portray his letters as attempts at persuasion rather than attempts at coercion. It is this very awareness that has led so many scholars to appreciate the rhetorical quality of Paul's correspondence.

10:16 Is not the cup of thanksgiving for which we give thanks a participation in the blood of Christ? And is not the bread that we break a participation in the body of Christ?

Keeping in mind that the eating and drinking of sacrificial food is at the heart of Paul's discussion in 8:1-11:1, it is no surprise that Paul brings up the issue of the eating and drinking of the Lord's Supper in 10:16ff. While Paul will spend more time on the issue of the Lord's Supper in 11:17-34, and there treat it in a totally different context, here he uses the issue of the Lord's Supper to help the Corinthians judge for themselves whether their participation in idolatry is proper.[11]

The reference to "cup of thanksgiving" in 10:16 is a reference to the drinking of the wine as a part of the Lord's Supper. As Paul explains that act in this verse, he goes beyond the notion of memorial (i.e., "do this in memory of me"). In this setting he wishes to emphasize the fact that the drinking of the cup is a participation (κοινωνία, *koinōnia*) in the blood of Christ. Christian history is replete with various theories and explanations of Paul's idea here. Witherington's analysis of this is worthy of consideration. He states, "apparently Paul believes that there is more than mere symbols involved in the Lord's Supper. There seems to be some sort of real spiritual communion with Christ, or one might say, an appropriation of the benefits of his death — forgiveness, cleansing, and the like."[12] Most commentators rightly point to the rich Jewish

---

[11]For the historical setting and Paul's theology of the Lord's Supper see esp. I.H. Marshall, "Lord's Supper," *DPL*, pp. 569-575.

[12]Witherington, *Conflict and Community in Corinth*, p. 225.

heritage of the "cup of blessing" and Fee, in particular, points out the fact that the NIV translation "cup of thanksgiving" rather than "cup of blessing" has sometimes "caused interpreters to miss the rich Jewish background of this language."[13]

Even though the sequence of partaking of the Lord's Supper according to 1 Cor 11 is bread followed by cup, in 1 Cor 10 Paul discusses these in reverse order. He next introduces the bread and comments that as Christians eat this bread they participate in the body of Christ. According to 11:24 the apostle Paul obviously knew that the bread of the Lord's Supper corresponded to Christ's broken body. Nevertheless, since the term "body" (σῶμα, sōma) can also refer to the body of Christians, we need to be open to that meaning in Paul's statement also.

10:17 Because there is one loaf, we, who are many, are one body, for we all partake of the one loaf.

It is in this verse that we find Paul referring to the corporate group of believers with the term "body."[14] The loaf that Paul refers to here surely is the loaf which is broken at the celebration of the Lord's Supper, and not just the common breaking of bread which would characterize regular meals. While early Christians often experienced fellowship with one another at regular mealtimes, the context of Paul's argument here would not be nearly as forceful if he had in mind only a regular meal. In order to argue successfully against Christian participation in religious meals in idolatrous situations, it is necessary for Paul to refer to the Christian meal in which one participates in a special way in communion with the Lord.[15] That the participation in this blood of Christ and body of Christ was a church-wide experience is evident in Paul's use of the word "all" in this verse.

---

[13]Fee, *First Epistle*, p. 467.
[14]R.Y.K. Fung, "Body of Christ," *DPL*, pp. 76-82.
[15]Ibid., p. 77.

2. The Lord's Table and the Table of Demons (10:18-22)

[18]Consider the people of Israel: Do not those who eat the sacrifices participate in the altar? [19]Do I mean then that a sacrifice offered to an idol is anything, or that an idol is anything? [20]No, but the sacrifices of pagans are offered to demons, not to God, and I do not want you to be participants with demons. [21]You cannot drink the cup of the Lord and the cup of demons too; you cannot have a part in both the Lord's table and the table of demons. [22]Are we trying to arouse the Lord's jealousy? Are we stronger than he?

10:18 Consider the people of Israel: Do not those who eat the sacrifices participate in the altar?

Paul reverts again to scriptural examples to undergird the point at hand. The spiritual reality of which Paul is needing to convince the Corinthians is the fact that eating sacrificial meals in a pagan cultic context has profound spiritual implications for the act of idolatry. The verbal link between Paul's affirmation in 10:18 and the preceding arguments in 10:15-17 is the Greek word κοινω-νοί (*koinōnoi*) and its cognates, which are translated in the NIV by the words "participation" and "participate." This is Paul's way of proving to the readership that there is an essential connection, attested by scriptural practice, between eating sacrificial food and solidarity with the religion and the deity to whom the food had been offered.

10:19 Do I mean then that a sacrifice offered to an idol is anything, or that an idol is anything?

At this point it is necessary for Paul to anticipate and refute possible objections from those Corinthian believers who are unpersuaded by his logic and reasoning. One of the counter arguments that could be made by a Corinthian idolater in the church is to say that Paul's argument falls apart because it assumes the existence of the deity associated with the altar. Therefore Paul raises the question of whether or not his own statement assumes the existence of these pagan deities. If Paul's argument does assume the existence of these pagan deities, then he has just lost his argument against these antagonists, and, in fact, contradicted the monotheistic affirmations which he made in 8:4-6.

Fee makes the observation that the NIV phrase "sacrifice offered to an idol" is incongruous with the flow of Paul's argument since this is the term which was translated in 8:1 as "food sacrificed to idols."[16]

10:20 No, but the sacrifices of pagans are offered to demons, not to God, and I do not want you to be participants with demons.

Paul answers with an emphatic "no" to the suggestion that his argumentation requires a belief in the existence of the gods of Greece and Rome. Nevertheless, he argues in this verse that there are malevolent spiritual forces associated with pagan altars even though they could not correctly be identified as the gods and goddesses of Greece and Rome.[17] By this strategic argument Paul is able to continue to affirm Christian monotheism while at the same time advocating a spiritual frame of reference that can justify his imperative to the Corinthians to flee from idolatry (1 Cor 10:14).

Paul then claims that when pagans worship their ostensible gods and goddesses they are in fact offering sacrifice to demons. Continuing to use his theme word *koinōnoi*, Paul teaches that participation in pagan idolatry is in fact participation in demons. Accordingly, the apostle is accusing these Christians who have been assimilated to their religious environment, or perhaps never completely left it, of worshiping demons. As Everett Ferguson makes clear in his important work on demonology in antiquity, Jews, Christians and pagans in the first century all believed in the existence of these malevolent spiritual beings.[18]

---

[16]Fee, *First Epistle*, p. 471, fn. 44.

[17]D.G. Reese, "Demons, New Testament," *ABD*, Vol. 2. 140-142, is not as helpful in regard to the significance of this text as he is with texts from the Gospels.

[18]E. Ferguson, *Demonology of the Early Christian World* (Lewiston, NY: E. Mellen Press, 1984).

10:21 You cannot drink the cup of the Lord and the cup of demons too; you cannot have a part in both the Lord's table and the table of demons.

In dogmatic tones and exclusivistic language, Paul makes clear that his gospel does not allow the kind of religious pluralism being practiced by those believers whom he is addressing in this section. The notion of religious exclusivism reflected in Paul's terse words here have their roots deep in the soil of Old Testament monotheism and covenant jealousy expressed in the Ten Commandments and other important Old Testament texts. In all probability some of these neophyte believers in Paul's churches at Corinth found this kind of religious exclusivism a difficult pill to swallow. They lived in a large metropolitan area in which one could find scores of temples, shrines, and altars to pagan deities, and there would not have been a single part of their education and upbringing that would have told them they could not worship all of these pagan gods and goddesses at the same time. Sounding much like one of the prophets of the Old Testament, the apostle Paul would not tolerate the kind of religious syncretism and pluralism manifested by believers who wish to participate in idolatrous feasts. For the apostle, loyalty to the Lord and loyalty to demons are mutually exclusive.

10:22 Are we trying to arouse the Lord's jealousy? Are we stronger than he?

It is precisely because Paul knows of the terrible consequences that can fall upon the people of God when they apostasize into immorality and idolatry that he raises the issue of the Lord's jealousy in this verse. The apostle is obviously drawing upon an Old Testament theme that arises from the character of Yahweh. As Fee rightly points out, "the term 'jealousy' is a reflection of the Old Testament motif of God's self-revelation (Exod 20:5), related to his holiness and power, in which he used to be understood as so absolutely without equal that he will brook no rivals to his devotion."[19]

---

[19]Fee, *First Epistle*, p. 474.

Because of the punitive character of God's actions described in the Old Testament Scriptures which Paul has drawn upon in his argument from 10:1-22, the apostle finishes this unit of thought with a rhetorical question. Do the Corinthians really believe that they are stronger than God? If they answer yes, then Paul would say they are fools. If they answer no, then they should consider the consequences of their idolatrous and immoral behavior. As Calvin noted on this verse, "anyone who fights with God is voluntarily inviting his own ruin, nothing less. Therefore, if we are afraid of having God for an enemy, we should have a greater fear of trying to make excuses for flagrant sins, i.e., anything that is in conflict with his Word. We should also shudder at the thought of calling in question things which he has told us."[20]

3. The Christian's Freedom (10:23-11:1)

[23]"Everything is permissible" — but not everything is beneficial. "Everything is permissible" — but not everything is constructive. [24]Nobody should seek his own good, but the good of others.

[25]Eat anything sold in the meat market without raising questions of conscience, [26]for, "The earth is the Lord's, and everything in it."[a]

[27]If some unbeliever invites you to a meal and you want to go, eat whatever is put before you without raising questions of conscience. [28]But if anyone says to you, "This has been offered in sacrifice," then do not eat it, both for the sake of the man who told you and for conscience' sake[b] — [29]the other man's conscience, I mean, not yours. For why should my freedom be judged by another's conscience? [30]If I take part in the meal with thankfulness, why am I denounced because of something I thank God for?

[31]So whether you eat or drink or whatever you do, do it all for the glory of God. [32]Do not cause anyone to stumble, whether Jews, Greeks or the church of God — [33]even as I try to please eve-

---

[20]Calvin, *First Epistle*, p. 220.

rybody in every way. For I am not seeking my own good but the good of many, so that they may be saved. [1]Follow my example, as I follow the example of Christ.

[a]26 Psalm 24:1   [b]28 Some manuscripts *conscience' sake, for "the earth is the Lord's and everything in it"*

10:23 "Everything is permissible" — but not everything is beneficial. "Everything is permissible" — but not everything is constructive.

In the unit of thought stretching from 10:23-11:1 the apostle introduces the last scenario under which he will analyze the matter of eating food offered to idols. Given the use of quotation marks at 10:23 in the NIV, one sees Paul giving rejoinders to slogans of freedom and liberty coming from believers in Corinth. The twofold repetition of the slogan "everything is permissible" (πάντα ἔξεστιν, *panta exestin*) is therefore understood to be the slogan for the philosophy of those who are unconcerned about the consequences of their freedom in the matter of eating food offered to idols. In a response that has some similarities to the contrast between knowledge and love in 8:1ff, Paul here teaches that permission is not the final and sole criterion when determining whether an action is right or wrong. While one certainly needs to ask the question regarding permissibility in ethical matters, Paul emphasizes that one must also ask the question about whether actions are beneficial.[21] Paul's second rejoinder in this verse "but not everything is constructive" has strong verbal parallels to Paul's wording in 8:1. The Greek verb (οἰκοδομέω, *oikodomeō*) translated "is constructive" in 10:23 was more accurately translated at 8:1 as "builds up."

10:24 Nobody should seek his own good, but the good of others.

Pauline interpersonal ethics rely heavily on the notion of service to others and loving one's neighbor as oneself (on this point see notes at 1 Cor 14).

---

[21]See esp. J. Paul Sampley, *Walking Between the Times. Paul's Moral Reasoning*, pp. 60-62.

10:25 Eat anything sold in the meat market without raising questions of conscience,

Even if a believer never enters a pagan temple and never participates in a religious sacrificial service to an idol, Paul knows that the believer must still deal with the issue of eating food that had been sold in meat markets which received their meat from idolatrous sacrifices. This fact is well established in classical literature. An amazingly high percentage of meat available in the public market made its way there after having been part of an animal sacrifice in honor of a particular Greek or Roman deity. Paul has no problem with the believer eating food that had been offered to a deity as long as the Christian did not participate in the sacrificial act itself. The fact that Paul has an indifferent attitude toward this kind of food is made evident by the fact that he refers to the issue of conscience in 10:25.

10:26 for, "The earth is the Lord's, and everything in it."

The radical monotheism expressed in Ps 24:1 and quoted by Paul here frees the believer from concerns about idolatrous contamination of the food he eats. As long as the believer is not involved in overt worship of an idol, Paul is able to cut the cord between the idolatrous contamination of the meat in a temple sacrifice and its adverse impact upon believers. Since the gods and goddesses of Greece and Rome do not exist, and since everything in the earth belongs to Yahweh, the believer in the Roman colony of Corinth is freed to participate without fear in the consumption of this food.

10:27 If some unbeliever invites you to a meal and you want to go, eat whatever is put before you without raising questions of conscience.

While it is clear in this verse that the invitation to dine comes from an unbeliever, Paul does not explicitly say where the meal will take place. Nevertheless, since this scenario assumes that the believer would not necessarily know the origin of the food, it seems unlikely that the unbeliever is inviting the believer to dine at a pagan temple. For in the temple context the believer would rightly assume that the food had been offered to the deity of the temple in which they were eating. Paul does not specify the particular occasion for this meal. Based upon the ancient evidence available to us, one could speculate about any number of possible occasions for a believer to be invited to dine with unbelievers. If the believer wants to go, Paul says, he may with a clear conscience eat what is put before him. Based upon the implications of the radical monotheism of 10:26, Paul says in 10:27 that the Christian is under no obligation to inquire about the nature of the food and its contact with temple ceremonies.

10:28 But if anyone says to you, "This has been offered in sacrifice," then do not eat it, both for the sake of the man who told you and for conscience' sake —

Paul's depiction of this scene becomes less clear now with his use of the term "anyone." In particular, scholars have debated about who this anyone is. Fee has summarized the options under the following categories. This anyone could be either the host who extended the invitation, or a pagan fellow guest at the same meal, or third, a fellow believer.[22] The line of reasoning and historical arguments used to defend any one of these three possibilities are usually extremely intricate, and none of them are problem free. There are cogent arguments, however, that the anyone of 10:28 is a pagan.

The support for this is philological and is based upon the Greek term which is rendered in the NIV as "has been offered in sacrifice." The term that Paul uses is ἱερόθυτον (*hierothyton*) and is the term a pagan would use to describe this food. This is a completely different term from that which Paul has been using throughout this section which reflects his Christian convictions and refers to idol food. The term that Paul has been using throughout this section is εἰδωλόθυτον (*eidōlothyton*) and is a pejorative term reflecting his Christian convictions that his food is not sacred food, but rather food that has been offered to an idol. The term "idol" is of course itself a negative term reflecting a Christian conviction and not the convictions of a pagan who believed in these deities.

---

[22]Fee, *First Epistle*, p. 484.

Once the believer then has learned from the pagan at the meal that this food had been offered to a deity, Paul says that the believer should not consume the food. Equally perplexing is Paul's reasoning when he says that the food should not be eaten both for the sake of the man who told you and for conscience' sake. If the person who told you was a pagan, in what way is Paul concerned about this person, and furthermore, what does conscience have to do with this onlooking nonbeliever? It seems to be the case, if Witherington's analysis is correct, that Paul is in fact concerned about the conscience of the pagan who has pointed out to the believer that it is idol meat. "In short, it would be a poor witness," as Witherington argues, "because the host was trying to be sensitive to the Christian's religious persuasion and perhaps assume that Christian's adherence to some derivative sort of Judaism, would like Jews, not partake of such food. . . . So Paul says to abstain for the pagan's sake so as to uphold a good image of moral consistency in the pagan's eye."[23]

10:29 the other man's conscience, I mean, not yours. For why should my freedom be judged by another's conscience?

Paul reiterates the fact that it is the conscience of another that he is concerned about. Paul may well have anticipated the fact that those at Corinth whom he is attempting to instruct would have claimed that their conscience was clear. If so, one can then see Paul's need to reemphasize that it is the conscience of another that concerns him. While we often think of the offended conscience as belonging to a fellow believer, 10:32ff makes it clear that Paul is concerned about the conscience both of the Christian and the non-Christian. Paul's use of the catchword "my freedom" in 10:29 alerts us to the fact that he is having to persuade fellow saints who are not accustomed to having their freedoms curtailed by the thoughts and opinions of others. The issue of the curtailment of personal freedoms picks up on Paul's treatment of this issue throughout ch. 9.

---

[23]Witherington, *Conflict in Community in Corinth*, pp. 227-228.

10:30 If I take part in the meal with thankfulness, why am I denounced because of something I thank God for?

This verse indicates that Paul understands how those whom he is attempting to persuade would respond to his counsel in this section. The occurrence of the two words "thankfulness" and "thank" in this verse points to a situation where believers (who were not so concerned about the good of others; 10:24) would have elevated their own thankful attitude as the sole criterion for whether it was right to eat or not. Once again the apostle is driving his readership to see the point that the sole criterion is not what pleases or satisfies self. Rather the believer must be concerned about how his actions impact others.

10:31 So whether you eat or drink or whatever you do, do it all for the glory of God.

At this point Paul leaves the prior style of giving specific stipulations and moves on to concluding comments where he gives general principles. The point is that the believer's behavior must be guided by a concern for a transcendent perspective. Unlike the Judaism contemporary with the Apostle Paul and many of the pagan religions of that period, early Christianity as conceived by Paul promulgated no dietary legislation. Accordingly, this correlation of 10:31 between the honor of God and the consumption of food and beverage should not be seen as reflecting first century Christian dietary codes. Rather, for Paul there is no area of life, even mundane meal considerations like those spelled out in 10:23-30, which should not be regulated by a concern for the glory of God.[24]

10:32 Do not cause anyone to stumble, whether Jews, Greeks or the church of God —

Paul's concern about causing anyone to stumble is related to three possible groups of people: Jews, Greeks, or the church of God. In light of the inclusion of the phrase church of God, it seems most natural to understand the term Jews and Greeks to refer to those individuals who are not in the church of God. Since

---

[24]Calvin, *First Epistle*, pp. 224-225.

the issue of ethnicity is almost non-existent in Corinthians, as opposed to a book like Romans or Galatians, the two terms Jews and Greeks is a euphemistic way of referring to those who are unsaved.

10:33 even as I try to please everybody in every way. For I am not seeking my own good but the good of many, so that they may be saved.

A proper interpretation of this verse requires that one perceives the rhetorical exaggeration involved in Paul's claim. Even a cursory knowledge of Paul's life and letters demonstrates that he made many choices which were not an attempt to please everybody in every way (see notes on 9:19-22). The Greek term σύμφορον (*symphoron*, translated here as "good") is a cognate of the word rendered "is beneficial" in 10:23. Accordingly, Paul begins and ends this section with his thoughts focused on the centrality in Christian ethics of the conviction that in matters of indifference the believer should be focused on the needs of others rather than himself. Paul's inexorable commitment to the good of others manifested in 1 Cor 8 and 1 Cor 10:23-11:1 is based ultimately on his concern about the salvation of others. Paul's use of a purpose clause (ἵνα [*hina*] + subjunctive) highlights this correlation between his practical ethical advice and his concern for others' relationship to the Lord. (See notes on a similar theme at 9:22.) The apostle realizes that his counsel that one should abdicate his own rights and preferences in deference to the salvation of others finds its genesis in the life and teaching of Jesus himself.

11:1 Follow my example, as I follow the example of Christ.

The chapter division at 1 Cor 11:1 is somewhat unfortunate since it gives the impression that 11:1 began the new section of 11:1-17. It has been universally acknowledged for centuries that the next unit of thought is found in 11:2-17. Calvin, for example, noted, "This shows us how badly the chapters have been divided, because this sentence [11:1] has been separated from the preceding sentences, to which it belongs by right, and joined to those which follow, to which it is quite irrelevant."[25]

This is the second time that Paul has explicitly urged the Corinthians to imitate his own example (cf. 4:16). This is a fitting way for Paul to conclude the three chapter section, 8-10, wherein we have seen him implicitly urge others to follow his own example in Christian ethics. By correlating his own life and example with that of the example of Christ, Paul is overtly anchoring his moral admonition here in the life and the teaching of Jesus of Nazareth. As Robertson and Plummer noted in this regard, "It is seldom that Saint Paul notes any of the details of our Lord's life on earth, and it is therefore unlikely that he is thinking of anything but the subject at hand — sacrificing one's own rights and pleasures for the good of others. Nevertheless, the knowledge which Saint Paul displays of details is sufficient to suggest that he knew a great deal more than he mentions."[26]

---

[25]Calvin, *First Epistle*, p. 226.
[26]Robertson and Plummer, *First Epistle of St. Paul*, p. 226.

1 CORINTHIANS 11

VI. LITURGICAL ABERRATIONS (11:2-34)

A. PROPRIETY IN WORSHIP (11:2-16)

1. Head Coverings in Worship (11:2-10)

[2]I praise you for remembering me in everything and for holding to the teachings,[a] just as I passed them on to you.

[3]Now I want you to realize that the head of every man is Christ, and the head of the woman is man, and the head of Christ is God. [4]Every man who prays or prophesies with his head covered dishonors his head. [5]And every woman who prays or prophesies with her head uncovered dishonors her head — it is just as though her head were shaved. [6]If a woman does not cover her head, she should have her hair cut off; and if it is a disgrace for a woman to have her hair cut or shaved off, she should cover her head. [7]A man ought not to cover his head,[b] since he is the image and glory of God; but the woman is the glory of man. [8]For man did not come from woman, but woman from man; [9]neither was man created for woman, but woman for man. [10]For this reason, and because of the angels, the woman ought to have a sign of authority on her head.

[a]2 Or *traditions*   [b]4-7 Or [4]*Every man who prays or prophesies with long hair dishonors his head.* [5]*And every woman who prays or prophesies with no covering ⌊of hair⌋ on her head dishonors her head—she is just like one of the "shorn women." * [6]*If a woman has no covering, let her be for now with short hair, but since it is a disgrace for a woman to have her hair shorn or shaved, she should grow it again.* [7]*A man ought not to have long hair*

11:2 I praise you for remembering me in everything and for holding to the teachings, just as I passed them on to you.

A few comments about the literary structure and themes of this new section of 1 Corinthians are in order. First, there is no occurrence of the "now about" (περὶ δέ, *peri de*) introductory phrase which many interpreters believe signal topics raised by the Corinthians that the apostle is answering (see Introduction; cf. 1 Cor 7:1; 8:1; 12:1; 16:1). Regardless of whether Paul is responding to inquiries in chapter 11, he clearly has two major issues before his readership, each of which begins with a form of verbal parallelism. The first section, 11:2-16, begins with the phrase "I praise you" while the second unit, 11:17-34, states "I have no praise for you." Another feature of both topics in this chapter is that they deal with matters related to the liturgical and devotional practices of the Corinthian believers. With the primary focus of 11:2-16 being on prayer and prophecy (see notes on 11:4-5), and the focus of 11:17-34 being on the Lord's Supper (11:20), one is constrained to see worship as the common denominator between these two blocks of Pauline instruction.

Consistent with Paul's words of praise in this first section, the reader notices the mild tone, relative to 11:17-34, in Paul's teaching. The apostle mentions two matters which serve as the basis (ὅτι, *hoti*) of his praise. They are the fact that the Corinthians remember him and that they embrace the religious traditions (παραδόσεις, *paradoseis*) with which he had instructed them in the past. All of this is to prepare them for additional religious tradition with which he hopes to correct the impropriety of their worship practices. This strategy of praising his readers prior to correction is not an uncommon rhetorical feature in Paul's letters or ancient Greco-Roman moral philosophers. The pagan author Plutarch encouraged this pattern of behavior in his philosophy. He wrote,

> We ought to keep close watch upon our friends not only when they go wrong but also when they are right, and indeed the first step should be commendation cheerfully be-

stowed. Then later . . . we should give them an application of frankness."[1]

11:3 Now I want you to realize that the head of every man is Christ, and the head of the woman is man, and the head of Christ is God.

Current literature on the issue of the Christian faith and its view(s) regarding the role, status, and function of men and women can easily be overwhelming and befuddling, particularly to the non-specialist. With the inundation of publications, all with differing agendas, scholars have found it helpful to categorize major schools of thought on the topic of the Bible and its view(s) about women. From the perspectives of a non-feminist (i.e., "believes hierarchical relationships based upon gender are still normative within the church,") Jack Cottrell has categorized feminist interpretations into four groups:[2]

---

[1]Plutarch "How to Tell a Flatterer from a Friend" 73C-74E, cited in Malherbe, *Moral Exhortation*, no. 21, p. 53.

[2]These summaries are taken from Jack Cottrell, *Gender Roles and the Bible: Creation, the Fall, and Redemption*, (Joplin: College Press, 1994; cf. Cottrell's earlier work, *Feminism and the Bible. An Introduction to Feminism for Christians*, 1992). The groupings would understandably have different labels when discussed by a feminist. The feminist Roman Catholic scholar Carolyn Osiek has surveyed representative literature in "The Feminist and the Bible: Hermeneutical Alternatives," (in *Feminist Perspectives on Biblical Scholarship*, ed. Adela Y. Collins, 1985, pp. 93-105) and gives these five alternatives:

1. Rejectionist. The Scriptures are no longer useful and "the entire Judeo-Christian tradition is hopelessly sinful, corrupt, and unredeemable" (p. 98).

2. Loyalist. The Scriptures are still essentially valid as the Word of God, and "need not be vindicated by human authority" (p. 99); the human happiness which is promised through the Scriptures "may not always conform to the standards of contemporary culture" (p. 99).

3. Revisionist. This perspective wants to hold to a Christian faith which acknowledges the ancient reality of the "male-dominated, androcentric, and discriminatory" characteristics of the biblical tradition, but believes that these were part of the historical, *but not theological and spiritual*, nature of biblical faith. This perspective becomes "the starting point for many feminist religious thinkers with liberal theologies of revelation who

1. Secular Feminism. These "have abandoned all religious belief as having any positive relation to feminist philosophy" and base their views "on human philosophy and humanistic theories of social justice" (p. 13).

2. Goddess Feminism. This approach believes "that Goddess worship was the original nearly-universal religion and that it fostered a matriarchal culture [and that] feminist goals can best be achieved through a 'return to the Goddess,' [a return that means becoming] an active part of the current revival of neo-pagan religions and witchcraft" (p. 15).

3. Liberal Feminism. This approach "shares the same general goals of secular and Goddess feminism, but it pursues these goals from within the Christian framework. . . .While granting that the Bible is mostly androcentric and patriarchal, they decline to abandon it altogether and to give up their connection with Jesus Christ. . . . Liberal Christian feminism does not accept the Bible as the revealed and inspired Word of God nor as any kind of canonical authority [but rather believes that] women's experience is the ultimate criterion of all truth" (pp. 16-17).

---

are not willing to abandon the tradition entirely as do the rejectionists" (p. 101).

4. Sublimationist. This hermeneutic is a form of gender separatism whose "basic premise is the otherness of the feminine," a feminine which "operates by its own principles and rules" which are decidedly "distinct from those of the male realm" (p. 101). Those who are attracted to this hermeneutic usually focus on the "glorification of the eternal feminine in biblical symbolism" such as "Israel as virgin and bride of God, the church as bride of Christ and mother of the faithful" and on "assertions of the stability and rightness of distinctive feminine and masculine modes of being" (p. 102).

5. Liberationist. As one can anticipate from the name of this perspective, this approach works from the broad assumptions of liberation theology. Redemption is interpreted fundamentally to mean that the Gospel "for women means liberation from patriarchal domination so that all human persons can be for each other partners and equals in the common task" (p. 103). Only biblical texts which "promote the full humanity of women" are granted much authority, while "this narrow criterion of revelation leads the liberationist method to eulogize the prophets, Jesus, and sometimes Paul while writing off other, particularly later New Testament, writers who do not meet the liberation criterion" (p. 104).

4. Biblical Feminism. This perspective accepts "the final authority of the Bible and . . . believes that feminism is the Bible's authentic teaching . . . [and] interprets the Bible as consistently teaching an egalitarian view of women" (pp. 18-19).

In light of the assumptions of a historical-exegetical method and the numerous exegetical abuses set forth both by feminists and anti-feminists, a few general observations are in order. First, when interpreters go beyond asking solely historical questions and attempt to isolate the differences between the temporary and the eternal in the teachings and affirmations of Paul, they must keep in mind that the apostle himself left no explicit guidelines for this task. That is, Paul did not employ some system of annotation, such as asterisks, to inform his original readers which instructions he thought were "only temporary." A historically honest interpretation ought at least acknowledge what the apostle thought his own doctrines, and their foundations, were.

Second, one needs to be cautious about the dangers of feminist alchemy, whereby the feminist interpreter attempts to transmute, based upon ill-informed historical reconstructions and tendentious philology, Pauline words and theology into something deemed to be more desirable and precious than the original. There are far too many examples in current publications where ideology is paraded about masquerading as exegesis.

Finally, in its more egregious forms, current feminist theories disregard any part of the Scripture that does not conform to their own cultural, philosophical, psychological, and social agendas.[3] It is no coincidence that feminist interpretations are often mere echos of whatever the currently popular social or political views happen to be.

Irrespective of what one chooses to do with the issue of feminism in the current setting, the intention of Paul can be more judiciously encountered and interpreted when his ideas are not jerked from the soil of his response to a first generation urban church in the Roman colony of Corinth.

---

[3]This type of disregard was seen early on in Luther's negative comments toward New Testament writings such as the Epistle of James or the Revelation of John.

The word "head" dominates in 1 Corinthians 11:3. The frequency of the term "head" (κεφαλή, *kephalē*) in this chapter (9×) is a significant indicator of the issue under discussion in 11:2-16. Specifically, Paul explains his position in this section on the basis of the alternation between the literal and the metaphorical use of the term. He does this in order to deal with two head-related ideas, namely, the liturgical head covering and the significance of hair (or lack of it) on one's head.

The occasional and contextual nature of Paul's choice of wording in this verse is important to notice. It is evident that the meaning of the term "head" in the paired formulations of 11:3 seems to be created for this particular section since it is found in this connection nowhere else in Paul's writings. Specifically, Paul nowhere else uses this term "head" (*kephalē*) to denote the relationship between Christ and every male. Nor is there corroborating evidence elsewhere in Paul for his use of this word to depict the relationship between men and women.[4] Most significantly, in all the Christological formulas and texts in Paul there are none which use the terminology of head to talk about the relationship between God and Christ. What stands before the interpreter, then, is another instance in which the apostle responds to a problematic situation with terminology and rhetoric which both arises from the *ad hoc* problem and corresponds to the occasional nature of the situation.

An important and detailed philological debate has arisen in the past few decades over the connotations of the Greek term *kephalē* as it is used metaphorically in this section of 1 Corinthians. The two basic interpretations are that the term should be understood as meaning either (1) source or (2) leader (=in authority over). The fact that the forceful impetus for promoting interpretation no. 1 typically comes from New Testament scholars (e.g., Gordon Fee) with strong feminist perspectives explains why this theory is still somewhat novel. Those interpreters who endorse the second view represent both scholars who support the ordination of women as well as those with no interest in supporting the ordination of women. English translations, as one

---

[4]Paul's teaching in Ephesians 5:21-33 is not about men and women, but rather about husbands and wives.

would expect, merely translate the word *kephalē* as "head" and leave it to the reader to interpret its metaphorical connotations. The evaluation of Witherington seems correct on this point when he reasons that, "since the context has to do with authority, authorization, and order in worship, it would seem more probable that *kephale* has the metaphorical sense" of leader.[5]

While the term "hierarchy" or "chain of command" will hardly do as a metaphor for the linking together of the three paired relationships (i.e., God-Christ; Christ-man; man-woman) in 11:3, one is not within earshot of this text if he cannot see that Paul, particularly in light of the following arguments of 11:2-16, is primarily focused on (re)affirming a certain liturgical propriety (see 11:13, "is it proper?" πρέπον ἐστίν, *prepon estin*) that employs a gender criterion.

In light of the fact that some of the Corinthian saints are not disposed to acquiesce to Paul's judgments in this matter, as he himself acknowledges (11:16), Paul attempts in 11:3 to prove the validity of his position by making an appeal to "the arrangements which God has appointed"[6] or, in more modern terms, "Paul's view is that the creation order should be properly manifested, not obliterated, in Christian worship. . . ."[7]

Due to the fact that Paul makes a correlation between "divine order" (i.e., God is the *kephalē* of Christ) and male "headship" (i.e., man is the *kephalē* of woman) at Corinth, some interpreters with feminist-egalitarian commitments end up promoting an egalitarian view of the Trinity in its depiction of the relationship between God and Christ. This view is obviously non-Pauline! (See 1 Cor 15:28.)

In order to keep the implications of Paul's argument clear, it is crucial to translate the pairing man/woman (ἀνήρ/γυνή, *anēr/gynē*) consistently in this particular rhetorical section. Accordingly, not only is it poor translation technique, but it also confuses the historical issues at Corinth to vacillate between man-

---

[5]Witherington, *Conflict and Community in Corinth*, pp. 237-38; Witherington depends here on the research of J. A. Fitzmyer, "Another Look at ΚΕΦΑΛΗ in 1 Cor. 11.3," *New Testament Studies* 35 (1989): 503-11.

[6]Calvin, *First Epistle*, p. 228.

[7]Witherington, *Conflict and Community in Corinth*, p. 236.

woman and husband-wife in this section, or to interpret this section through the situation addressed in Eph 5:21ff where marriage is clearly meant.

11:4 Every man who prays or prophesies with his head covered dishonors his head.

The history of the interpretation of 1 Cor 11:4 manifests a wide diversity of methodologies and corresponding conclusions. [8] Two major methodological problems explain most of the incorrect interpretations of this section. Either the interpreter is:

1. remiss in understanding and using the appropriate sources from ancient cultures or

2. preoccupied with demonstrating that Paul's principal complaint is with Christian women at Corinth.

1. John C. Hurd, for example, questions the necessity of knowing the historical information about the background to this situation when he writes, "It is not necessary to decide the difficult historical problem of the actual social *mores* which were current at that time."[9] Others, such as Gordon Fee, have misjudged the availability of the pertinent evidence. Contrary to the evidence of a plethora of literary and archaeological evidence Fee concluded, "There is almost no evidence (paintings, reliefs, statuary, etc.) that men in any of the cultures (Greek, Roman, Jew) covered their heads." After abandoning the hope of finding a historical and cultural matrix that would provide insight into the Corinthian situation, he is drawn inevitably to conclude, "In the final analysis, however, we simply have to admit that we do not know. In any case, it is hypothetical, whatever it was."[10]

These conclusions by Fee and others simply do not acknowledge the relevant archaeological and literary evidence from antiquity. Notwithstanding this neglect, the ancient evidence is incontestible and widespread. Plutarch, a Greek writing author who lived during the early Roman Empire, wrote that the Romans, as

---

[8]Oster, "When Men Wore Veils to Worship: Historical Context of I Cor. 11:4." *New Testament Studies* 34 (1988):481-505.

[9]John C. Hurd, *The Origin of 1 Corinthians* (New York: Seabury Press, 1965), p. 184.

[10]Fee, *First Epistle*, pp. 507-508.

opposed to Greeks, "thus worshipped the gods, either humbling themselves by concealing the head, or rather by pulling the toga over their ears."[11] The later author Dionysus of Halicarnassus likewise observed that this use of the devotional head covering was an important Roman religious practice used when participating in prayer, prophecy, or sacrifice.[12] The Latin author Valerius Flaccus, writing in the late first century A.D., mentions the pagan prophet Mopsus who "veiling his head" worships by offering a libation.[13] Virgil, the famous Latin author who wrote shortly after the time of the refounding of Corinth as a Roman colony, also sheds light on this significant Roman liturgical practice. In the epic story of Rome's beginnings recorded in the *Aeneid*, one learns that it was sacred law for the Romans to veil their heads when worshiping and sacrificing to their gods and goddesses. Regarding this custom and tradition the prophet Helenus proclaims that "This mode of sacrifice do thou keep, thou and thy company; by this observance let thy children's children in purity stand fast."[14] Both the frequency and the significance of this pietistic head covering gesture is attested by the Latin author Lucretius who ridicules Roman piety with these words,

> It is no piety to show oneself often with head covered, turning towards a stone and approaching every altar, none to fall prostrate upon the ground and to spread open the palms before shrines of the gods, none to sprinkle altars with the blood of beasts in shows and to link vow to vow.[15]

In addition to an enormous amount of literary data that depicts this Roman devotional head-covering, it is also attested by

---

[11]*Roman Questions* 266d. Cited according to Frank C. Babbitt, *Plutarch's Moralia* (Loeb Classical Library. Cambridge: Harvard University Press, 1972), p. 23.

[12]*Roman Antiquities* 12.16.22-23.

[13]*Argonautica* 5.95-97.

[14]*Aeneid* 3.403-09. Translation from *Virgil* (Loeb Classical Library. Cambridge: Harvard University Press, 1956), Vol. 1, p. 374.

[15]*Concerning the Nature of Things* 5.1198-1200. Translation from *Lucretius de Rerum Natura* (Loeb Classical Library. Cambridge: Harvard University Press, 1982), p. 424.

visual evidence on ancient Roman coins, Roman statues, and Roman altar reliefs from around the Mediterranean world. Even though some interpreters of this Corinthian text are yet unconvinced that this widespread Roman practice should be seen as the backdrop for this verse,[16] other scholars are now convinced that this provides the most plausible explanation for the situation assumed by this opening section of 1 Cor 11:2ff.[17] All things considered, it is not a radical conclusion to affirm that a congregation in a large Roman colony would have some Roman members who would have been converted from Roman paganism and would have brought some of their devotional and liturgical traditions with them into the worship assemblies of the church of God.

2. Probably because of the gender of most interpreters of 1 Corinthians, many have thought that the only aberrant believers whom the apostle was addressing in this section were women. As Jerome Murphy-O'Connor has shown, it is a masculine bias that has focused on Paul's injunctions in 11:2-16 and concluded that no men were at fault.[18] Typical of the history of this sexist exegesis were comments by:

a. Archibald Robertson and Alfred Plummer: "There is no reason for supposing that men at Corinth had been making this mistake in the congregation. The conduct which would be improper for men is mentioned in order to give point to the censure on women, who in this matter had been acting as men."[19]

b. Charles Hodge: "The thing to be corrected was women appearing in public assemblies unveiled . . . . Men are mentioned only for the sake of illustrating the principle."[20]

c. Hans Conzelmann: "The parallelism between vv 4 and 5 expresses the fundamental equality of rights although it is only the *woman's* conduct that is at issue."[21]

---

[16]E.g., M. Black, "1 Cor. 11:2-16—A Re-investigation," *Essays on Women in Earliest Christianity*, Vol. I.

[17]Witherington, *Conflict and Community in Corinth*, pp. 231-240.

[18]Jerome Murphy-O'Connor, "Sex and Logic in I Corinthians 11:2-16," *CBQ* 42 (1980) 483.

[19]Robertson and Plummer, *First Epistle of St. Paul*, p. 229.

[20]Charles Hodge, *An Exposition of the First Epistle to the Corinthians* (Grand Rapids: Eerdmans, 1965), pp. 207-208.

d. F.F. Bruce: "It is improbable that Christian men were actually veiling their heads in Corinth; the reference to their
(hypothetically) doing so is necessary to complete the argument."[22]

An overview of 11:2-16 makes it clear that Paul is quite even-
handed in his directives and arguments about both men (ἀνήρ,
anēr) and women (γυνή, *gynē*) in this chapter:

Verses	mentions of *anēr*	mentions of *gynē*
11:3	2	1
11:4	1	0
11:5	0	1
11:6	0	2
11:7	2	1
11:8	2	2
11:9	2	2
11:10	0	1
11:11	2	2
11:12	2	2
11:13	0	1
11:14	1	0
11:15	0	1
TOTAL	**14**	**16**

Another clear implication of this statistical evidence is that in
Paul's mind gender is the controlling issue of the paradigm with
which he is operating. This means that social status issues were
not what the apostle was striving to counter.[23]

There are three exegetical points in the text that need to be
mentioned. First, in light of the Greek words used by Paul for the
phrase "with his head covered," (κατὰ κεφαλῆς ἔχων, *kata kephalēs
echōn*) there is no need to question whether he had the idea of a
head covering in mind. In light of the ancient philological evi-

---

[21]Hans Conzelmann, *I Corinthians* (Philadelphia: Fortress Press, 1975)
p. 184, note 35.

[22]F.F. Bruce, *1 and 2 Corinthians* (London: Butler & Tanner Ltd., 1971)
p. 104.

[23]Contrary to D.W.J. Gill, "The Importance of Roman Portraiture for
Head-Coverings in 1 Corinthians 11:2-16," *Tyndale Bulletin* 41 (1990),
245ff.

dence, the words and idioms used by Paul most naturally refer to the Roman toga which would have covered the head of someone worshiping. Second, given the Roman cultural setting of this custom, it is extremely doubtful whether the acts of praying and prophesying mentioned here ought to be identifed with the "charismatic" praying and prophesying recounted in 1 Cor 14. Finally, the second reference to the head (i.e., the dishonored head) in this verse is the literal head of the man who prays and prophesies and not Christ as the head.

11:5 And every woman who prays or prophesies with her head uncovered dishonors her head — it is just as though her head were shaved.

Since the apostle specifies the exact circumstance he has in mind and this is participation in liturgy (i.e., praying and prophesying), one has clearly left Paul's agenda to take this text to refer to what a believing woman should wear when she goes outside her home. Admittedly there were ancient dress codes of modesty that were concerned about the modesty of a woman's attire in public. A pagan philosophical document coming from a time generally contemporary with early Christianity asserts that,

> The temperate, freeborn woman must live with her legal husband adorned with modesty, clad in neat, simple, white dress without extravagance or excess. She must avoid clothing that is either entirely purple or is streaked with purple and gold.[24]

Paul has no interest in the issue mentioned in the above quotation. Moreover, he is not even addressing a situation concerning what women should wear "to the assembly."

Several preposterous suggestions have been offered about the background of Paul's concern here. One such idea states that Paul is combatting a situation where the women believers were appearing like prostitutes since they were unveiled. Another perspective states that there were women running around unclothed in the

---

[24]Pseudo-Melissa, "Letter to Kleareta," cited in Malherbe, *Moral Exhortation*, no. 34, p. 83.

assembly in some orgiastic like demeanor. These types of suggestions and reconstructions stem from a fertile imagination rather than any exegetical or historical evidence.

The apostle's observations in this verse are solely about women's devotional attire in the presence of men during periods of worship in which some woman participated. Since women prophets are also attested in the Acts of the Apostles, a reference here to women prophesying should come as little surprise. Since prophecy was a gift for corporate worship (1 Cor 14), he can hardly have in mind at 11:5 some worship that is performed alone or without the presence of men. In fact, had there been no men present (1 Cor 11:4) when these sisters were praying and prophesying, this issue would not have even arisen for Paul to correct.

Interpreters differ over the various possible connotations of the threefold use of the word "head" in this verse. While all take the first and third occurrences to be literal, many view the second occurrence (dishonors her head) to be a metaphorical reference. This use of head does not likely refer metaphorically to the woman's husband as Kistemaker[25] and Gill[26] believe since in this section *anēr* refers to man and not to a husband. Another metaphorical view interprets the reference back to head in 11:3 and takes 11:5 as a reference to the woman's man "in terms of male/female relationships."[27] This view is likewise not without problems. In my judgment Paul uses this term *kephalē* in the literal sense all three times in 11:5. As Robertson and Plummer noted, "The unveiled woman dishonours her head, because that is the part in which the indecency is manifested."[28] The connecting Greek word *gar* (for; omitted in the NIV translation) between the second and third occurrences of the word "head" reveals the connection in Paul's mind between dishonoring one's literal head and the similar meaning manifested when the literal head is shaved. Barrett sees the same connection and notes about the

---

[25]Kistemaker, *First Corinthians*, pp. 369-371.
[26]Gill, "The Importance of Roman Portraiture" *Tyndale Bulletin*.
[27]Fee, *First Epistle*, p. 508.
[28]Robertson and Plummer, *First Epistle of St. Paul*, p. 230.

meaning of the phrase "dishonors her head" that "the subsequent reference to shaving suggests that her physical head is meant."[29]

11:6 If a woman does not cover her head, she should have her hair cut off; and if it is a disgrace for a woman to have her hair cut or shaved off, she should cover her head.

The interpreter finds himself, somewhat unexpectedly, in the midst of references to hair, or its absence, on women's heads. In light of the dual references in this section to bald women and men with long hair, scholars have wondered exactly what Paul is referring to. There are two main schools of thought regarding Paul's intent in introducing issues of hair and hair length.

One school of thought believes that some of the Corinthians are manifesting concrete problems with the length of their hair. Interpreters mention the ancient phenomenon of men, either homosexuals or disheveled cynic philosophers, having long, stringy, and unkempt locks, and the phenomenon of women, usually prostitutes, adulteresses, or priestesses in pagan cults, with shorn heads. In light of this perspective, Paul is admonishing the men and women believers to abandon these unacceptable hair styles because of their dishonorable reputation.

A second understanding views the arguments about the respective hair lengths as not directed to any concrete problems that the Corinthian saints have, but as arguments used to buttress Paul's contention that head coverings, hair or otherwise, do make a difference. This second interpretive approach seems more cogent to me. It does not have the liability of having Paul introduce an issue which has nothing essential to do with the topic of worship, a topic which is the focus of the entirety of the rest of chapter 11.

Moreover, at the rhetorical level this second understanding makes the best sense of Paul's strategy of connecting the issue of artificial head coverings with the issue of the natural covering provided by human hair, especially in 11:13-15. Paul anticipates the problems that some of his readers will have with his admonitions on the head veils (11:16) and he intends to persuade them on the basis of an appeal to commonly held values. That is,

---

[29]Barrett, *First Epistle*, p. 251.

Paul's thesis that liturgical head coverings should differ according to gender will not appear cogent to Roman believers for whom the devotional head covering was never a gender-related practice. In this situation Paul wants to argue, based upon the authority of the everyday perceptions and values of his readers, that everyone knows that shame and dishonor can be attributed to a person's literal head based upon the presence or lack of a natural covering.

In light of the premise at the end of the preceding verse (a woman's uncovered head is like a shaved head), Paul argues that the logic of the situation demands that the sisters at Corinth who are uncovered during their participation in praying and prophesying in worship should be consistent and have their "hair cut off." Conversely, if it is a correct premise (and Paul's audience would have certainly consented to this premise) that a woman with a shaven head is a disgrace, then, Paul concludes the argument, the women at Corinth who wish to avoid a disgraceful demeanor must cover their heads during the liturgical circumstances set forth in 11:5.

11:7 A man ought not to cover his head, since he is the image and glory of God; but the woman is the glory of man.

In this verse Paul cannot employ an argument against men's improprieties that is identical with the one that he used against women in the preceding verse. Given the realities of human genetics (men have a greater propensity for balding) and the fact that the cultural image of a man with a shaven head did not engender concepts of disgrace, the apostle's reasoning turns at this point to other arguments and resources.

As mentioned above, the Greek author Plutarch reports important information about this Roman practice of head covering. In his discussion he makes it clear that there were several distinct and at times conflicting interpretations about the meaning and significance of the wearing of the liturgical veil.[30] One of the stronger interpretations was that the wearing of the devotional head covering was a sign of giving honors to the gods (τιμή, *timē*).

---

[30]*Roman Questions* 266c-e.

The apostle himself will reveal more than one reason about the divine necessity (ὀφείλω, *opheilō*) involved in his instruction.

The justification, indeed demand, that male participants in worship keep heads uncovered is first argued on the basis of the terms "image" (εἰκών, *eikōn*) and "glory" (δόξα, *doxa*). In light of the explicit reference to the creation account of Genesis in 1 Cor 11:8-9, there is no justification for denying the implicit reference to it in 11:7. In fact, if one were looking for Scripture attestation to issues related to men and women one would be hard pressed to find a more natural place to begin than Genesis.

The internal "logic" of Paul's argumentation has not always been readily apparent. This is understandable since the attribute of glory in the case of the man requires unveiling while praying and prophesying though in the case of the woman it requires veiling. The upshot of the apostle's reasoning seems to be that man can worship God without a head covering since he is the glory (*doxa*) of God's creation. Woman on the other hand is the glory (*doxa*) of man and not of God. Therefore, she must pray and prophesy in the presence of men with head covered.

Most interpreters rightly observe that the apostle did not say that woman was the image (*eikōn*) of man, but only his glory. It is surely, however, a trivialization of Paul's thought to suggest no more than that, "Perhaps he means that women's uncovered heads are drawing men's attention to humanity instead of to God; as one would say today, they were turning men's heads."[31]

11:8 For man did not come from woman, but woman from man;

By his use of the term "for" (γάρ, *gar*) he offers 11:8 as an explanation of how woman is the glory of man. Specifically, Paul has in mind limiting this perspective of glory to the priority of man's creation to woman's. This is an obvious allusion to Gen 2:22-23 which states, "Then the Lord God made woman from the rib he had taken out of man, and he brought her to the man. The man said, 'This is now bone of my bones and flesh of my flesh; she shall be called "woman," for she was taken out of man.'"

---

[31]Craig S. Keener, *The IVP Bible Background Commentary, New Testament* (Downers Grove: InterVarsity, 1993), p. 476, at 1 Cor 11:7.

11:9 neither was man created for woman, but woman for man.

Having given an argument in 11:8 based upon the relative origin of the female species (from man), Paul now turns to an argument based upon the cause (διά, *dia* plus the accusative case) for the creation of the woman. Paul again draws his theological perspectives from the Genesis narrative, this time from Gen 2:18-20. God observed the loneliness of the man and decided to create an appropriate helper for him to remedy this problem, a helper whose role in this regard, according to the narrative of Gen 2:18-24, is completed in marital union.

Since Adam and Eve are presented in Genesis as both the first married couple and the first man and woman, it is crucial to keep in mind which perspective Paul is focused on in 1 Cor 11. As Witherington correctly concluded, Paul's "argument [in this section] is not about family relations but about praying and prophesying in Christian worship."[32] It is especially difficult to follow Paul's argument if we read husband and wife rather than man and woman into 11:8.

11:10 For this reason, and because of the angels, the woman ought to have a sign of authority on her head.

This one brief sentence is replete with grammatical, philological, and exegetical difficulties. One of the less significant of these problems is how to understand the opening words "for this reason" (διὰ τοῦτο, *dia touto*). Does this prepositional phrase point back to the preceding sentence or to the following thoughts or to both? Fee is of the opinion that the meaning of this phrase functions "in both directions at once," which means that "the woman ought to have authority over her head because she is man's glory" and also "because of the angels."[33]

A more difficult and significant issue is the proper understanding of the Greek wording behind the NIV's translation "have a sign of authority" (ἐξουσίαν ἔχειν, *exousian echein*). At the most rudimentary level the Greek merely says "have authority" on her head. The difficulty is that Paul's general contextual view seems to point in the direction of women wearing head coverings. Since

---

[32]Witherington, *Conflict and Community in Corinth*, p. 235.
[33]Fee, *First Epistle*, p. 518.

Paul has established (11:3) that man is the head of woman, how does the woman's wearing of the head covering signify *her* authority? If it is man's authority that he wishes to advocate (as the context clearly indicates), then why use the word "authority" (*exousia*), which has implied to certain interpreters that Paul is acknowledging that the woman does "wear authority"? A host of explanations for this irregularity have been offered. In a famous article by Morna Hooker[34] she advocates that the woman does have new authority in the Christian faith to pray and prophesy in public worship when wearing the head covering. Many interpreters and most translations take "authority" to mean "sign of authority" or "sign of submission" and correlate that with the veil as such a sign. Robertson and Plummer take Paul to be saying that the woman does in fact have authority over what is on her head. Since she is in charge of what she wears on her head, she should not expose it so as to put herself to shame.[35] Fee surveys the several possibilities that have been advocated over the years, and opts for the meaning "The woman ought to have the freedom over her head to do as she wishes," and then confesses "what that means in this context remains a mystery."[36]

The third troublesome part of this verse is the final prepositional phrase "because of the angels." The older concept that Paul's reference to angels is an adaptation of the Gen 6:2 text ("the sons of God saw that the daughters of men were beautiful"), understood in ancient Judaism as a saga where heavenly beings were sexually attracted to women, is highly problematic since the head covering provided by the Roman toga did not particularly cover up erogenous areas. A very interesting theory is one found in, among others, Robertson and Plummer, who comment that the apostle is reminding women that "she must remember that she will also be shocking the angels, who of course are present at public worship."[37] The investigation of the archaeological materials

---

[34]Morna Hooker, "Authority on Her Head: An Examination of 1 Cor. XI.10," *New Testament Studies* vol 10 (1963-1964), pp. 410-416; Hooker's view is adapted by C.K. Barrett, *First Epistle*, pp. 254-255.

[35]Robertson and Plummer, *First Epistle of St. Paul*, p. 232.

[36]Fee, *First Epistle*, pp. 520-21.

[37]Robertson and Plummer, *First Epistle of St. Paul*, p. 233.

from the Dead Sea Scrolls has yielded a similar motif of angelic presence at worship.[38]

While certitude hardly seems possible at this juncture in research, the function of this text seems discoverable. The purpose of this verse is to keep the heads of the women participants covered and to base that appeal upon certain divine realities.

2. Hair in the Nature of Things (11:11-16)

[11]**In the Lord, however, woman is not independent of man, nor is man independent of woman. [12]For as woman came from man, so also man is born of woman. But everything comes from God. [13]Judge for yourselves: Is it proper for a woman to pray to God with her head uncovered? [14]Does not the very nature of things teach you that if a man has long hair, it is a disgrace to him, [15]but that if a woman has long hair, it is her glory? For long hair is given to her as a covering. [16]If anyone wants to be contentious about this, we have no other practice — nor do the churches of God.**

11:11 In the Lord, however, woman is not independent of man, nor is man independent of woman.

In spite of all the differences between man and woman and notwithstanding the "headship" relationship that exists between them, Paul will not allow this to promote a gender-based sense of autonomy and gender self-sufficiency. Since there is no historical evidence that Paul is attempting in this section of Corinthians to suppress "uppity women" or first century "women libbers" there is no need to see Paul's plea for interdependence as a constraint on some woman's radical misunderstanding of her new freedom in Christ. Though it is assumed with some regularity in current interpretation, there is no historical evidence that some of the Corinthian sisters were taking the affirmation of Gal 3:28 — In Christ there is neither male nor female — to some aberrant extreme.

---

[38]J. Fitzmyer, "A Feature of Qumran Angelology and the Angels of 1 Cor. xi.10," *New Testament Studies* 4 (1957-1958), pp. 52ff.

Calvin was of the opinion that Paul wrote this verse "partly to restrain men from treating women badly, partly to give encouragement to women, so that their subjection may not be a source of annoyance to them."[39] Some interperters see these thoughts as representing "an about-face" from the preceding Pauline ideas since "if taken at face value, [they] controvert his remarks immediately preceding." Accordingly, Holladay concludes that if they are taken as the words of "an imaginary opponent, expressing the views of the 'enlightened' within the church, they are more comprehensible."[40] Fee, on the other hand, suggests that this verse is designed to qualify the woman's understanding of her own authority (*exousia*) mentioned in 11:10 as well as "to keep the earlier argument from being read in a subordinationist way."[41]

One's understanding of the prepositional phrase "in the Lord" should impact one's interpretation of the apostle's statement here. While it is almost universally believed that Paul is talking about gender relationships between fellow believers (because of the phrase "in the Lord"), this view is not without problems. First, is Paul setting up a double standard whereby the benefits of the suggested abolition of the male hierarchy in 1 Cor 11:11-12[42] is only for believing women? Must a woman or a man be "in the new age"[43] in order to receive such treatment from a follower of Christ? Second, if this prepositional phrase refers to Christian relationships, why is Paul's explanation (γάρ, *gar*, 11:12) and illustration taken from the creation account of Genesis and the natural world of human reproduction?

11:12 For as woman came from man, so also man is born of woman. But everything comes from God.

Paul now demonstrates by an argument from Scripture and an argument from nature that there does exist a divinely directed mutuality between men and women. The fact that a woman is not independent of man (11:11) is shown by the fact that in the crea-

---

[39]Calvin, *First Epistle*, p. 233.
[40]Holladay, *First Letter*, p. 142.
[41]Fee, *First Epistle*, pp. 523-524.
[42]Witherington, *Conflict and Community in Corinth*, p. 238.
[43]Fee's terminology, *First Epistle*, p. 523 note 41.

tion of mankind woman was taken from man (identical to the observation made in 11:8). Moreover, man's dependence on woman is manifested, Paul argues, in the fact that men are conceived in and born of women.

Paul's concluding phrase in this verse is typically theocentric. It certainly removes any misplaced emphasis upon the man or woman isolated and removed from his or her theocentric origin. This may be his way of restating in summary form the headship paradigm of 1 Cor 11:3 in which God clearly stood at the zenith of headship over both Christ as well as men and women.

11:13 Judge for yourselves: Is it proper for a woman to pray to God with her head uncovered?

Paul had earlier challenged the readers to judge for themselves what he was saying (see 1 Cor 10:15). The fact that he mentions only the woman at this juncture does not negate the entirety of the preceding eleven verses in which he also focused attention on men.[44] In fact, this verse is parallel to 11:5 except that here Paul's argument shifts to an argument based upon propriety (πρέπον, *prepon*, cf. Eph 5:3; 1 Tim 2:10). With his reference to a woman praying Paul obviously has in mind the liturgical setting assumed in 1 Cor 11:4-5 and not just any setting of personal devotion and piety.

11:14 Does not the very nature of things teach you that if a man has long hair, it is a disgrace to him,

Here the apostle shifts to yet another form of argumentation, namely an argument from nature (ἡ φύσις, *hē physis;* cf. Rom 1:26). This type of argumentation was relatively well known and popular at Paul's time. In fact, the important Stoic author Epictetus appeals to the fact that God had given men and women different amounts of hair to distinguish the two sexes from each other.[45] But what did Paul mean with this mention of the didactic character of "the very nature of things"? According to Calvin, with this reference to nature, Paul is pointing to "what was accepted by

---

[44]M. Black thinks otherwise, "1 Cor. 11:2-16—A Re-investigation," p. 195.
[45]Epictetus 1.16.9ff.

common consent and usage at that time."[46] Thus, one learns from
both the literary and archaeological evidence of that period that
acceptable men, indeed, men of propriety, used barbers and typically had short hair. In the routine experience of an urbane Corinthian believer, it would be disgraceful (ἀτιμία, *atimia*) men such
as the male homosexual or the unkempt Cynic philosophers who
"typically" might have long hair.

**11:15 but that if a woman has long hair, it is her glory? For long
hair is given to her as a covering.**

Paul's explicit point here is not to get the Corinthian sisters to
let their hair grow longer, but to reinforce his argument upon the
basis of a pre-existing conviction and experience of the Corinthians about "natural" head-coverings on women. It is a glory to a
woman to have long hair because it serves as a covering (ἀντὶ περι-
βολαίου, *anti peribolaiou*) for her. Paul is not saying, as is sometimes suggested, that the woman can have long hair in place of
the liturgical head-covering.[47] Rather, since natural hair is a glory
and serves as a covering, they ought to embrace Paul's emphasis
upon a liturgical head-covering.

**11:16 If anyone wants to be contentious about this, we have no
other practice — nor do the churches of God.**

Paul's concern about contentiousness (φιλόνεικος, *philoneikos*) is
focused upon the original issues raised in 11:4-5. If some of the
Corinthian readers are still at loggerheads with Paul's position
and instruction about devotional head-coverings they should
know how out-of-step they are with both Paul and the rest of the
churches. The designation "churches of God" fits well with this
widespread designation used by Paul in the Corinthian letters
(e.g., 1 Cor 1:1; 10:32; 11:22; 15:9). By the nature of this appeal,
Sampley states, "Paul recognizes a nascent sense of collectivity of

[46]Calvin, *First Epistle*, p. 235.
[47]Fee, *First Epistle*, pp. 528-529 demonstrates the inadequacies of the
view that says that the hair can take the place of the head covering.

his congregations. Insofar as individual churches are supposed to be swayed by practices that prevail 'in all the churches.'"[48]

The translation "no other practice" is infamously imprecise since the word translated "other" (τοιαύτην, *toiautēn*) never means that except in the translation of this verse.[49] Paul stated that we have no such practice (συνήθειαν, *sunētheian*), referring to the head-covering practices corrected in 11:2-15, though some interpreters believe that Paul refers to the practice of being contentious.[50]

B. THE LORD'S SUPPER (11:17-34)

1. The Corinthians' Practice (11:17-22)

[17]In the following directives I have no praise for you, for your meetings do more harm than good. [18]In the first place, I hear that when you come together as a church, there are divisions among you, and to some extent I believe it. [19]No doubt there have to be differences among you to show which of you have God's approval. [20]When you come together, it is not the Lord's Supper you eat, [21]for as you eat, each of you goes ahead without waiting for anybody else. One remains hungry, another gets drunk. [22]Don't you have homes to eat and drink in? Or do you despise the church of God and humiliate those who have nothing? What shall I say to you? Shall I praise you for this? Certainly not!

11:17 In the following directives I have no praise for you, for your meetings do more harm than good.

The first century A.D. philosopher and moralist Musonius Rufus noted that Greco-Roman meal times provided the opportu-

---

[48]J. Paul Sampley, *Walking Between the Times. Paul's Moral Reasoning*, p. 110.

[49]Fee, *First Epistle*, p. 530.

[50]See Witherington, *Conflict and Community in Corinth*, pp. 238-239.

nity for not one but for many sins (ἁμάρτημα, *hamartēma*).[51] This acknowledgment sets the stage for the modern interpreter's understanding of how such flagrant misbehavior could have taken place at the communal meal of believers in ancient Corinth. It required no special effort on the part of the Corinthian church of God to conduct the Lord's Supper in the way Paul describes it in 11:17-34. In fact, as the ancient literary and archaeological record makes abundantly clear, the very abuses which the apostle Paul addressed and censured in this section were widespread in Greco-Roman culture and practice.

In contrast to the praise given by Paul in 11:2, he has no praise for their attitudes and actions at the Lord's meal. Paul's statement that their meetings do more harm than good reveals the depth of his displeasure with the Corinthians' behavior. Paul's doctrinal understanding of the assembly does not include a belief in the virtue of assembling for its own sake. As a student of Scripture he knew well God's hatred of religious assemblies and ceremonies when those in attendance had lives and hearts out of step with God's will (cf. Isa 1:10-15; Mal 1:10; Matt 5:23-24).

11:18 In the first place, I hear that when you come together as a church, there are divisions among you, and to some extent I believe it.

In this verse Paul spells out the harmful actions which he referred to in 11:17. In particular, their assembly at the time of the communal meal is characterized by divisions (σχίσματα, *schismata*, cf. 1:10;12:25). Since the Greek term which is translated "church" (*ekklēsia*) was also used in Greek literature, inscriptions, and papyri for non-Christian gatherings and assemblies (cf. the use of *ekklēsia* in Acts 19:32, 39, 40), it is not surprising to find that the Pauline expression of "coming together as a church" (συνερχομένων ἐν ἐκκλησίᾳ, *synerchomenōn en ekklēsia*) is a well documented Greek phrase.

The potentially divisive character of Greek and Roman meal time gatherings is well documented in ancient literary testimony,

---

[51]Musonius Rufus *Lesson* 18B. 31-33 in C.E. Lutz, "Musonius Rufus. The Roman Socrates." *Yale Classical Studies* 10 (1947), pp. 116-117.

from authors such as Plato, Plutarch, Juvenal, Pliny, and Lucian.[52] We also have a handful of archaeological artifacts that mention the need for religious and non-religious assemblies and guilds to regulate the problems associated with meal times. As one Latin inscription from Pompeii stated it, "Be sociable and put aside, if you can, annoying quarrels. If you can't, go back to your own home."[53]

Given the lack of internal evidence in 1 Corinthians that there was any Jew-Gentile division in the Corinthian fellowship, it is only speculation to suggest that "a meal may also have provided Jewish Christians, if they insisted on *kosher* food, with an occasion for separating themselves from their Gentile brothers."[54]

Because of Paul's use of the words "I hear" and "I believe" in this verse, it seems improbable that he learned about this issue from the letter the Corinthians had written to him (cf. 7:1).

11:19 No doubt there have to be differences among you to show which of you have God's approval.

In light of Paul's intense dissatisfaction with some of the Corinthians in this section, it is best to understand this verse as reflecting mild irony (and perhaps sarcasm). The very carnal disposition that characterizes some of these Corinthians serves as the catalyst for making evident those who are pleasing to God.

11:20 When you come together, it is not the Lord's Supper you eat,

The opening words of this verse make it clear that Paul has in mind the occasion at which all the believers come together at one place (ἐπὶ τὸ αὐτό, *epi to auto*, omitted in the NIV translation). Due to the aberrant Corinthian behavior which Paul is about to highlight in 11:21ff, he is compelled to inform the Corinthians that the

---

[52]In general see the popular summary of these issues in D.E. Smith and H.E. Taussig, *Many Tables. The Eucharist in the New Testament and Liturgy Today* (Philadelphia: Trinity Press International, 1990), pp. 21-35.

[53]The translation of this Latin inscription from Pompeii is taken from *As the Romans Did*, no. 317, p. 319.(= *Corpus Inscriptionum Latinarum* IV.7698). The author of this inscription, like the apostle Paul (11:22), told those who came to eat to either behave or go back to their own homes.

[54]Barrett, *First Epistle*, p. 261.

meal they are conducting is not the Lord's meal (κυριακὸν δεῖπνον, *kyriakon deipnon*). This Pauline evaluation would surely have startled his readers since they thought that this was the very meal they were conducting.

11:21 for as you eat, each of you goes ahead without waiting for anybody else. One remains hungry, another gets drunk.

The apostle now spells out just why this corporate meal is not at all what they think it is. The problem is not with inappropriate believers participating in the meal or officiating at it. Nor is the difficulty that Paul has with a deviation by the Corinthians from some pre-determined liturgical pattern for the Lord's supper.

The specific problem, according to Paul, is that this meal that is supposed to engender and reflect corporate unity (10:16-17) has become completely individualistic. If it were a true meal of the Lord the participants would partake in a way that manifested their fellowship in the Body of Christ. As it is being practiced by the Corinthians, they have allowed the typical Greco-Roman mores of social class distinctions and inebriation at meals to prevail. These types of problems were so prevalent at large meals in Greco-Roman antiquity that pagan philosophers and moralists complained about them.

Some of the Corinthian believers have so lost any sense of the Lord's meal as having a horizontal or communal dimension that they are not waiting for anyone else when they partake of this Lord's meal.

One of the reasons that there has been and will continue to be debate over whether the Corinthians partook of the Lord's meal in the context of a larger fellowship meal (the *agapē* banquet) is that the text itself is ambiguous.[55] My own judgment is that the Lord's meal was originally eaten in conjunction with other food, as was the case when it was instituted (note the phrase "after supper," μετὰ τὸ δεῖπνῆσαι, *meta to deipnēsai* in 11:25.). Since the bread and wine together were called a meal (11:20, δεῖπνον, *deipnon*) the quantity of these two elements consumed probably exceeded what is contemporary practice in churches.

---

[55]Fee, *First Epistle*, pp. 540-543, summarizes the various options in this regard.

Paul is not specifically concerned in this setting whether the Lord's supper is eaten at the same time of day and at the same gathering with other foods. Rather, the apostle is agitated about the individualistic attitude of some believers which allows them to eat their own food (τὸ ἴδιον δεῖπνον, *to idion deipnon*) and not be concerned about those who do not have food (see esp. 11:22). Because of differing economic and social status some of the believers, Paul observes, remain hungry. In this setting the economic and social class distinctions which characterized the various members of the church of God in their work-a-day world were being maintained during the Lord's meal in the assembly.[56] To the apostle this situation is unacceptable!

Moreover, drunkenness was a problem for some of the believers. Paul had already indicated to his readers that drunkards cannot inherit the kingdom of God (1 Cor 6:10). The excessive volume of wine often consumed at Greco-Roman banquets and meals was even commented upon by pagan moralists. One of the jobs of banquet organizers and supervisors in antiquity was to regulate the amount of wine consumed (cf. John 2:9, the master of the banquet).

11:22 Don't you have homes to eat and drink in? Or do you despise the church of God and humiliate those who have nothing? What shall I say to you? Shall I praise you for this? Certainly not!

Paul's reference to houses has led some interpreters to think that it is the wealthy in church who are causing some of these problems. After all, the argument goes, the slaves and poor of the church would not have houses. Moreover, it is the "have nots" who are the victims of humiliation in this situation according to this verse.

Paul is stating that if those who are guilty of the major offenses in the preceding verse cannot wait for other believers and share their food with others, then they should eat and drink at home. By his contrasting use of homes (οἰκίας, *oikias*) and church of God (ἐκκλησίας τοῦ θεοῦ, *ekklēsias tou theou*), Paul is acknowledging the

---

[56]One should consult the seminal work by G. Theissen, *The Social Setting of Primitive Christianity*.

rightful distinction between the public and private spheres of life (cf. 14:34-35) in this regard.

With his explicit reference to those who have nothing (τοὺς μὴ ἔχοντας, *tous mē echontas*) Paul reveals the socio-economic nature of this problem.

Paul reaffirms his previous judgment (11:17) that he cannot possibly praise the Corinthians for their type and style of banqueting and participation in the Lord's meal.

2. The Lord's Supper As Instituted (11:23-26)

[23]For I received from the Lord what I also passed on to you: The Lord Jesus, on the night he was betrayed, took bread, [24]and when he had given thanks, he broke it and said, "This is my body, which is for you; do this in remembrance of me." [25]In the same way, after supper he took the cup, saying, "This cup is the new covenant in my blood; do this, whenever you drink it, in remembrance of me." [26]For whenever you eat this bread and drink this cup, you proclaim the Lord's death until he comes.

11:23 For I received from the Lord what I also passed on to you: The Lord Jesus, on the night he was betrayed, took bread,

Even though pagan banquets and meals often had serious religious overtones, the Corinthians' model of the Lord's meal was void of religious perspectives from their Lord. Consequently, Paul turns to the setting and the theology of the institution of the Lord's supper to remind and inform the Corinthians what the supper of the Lord Jesus was all about. By doing this he hopes to once again "Christianize" their meal, since evidently its practice had fallen under the influence of Greco-Roman practices and attitudes.

Paul claims that this instructional material came from the Lord and states that at some past time he had given it to the church of God at Corinth. It is immediately apparent that Paul is taking the Corinthians back to the setting of the Last Supper (cf. Matt 26:26-29; Mark 14:22-25; Luke 22:14-20) shortly before Jesus' trial and execution.

With his reference to the bread (ἄρτον, *arton*) Paul is introducing the first of the two elements of the Lord's meal (cf. 10:16-17).

11:24 and when he had given thanks, he broke it and said, "This is my body, which is for you; do this in remembrance of me."

Paul cites Jesus' statement which associates the bread of the Lord's meal with Jesus' personal body that was vicariously sacrificed for believers (τὸ σῶμα τὸ ὑπὲρ ὑμῶν, *to sōma to hyper hymōn*). The apostle includes within the quotation of Jesus' words Jesus' imperative to perpetuate this meal. These words about remembrance arise from Jesus' own understanding of the role of remembrance in the Passover Feast, though as C.K. Barrett points out, there would be nothing strange about a meal of remembrance for pagans.[57] Even though the theme of remembrance is central in Paul's teaching in 11:23-25, there is no justification for elevating this understanding over the participation theme (κοινωνία, *koinōnia*) found earlier in 10:15-17.

11:25 In the same way, after supper he took the cup, saying, "This cup is the new covenant in my blood; do this, whenever you drink it, in remembrance of me."

Next Paul moves to the second element of the Lord's meal, namely the beverage. The place of the cup (cf. 10:16) needs to be seen in the setting of Jesus' celebration of the Passover according to contemporary Jewish custom (cf. Luke 22:17-20). In that historical context Jesus associates the cup with the New Covenant (cf. Jer 31:31; Heb 8:8-13; 2 Cor 3:1-18). Jesus specifically associates the cup (in which there was wine) with the blood he was about to shed. When believers drink of this cup at the Lord's meal, they should do so in remembrance of Jesus whose life and ministry culminated in his redemptive death. This perspective which is rooted in the words of Jesus and passed on by the apostle Paul was obviously totally forgotten (hence the need to remember) by Corinthian believers whose experience of the cup of wine was as a source of inebriation (see 11:21).

---

[57]Barrett, *First Epistle*, p. 267.

11:26 For whenever you eat this bread and drink this cup, you proclaim the Lord's death until he comes.

In this verse Paul forcefully jerks the Corinthians' current practice of the Lord's meal from the damning perspectives of Greco-Roman meal customs and firmly replants it in the soil of redemptive history. Whenever believers participate in the Lord's supper (not just any supper), it is a proclamation of the death of the Lord. The supper as a whole points to Jesus' death since the two essential elements commanded by Jesus (bread and cup) both are interpreted in terms of his redemptive work at his death. The centrality of this meal to the life of the church is seen in the fact that the church is commanded to eat and drink of the Lord's meal until the Lord's return.

3. Self-examination to Avoid Judgment (11:27-34)

[27]Therefore, whoever eats the bread or drinks the cup of the Lord in an unworthy manner will be guilty of sinning against the body and blood of the Lord. [28] A man ought to examine himself before he eats of the bread and drinks of the cup. [29]For anyone who eats and drinks without recognizing the body of the Lord eats and drinks judgment on himself. [30]That is why many among you are weak and sick, and a number of you have fallen asleep. [31]But if we judged ourselves, we would not come under judgment. [32]When we are judged by the Lord, we are being disciplined so that we will not be condemned with the world.

[33]So then, my brothers, when you come together to eat, wait for each other. [34]If anyone is hungry, he should eat at home, so that when you meet together it may not result in judgment.

And when I come I will give further directions.

11:27 Therefore, whoever eats the bread or drinks the cup of the Lord in an unworthy manner will be guilty of sinning against the body and blood of the Lord.

Having made clear to the Corinthians the cross-centered nature of the Lord's meal, Paul then begins to draw out the punitive consequences when believers participate in the meal in an unworthy manner. Since for Paul the elements of the bread and cup are undeniably and inextricably tied to the death of Jesus as manifested in his broken body and shed blood, to handle these elements as the Corinthians have is to place oneself "under the same liability as those responsible for that death in the first place."[58]

11:28 A man ought to examine himself before he eats of the bread and drinks of the cup.

As Robertson and Plummer point out, the grammar and wording of this verse "shows that the individual Christian can do it [examination] for himself and perhaps implies that this is the normal condition of things."[59] Paul is calling for each believer to evaluate his behavior at the supper (not his behavior throughout the week) to discern if it is appropriate to the doctrine of the Lord's meal that Paul has given.

11:29 For anyone who eats and drinks without recognizing the body of the Lord eats and drinks judgment on himself.

The apostle here specifies the concrete sin an individual Corinthian should think about. If a believer partakes of the Lord's dinner (eats and drinks) he will ensure his own condemnation if he has not properly recognized the body (τὸ σῶμα, *to sōma*).

According to Fee, there have been at least three major interpretations of what Paul means by not recognizing the body.[60] One view takes this to mean that Paul is concerned that the Corinthians are not properly discerning the difference between the sacred elements of the Lord's supper and the common food. A second perspective proposes that the Corinthians are guilty of not appropriately meditating on the death of Jesus, particularly his body on the cross, when they take the elements of his meal. A third major understanding is to take body as the congregation (= Body of

---

[58]Fee, *First Epistle*, p. 561. The NIV wording "will be guilty of sinning against" is one possible interpretation of the Greek words ἔνοχος ἔσται (*enochos estai*).

[59]Robertson and Plummer, *First Epistle of St. Paul*, p. 251.

[60]Fee, *First Epistle*, pp. 563-564.

Christ) and to view Paul continuing his critique of Corinthian neglect of one another during the Lord's dinner.

This third perspective has more evidence in its favor. This includes the fact that contextually the focus of Paul's criticism has
been about mistreatment of fellow believers at the meal (11:21, 22,
33). In addition, Paul's readers have already been introduced to
the terminology of body = fellow believers in the context of the
Lord's meal at 10:17. Finally since Paul shifts from his previous
idiom of body and blood (= bread and cup, 11:27) to only one
body, one cannot cogently argue that body must mean the same
thing in 11:27 and 11:29. Since Paul did not write "without recognizing the body and the blood of the Lord" but rather "not recognizing the body"[61] one must be very cautious in turning Paul's
criticism into an attack upon the lack of devotional focus during
the Lord's supper. Lack of devotional focus may or may not be
grounds for contemporary concerns, but this hardly seems to me
to be the issue that Paul is attacking in the congregation at Corinth.

**11:30 That is why many among you are weak and sick, and a
number of you have fallen asleep.**

Paul's earlier warnings about receiving punitive judgment because of actions such as despising the church of God and humili-
ating the "have nots" were no idle threats. In this verse Paul specifically mentions three manifestations of the self-engendered
judgment of 11:29. Many of the Corinthian believers (ἐν ὑμῖν πολλοί, en hymin polloi), Paul asserts, have become weak and sick and
another group has fallen asleep.

It is impossible to know the details of the events to which Paul
refers. Calvin noted, "We do not know if a plague was raging there
at the time, or whether they were afflicted by other kinds of dis-

---

[61]The NIV translators have done Bible students a great disservice by
rendering this phrase as "without recognizing the body of the Lord." This
particular wording "body of the Lord" is found only in inferior textual
witnesses. In light of the strong manuscript evidence for "body" rather
than "body of the Lord," I can only assume that the NIV committee gave
in to doctrinal presuppositions rather than follow the normal rules for
the evaluation of variant readings.

eases,"[62] while Fee takes the contrary position that, "In any case, Paul is not saying that sickness among Christians is to be viewed as present judgment, nor that such sickness is necessarily related to an abuse of the Supper."[63]

Since both the Old Testament and New Testament recognize the role of punitive miracles, there is certainly no reason to conclude that Paul's words should or cannot be taken at face value.

11:31 But if we judged ourselves, we would not come under judgment.

Paul is here encouraging the readers to participate in continued self-evaluation so that they will mend their ways and no longer be recipients of the judgment of God as described in 11:30.[64]

11:32 When we are judged by the Lord, we are being disciplined so that we will not be condemned with the world.

This verse makes it clear that God intends there to be a therapeutic consequence for his judgment. The purpose of this stern discipline of the church of God is to spare believers from God's eschatological judgment of the world (μὴ σὺν τῷ κόσμῳ, *mē syn tō kosmō*). The implication is that if these Corinthians do not repent and receive the discipline of God, then they will be judged with the world.

11:33 So then, my brothers, when you come together to eat, wait for each other.

Paul here begins to bring his thoughts to a conclusion. When the saints at Corinth assemble to eat (εἰς τὸ φαγεῖν, *eis to phagein*), presumably both a communal meal and Lord's dinner, they must wait for one another. Since the New Testament does not acknowledge clergy ordination in the modern sense, "Paul does not say, Wait for so-and-so, or for such-and-such an official, to preside

---

[62]Calvin, *First Epistle*, p. 254.
[63]Fee, *First Epistle*, p. 565.
[64]Robertson and Plummer, *First Epistle of St. Paul*, p. 254.

over your gathering."[65] Rather, the apostle urges them to wait until all who have assembled have food to eat.

11:34 If anyone is hungry, he should eat at home, so that when you meet together it may not result in judgment. And when I come I will give further directions.

Paul gives here an alternative for the believer who would dispute his apostolic counsel in 11:33. If, without concern for others, someone argues on the basis of hunger that they need to eat, Paul grants them permission as long as it is done in the privacy of their home (ἐν οἴκῳ ἐσθιέτω, *en oikō esthietō*) and not at the public assembly of the church. If hungry church members reject Paul's warning and eat selfishly when they have assembled (συνέρχεσθε, *synerchesthe*), then they will experience the judgment of God.

Although the apostle has more directives and instructions to give (on the issue treated in 11:17-34?), he informs the Corinthians that he must wait until he can see them face-to-face. On his next visit to Corinth they will take care of the remaining matters (τὰ δὲ λοιπά, *ta de loipa*), whatever they were.[66]

---

[65]Barrett, *First Epistle*, p. 276.

[66]Robertson and Plummer, *First Epistle of St. Paul*, p. 255 comment, "One may guess forever, and without result, as to what things the Apostle was going to set in order. . . ."

1 CORINTHIANS 12

VII. MISUNDERSTANDING OF SPIRITUAL GIFTS (12:1-14:40)

A. SPIRITUAL GIFTS (12:1-11)

1. Influence of the Spirit (12:1-3)

[1]Now about spiritual gifts, brothers, I do not want you to be ignorant. [2]You know that when you were pagans, somehow or other you were influenced and led astray to mute idols. [3]Therefore I tell you that no one who is speaking by the Spirit of God says, "Jesus be cursed," and no one can say, "Jesus is Lord," except by the Holy Spirit.

12:1 Now about spiritual gifts, brothers, I do not want you to be ignorant.

This verse introduces a three-chapter section that includes chapters 12-14.[1] Since Paul uses the "now about" phrase (περὶ δέ, *peri de*) which we have seen earlier in 1 Corinthians, it is likely that he is now addressing an issue brought forward by the Corinthians in their letter to him. It is not as clear in the Greek text that Paul is specifically addressing the issue of spiritual gifts. The Greek text has only the adjective "spiritual" (πνευματικῶν, *pneumatikōn*) and the interpreter is left to decide whether Paul is referring to spiri-

---

[1]A very helpful guide to this three chapter section is available in D.A. Carson, *Showing the Spirit, A Theological Exposition of I Corinthians 12-14* (Grand Rapids: Baker Book House, 1987).

tual matters, spiritual individuals or spiritual gifts.[2] It is clear from the last half of verse 1 that Paul believes that some of the readers of this letter are operating with less than a complete and clear understanding of these spiritual issues. This three-chapter section has probably been more misinterpreted than any other section of 1 Corinthians. A major problem in many of the interpretations of this section is that later Christian authors impose upon the Corinthian situation issues which are much later in the history of Christian thought. It should be obvious that Paul is not concerned here about a debate within the church at Corinth regarding Pentecostalism. Any attempt to understand these three chapters against a backdrop of either a pro-Pentecostal or anti-Pentecostal debate has failed to appreciate the historical setting in the church of God at Corinth.[3]

12:2 You know that when you were pagans, somehow or other you were influenced and led astray to mute idols.

The full significance of this verse has often been overlooked by interpreters. It seems that in this verse Paul makes it clear that the origin of the problem that the Corinthians have is their pre-Christian spiritual experiences in pagan idolatry.[4] Even though the Greek word ἔθνη (*ethnē*, pagans) found in verse 2 can mean Gentiles, it is obvious in this context Paul intends for it to mean pagan. By this use of the word *ethnē* as well as the accompanying term "idols" Paul makes it abundantly clear that this problem cannot have arisen out of a Jewish background, or simply out of immature thinking among Christians who had no connection with pagan religious experiences.

The fundamental problem on this issue with the Corinthians is not that they had misunderstood what was taught or manifested on the day of Pentecost or what were the implications of the work-

---

[2]Fee, *First Epistle*, p. 576, believes "the better translation might be 'the things of the Spirit,' which would refer primarily to spiritual manifestations."

[3]To my knowledge there is still no major theological or exegetical treatment of chapters 12-14 that seriously interacts with the cultural background of these chapters.

[4]While Paul may not be thinking specifically of pagan ecstasy, it is clear in the wording of 12:2 that he has general pagan piety in mind.

ing of the Holy Spirit in sanctification. It is clear by the connection between verses 1 and 2 that the source of the misunderstanding among the Corinthians that Paul is attempting to solve arises uniquely from their pagan spiritual worldviews, which many of them are still carrying as baggage in their Christian lives. We see once again then a problem among the converts at Corinth which has arisen because of the residual impact of their pre-Christian polytheistic idolatry upon them.[5]

12:3 Therefore I tell you that no one who is speaking by the Spirit of God says, "Jesus be cursed," and no one can say, "Jesus is Lord," except by the Holy Spirit.

The contextual point of v. 3 is to help these new Christians, still operating out of a worldview founded in their pagan religious experiences, clarify the misunderstandings and the confusion they have about spiritual matters.[6] One will come much closer to understanding Paul's historical meaning in this verse if one understands what it would be like to work with a congregation of people who live within a syncretistic environment and continue to be influenced by religious beliefs flowing from the pagan setting in their own personal backgrounds.[7] What Paul is attempting to do in verse 3 is to help these young Christians from a pagan background cut through a lot of the confusion in their own minds and spiritual experiences. Paul wants to inform these young Christians regarding the matter of how they can know where God is at work and where God is not at work. The need to address the question only arises when young Christians find themselves in a syncretistic multicultural spiritual environment replete with animism and

---

[5]The interpreters who overlook this point are usually the same as those who fail to point out the fact that pagan religion also claimed to practice prophecy, healings, miracles, interpretations, and some forms of speaking in tongues.

[6]Carson, *Showing the Spirit*, p. 26, attempts to prove on grammatical grounds that "we no longer have to interpret verse 3 in light of verse 2, and vice versa."

[7]This is of course the assumption most interpreters rely upon when they attempt to understand the Corinthians' problems with incest, fornication, problems at the Lord's Supper, liturgical head coverings/hair, denial of the resurrection, etc.

polytheism. As we will point out later in this chapter, many of the activities which Paul credits to the work of God among Christians had general analogies within pagan religious experience.[8] By this I mean there were many temples and religions in the ancient world which also claimed to offer prophecies, the interpretation of prophecies, miracles, and gifts of healing. One can imagine, then, how confusing it would be for a young Christian to understand where and when the true God was at work.

If anyone doubts that this kind of confusion could go on in the mind of a recent convert and impact his thoughts and practices, one need only restudy the text of Acts 8 where the story of Simon the Magician is set forth by Luke. Not only were the Gentile converts in the Corinthian church all young Christians, but we also know, based upon the evidence in chapters 8-10, that some of them still had one foot in the conceptual world of practicing idolatry.[9]

In light of this situation, Paul wants them to know in this verse that if anyone curses Jesus, if anyone opposes the cause of Christ, that person is not speaking by the Spirit of God.[10] On the other hand, anytime one affirms that Jesus is Lord, that must be attributed to the work of God's Spirit. In this way, the affirmation of the Lordship of Jesus serves as the litmus test of the presence of God and the working of his Spirit. This understanding of the function of 12:3 seems to take much more seriously the historical and cultural setting of this Corinthian church than other non-historical interpretations do.

When one takes 12:1-3 as an introduction to chapters 12-14, it becomes clear that one must always be open to the possibility that Paul's instruction in these chapters should be read against the

---

[8]These analogies were readily acknowledged by the Christian Apologists of the 2nd century A.D. A helpful treatment of pagan, Jewish, and Christian prophecy is David E. Aune, *Prophecy in Early Christianity and the Ancient Mediterranean World* (Grand Rapids: Eerdmans, 1983).

[9]This is not to suggest that the same Gentile believers were involved in the issue of chapters 8-10 and of 12-14.

[10]There is no historical evidence either in Scripture or in the secular record to substantiate the argument that the statement "Jesus be cursed" would have been part of synagogue or state persecution of believers in Corinth at that time.

setting of believers who are misunderstanding the way God is working in their midst because of prior spiritual religious experiences; and in some cases, the residual influence of polytheistic beliefs and animism was still strong. By his triune reference in v. 3 to God, to Jesus, and to the Holy Spirit,[11] Paul is beginning a transition into vv. 4-6.

2. Different Gifts for a Common Good (12:4-11)

[4]There are different kinds of gifts, but the same Spirit. [5]There are different kinds of service, but the same Lord. [6]There are different kinds of working, but the same God works all of them in all men.

[7]Now to each one the manifestation of the Spirit is given for the common good. [8]To one there is given through the Spirit the message of wisdom, to another the message of knowledge by means of the same Spirit, [9]to another faith by the same Spirit, to another gifts of healing by that one Spirit, [10]to another miraculous powers, to another prophecy, to another distinguishing between spirits, to another speaking in different kinds of tongues,[a] and to still another the interpretation of tongues.[a] [11]All these are the work of one and the same Spirit, and he gives them to each one, just as he determines.

[a]10 Or languages; also in verse 28

12:4 There are different kinds of gifts, but the same Spirit.

Most interpreters rightly notice that verses 4-6 contain references to the three personalities in the Godhead, namely the Spirit, the Lord, and God. It would be a mistake, however, to impose upon these three references later developments in Christian

---

[11]It seems to me that Evangelical interpreters such as Fee (First Epistle, pp. 581-582) and Carson (Showing the Spirit, pp. 25-28) are so intent on applying these verses to modern ecclesiastical problems, their views about 12:1-3 are anachronistic. The Corinthian church of God had enough of its own problems and demons without our foisting others on them.

thought which advocated a Trinitarian doctrine. Even though Fee is fond of "finding" references to the concept of the Trinity in 1 Corinthians, the words of Victor Furnish are judicious, "There is no reason to think that his successive and parallel references to the Spirit, the Lord, and God (12:4-6) either echo or constitute a specific 'trinitarian' formula, or that they represent some incipient Pauline doctrine of the Trinity."[12]

It is clear, however, by Paul's use of the word "same" in verses 4, 5, and 6, that he intends to counter any polytheistic notions that are embraced by the readership. In the world of polytheism, which was the dominant religious view in the Greek and Roman worlds, different activities were attributed to operations of different gods and goddesses. Paul will have none of that since overt idolatry excludes individuals from the Kingdom of God (see 5:11; 6:9). For him the variety of experiences within the church of God at Corinth are not to be explained against the background of a variety of gods and goddesses. For Paul, all the experiences that the Christians are having come from the same Godhead. The background, then, for Paul's focus on the triune Godhead here is not merely a development in early Christian thought, but a response to the threat from syncretism and polytheism within the church at Corinth.

In this verse Paul uses the word "gifts" (χαρισμάτων, *charismatōn*) and acknowledges that there is a variety and a difference in the various gifts that are found within the members at Corinth. For Paul, however, these different kinds of gifts do not point to a variety of spirits.[13] For Paul the same Spirit is at work in the distribution of all of these gifts.

---

[12]Victor Furnish, "Theology in First Corinthians," in *Pauline Theology*, Vol. II: 1 & 2 Corinthians, ed. David M. Hay, p. 72; in fn. 39 of p. 72 he continues, "I find no exegetical warrant at all for the claim that Paul has 'grounded his appeal for diversity in the Triune God himself,'" (Fee, *First Epistle*, p. 588).

[13]On the Corinthians' misconceived ideas about the relationship between gifts and spirits cf. 1 Cor 14:12.

12:5 There are different kinds of service, but the same Lord.

In language and structure that is very similar to v. 4, Paul also admits that there are different kinds of service in the Christian community. But he emphasizes the fact that these different kinds of services are not from or rendered to different lords. While it might strike the modern reader as peculiar that Paul has to affirm that there are not many lords, one needs to keep in mind Paul's characterization of idolatry in 8:5. In that location Paul acknowledged that from the point of view of "Christian polytheism" there was an understanding of many lords and many gods. In 12:5, however, he makes it clear that there is only one Lord for Christians and that this Lord is the origin of all the varieties and kinds of service.

12:6 There are different kinds of working, but the same God works all of them in all men.

Continuing the same basic approach that he had in 12:4-5 Paul now moves to the term God in this triune presentation. Paul's phrase here, "different kinds of working" (διαιρέσεις ἐνεργημάτων, *diaireseis energēmatōn*), may refer in the context of 1 Cor 12 specifically to the gifts that will be discussed in this chapter, but there is nothing intrinsic in the word or in Paul's use of the word in other contexts which requires that the word "work/working" refers to spiritual gifts or supernatural occurrences. The Greek word for all men (πᾶσιν, *pasin*) need not refer specifically only to males. Paul has here in mind God's working among all believers.

12:7 Now to each one the manifestation of the Spirit is given for the common good.

Even though Paul's purpose is not to set forth in verses 4-6a Trinitarian doctrine, he does clearly set forth a monotheistic foundation for his doctrine of gifts in the Corinthian church. In verses 7-11 Paul's references to Christ and to God recede, and all of Paul's attention is focused upon the work of the Spirit. The degree to which this discussion of gifts in 1 Cor 12-14 is controlled by the preoccupation with the Spirit and spiritual matters comes to light when one compares the treatment of 1 Cor 12 with Paul's treatment of similar topics in Rom 12 and Eph 4. It is only here that Paul gives such an intense focus upon this topic and brings together gifts with the work of the Spirit. Even though in contemporary Christian jargon one is accustomed to referring to spiritual gifts, or gifts of the Spirit, it is clearly seen in Paul's other treatments in Romans and Ephesians that Paul is just as comfortable in referring to these as the gifts of Christ or gifts of God.

A comparison of 1 Cor 12 with Rom 12 and Eph 4 also reveals that the discussion of 1 Cor 12 is just as contextually limited as the other two presentations are. This means that we should not expect to find in 1 Cor 12 a complete listing of all the gifts of God or his Spirit. Those particular gifts that will be mentioned in this section of 1 Cor 12 are there because they relate specifically to the problem that the Corinthians have raised and the situations with which they are dealing. As is true with all the other problems that Paul has dealt with in 1 Corinthians and will continue to deal with in later chapters, we have no way of knowing what percentage of the congregation participated in these particular problems or manifested the shortcomings that Paul is addressing here. Regardless of what the Corinthians themselves think they are experiencing from the manifestation of God's Spirit, Paul is very direct in his interpretation. Paul says that when a manifestation of the Spirit is given to a believer it is for the common good. The concept of the common good clearly reflects Paul's concern about the interpersonal or horizontal dimensions of spiritual gifts in this section. Though Paul's wording will change from section to section, it is clear that this is a constant thread throughout chapters 12, 13, and 14. In this three-chapter section Paul shows no sympathy for a highly individualistic and self-satisfying experience of God's Spirit. In his address to the Corinthians Paul is much more focused upon the interpersonal and edifying character of these manifestations. By putting forth this emphasis Paul is clearly bringing these spiritual experiences under the guidelines mandated by the prime directive of both the Old and New Testaments, which says that one must love his neighbor as himself.

12:8 To one there is given through the Spirit the message of wisdom, to another the message of knowledge by means of the same Spirit,

Having set the tone in 12:7 with his reference to the fact that manifestations of the Spirit are to be for the common good, Paul now begins to list particular manifestations of God's Spirit through gifts. Notwithstanding all the sermons and lessons that have been built upon the terminology in verse 8, we in fact know amazingly little about what these individual gifts looked like in practice. To be sure there is no doubt that both Paul and the Corinthians knew what he was talking about, but from our historical distance it is extremely difficult to fill in the details. Typically we can do little more than re-create a skeleton based upon general etymology and basic meanings of the words. We are certainly not on solid interpretive ground when we merely flesh out these terms by twentieth-century spiritual and pietistic experiences.

The first gift Paul mentions in verse 8 is the message of wisdom. It is worth noting that beyond this occurrence in 12:8, all other references to the noun "wisdom" (σοφία, *sophia*) in 1 Corinthians occur in the first four-chapter section where Paul deals with community fragmentation. In that context the word is found both in a positive and negative light. Paul obviously expects "wisdom" in 12:8 to be understood in the positive sense rather than the pejorative sense. The phrase "message of wisdom" could perhaps reflect a wisdom teaching based on Old Testament wisdom precepts, or it could be a message more focused on Christ in light of what Paul says in 1 Cor 1:30 when he writes that "Christ Jesus has become for us wisdom of God."

Paul ends verse 8 by pointing out that there will be another Christian who by the same Spirit receives a message of knowledge. As was true with regard to the noun "wisdom," it is also true to the noun "knowledge" (γνῶσις, *gnōsis*) that Paul uses this both in a positive as well as a pejorative sense in 1 Corinthians. Rather than the more broadly conceived idea of knowledge such as Paul commented on in 1:5, and rather than the quite narrowly defined use of knowledge we found in 8:1, Paul is probably using knowledge here in a sense related to his other uses of this noun in the unit of thought of chapters 12, 13, and 14. It seems that the

knowledge referred to in 12:8 would not be a knowledge possessed by all Christians or which was part of the general Christian
message. It seems rather that this would be a special kind of
knowledge given through the Spirit to individual Christians. This
same outlook in regard to the use of the word "knowledge" is also
reflected in 13:2, 18, and 14:6. The occurrence of knowledge in
14:6 seems to provide the most specific background in that it refers to a message of knowledge given through God's Spirit only to
certain Christians, who are then to share it with others in the assembly. I know of no evidence in the text that would inform us
about the specific content of this message of knowledge.

**12:9 to another faith by the same Spirit, to another gifts of heal-
ing by that one Spirit,**
     To another Christian, or perhaps another group of Christians,
Paul says that faith is given by the same Spirit. The reader needs
to be aware that Paul uses the noun "faith" (πίστις, *pistis*) in more
than one way in his letters.[14] As we approach v. 9 it is important to
keep in mind at least three of the different ways Paul uses this
word. One of the ways the apostle uses "faith," and the one that is
best known, focuses on the idea of trust in God. This is best
known through Paul's discussion of the faith of Abraham. A second use in Paul's letters of the term "faith" is when it relates to the
concept of conscience, e.g., Rom 14:1, 22, 23. Because of Paul's
use of the word "faith" at 1 Cor 13:2, it is probable that in our
verse here he has in mind a third use of the term to refer to supernatural faith to move mountains. Next Paul mentions gifts of
healing. The apostle does not specify which kind of healing he
has in mind, but we can only assume that it would include the
kinds of healings that Jesus performed in the Gospels and which
the apostles and others performed as recorded in the Acts of the
Apostles. Both the Jewish and pagan converts in the church of
God at Corinth would have been familiar with the claims in their
previous religions regarding the ability to work miracles. Both the
Jews of this period of history as well as pagan religions believed in
the possibility of supernatural religious healings. In fact there

---

[14]A convenient summary is given by Leon Morris, "Faith," *DPL*, pp. 285-
291.

were large pagan temples constructed for this particular purpose, some of which have been excavated in the city of Corinth.

12:10 to another miraculous powers, to another prophecy, to another distinguishing between spirits, to another speaking in different kinds of tongues, and to still another the interpretation of tongues.

Paul's reference to miraculous powers (ἐνεργήματα δυνάμεων, *energēmata dynameōn*) is somewhat ambiguous in this verse. We are uncertain, for example, which miraculous powers Paul has in mind which would not overlap with the gift of healing mentioned in the previous verse. Perhaps the apostle is referring to some types of nature miracles wherein Christians were able to exercise God's authority over the natural world.

In the context of this verse it is easier to understand what Paul has in mind by his reference to prophecy. The possession of this gift by believers is attested not only in Acts and the other Pauline letters, but has also been previously referred to in 1 Cor 11:4-5. Once again both the Jewish and pagan cultures of the first century were well aware of prophecy and prophets in their respective religions. In the world of Greek and Roman polytheism there were even gods and goddesses who specialized in prophecy and prophetic gifts. In an inscription from one pagan shrine in Asia Minor there is a reference to the belief in the "gift of prophecy." The Jewish writings of Josephus as well as numerous pagan authors of the early Roman period contain many references to the dissemination of this belief in prophets and prophetesses at this time.

It is not a coincidence that the next gift which Paul mentions is one that relates to the ability to distinguish between spirits. What he probably has in mind is the ability to discern the difference between true and false prophecy. Since prophecy was seen as arising from the work of God's Spirit in the life of the believer, Paul recognizes, as other Christian writers also did, the need for Christians to know whether a prophecy was truly from God or from an evil spirit. In a religion like early Christianity where the gift of prophecy was not relegated to a small professional clergy, it was understandably important that Christians had ways to discern the difference between prophecy and messages which came from God and those which came either from the devil or just from human ignorance. This is the gift that Paul has in mind when he mentions the discernment of spirits.

Paul concludes this verse with a reference to different kinds of tongues (γένη γλωσσῶν, *genē glōssōn*). There has been much debate regarding the question of what kind of tongue Paul is referring to in 1 Corinthians.[15] Some insist that it is a foreign language and understand this in light of Acts 2. Other interpreters prefer to see this as a reference to ecstatic language. Since the apostle uses the plural and refers to different kinds of tongues, the interpreter should be cautious and not make Paul fit into either one of these categories. Since Paul refers to kinds of tongues, the interpreter needs to be open to the possibility that the practice at Corinth included both foreign languages as well as ecstatic utterances. Once again, these recent converts would have had some familiarity with similar phenomena in their pre-Christian religious experiences since claims of ecstatic language and foreign languages are also found in pagan and Jewish literature of antiquity.

Paul brings this list of different kinds of gifts to an end with a reference to the interpretation of tongues. Paul would have been remiss had he left it out of this list since the gift of interpretation is related to an important part of his argumentation in chapter 14 when he downplays the significance of tongues if there is no one to interpret them.

12:11 All these are the work of one and the same Spirit, and he gives them to each one, just as he determines.

With this verse, Paul brings to a conclusion this unit of thought which he started in 12:7. He emphasizes once again that all of these gifts are the result of the work of the one and same Spirit and that the distribution of these gifts among the various believers in the Corinthian fellowship is based upon the election and prerogative of God's Spirit. This Pauline outlook obviously undermines any Corinthian belief that their possession of a particular gift was based upon their merit or innate spirituality.

---

[15]See the comments by C.M. Robeck, Jr. on "Tongues" in *DPL*, pp. 939-943.

B. ONE BODY, MANY PARTS (12:12-31a)

1. One Body in Christ (12:12-13)

[12]The body is a unit, though it is made up of many parts; and though all its parts are many, they form one body. So it is with Christ. [13]For we were all baptized by[a] one Spirit into one body — whether Jews or Greeks, slave or free — and we were all given the one Spirit to drink.

[a]13 Or *with*; or *in*

12:12 The body is a unit, though it is made up of many parts; and though all its parts are many, they form one body. So it is with Christ.

Paul now joins his doctrine of gifts to his doctrine of the body of Christ. It is worth underscoring that during each of the three occasions in Paul's letters where he discusses gifts (Rom 12, Eph 4, and 1 Cor 12), Paul always includes a discussion of these gifts and their relationship to the body of Christ, namely the church. For Paul there is no idea of a church which has no gifts, and conversely there is no idea in Paul of gifts that do not operate in the context of the body of Jesus Christ.

The general metaphor in 12:12 of a body and its many members was well known in the ancient Roman world. It was sometimes used in political theory as a metaphor to explain the unity that should exist among different individuals in a state and city. The genius of the metaphor for Paul's purposes is seen in the fact that it allows him to explain the organic relationship among Christians, and it also allows him to stress the issues of individuality and unity, two concepts which should not be confused with individualism and uniformity. In Christ the individuality of gifts in no way undermines the organic unity which exists among all the believers.

**12:13 For we were all baptized by one Spirit into one body —
whether Jews or Greeks, slave or free — and we were all given the
one Spirit to drink.**

The common experience in which all believers at Corinth
shared and through which they were brought into an organic relationship with one another is expressed by Paul in this verse. Paul
says that by one Spirit all the believers in Corinth were brought
into the body of Christ. The English phrase "baptized by one
Spirit" (ἐν ἑνὶ πνεύματι . . . ἐβαπτίσθημεν, *en heni pneumati . . .
ebaptisthēmen*) represents a Greek expression found seven times in
the New Testament. It is exceedingly clear in 12:13 as well as in
the surrounding verses that Paul does not have in mind here any
kind of special baptism or any kind of special spiritual experience
available only to a certain group of believers. The baptism to
which Paul refers is one that was experienced by every believer in
the church of God at Corinth.

There has been much debate about what Paul means by his
phrase "all were given the one Spirit to drink." It seems unlikely
that Paul is referring to a participation in the Lord's Supper. It
seems to me that this is just an additional metaphor used by Paul
to refer to the initial experience which all believers participated in
when they came into the body of Christ. This interpretation
would be in harmony with other metaphorical uses that Paul employs when discussing baptism. When Paul says in the first part of
12:13 that Christians have been inundated by the Spirit and at the
end of the verse says they have drunk one Spirit, Paul is working
within the same field of images.

2. Body Members Not Independent (12:14-20)

[14]Now the body is not made up of one part but of many. [15]If
the foot should say, "Because I am not a hand, I do not belong to
the body," it would not for that reason cease to be part of the
body. [16]And if the ear should say, "Because I am not an eye, I do
not belong to the body," it would not for that reason cease to be
part of the body. [17]If the whole body were an eye, where would
the sense of hearing be? If the whole body were an ear, where

would the sense of smell be? [18]But in fact God has arranged the parts in the body, every one of them, just as he wanted them to be. [19]If they were all one part, where would the body be? [20]As it is, there are many parts, but one body.

12:14 Now the body is not made up of one part but of many.

By the use of terms such as body, one part, and many, it is clear that Paul's admonitions in this section are rooted in the spiritual affirmations of 12:12. In addition the apostle is providing the setting for the specific details of 12:15-26.

12:15 If the foot should say, "Because I am not a hand, I do not belong to the body," it would not for that reason cease to be part of the body.

As John Calvin pointed out in his commentary, "everything in this section corresponds to the fable of Menenius Agrippa."[16] This fable or illustration, used by the Roman Menenius Agrippa to advocate unity and tranquillity in the midst of social and political discord, shares in common with Paul's argument here not only the use of an organic model to advocate concord and cooperation but also the personification and monologue of body parts.

> In the days when man's members did not all agree amongst themselves, as is now the case, but had each its own ideas and a voice of its own, the other parts thought it unfair that they should have the worry and the trouble and the labour of providing everything for the belly, . . . they therefore conspired together that the hands should carry no food to the mouth, nor the mouth accept anything that was given it, nor the teeth grind up what they received. While they sought in this angry spirit to starve the belly into submission, the members themselves and the whole body were reduced to the utmost weakness. Hence it had become clear that even the belly had no idle task to perform, and was no more nourished than it nourished the rest, . . . Drawing a parallel from this to show how like was the internal dissen-

---

[16]Calvin, *First Epistle*, p. 266.

sion of the bodily members to the anger of the plebs against
the Fathers, he prevailed upon the minds of his hearers.[17]

In terms of Paul's illustration, it is interesting that the monologue he begins with is not by domineering body parts but rather
by those who question whether they belong to the body. It is clear
at 12:21 that the ideas of the foot are a result of the demeaning
response from arrogant body parts. It is significant in my judgment that Paul's illustration also reflects a conviction that the
foot's diffidence and self-criticism does not remove it from the
body, even when other body parts are the source of such lack of
self-confidence. (See comment on 12:18.)

**12:16 And if the ear should say, "Because I am not an eye, I do
not belong to the body," it would not for that reason cease to be
part of the body.**
Paul switches here to two sensory organs of the body. The
same fundamental perspectives are expressed here as in 12:15,
only this time through a different set of parts.

**12:17 If the whole body were an eye, where would the sense of
hearing be? If the whole body were an ear, where would the sense
of smell be?**
The intended force of Paul's rhetorical questions in this verse
is clear. As John Calvin observed, "it is impossible for the body to
remain healthy and sound, unless its members have different
functions. . . . Equality is therefore in conflict with the well-being
of the body."[18]
The use of the word "eye" here anticipates the pride and boasting of the personified eye in 12:21.

**12:18 But in fact God has arranged the parts in the body, every
one of them, just as he wanted them to be.**
In his instruction to correct Corinthian attitudes Paul wants his
teaching to rest upon more than human observation about how

---

[17]Livy 2.32.9-12, Loeb Classical Library, p. 325. A similar use of this illustration is found in Xenophon, *Memor.* 2.3.18 and Cicero, *Duties* 3.5.22.
[18]Calvin, *First Epistle*, p. 267.

human bodies function. The body illustration is helpful to explain the truth, but the truth Paul is communicating here is grounded specifically in divine actions and intentions. The apostle makes three important affirmations in 12:18.

Paul's first affirmation is that the church of God at Corinth, unlike other associations, guilds, or religious communities at Corinth, is a manifestation of divine arrangement. In the context of the argument of chapter 12 the apostle is establishing the truth that the believers at Corinth must see the various gifts in the Corinthian church as a result of divine and transcendent orchestration.

Second, the apostle teaches that everyone of the Corinthian believers received his or her gift from God. Unlike the concepts of "superior" or "outstanding" which are associated with the English word "gifted," Paul's concept of gifted included all believers. When Paul asserts in 12:22ff. that even weak and dishonorable body parts are important, he is making explicit what is stated here. Namely, all believers and their God-given gifts, irrespective of their prestige in human eyes, are a work of God and belong exactly where God has placed them.

A final point that is made regards the issue of the sovereignty of God. When Paul writes of something being the way God wanted it to be, he reflects the Biblical conviction of God's sovereign will reflected in texts such as Ps 115:3 and 135:6.

12:19 If they were all one part, where would the body be?

This is one of Paul's strongest statements, by means of a rhetorical question, against those who would equate unity with uniformity. There can never be a healthy example of a body, either human or Christ's, where all the members walk lockstep or look like they were manufactured from the same cookie cutters.

12:20 As it is, there are many parts, but one body.

The truth in God's church, Paul writes, is that a plurality of gifts is the divine mandate. And furthermore, each gifted believer ought to see himself or herself in a bodily (= organic) relationship to other gifted believers.

3. Special Honor for Weaker Parts (12:21-26)

[21]The eye cannot say to the hand, "I don't need you!" And the head cannot say to the feet, "I don't need you!" [22]On the contrary, those parts of the body that seem to be weaker are indispensable, [23]and the parts that we think are less honorable we treat with special honor. And the parts that are unpresentable are treated with special modesty, [24]while our presentable parts need no special treatment. But God has combined the members of the body and has given greater honor to the parts that lacked it, [25]so that there should be no division in the body, but that its parts should have equal concern for each other. [26]If one part suffers, every part suffers with it; if one part is honored, every part rejoices with it.

12:21 The eye cannot say to the hand, "I don't need you!" And the head cannot say to the feet, "I don't need you!"

In this verse the apostle fights against the attitude of certain Corinthian believers that they can go it alone, or at least that they have no need of fellow saints whom they regard as beneath them. This seems to be a clear instance of the social stratification of urban Corinth penetrating the ranks of the church, resulting in some believers assuming a posture of superiority in terms of gifts. It is surely not an accident that in Paul's social setting where manual labor was judged inferior in the minds of upper crust people, that it was hands and feet that were being snubbed. While eyes and head reflected the body parts more symbolized by affluence and educational elitism, hands and feet were the essential body parts for the mass of urban lower classes and slaves. Paul emphatically repudiates any efforts to bring into the church and its ministries of gifts a Roman elitism and parochialism based upon ideas of self-sufficiency and superiority.

12:22 On the contrary, those parts of the body that seem to be weaker are indispensable,

While Paul's use of the term "weaker" (ἀσθενής, *asthenēs*) fits naturally in the metaphor of a body, he probably has not used this term without a backward glance to his use of the word "weak" (and its cognates) in 1:2, 27; 8:7, 9, 10, 11, 12; and 9:22. The apostle's use of the term "weak" to describe a recognizable group of Corinthian believers in chapters 8-9 provides a striking analogy to his use in 12:22, where it must certainly refer metaphorically to a recognizable group within the body of Christ. God has often used weak individuals to play an indispensable role in his plans (see notes on 1 Cor 1:25-27).

12:23 and the parts that we think are less honorable we treat with special honor. And the parts that are unpresentable are treated with special modesty,

In a Roman urban setting which was mesmerized by recognition and bestowal of honor, Paul must argue decisively and boldly to carve out a place for the less honorable within the community of faith. Banquets were held, statues and inscriptions were erected, crowns were awarded, and orations were given throughout Paul's world to bestow honor and acclaim. In this instance Paul must inculcate within his readers the novel idea of giving honor to whom (from a cultural point of view) honor is not due. The apostle's metaphor of body provides a perfect object lesson. From the treatment of the human body, where the genitalia are regarded as less honorable and unpresentable but are given a special honor and modesty, Paul is able to argue that in God's plan those at church who appear honorless should receive special honor.

12:24 while our presentable parts need no special treatment. But God has combined the members of the body and has given greater honor to the parts that lacked it,

The body's presentable parts (e.g., face, arms) need no special treatment. The acknowledgment in 12:24 that God is responsible for the mixture and combination of different types of body members is clearly designed to address the Corinthians' ignorance about the nature of the church and not about human biology. Not only is God responsible for the diversity but, according to the apostle, he is also the reason that the community of faith at Cor-

inth must give honor (τιμή, *timē*) to the honorless (ἄτιμος, *atimos*) in
its midst.

**12:25 so that there should be no division in the body, but that its
parts should have equal concern for each other.**

Since God is the author and source of unity among believers,
he obviously supplies the church with those things necessary for
unity. In 12:25 Paul explains why God gave greater honor to those
who lacked it. God's purpose was to preclude (ἵνα + μή, *hina* + *mē*)
division in the body of Christ. This is the third time in
1 Corinthians that Paul has acknowledged that he is dealing with
a problem of division. The first occurrence was in the matter of
party loyalty (1:10), the second was in regard to social stratification and disorderliness interjected into the Lord's Supper (11:18),
and the final instance relates to misunderstandings about gifts and
their correct use (12:25).

The opposite of division in the context of the Corinthians'
misunderstanding and misuse of gifts is a spirit of reciprocal concern. A dynamic and organic unity where the various limbs and
organs of a body tend to the needs of one another is Paul's antidote for divisive thoughts and actions arising from the possession
of gifts.

**12:26 If one part suffers, every part suffers with it; if one part is
honored, every part rejoices with it.**

This verse contains two conditional (if) sentences. In the first
one Paul draws out of the implication from the body's response
to pain. If one suffers pain through a broken bone, a headache, a
sunburn, or a cut, the entire body is aware of the pain and the
ability of the whole to function is impaired. This is Paul's analogy
to support the previous notion (12:25) that the members of the
body should show equal concern for each other.

Paul's specific meaning in the second conditional sentence has
been less clear to interpreters. It may be the case that Paul's sense
is that when a fellow believer (= one part of the body of Christ) is
honored all the members should rejoice. On the other hand, he
may be remaining in the analogy of the body and stating that
when a human body part is honored (cf. 12:23, 24 for the genitalia

being honored), all the other body parts, understood as a collective personification, rejoice with the honored part. In either case, the upshot of this analogy is clear for the church in Corinth.

4. Application to the Body of Christ (12:27-31a)

[27]Now you are the body of Christ, and each one of you is a part of it. [28]And in the church God has appointed first of all apostles, second prophets, third teachers, then workers of miracles, also those having gifts of healing, those able to help others, those with gifts of administration, and those speaking in different kinds of tongues. [29]Are all apostles? Are all prophets? Are all teachers? Do all work miracles? [30]Do all have gifts of healing? Do all speak in tongues[a]? Do all interpret? [31]But eagerly desire[b] the greater gifts.

[a]*30 Or other languages*   [b]*31 Or But you are eagerly desiring*

12:27 Now you are the body of Christ, and each one of you is a part of it.

At this juncture the apostle moves from the illustration and analogy of the human body. Paul now declares that the church of God at Corinth should not only work together like a body, but in fact that it is the body of Christ. The saints in this colonial Roman capital of Achaia are reminded (or perhaps told for the first time) that each one of them is an organic part, a corporeal member, of Christ's body. It is on the basis of Paul's doctrinal statement here that some interpreters have argued that the church, as the body of Christ, is an extension of the Incarnation or is the Second Incarnation. To the extent that this understanding is faithful to Paul's overall theology, it would be better to locate it in other texts where he uses body of Christ imagery. Given the issue under discussion in 1 Cor 12 and the rhetorical context of 12:27, it seems improbable that Paul is making an explicit point about ecclesiology or the church's connection to the enthroned Lord (as in Eph 1:19-23; Col 1:15-20) when he writes "you are the Body of Christ."

12:28 And in the church God has appointed first of all apostles, second prophets, third teachers, then workers of miracles, also those having gifts of healing, those able to help others, those with gifts of administration, and those speaking in different kinds of tongues.

While the basic intent and function of this verse is clear, the verse bristles with difficulties when the details are investigated. The function of the section 12:28-31 is to serve as a transition to chapter 13 by bringing to an end his discussion of gifts and the body of Christ. He also highlights a final time that the variety of gifts is from God and that uniformity of gifts has never been the plan of God or the experience of the Corinthian saints.

The first point of controversy is the meaning of Paul's use of the terms "first . . . second . . . third . . . then." Do these terms refer to the chronological sequence in which they appeared in the primitive church or in which they appeared at Corinth, or do the terms point to a qualitative value of these gifts? That is, are apostles of first importance, prophets second, teachers third, etc.? Although it is not without problems, the qualitative interpretation seems to be the best one. One must keep in mind that the kingdom of God is not a democracy and that gifts are neither identical in nature nor equal in function. Paul is teaching that some gifts and the ministries of those who have them have a higher priority than others. The concept of priority expressed here by the use of numbers is expressed at other places in the Pauline letters by terms such as master builder (1 Cor 3:10-12) and apostles and prophets (Eph 3:5).

It is not certain whether the term "apostle" (ἀπόστολος, *apostolos*) here refers to the Twelve or to other workers known by the term *apostolos* (e.g., 1 Cor 4:9; 15:7-11; Gal 1:19; Phil 2:25; 1 Thess 2:7; cf. Acts 14:4,14).

On the role of prophets see notes on 12:10.

The gift of teachers is recorded in Rom 12:7 and Eph 4:11, making it and the gift of prophecy the two gifted ministries found in the three lists of gifts in Rom 12:6-8; 1 Cor 12, and Eph 4:11.

In light of the contextual influence exerted on the details of Paul's list of gifts, the two gifts of helping others and of administration seem to be out of place. These two do not seem to belong quite as naturally in the list, nor do they seem to play a role in the Corinthian problem that Paul is responding to in 1 Cor 12-14. The gifts of miracle working, healing, and speaking in different kinds of tongues, on the other hand, fit naturally and quickly into the lists of 12:8-10, 29-30 as well as into the Corinthian problem set forth in chapters 12-14.

12:29 Are all apostles? Are all prophets? Are all teachers? Do all work miracles?

Both in 12:29 and 12:30 Paul rapidly sets out a series of rhetorical questions intended to address the divisive attitude of some of the Corinthians regarding various spiritual gifts (cf. 12:25, so that there may be no division (σχίσμα, *schisma*). There is an important feature in the Greek grammar of these questions which is not always appreciated in English language translations of the New Testament. Based upon the details of the Greek text, Paul's question implies that he expects a negative answer. Accordingly, when Paul writes "Are all apostles?" the answer is to be "no." While common sense might tell most interpreters that God did not expect all believers to be apostles, the issue would be less obvious in regard to other gifts (e.g., tongues). It is helpful to realize, therefore, that the correct answer to all the questions of 12:29-30 is "no." By examining the other references in the Pauline letter to apostolic, prophetic, didactic, and miracle-working activities, it is manifest that God never intended for all believers to have any one of these gifts. In regard to the gift of prophecy, the point Paul makes here should not be lost when interpreting chapter 14.

12:30 Do all have gifts of healing? Do all speak in tongues? Do all interpret?

As mentioned earlier (see notes on 12:9), we do not know the details of these healing gifts at Corinth, nor do they come up again in the subsequent instructions in chapters 13-14.

The gift of speaking in tongues, in its variety, is known to us from chapters 13-14 as well as from the Acts of the Apostles and the longer ending of Mark 16. Even though some Pentecostal interpreters are not yet convinced, 12:30 makes it clear that God did not supply this gift to all believers. Given the rhetorical context of

Paul's argument at 12:27-30, Paul is here focusing primarily on the fact of the diversity of gifts in the Body of Christ. It will only be possible after laying down the foundational principle of *agapē* in 13:1-14:1 that Paul can use that to guide the correct practice of tongues. Furthermore, the gift of interpretation, whose significance is made clear in chapter 14 (cf. 12:10) is likewise not given to every "baptized-by-one-Spirit" (12:13) member of the church of God.

12:31 But eagerly desire the greater gifts. And now I will show you the most excellent way.

Here the interpreter is faced with an immediate translation problem, the details of which are traced by R.P. Martin.[19] The phrase "eagerly desire" represents the Greek word ζηλοῦτε (*zēloute*) which could be translated: (1) as an imperative ("you must desire," as the NIV translates it); (2) as an indicative ("you are currently seeking"); (3) as an interrogative indicative ("you are seeking then the 'greater gifts', are you?").[20] This study will follow the imperative option taken by the NIV.

It is apparent from the imperative verb "desire" that the Corinthians have control over their possession of at least some of the gifts. This is certainly in harmony with Paul's teaching that "spirits of prophets are subject to the control of prophets" (1 Cor 14:32). Fee is correct to link the reference to greater gifts in 12:31 with the connected thought of 14:5 that affirms that he who prophesies is greater than he who speaks in tongues. The greater gifts which the Corinthians should eagerly desire would be those that edify and serve other believers rather than those that are self-serving.

This train of thought anticipates the details of ch. 14 and moves quite quickly and naturally in the focus of 13:1-6 on the necessity of love. Even though some interpreters have imagined that Paul is offering *agapē* as a superior substitute for gifts, this is quite unlikely. In the first instance, Paul affirms that gifts are part and parcel of the church's equipment until the day of Christ's return (1 Cor 1:6-8). Moreover, since Paul has pointed out the inextricable connection between members of the body of Christ and

---

[19]Martin, *The Spirit and the Congregation*, pp. 17, 33-35.
[20]Ibid., p. 17.

gifts (1 Cor 12), he could hardly conceive a body without body parts. Finally, as the logic of the conditional sentences of 13:1-4 makes clear, the apostle is concerned that love accompany, not replace, gifts.

For Paul the most excellent way is not to be a giftless church — an ecclesiastical amputee, to adapt the metaphors of chapter 12 — but a community of believers whose use and understanding of the gifts of God is loving and other-centered.

1 CORINTHIANS 13

C. LOVE (12:31b-13:13)

1. Gifts Without Love Pointless (12:31b-13:3)

And now I will show you the most excellent way.
[1]If I speak in the tongues[a] of men and of angels, but have not love, I am only a resounding gong or a clanging cymbal. [2]If I have the gift of prophecy and can fathom all mysteries and all knowledge, and if I have a faith that can move mountains, but have not love, I am nothing. [3]If I give all I possess to the poor and surrender my body to the flames,[b] but have not love, I gain nothing.

[a]*1* Or *languages*   [b]*3* Some early manuscripts *body that I may boast*

13:1 If I speak in the tongues of men and of angels, but have not love, I am only a resounding gong or a clanging cymbal.
Due to the obvious impact of the Protestant Reformation, Paul's doctrine of *agapē* (ἀγάπη) is not as influential as his doctrine of justification. Nevertheless, this chapter is the most quoted and best known chapter from the Pauline corpus of letters.

In light of the occasional nature of Paul's letters and the location of 1 Cor 13 in the rhetorical setting of chapters 12-14, both the details of this chapter as well as its overall arguments must be interpreted in light of the epistle's historical-cultural setting. Accordingly, the dichotomy "tongues of men" and "tongues of angels" ought to be interpreted in the frame of reference provided by ancient practices of Jewish and non-Jewish religions (cf. 12:2 and notes there) and the apostolic teaching given by Paul, especially in 1 Corinthians. To begin, there is little support for the view that Paul's doctrine of tongues expressed in 1 Corinthians requires that tongues be either glossalalia or foreign languages. This kind of rigid either/or choice is certainly at odds with the seemingly straightforward meaning of 13:1a. It must be remembered that Paul already acknowledged in 12:10, 28 that believers who spoke in tongues had the gift of kinds of tongues (γένη γλωσσῶν, *genē glōssōn*). Contextually, then, the two types of tongues mentioned in 13:1a might reflect the types of gift-tongues mentioned in the preceding chapter.

In addition, there is clear historical evidence from antiquity that points to the existence of similar phenomena in both Jewish and Gentile religions. That is, the idea of a religious experience which included the speaking of heavenly (non-human) words as well as the speaking of foreign (to the speaker) words circulated in the literature and practices of the world contemporary with early Christianity. The long known Jewish document entitled *Testament of Job* contains a scene with the daughters of Job. While in an ecstatic state they speak in an "angelic language," in "the language of the Cherubim," and "the language of principalities."[1] The early Christian author Clement of Alexandria affirmed that even Plato believed that the gods had their own language which they used in communications with mortals in the form of dreams, oracles, and demonic possession of individuals.[2]

Paul's point in his contrast of tongues without love is to teach the Corinthians that when they engage in tongue speaking that is self-centered rather than other-centered it results in a cacophony. Discordant sounds are the fruit of loveless tongue speaking in a congregational setting.

---

[1]*Testament of Job* 48-50, cited according to R.P. Spittler, *Testament of Job* in *The Old Testament Pseudepigrapha* Vol. 1, Apocalyptic Literature and Testaments, ed. J.H. Charlesworth (Garden City: Doubleday, 1983), pp. 865-866.

[2]Clement, *Stromata* 1, 21.

13:2 If I have the gift of prophecy and can fathom all mysteries and all knowledge, and if I have a faith that can move mountains, but have not love, I am nothing.

This verse continues the style and theme begun by the Apostle in 13:1. Even though prophecy has high visibility in 1 Corinthians and is highly ranked by Paul himself (cf. 12:28; 14:1,5) possession of it accrues to nothing if it is practiced by one not controlled by love. The decision to include prophecy in this verse is made on the basis of its role in the problem issues of ch. 12-14 and not because all believers at Corinth had received this gift from God (cf. 12:29).

While reference to a negative understanding of knowledge can be found outside the rhetorical unit of chapters 12-14 (e.g., 8:1), Paul's use of the term in 13:2 is best understood against the background of 12:8 where the gift of knowledge is attested. The notion of knowing all mysteries could be traced back to ideas of 4:1ff or, given the residual pagan theology Paul is opposing among certain of the Corinthians, it may refer to a religious preoccupation with arcane and mystical religious information and experiences.

The final item in 13:2, faith that can move mountains, clearly points to supernatural and miraculous activity (cf. 12:9-10). The wording of this concept can surely be traced to the words of Jesus in Matt 17:20; 21:21, and Mark 11:23. While this phrase obviously points to extraordinary miraculous power, there is a question whether it was understood literally by Jesus and the Apostles. This phrase clearly points to a nature miracle rather than a healing miracle (cf. 12:9-10). It is no coincidence, in my judgment, that Jesus himself never performs this particular miracle and that nature miracles of this sort are astonishingly rare in the lives of the Twelve, Paul, and the early Christian communities. These facts point to the hyperbolic character of this concept and phrase. Similar verbal hyperboles were known in the Greek world as pagans spoke of someone's miraculous powers over nature. Martin[3] believes that this idiom reflects "use of a Jewish proverbial phrase."

---

[3]Martin, *The Spirit*, p. 44.

For those at Corinth who are promoting division over the worthiness of gifts (cf. 12:24-25), Paul's analysis is devastating. Could it be that possession of the three alls — all mysteries, all knowledge, all faith (this final "all" is left out by the NIV) — was less than impressive to God if these were not accompanied by *agapē*? The apostle answers in the affirmative by his words, "I am nothing."

13:3 If I give all I possess to the poor and surrender my body to the flames, but have not love, I gain nothing.

Paul has left more than one interpreter wondering about the point of reference the apostle had in mind in 13:3. With the words "but have not love, I gain nothing" it is easy enough to recognize the similarity between the upshot of 13:3 and 13:1-2. The problem issues, however, are the references to "giving to the poor" and "body to the flames." There is little doubt that Paul is here attacking misplaced Corinthian values. The initial problem, however, is whether and how these two relate to the issues that characterize 1 Cor 12-14.

At least two suggestions should be considered. The first is that 13:1-3 are intended by Paul to be regarded as autobiographical rhetoric. Just as he had used autobiographical materials earlier in this epistle to bolster the persuasiveness of his argument (e.g., 2:1-5; 9:1-23; 10:30-11:1), so here he expects the readers to see his own life in the statements of 13:1-3. In light of the repeated use of the pronoun "I" in 13:1-3, it is easy to see that 13:3a might refer to characteristics of the apostle's life which would not necessarily be part of the problems under discussion in chapters 12-14.

A second possibility is to see the issues of 13:3a as related to the Corinthian situation, but not as centrally as prophecies, tongues, etc. If it is indeed this latter case, then the two issues of donating possessions and throwing oneself to the flames would need to be documented as hallmarks of boasting and of religiosity in the world of the Corinthian converts. Denunciation of possessions was clearly viewed by certain Greco-Roman philosophers and miracle-workers as emblems of their self-importance and divine superiority to others. The denunciation of this world would reach a climax in suicidal immolation. An example of this type of understanding is evident in the biography of a philosophic guru of the second century who began as a pagan, converted to Christianity, lapsed back into paganism and finally ended his life intentionally by throwing himself into the flames. In the case of this particular pagan, Proteus Peregrinus, this fiery death was a means of his metamorphosis into immortality.

2. The Virtues of Love (13:4-7)

⁴Love is patient, love is kind. It does not envy, it does not boast, it is not proud. ⁵It is not rude, it is not self-seeking, it is not easily angered, it keeps no record of wrongs. ⁶Love does not delight in evil but rejoices with the truth. ⁷It always protects, always trusts, always hopes, always perseveres.

13:4 Love is patient, love is kind. It does not envy, it does not boast, it is not proud.

If 13:1-3 is designed to teach the emptiness of gifts not controlled by love, then 13:4-7 enumerates characteristics of love.[4] There are many facets to love and numerous images and idioms used in Scripture to teach about it (cf. Rom 5:6-8; 8:37-39; 2 Cor 5:14-15). The ideas and terms recorded here are especially germane to the congregational and liturgical problems evident in Corinth. For example the reference to "envy" (ζηλόω, *zēloō*) echoes the noun cognate in 1 Cor 3:3 (ζῆλος, *zēlos*) and the term "proud" (φυσιόω, *physioō*) reminds one of the apostle's remarks about this trait among Corinthian believers (4:6, 18, 19; 5:2; 8:1).

More than one of the traits listed here can be found in other sections of Pauline letters (e.g., Gal 5:19-23). Since the Corinthians' misunderstanding of spiritual matters lies primarily in their failure to live as a body, Paul draws attention to those characteristics of love most important for harmonious relationships.

---

[4]In general see R. Mohrlang, "Love," *DPL*, pp. 577-578.

13:5 It is not rude, it is not self-seeking, it is not easily angered, it keeps no record of wrongs.

It is helpful when interpreting this verse to reflect on the dynamics of party loyalty (ch. 1-4), the personal struggles involved in getting the strong to defer to the weak (ch. 8-10), or the pride and emotions which were so evident in the competition among prophets and tongue speakers (14:26-40). Against this backdrop the interpreter easily visualizes the relevance and application of this verse to the Corinthian readers. Ralph Martin correctly observed in this matter that the verbs of these verses "unite to form a coherent profile of the trouble at Corinth, and Paul submits a theological critique in the name of *agapē*."[5]

13:6 Love does not delight in evil but rejoices with the truth.

The contextual background to Paul's inclusion of evil and truth is the problem of immorality addressed in chapters 5-6. The Greek word (along with its cognates) used here for evil (ἀδικία, *adikia*) is found in 6:1, 7-9 where the apostle teaches that the unrighteous (ἄδικος, *adikos*) will not inherit God's kingdom. There is no place in God's kingdom, according to Paul, for those who are in love with evil and its manifestations as enumerated in 6:9-10.

Conversely, those who celebrate the Christian's Passover and the believer's feast of Unleavened Bread do so in truth (5:8) and rejoice, with no apologies, with the truth.

13:7 It always protects, always trusts, always hopes, always perseveres.

Some interpreters divide the four verbs of this verse into two categories. In this arrangement the first and last deal with the present circumstances, while the second and third verbs look to the future.[6]

The direction the NIV goes with this first verb (στήγω, *stēgō*) is perhaps misleading. If there is any autobiographical element in this section of chapter 13 (see comments on 13:3), then the only other use of this verb in 1 Corinthians might provide interpretive clues. In another autobiographical section of this epistle Paul

---

[5]Martin, *The Spirit*, p. 50.
[6]Fee, *First Epistle*, pp. 639-640.

writes, ". . . we put up (στήγομεν, *stēgomen*) with anything (πάντα, *panta*) rather than hinder the gospel of Christ" (9:12). In this light, 13:7, (πάντα στήγει, *panta stēgei*) might better be translated "love puts up with anything" instead of love "always protects."

The phrase "always trusts" (πάντα πιστεύει, *panta pisteuei*) probably anticipates the faith (13:13), just as "always hope" anticipates the endurance of hope in 13:13. The notion of "always perseveres" (πάντα ὑπομένει, *panta hypomenei*) points to the quality of love that expresses patience in the face of all situations.

3. The Permanence of Love (13:8-13)

[8]Love never fails. But where there are prophecies, they will cease; where there are tongues, they will be stilled; where there is knowledge, it will pass away. [9]For we know in part and we prophesy in part, [10]but when perfection comes, the imperfect disappears. [11]When I was a child, I talked like a child, I thought like a child, I reasoned like a child. When I became a man, I put childish ways behind me. [12]Now we see but a poor reflection as in a mirror; then we shall see face to face. Now I know in part; then I shall know fully, even as I am fully known.

[13]And now these three remain: faith, hope and love. But the greatest of these is love.

13:8 Love never fails. But where there are prophecies, they will cease; where there are tongues, they will be stilled; where there is knowledge, it will pass away.
This verse begins the third and final major argument of chapter 13, one in which the author demonstrates the superiority of love. The first part of this argument is based upon the temporal superiority of love. To state it briefly, the Corinthians need to tone down their preoccupation with squabbling over tongues, prophecies, and special knowledge, because none of these is destined for a long life. The three phrases "they will cease," "they will be stilled," and "it will pass away" are all set temporally in juxtaposition to the unfailing nature of love.

13:9 For we know in part and we prophesy in part,

The two issues of knowledge and prophecy mentioned in 13:9 arise from references to them in 13:8 (notice the connecting word for (γάρ, *gar*). For reasons of English style the NIV covers up a verbal connection between 13:9 and 13:10 that is obvious in the Greek text. The reader should know that the prepositional phrase (ἐκ μέρους, *ek merous*) rendered "in part" twice in 13:9 and once in 13:12 is translated as "imperfect" in the phrase "the imperfect" in 13:10. Since the *ek merous* of 13:10 is contrasted with "the perfect" (τὸ τέλειον, *to teleion*) this phrase points in the direction of meaning "imperfectly" in 13:9.

In light of the fact that in the context of 1 Cor 12-14 the idea of knowledge generally refers to the gift known as the "word of knowledge" (12:8) or having "all knowledge" (13:2), Paul is probably referring to such in 13:9. This would surely make sense of the reference to the Spirit given knowledge in 13:8. The gift of prophecy is likewise experienced only in part. Irrespective of the quantity and quality of one's prophecies, for Paul the prophet has still only touched the hem of the garment in regard to understanding the mind of God, discerning his will, and knowing the fullness of his presence (cf. 13:12).

13:10 but when perfection comes, the imperfect disappears.

While it has been relatively obvious to most interpreters that the disappearance of the imperfect refers to the cessation of spiritual gifts, there has not been as much unanimity regarding the meaning of the term "perfection" (τὸ τέλειον, *to teleion*). The four most popular views seem to be the following:

1) The idea of the arrival of perfection and the cessation of these gifts points to the full revelation of doctrine which is to be found in the New Testament Scriptures (cf. Eph 4:11-13; Heb 2:1-4). Accordingly, these gifts would pass away during the era of the primitive church, not lasting any longer than a few generations past the deaths of the Apostles (= Paul + the Twelve).

2) The concept of perfection is associated with the acquisition of love by the church. Viewing love as the more excellent way and a replacement for spiritual gifts, this approach attaches the cessa-

tion of gifts to the church's timetable in its following the path of *agapē*.

3) A closely related interpretation is that which believes that the mature church no longer needs the contributions made by these gifts of the Spirit. This view is especially compelling to some because of the mature-immature imagery in 1 Cor 2:6; 3:1-3 and a correlation of the topics of gifts and maturity in Eph 4:7-16 (esp. 4:13).

4) The fourth view is that gifts are part of the ministry of God to strengthen the church until the Second Coming of Christ (1 Cor 1:5-9). This means that the perfection in 13:10 refers to the time and conditions following the End. D.A. Carson noted in his support of this view that this eschatological interpretation is strengthened by 1 Cor 13:12b where "Perfection entails a state of affairs where my knowledge is in some ways comparable with God's present knowledge of me" and by the fact that the wording "we shall see face to face" is "almost certainly a reference to the new state brought about by the parousia."[7]

This fourth view has, in my judgment, much to commend it. Even though the first view has a long and widespread acceptance in Protestant interpretation even to this day, it does seem to have been kept alive more by polemical necessity than exegetical soundness. One should not, however, leap to the false conclusion that the abandonment of position one (the perfect = the completed Canon) is tantamount to an abdication to Pentecostal theology and experience. Numerous religious fellowships and denominations have accepted interpretation four (i.e., the eschatological) and yet remained firmly opposed to classical Pentecostalism. It seems to me that advocates of Pentecostalism would have to work vigorously on at least three issues before the eschatological interpretation could be used to buttress their own classical doctrinal views. I would call these the issues of (1) selectivity of gifts, (2) sectarian and carnal fruit, and (3) scriptural practice of tongues and prophecy.

(1) *Selectivity of gifts.* If those who advocate that God dispenses the same gifts today as 2000 years ago were correct, then why is

---

[7] Carson, *Showing the Spirit*, pp. 70-71.

the primary Pentecostal gift today one that is so easily counter-feited? As the renowned Charismatic scholar Michael Green observed in regard to tongue speaking, "Of course, there are counterfeits. . . . In the case of tongues [God takes over] a psychological phenomenon that was and is widely experienced. . . . Moslem mystics speak in tongues; . . . tongues can be psychologically induced in men who have no faith at all."[8] In this day of global communication and instant replays, why are non-charismatics not given access to contemporary examples of individuals being raised from the dead or samplings of nature miracles, rather than primarily charismatic worship services where those items put forth as proof of the working of the "Holy Ghost" are exceedingly unrepresentative of the full number of gifts and miraculous powers demonstrated in the early church.

(2) *Sectarian and carnal fruit.* As D.A. Carson noted, more than one fellowship has been torn apart or divided by the carnal spiritual elitism of those who claimed to have been blessed by a special measure of spiritual gifts.[9] Moreover, while every doctrinal orientation has its Achilles' heel, the notoriety of the shams, the sexual immorality, and the criminal financial dealings that have risen from modern Pentecostalism surely leave one with the impression that this group needs to get its own house in order before it claims exemplary blessings from or insight into the Holy (!) Spirit.

(3) *Scriptural practice of tongues and prophecy.* It is difficult for many on the outside of the Pentecostal Movement (a movement that desires to be Scripture-based) to understand why there is such an apparent disregard for Paul's explicit teaching that tongues are to be accompanied by interpretation of tongues, as well as his statement that only a few at a time should be allowed to speak in tongues or to prophecy.

---

[8]Michael Green, *I Believe in the Holy Spirit* (Grand Rapids: Eerdmans, 1975), p. 199.
[9]Carson, *Showing the Spirit*, pp. 185-188.

13:11 When I was a child, I talked like a child, I thought like a child, I reasoned like a child. When I became a man, I put childish ways behind me.

Since the apostle Paul himself was a tongues-speaker, since he forbade any efforts to squelch tongue-speaking (done correctly), and since love and maturity are not a substitute for spiritual gifts, it is unlikely that Paul is directing this verse against Corinthian tongue-speaking. The apostle is not, in my judgment, teaching that tongue speaking is only for infantile believers or that the "childish ways" are ephemeral supernatural gifts. The contextual meaning of 13:11 is to tell the Corinthians that certain thinking and behavior are appropriate for certain ages. Compared to the age-to-come the present age is childlike. This reminder to the Corinthians, who believe they know far more than they actually do, anticipates the connection in 13:12 about the poor reflection of reality experienced in the "now." It is only when "time will be no more" that the Corinthians will fully recognize their earlier adolescence.

13:12 Now we see but a poor reflection as in a mirror; then we shall see face to face. Now I know in part; then I shall know fully, even as I am fully known.

Lamentably the NIV chose not to translate the Greek word γάρ (*gar*, for) in 13:12, thereby lessening the explicit connection between 13:11 and 13:12. The function of this verse is to challenge the readers at Corinth to recognize the relative inferiority of their current situation. By his twofold use of the "now/then" (ἄρτι/τότε, *arti/tote*) temporal contrast, the apostle is attempting to diminish the misplaced security some of the Corinthian believers have. In Paul's judgment, if a diversity of gifts is allowed to bring about division (12:25) and impede edification (ch. 14), one's evaluation of gifts needs to be recalibrated. We can only hypothesize whether these Corinthians had an overt problem in their eschatology. It is clear, however, that Paul employs his own eschatological perspectives to attempt a correction. By his references to the eschatological future (then) and its superiority, Paul hopes to shift the Corinthians out of their carnal thinking.

Specifically, Paul wants to challenge those who might be self-deceived through their tongue speaking, prophecies, or gifts of knowledge (13:2, 8-9) and who think they can justifiably boast, be proud, be self-seeking, and impatient (cf. 13:4-5). Paul's verdict to everyone in this situation is that all that they have, regardless of its source, is but a poor reflection. The experience of the divine world claimed by the readers is nothing, in the apostle's opinion, compared to the eschatological experience when all believers, unassisted by tongues and prophecy, commune with God face to face. While there are some dissenters, most interpreters rightly regard the phrase "face to face" as a divine encounter (e.g., Gen 32:30; Exod 33:11; Num 14:14; Deut 5:4; 34:10; Ezek 20:35; cf. Judg 6:22).

Paul's affirmation here of the partial knowledge of the believer (even of an apostle) in the present age goes hand-in-hand with other texts where Paul makes the same point, though in different congregational settings. In light of the congregational needs at Corinth and in light of the rhetorical character of 1 Cor 13, Paul's statement is not intended to foster doubt or agnosticism, but to collapse the theology of those who claim to have "all knowledge" (v. 2).

13:13 And now these three remain: faith, hope and love. But the greatest of these is love.

The triad of "faith, hope, and love" was, in R.P. Martin's opinion, "a pre-formed triad of Christian 'virtues' attested in Paul, who in turn derived it from his predecessors" . . . [and] "reads here in a way that suggests that Paul is appealing to a well-known formula."[10]

There seem to be two distinct approaches to the interpretation of this verse, both of which are related to one's understanding of the phrase "and now" (νῦν δέ, *nun de*). One approach interprets this as a temporal phrase, keeping it in the same "now-then" eschatological framework as we have seen in the preceding verses. From this point of view, faith, hope, and love are the supreme

---

[10]Martin, *The Spirit*, p. 55.

virtues of this age since they remain, while love is the greatest since it goes on into eternity.

A second approach, argued by D.A. Carson, takes the phrase "and now" logically and not temporally. He translates the Greek at this location with the words "now in fact."[11] From Carson's perspective all three virtues continue into eternity, but love is the greatest "presumably because God himself displays love but neither faith nor hope."

The first of these two approaches has appealed to the greatest number of interpreters and correctly so. The eschatological interpretation more fully appreciates the radical nature of the coming perfection and consummation when "faith will become sight and hope will be fulfilled" and love will "bridge this age and the eschatological reality."[12]

As the reader gives a backward glance over the preceding verses of ch. 13 there can be little doubt why the apostle regards love so highly. As Fee succinctly observed about this chapter, the apostle argued and taught the "absolute necessity of love" (13:1-3), "the character of love" (13:4-7), and "the permanence of love" (13:8-13).[13] As the reader looks ahead to the pleas, arguments, and details of ch. 14, it should not go unnoticed that agapē is that bridge (14:1a) on which Paul walks as he enters into that stage of his letter.

---

[11]Carson, *Showing the Spirit*, p. 73.
[12]Witherington, *Conflict and Community in Corinth*, p. 272.
[13]Fee, *First Epistle*, p. 628.

1 CORINTHIANS 14

D. GIFTS OF PROPHECY AND TONGUES (14:1-25)

1. Tongues and Prophecy Compared (14:1-5)

¹Follow the way of love and eagerly desire spiritual gifts, especially the gift of prophecy. ²For anyone who speaks in a tongue^a does not speak to men but to God. Indeed, no one understands him; he utters mysteries with his spirit.^b ³But everyone who prophesies speaks to men for their strengthening, encouragement and comfort. ⁴He who speaks in a tongue edifies himself, but he who prophesies edifies the church. ⁵I would like every one of you to speak in tongues, but I would rather have you prophesy. He who prophesies is greater than one who speaks in tongues,^c unless he interprets, so that the church may be edified.

^a2 Or *another language*; also in verses 4, 13, 14, 19, 26 and 27   ^b2 Or *by the spirit*
^c5 Or *other languages*; also in verses 6, 18, 22, 23 and 39

14:1 Follow the way of love and eagerly desire spiritual gifts, especially the gift of prophecy.

A few observations are in order as one moves into this new chapter. Even though 14:1 is linked to 12:1 by the common use of the plural adjective πνευματικά (*pneumatika*, spiritual things), Paul has clearly narrowed his focus. The gifts of tongues and prophecy are easily lost in the larger cluster of gifts enumerated in 12:4-10 and 12:28-30. By the time Paul has carried forward his argument through chapter 13, the list of gifts has shrunk so that tongues and prophecy are a bit more prominent (cf. 13:1-3, 8-12). With chapter 14, however, there can be no doubt that Paul is now ready to focus intently on the gifts of tongues and prophecy. Paul's term for tongues (γλῶσσαι, *glōssai*) is found approximately twenty times in

327

1 Corinthians and fifteen of these are in this one chapter. When one looks at the issue of prophecy the evidence is equally stark. The verb "to prophesy" (προφητεύω, *prophēteuō*) occurs eleven times in 1 Corinthians with eight of these found in chapter 14.

It is universally acknowledged that in this chapter Paul is dealing with the misuse of these two gifts in the congregational setting of the church of God at Corinth. A clear indication of this is the dramatic increase in the frequency of the Greek word ἐκκλησία (*ekklēsia*) in 1 Cor 14, a word which points to a congregational assembly. This word occurs three times in ch. 11, once in ch. 12, no occurrences in ch. 13, and nine occurrences in ch. 14.

The weight of Paul's response to the abuses in the assembly falls clearly on tongue speaking. The apostle's preference throughout this chapter is for the priority of prophecy (e.g., 14:39). In light of the Corinthian situation, which is virtually the only place Paul treats these two gifts at length, Paul is patently an advocate of prophecy and tolerant toward tongues (see 14:5). No doubt the apostle's statements about the lesser value of tongues would have been more irenic and encouraging to tongue speakers had the situation not been so deleterious. If the number and frequency of Paul's use of imperatives is any indication of the depth and breadth of this problem, then the issues of 1 Cor 14 are not insignificant to Paul.

The apostle clearly has no interest in outlawing tongues in general, but he does want to demonstrate emphatically what the inadequacies of tongue speaking are (as practiced by the Corinthians) and why for very practical reasons he promotes prophecy over tongues.

14:2 For anyone who speaks in a tongue does not speak to men but to God. Indeed, no one understands him; he utters mysteries with his spirit.

Time and again the apostle will explain his overriding preference for prophecy and his displeasure with the Corinthian tongue speakers. The use of the word "for" (γάρ, *gar*) leads into one such explanation. Since corporate worship is an important and natural part of the life of believers, Paul is sensitive to the horizontal dimension of activities in the assembly of the saints. Since tongue speaking is vertically directed to God rather than horizontally addressed to men, it is totally inappropriate for *ekklēsia* (assembly) worship. Moreover, since it is addressed to God, it is unintelligible to humans. The tongue speaker is speaking mysteries (μυστήρια, *mystēria*) with his spirit, a phenomenon with little value for others within earshot.

14:3 But everyone who prophesies speaks to men for their strengthening, encouragement and comfort.

By contrast, the prophet directs his message toward other people at church and thereby contributes to their strengthening, encouragement, and comfort. Of the three items which Paul lists as coming from the words of the prophet, the first is the most dominant in 1 Corinthians. The concept of strengthening is based upon the Greek term οἰκοδομή (*oikodomē*) and its cognates, which occurs seven times in this chapter (vv. 3, 4 [2×], 5, 12, 17, 26). While this concept has a variety of usages in the Pauline letters, in this setting it is tightly related to an ethical consideration. The apostle has obviously designated prophecy as the ethical high ground since it is the prescribed manifestation of the pursuit of love (esp. 14:1). Based upon Lev 19:18 Pauline theology sets love of neighbor at center stage (cf. Rom 13:8-10) and realizes that a concrete manifestation of this love of neighbor (cf. 1 Cor 13:7) is actions that promote the strengthening of one's fellow believer. This connection between *oikodomē* and love for others is made clear by the use of *oikodomē* in particular ethical situations among believers such as those depicted in Rom 14:19 and 15:2. What Paul has done, probably to the dismay of tongue speakers, is normalized *agapē* for liturgical practices at Corinth and made *oikodomē* into the essential criterion for acceptable worship assemblies.

Encouragement and comfort are two additional concepts which are part and parcel of the Spirit's activity through prophetic activity among believers. Encouragement is mentioned numerous times in 2 Corinthians as an attribute and activity of God (noun παράκλησις, *paraklēsis*, 2 Cor 1:3-7), while the verb form (παρακαλέω, *parakaleō*) is used of prophetic activity in 1 Cor 14:31. The term for "comfort" (παραμυθία, *paramythia*) is found only here in the

New Testament, though cognates are used by Paul in Phil 2:1 and
1 Thess 2:12 and 5:14.

**14:4 He who speaks in a tongue edifies himself, but he who
prophesies edifies the church.**

Paul acknowledges that a form of edification occurs during
unacceptable tongue speaking. Lamentably, this is self-edification
which is of no value for the whole. Once again the prophetic ministry is preferable in this setting since it seeks the good of others
and edifies the assembled church.

**14:5 I would like every one of you to speak in tongues, but I
would rather have you prophesy. He who prophesies is greater
than one who speaks in tongues, unless he interprets, so that the
church may be edified.**

In this verse the apostle maintains the superiority of prophecy
over tongues by a rhetorical statement that only apparently promotes tongue speaking. Given the realities of the assemblies of
saints at Corinth, and this is the background for Paul's directives,
there is no way that Paul can give an unqualified affirmation of
tongue speaking. Accordingly, he once again prefers prophecy
over tongues based upon the criterion of edification.

There is an exegetical debate regarding how to understand
Paul's use of the phrase "every one of you" (πάντας ὑμᾶς, *pantas
hymas*). Since he has earlier ruled out the notion that every believer speaks in tongues (see 12:29-30) and since he will shortly
limit the number of tongue speakers at an assembly to three
(14:27-28), it seems quite improbable that he wants all the believers at Corinth to acquire the gift of tongues. Either the church at
Corinth is incredibly smaller than any scholar ever imagined or,
equally implausible, Paul wants them to acquire a gift they can
rarely employ.

The very practical nature of Paul's evaluation of tongues and
prophecy is evident in the "unless he interprets" phrase. Paul
teaches by this that the tongue speaker will no longer have the
lesser gift if, in fact, he also can interpret his tongues and thereby
edify the assembly (cf. 14:13). If the practical benefit of tongues
(edification) becomes the same as prophecy, then tongues, though

not identical with the gift of prophecy, would receive increased praise from Paul.[1]

2. Tongues and Clarity (14:6-12)

[6]Now, brothers, if I come to you and speak in tongues, what good will I be to you, unless I bring you some revelation or knowledge or prophecy or word of instruction? [7]Even in the case of lifeless things that make sounds, such as the flute or harp, how will anyone know what tune is being played unless there is a distinction in the notes? [8]Again, if the trumpet does not sound a clear call, who will get ready for battle? [9]So it is with you. Unless you speak intelligible words with your tongue, how will anyone know what you are saying? You will just be speaking into the air. [10]Undoubtedly there are all sorts of languages in the world, yet none of them is without meaning. [11]If then I do not grasp the meaning of what someone is saying, I am a foreigner to the speaker, and he is a foreigner to me. [12]So it is with you. Since you are eager to have spiritual gifts, try to excel in gifts that build up the church.

14:6 Now, brothers, if I come to you and speak in tongues, what good will I be to you, unless I bring you some revelation or knowledge or prophecy or word of instruction?

In commenting upon 14:6ff D.A. Carson correctly observed that, "Paul introduced the question of intelligibility; now he stresses and enlarges upon it."[2] Paul reverts (14:6, 11, 14, 15, 18, 19) again to the use of the first person (autobiographical) style to provide a rhetorical buffer to the criticism he is giving to the tongue speakers (see notes on 13:1-3).

Paul affirms again that the current Corinthian practice of tongue speaking, that is, without interpretation, is of no value to the other saints. The apostle then lists, for the sake of contrast,

---

[1]Fee, *First Epistle*, p. 659.
[2]Carson, *Showing the Spirit*, p. 103.

four examples of spiritual gifts which do have value for fellow believers in the assembly. This list of four items both builds upon gifts already mentioned in chapters 12 and 13 and anticipates the similar list given at 14:26.

Generally speaking Paul did not confine the reception of divine revelation only to apostles (cf. 1 Cor 2:10; 14:26, 30; Eph 1:17, 3:5; Phil 3:15) or to periods of corporate worship (Eph 1:17; 3:5; Phil 3:15). The idea of divine knowledge (γνῶσις, *gnōsis*) was introduced by Paul earlier with the phrase "word of knowledge" (1 Cor 12:8) and "all knowledge" (1 Cor 13:2). Just like the mention of revelation, the mention of knowledge is appropriate here since it is intelligible and does not require interpretation. The manifestation of prophecy and its inherent intelligibility is central to the argument of this entire chapter. In an earlier reference to God's arrangement of offices in the church, Paul lists teachers as third (12:28) and observed that all believers should not expect to be teachers (12:29). Paul now mentions the related idea of teaching (NIV "word of instruction"). The NIV's translation decision obscures the possible connection in Paul's theology between the gift of teachers (διδάσκαλος, *didaskalos*) and the gift of teaching (διδαχή, *didachē*), by rendering the latter by the phrase "word of instruction." In 14:6 the apostle clearly has in mind the content of the teaching and not the activity of teaching per se. The modern reader would do well, in my judgment, to remember the verbal connection between the ideas of 12:28-29 (teachers) and the gift of bringing a teaching (14:6, 26) before the congregation.

14:7 Even in the case of lifeless things that make sounds, such as the flute or harp, how will anyone know what tune is being played unless there is a distinction in the notes?

The apostle now uses an illustration from everyday life to underscore the significance of intelligibility. The two lifeless things he employs in his illustration are the flute and the harp, common wind and stringed instruments of the Greco-Roman world. Fee rightly interprets Paul's point when he observes, "The analogy is clear. Tongues, Paul is arguing, is like the harpist running fingers over all the strings, making musical sounds but not playing a pleasing melody. . . ."[3]

As 14:9a makes explicit, this and the following illustrations are given to apply directly to the ecclesiastical problem of uninterpreted tongues. The apostle Paul is not, like later Church Fathers and Hellenistic Jewish authors, using the illustration of a musician playing on a passive instrument to explain how miraculous gifts, especially the mechanics of the inspiration of Scripture, should be understood.

14:8 Again, if the trumpet does not sound a clear call, who will get ready for battle?

Another illustration toward the same point is given with the sound of the battle trumpet. If the notes played are inappropriate, not clear, or generally unintelligible, how can soldiers prepare for combat?

14:9 So it is with you. Unless you speak intelligible words with your tongue, how will anyone know what you are saying? You will just be speaking into the air.

With his reference to the Corinthian readers in 14:9a, Paul makes clear application of his metaphors and illustrations from the world of musical instruments. If the other Corinthians who are not tongue speakers are subjected to a concert of cacophonous and unintelligible tongue speaking, how will they know what is being said? As a consequence, how can they be edified? The idea of speaking into the air is the apostle's way of contrasting the value of speech which is edifying with that which is unintelligible.

14:10 Undoubtedly there are all sorts of languages in the world, yet none of them is without meaning.

Paul now turns from the illustrations of musical instruments, lifeless metaphors, to illustrations that come from human speech. The phrase "all sorts of languages" refers to the numerous languages known about in the Greco-Roman world. Paul does not use here the well known word γλῶσσαι (*glōssai*) for languages since

---

[3]Fee, *First Epistle*, p. 664.

in this section *glōssai* is the term he uses for speaking in tongues (12:10, 30; 13:1; 14:2, 4, 5, 6, 9, 13, 14, 18, 19, 22, 23, 26, 27, 39). The term rendered "languages" is from φωνή (*phonē*). This word serves as a verbal thread that links together several of Paul's illustrations in this section since its broader meaning is "sound" (cf. 14:7, 8, 11). Paul is obviously referring to human languages and stating the obvious, just as he had regarding lifeless instruments, namely, all languages have intended meaning.

It would be pressing the details of Paul's language illustration too hard to suggest that he is indicating that tongues are foreign languages. As Witherington noted on this section, "It does not follow from this that he thought of tongues as simply another foreign language. He is thinking of the analogous effect of listening to a completely unknown foreign language."[4]

14:11 If then I do not grasp the meaning of what someone is saying, I am a foreigner to the speaker, and he is a foreigner to me.

This commonplace illustration would ring true to all denizens of a city such as Corinth. Even though the Greek language was the *lingua franca* of Paul's world, the Mediterranean world was a polyglot region where one could encounter any number of individuals who spoke a non-Greek language. This fact is evident in the numerous languages found in the ancient archaeological record of papyri and inscriptions (cf. Acts 14:11).

14:12 So it is with you. Since you are eager to have spiritual gifts, try to excel in gifts that build up the church.

This is the second time Paul has used this phrase "So it is with you" in this section (cf. 14:9). He is once again applying the implications of the preceding verses to the abusing tongue speakers. The nuance of the Greek words rendered "you are eager to have spiritual gifts" is sometimes overlooked in commentaries. What, in fact, Paul wrote was, "you are desirous of spirits" (ζηλωταὶ πνευμάτων, *zēlōtai pneumatōn*, eager for spirits). This observation by the apostle Paul is one of those explicit comments, plastered over in translations, that highlight the pagan and idolatrous spirituality

---

[4]Witherington, *Conflict and Community in Corinth*, p. 283.

that was still misleading certain Corinthian believers in their understanding and practice of spiritual gifts (see notes on 12:1-3).
Paul, in my judgment, is alluding to an animistic perspective that
still has a hold on some of the Corinthian saints and which leads
them to associate the supernatural spiritual gifts with the activity
of various spirits.

This conclusion is not to reduce Corinthian tongue speaking
to some Hellenistic phenomenon that is the Christian clone of
pagan oracles and ecstatic piety. Nevertheless, it is indefensible to
doubt (as some scholars do) that certain young pagan converts in
a young church, the majority of whose problems are directly
traceable to abiding pagan values and residual polytheistic beliefs,
would have had beliefs and practices about spiritual gifts still influenced by their surrounding indigenous culture.[5]

The majority of scholars acknowledge that Paul's choice of the
Greek term for spirits (πνεύματα, pneumata) is confusing, but conclude, nevertheless, that Paul clearly has spiritual gifts in mind.[6]
John Calvin, for example, judged that "The term spirits, he employs here, by metonymy, to denote spiritual gifts."[7]

The upshot of Paul's words in this verse is apparent. With
some mild sarcasm he contrasts the eagerness (ζηλωτής, zēlōtēs) of
the wrongheaded tongue speakers with their true need to seek to
excel in serving others by using gifts that edify (oikodomē). Having
made the decision to translate pneumata (spirits) as spiritual gifts
in 14:12a, the NIV inserts the phrase "in gifts" in 14:12b.

3. The Spirit and the Mind (14:13-19)

[13]**For this reason anyone who speaks in a tongue should pray
that he may interpret what he says. **[14]**For if I pray in a tongue, my
spirit prays, but my mind is unfruitful. **[15]**So what shall I do? I will
pray with my spirit, but I will also pray with my mind; I will sing
with my spirit, but I will also sing with my mind. **[16]**If you are**

---

[5]Cf. Witherington, Conflict and Community in Corinth, pp. 276-283.
[6]Fee, First Epistle, p. 666.
[7]Calvin, First Epistle, at 1 Cor 14:13.

praising God with your spirit, how can one who finds himself among those who do not understand[a] say "Amen" to your thanksgiving, since he does not know what you are saying? [17]You may be giving thanks well enough, but the other man is not edified.

[18]I thank God that I speak in tongues more than all of you. [19]But in the church I would rather speak five intelligible words to instruct others than ten thousand words in a tongue.

[a]16 Or *among the inquirers*

14:13 For this reason anyone who speaks in a tongue should pray that he may interpret what he says.

If edification of the assembly is the desired goal, as Paul just asserted, then the Corinthians who speak in tongues are directed to seek the gift of interpretation. In reading 12:10 and 14:26-28 one is left with the distinct impression that the two gifts of tongues and the interpretation of tongues are normally distributed by God to different individuals. Yet, the apostle's solution at this juncture is to counsel the tongue speakers to petition God, who appoints gifts in the church (12:28), to provide them with the gift of interpretation also.

14:14 For if I pray in a tongue, my spirit prays, but my mind is unfruitful.

In 14:14-15 Paul enters into specific instruction which, in my judgment, makes the most sense when viewed against the backdrop of residual pagan thinking among certain converts. Specifically, Paul's corrective use of the mind (νοῦς, *nous*)/spirit (πνεῦμα, *pneuma*) dichotomy seemingly assumes a situation where the tongue speakers are relying only on their "spiritual" component to the neglect of their rational self. Even though there is no such radical antithesis between mind and spirit in Pauline anthropology, there is apparently such in the thinking and practice of these Corinthian saints. Accordingly, Paul's observation about the unfruitfulness of the mind of the Corinthian tongue speakers during their prayers-in-tongues implies an "irrational" dimension to their spirituality and piety that the apostle finds unacceptable. Ralph

Martin summarized the significance of this unfruitful mind in this way:

> The last word implies that the human intellect in this kind of ecstatic praying lies dormant, contributing nothing to the process of articulating thoughts into words. . . . It suggests an enraptured fellowship with God when the human spirit is in such deep, hidden communion with the divine Spirit that "words" — at best broken utterances of our secret selves — are formed by a spiritual upsurge requiring no mental effort. [8]

This type of "irrational" focus in communion with the divine was well known in Greco-Roman and Hellenistic Jewish materials of antiquity. E.R. Dodd's classic work entitled *The Greeks and the Irrational*, unfortunately neglected by most interpreters of 1 Cor 14, shows how widespread and deeply rooted the notion of the "irrational" was in the pagan concepts of prophecy, enthusiasm, and oracular possession. This is the very reason why pagan visitors to the worship service can so readily interpret this aberrant tongue speaking in light of the pagan oracular experiences and presume a deity is also in the midst of these tongue speakers in the church of God (see notes on 14:23). Even a Jewish contemporary of Paul like Josephus could think in terms of prophecy arising in an individual "who was no longer his own master, but was overruled by the divine spirit."[9]

14:15 So what shall I do? I will pray with my spirit, but I will also pray with my mind; I will sing with my spirit, but I will also sing with my mind.

Keeping the same corrective principle before his readers, Paul declares that when he prays in a tongue it will include his rational faculties — both spirit (*pneuma*) and mind (*nous*) will be at work. Paul's insistence on the rational, but not rationalistic, character of acceptable tongue speaking lines up nicely with his preferences in

---

[8]Martin, *The Spirit*, p. 69.
[9]θείῳ πνεύματι, *theio pneumati*; Josephus, *Jewish Antiq* 4.6.5 (118).

the earlier contrast between tongues and more cognitive gifts such as revelation, knowledge, prophecy and teaching (14:6).

Even though the Greek word for "my" is not in 14:15, it should obviously be brought forward from the context of 14:14 where "my" accompanies both spirit and mind. Accordingly, the prepositional phrase ("spirit" in the dative case) "with spirit" can only refer to the individual's spirit and not the Holy Spirit. One ought not, therefore, parallel this phrase directly to texts which speak of praying in (with, by) the Holy Spirit (e.g., Rom 8:26-27; Jude 20; cf. Eph 6:18).

There seems insufficient evidence to be dogmatic regarding the question whether the "praying with my spirit" and "singing with my spirit" is just another way to describe uninterpreted tongues. D.A. Carson is of the opinion that "speaking in tongues is a form of prayer" and that "singing with the spirit" is basically tongue speaking which has "a more melodious or metrical form."[10] However, it should be kept in mind that the acts of singing and tongue speaking seem to be quite distinct in 14:26.

The reference to singing in an early Christian assembly should come as no surprise, nor should anyone familiar with the Spirit directed hymns of the Old Testament, the Gospels, and Eph 5:18ff be taken back by "charismatic hymnody" in the Corinthian setting.[11] What is noteworthy, however, is that unlike the hymnic materials of the Old Testament, the hymnic materials in the Infancy Narratives of Luke, the supposed hymnic materials in the Pauline letters, and the hymnic materials in the Apocalypse of John, these Corinthian singers were apparently using "irrational," that is unintelligible, songs. The apostle's rejoinder to this practice is to demand intelligibility. More light on the dynamics of this kind of Corinthian singing will probably have to wait until further historical research is done and interpreters commit themselves to investigating this phenomenon in light of ancient practices rather than 20th century Pentecostal religious phenomena.

---

[10]Carson, *Showing the Spirit*, p. 104.
[11]Fee, *First Epistle*, p. 671.

14:16 If you are praising God with your spirit, how can one who finds himself among those who do not understand say "Amen" to your thanksgiving, since he does not know what you are saying?

Paul next applies the litmus test of intelligibility and rationality to the act of praising God. This act of praise is also called thanksgiving (εὐχαριστία, *eucharistia*). Because some of the Corinthians are doing this "in the spirit" the "uninitiated" don't have a clue about what is being said. How is it possible, the apostle asks, for someone in this situation to say "Amen" to the statements of praise and thanksgiving? The NIV's translation "one who finds himself among those who do not understand" is somewhat non-committal on a particularly thorny historical question. Paul's sentence refers to the one who fills the place (τόπος, *topos*) of the *idiōtēs* (= interested non-member). Because of the ambiguities of the Greek term *idiōtēs* (ἰδιώτης) and the occurrence of the same word in 14:23 (in connection with unbelievers), scholars are divided over Paul's meaning here.[12] In my own judgment the word *idiōtēs* in 14:16, 23-24 refers to the same type of person, and this person would be somewhat like God-fearers in Jewish synagogues or pagans who were sympathetic to Judaism but were never fully converted. Given the openness of early Christian assemblies, at least in Corinth (14:22-25), and the religiously mixed households in attendance, there are no historical, theological, or exegetical impediments to viewing this person who cannot say "Amen" as an unbaptized, though quite interested, individual who attends the church of God at Corinth (see notes on 14:23-25).

14:17 You may be giving thanks well enough, but the other man is not edified.

Paul acknowledges, though perhaps with some sarcasm, that the self-centered believers are doing a good job in their individualistic "praise and thanksgiving" worship. They have, however, taken their eyes off of the compass that always guides believers in the direction of serving and edifying the other person (ὁ ἕτερος, *ho heteros*).

---

[12]Fee, *First Epistle*, pp. 672-673 sets out the details of the various interpretations.

14:18 I thank God that I speak in tongues more than all of you.

The content of this verse removes any question about the "charismatic" nature of Paul's own piety. Paul himself was an enthusiastic tongue speaker and an individual who experienced divine revelations (2 Cor 12:1-7). It is the apostle's own extensive experience as a tongue speaker that allows him both to chastise tongue speakers and to protect them (14:39) on the issue of their own abuse of tongue speaking. The superlative claim of this verse, whose rhetorical nature should not be forgotten, ought not be construed in such a way that this particular Pauline gift of tongues is "discovered" in other Pauline texts where it is not mentioned. We can say with some certainty that this gift of tongues is broached by Paul only this one time, when he had to deal with an abuse of it in the church of God. One must assume that Paul's experiences of tongue speaking were either done outside the assembly, in private, or were interpreted for the benefit of others.

14:19 But in the church I would rather speak five intelligible words to instruct others than ten thousand words in a tongue.

The beginning words of this verse (in the church) refer to the assembled saints and not to a place or building where they met.[13] The premium Paul places on intelligibility and edification is so high that five words with one's mind (*nous*; same term used in 14:14, 15) are greater than (cf. 14:5) ten thousand words which are only self-focused and do not instruct others. While there has been some speculation about the phrase "five words," there is no indication that Paul has a particular five words in mind.

This is not the first nor the final time that Paul will use a "different standard" to evaluate the acceptability of a practice. For the apostle the concept encapsulated in the prepositional phrase ἐν ἐκκλησίᾳ (*en ekklēsia*, in the assembly) reveals that a different set of rules and judgments are to be observed. A similar use of a different standard involving the concept of *en ekklēsia* is seen at 11:18, 22, 34 and 14:34-35.

---

[13]Fee, *First Epistle*, p. 675.

4. Maturity and Spiritual Gifts (14:20-25)

[20]Brothers, stop thinking like children. In regard to evil be infants, but in your thinking be adults. [21]In the Law it is written:
"Through men of strange tongues
and through the lips of foreigners
I will speak to this people,
but even then they will not listen to me," [a]
says the Lord.
[22]Tongues, then, are a sign, not for believers but for unbelievers; prophecy, however, is for believers, not for unbelievers. [23]So if the whole church comes together and everyone speaks in tongues, and some who do not understand[b] or some unbelievers come in, will they not say that you are out of your mind? [24]But if an unbeliever or someone who does not understand[c] comes in while everybody is prophesying, he will be convinced by all that he is a sinner and will be judged by all, [25]and the secrets of his heart will be laid bare. So he will fall down and worship God, exclaiming, "God is really among you!"

[a]21 Isaiah 28:11,12   [b]23 Or some inquirers   [c]24 Or or some inquirer

14:20 Brothers, stop thinking like children. In regard to evil be infants, but in your thinking be adults.

The childlike thinking that Paul has in mind is the self-centeredness of the abusing tongue speakers. Infantile thinking is desirable among believers when it is in regard to evil. With this small colony of believers in mind, Paul exhorts them to retain a certain innocence and childlike naiveté in matters of evil. Mature thinking — seeking the good of others (14:19b) — is what Paul demands from the factious members of the Corinthian church.

14:21 In the Law it is written: "Through men of strange tongues and through the lips of foreigners I will speak to this people, but even then they will not listen to me," says the Lord.

Verses 21-25 form one of the more enigmatic sections in chapter 14. The difficulties are caused by Paul's choice and interpretation of an Old Testament Scripture for addressing this assembly problem at Corinth. In addition, some interpreters have been unable to reconcile Paul's theoretical understanding of prophecy and tongues (v. 22) and his description of how, in fact, they impact various segments of those in attendance (vv. 23-25).

The unit of thought contained in 14:21-25 is totally in step with the upshot of the preceding verses. Just as he has argued in 14:1-19 that prophecy is greater in the assembly since it edifies, so also in 14:21-25 Paul wants to demonstrate that prophecy is greater than tongues since it convicts non-Christians. Just as intelligibility was the *sine qua non* for prophecy's advantage over tongue speaking in building up the assembly, so intelligibility is the *sine qua non* for prophecy's advantage over tongue speaking in benefiting the spiritual needs of the non-Christian in attendance. With this perspective in mind, Paul's strategy and argumentation in 14:21-25 become more transparent.

Paul's use of this Old Testament Scripture fits comfortably into the typical interpretive perspectives and guidelines we find him using elsewhere (see notes on 10:11). What the apostle is doing here is reasoning from the realities of the Corinthian assemblies back to the verses which contain the keywords and logic that reflects his own position. Accordingly, the phrases "strange tongues" and "lips of foreigners" correlate to the Corinthian phenomenon of speaking in uninterpreted tongues (notice "foreigner" imagery used of uninterpreted tongues in 14:11). The scriptural concept of "speaking to a group of people who will not listen" becomes in the Corinthian experience a sign for unbelievers (14:22). The clarity of this correlation is evident in the grammatical connectors Paul uses in 14:22 (ὥστε, *hōste*) and 14:23 (οὖν, *oun*).

Since the contextual function of 14:21 is to set forth a scriptural basis for the observable advantage of prophecy over tongues in regard to nonbelievers, little is to be gained by attempting to "harmonize" the Corinthians' context in this Roman colony with that of Isaiah centuries earlier.

14:22 Tongues, then, are a sign, not for believers but for unbe-lievers; prophecy, however, is for believers, not for unbelievers.

Paul's use of the term "sign" (σημεῖον, *sēmeion*) is significant in this verse, for it is one of the things that distinguishes the impact of tongues for unbelievers from prophecy for believers. In deter-mining what specifically the apostle has in mind, it is important to remember that he is formulating his observation in this verse in light of the experiences he mentions in 14:24-25. Consequently, the concept that tongues are a sign for unbelievers must be corre-lated with the unbelievers' reaction to tongues described in 14:23b. In similar fashion, the statement that prophecy is for be-lievers must be correlated with the actions described in 14:24-25 when prophecies are given. The details of this are discussed in the commentary at 14:23-25.

14:23 So if the whole church comes together and everyone speaks in tongues, and some who do not understand or some unbeliev-ers come in, will they not say that you are out of your mind?

Since we do not know either the size of the church at Corinth or the size of its meeting places, it is difficult to interpret the phrase "the whole church." This coming together of the whole church would certainly include the regular "first day of every week" (16:2) setting, though there is no reason to assume it would include only that. A similar idea is located in 11:20 in the context of the eating of the Lord's Supper. Based upon word and phrase usage in the Old Testament when it speaks of the assembly of "all Israel" or the gathering of the "whole congregation," one should recognize the hyperbole that sometimes characterizes words such as "all," "every," and "whole."

This Corinthian setting of coming together (from συνέρχομαι, *synerchomai*) as "the whole church" is the backdrop for the rest of the instruction in 1 Cor 14, a fact made clear by the continued use of "coming together" (*synerchomai*) in 14:26 as well as the func-tion of the rhetorical question in 14:26a that looks backward to 14:20-25.

In light of the fact that Paul has made it clear that it is contrary to the nature of the working of God's Spirit to give tongues to every believer (see notes on 12:29-30), he can hardly be advocating that position now. Moreover, if every member of the Corinthian congregation spoke in tongues, one wonders why Paul needs to protect tongue speakers from spiritual assailants as he does in 14:39. It seems most reasonable to understand "everyone" (πάντες, *pantes*) as meaning everyone who has the gift of tongue speaking. It is quite clear that Paul's statement that "everyone speaks in tongues" is descriptive rather than prescriptive. If the latter were true, that he wanted all of them to speak in tongues, it would pose grave problems since in 14:27 he limits the number of tongue speakers to three at most.

The two groups Paul describes as those "who do not understand" and as "unbelievers" are patently non-Christian (see notes on 14:16). The apostle next reports what these two groups will say in response to a worship situation characterized by a mass of uninterpreted tongue speakers. They will respond, Paul writes, that you are out of your mind. Since these outsiders are probably pagan and since wildly emotional and irrational worship was well known in certain aspects of pagan religiosity, these outsiders may not have been responding negatively. As D.A. Carson observed, "it will not be surprising if they [i.e., outsiders and unbelievers] simply conclude that the believers are possessed."[14] Consequently, the Scripture cited in 14:21 is fulfilled, for tongue speaking has served only as a signpost; but no one listened to God (how could they?).

14:24 But if an unbeliever or someone who does not understand comes in while everybody is prophesying, he will be convinced by all that he is a sinner and will be judged by all,

Paul now paints a scene which is quite distinct from that of 14:23. When the outsiders are confronted by a cacophony (from Paul's perspective) of uninterpreted and therefore unintelligible tongues, they can hardly listen to the true voice of God. Things are significantly different, however, when these non-Christians are exposed to rational and intelligible words from the Spirit of God.

It is important to notice that Paul's earlier quotation from the law (14:21) is not as directly related to prophecy as it had been to

---

[14]Carson, *Showing the Spirit*, p. 115.

tongue speaking, though Calvin thinks otherwise.[15] At least since the time of Chrysostom there have been numerous solutions suggested to explain the ostensible contradiction between Paul's statement that prophecy is not for unbelievers but for believers (14:22) and the description in 14:24-25 where it is precisely the unbelievers who are positively affected by the prophecy of the saints. Most interpreters would agree with Carson's assessment that "these verses are extraordinarily difficult," and all would benefit from reading his survey of the several different interpretations of this issue.[16]

Fee's solution is to suggest that the response of the outsider to prophecy (14:25 "God is really among you") serves as a sign of divine knowledge to believers, since it would be an "indication of God's favor resting upon them."[17] Another view looks for the remedy in this way. In 14:23b Paul states, as he had numerous other times in chapter 14, that prophecy is for edification of the assembly. In the context of assemblies where prophecy is for believers, non-believers are occasionally present. As these non-believers overhear God's words in the prophecy of the saints, they undergo the experiences described in 14:24-25. Thus, as Ralph Martin wrote, the act of prophecy "builds up the church, but also has a signal and salutary effect on the non-believer."[18] All of this demonstrates once again the greater value of prophecy in the assembly, not only in regard to the saints, but even in regard to the outsiders who benefit from it.

14:25 and the secrets of his heart will be laid bare. So he will fall down and worship God, exclaiming, "God is really among you!"

This work of the Spirit in judgment anticipates the nature of God's eschatological judgment. "Exposing the motives of men's hearts" (4:5) underscores the importance of the condition of the human heart in the mind of God (cf. Acts 1:24; 15:8 for God knowing the heart). The prophet Jeremiah's profound awareness

---

[15]Calvin, *First Epistle*, p. 299.

[16]Carson, *Showing the Spirit*, pp. 108-117.

[17]Fee, *First Epistle*, p. 683.

[18]Martin, *The Spirit*, p. 73; similar view is given by Carson, *Showing the Spirit*, pp. 116-117.

that, "The heart is deceitful above all things and beyond cure. Who can understand it?" points to the reality of mankind's need for revelation in order to understand the gravity of his own situation.

There is plenty of evidence, however, in both the pagan religions and in the writings of moral philosophers of antiquity to realize that non-Christians knew of their own guilt and shortcomings in the sight of their gods. The NIV's added phrase in 14:24 "that he is a sinner" probably reflects modern evangelistic piety more than it does an ancient pagan's response to prophecy directed to edifying the church.

Paul's description in 14:25 portrays non-believers whose hearts are touched in such a way by the words of God that they are led to fall down and worship God. In a pluralistic and polytheistic setting it is anachronistic to depict this as a Corinthian revival meeting wherein the unsaved are saved. The texts from the Old Testament and the other arguments which Fee assembles do not fully demonstrate that these verses depict the unsaved in Corinth being converted and joining the people of God.[19]

The act of worship and the confession "God is really among you" described by Paul remind one more of Naaman's response in 2 Kings 5:15 than of the "what must I do to be saved?" picture so reminiscent of the Acts of the Apostles. If Paul is alluding to conversions, his language is especially oblique.

E. ORDERLY WORSHIP (14:26-40)

1. Control of Tongues and Prophecy (14:26-33)

[26]**What then shall we say, brothers? When you come together, everyone has a hymn, or a word of instruction, a revelation, a tongue or an interpretation. All of these must be done for the strengthening of the church. [27]If anyone speaks in a tongue, two — or at the most three — should speak, one at a time, and some-**

---

[19]Fee, *First Epistle*, p. 687.

one must interpret. [28]If there is no interpreter, the speaker should keep quiet in the church and speak to himself and God.

[29]Two or three prophets should speak, and the others should weigh carefully what is said. [30]And if a revelation comes to someone who is sitting down, the first speaker should stop. [31]For you can all prophesy in turn so that everyone may be instructed and encouraged. [32]The spirits of prophets are subject to the control of prophets. [33]For God is not a God of disorder but of peace.

As in all the congregations of the saints,

14:26 What then shall we say, brothers? When you come together, everyone has a hymn, or a word of instruction, a revelation, a tongue or an interpretation. All of these must be done for the strengthening of the church.

At this juncture the apostle leaves the strategy and style of the previous sections where he argued on the basis of principles and illustrations. He will now focus his comments and directives on specific liturgical rules and legislation. The opening words and question of 14:26 obviously are intended to draw upon the style and content of the preceding 25 verses. But now, in 14:26-36, 39-40, Paul will articulate the concrete and acceptable practices based upon the earlier stated principles; in addition, he will claim divine authority for these practices and denounce any and all who challenge them (14:37-38).

Paul has in mind the same worship assembly that was mentioned in 14:23 (see notes on 14:23). He makes reference to five particular spiritual gifts which are distributed among [some of] the believers. All five of these have been referred to earlier in this chapter: hymn (singing, 14:15), word of instruction (14:6, see notes at 14:6), revelation (revelation, 14:6), tongues (14:2ff), and an interpretation (14:5, 13).

The term "hymn" (literally "psalm," ψάλμος, *psalmos*) in another setting might refer to the scriptural psalms of the Old Testament (cf. Luke 24:44), but its contextual connection with the singing (ψάλλω, *psallo*) of 14:15 makes this improbable. These five items are grammatically the objects of indicative rather than imperative verbs. The point of this observation is to make it clear that Paul is acknowledging the presence of these rather than commanding that all five be part of the Corinthian worship experience when they come together. It would be misguided to suppose that these verses provide some kind of absolute list or description of an early Christian worship service. Noticeable by their absence from these verses are items such as the reading of Scripture and the Lord's Supper.

After the five item list of liturgical gifts, the apostle does impose an imperative. His corrective to the current situation is to mandate that all five of these must be practiced from the perspective of edification and strengthening of others. The NIV's phrase "of the church" is not a translation of any words in the Greek text, but that is surely Paul's idea.

14:27 If anyone speaks in a tongue, two — or at the most three — should speak, one at a time, and someone must interpret.

The apostle next moves to correct, censure, and give order to three subgroups whose verbal activities in the assembly are inappropriate. The connecting thread of Paul's imperatives to these three groups is the imperative "be silent" (σιγάτω, *sigatō*) of v. 28. The three groups are: (1) disorderly tongue speakers, (2) disorderly prophets, and (3) disorderly women (14:2, 30, 34). In this section Paul is still obviously concerned about edification, but the perceived impediment is not so much unintelligibility as it is with liturgy not being done "in a fitting and orderly way" (14:40).

A second connecting thread between Paul's treatment of these three groups is the prepositional phrase "in church(es)." Paul's divinely given (14:37) directives at this juncture are related to abuses occurring "in the assembly." Consequently, his rules for the Corinthians are specifically related to their demeanor and activity in worship assemblies when the whole church (14:23) comes together. The fact that Paul's commands on these three issues (i.e., tongue speaking, prophets, women) relate only to activities "in church" has led some to question the validity and consistency of his teaching. The fact is, this division between "public" assembly and more "private" activities made complete sense to most people in the Greco-Roman world. In fact, had Paul himself not adapted the "public" versus "private" paradigm, it is hard to imagine how the assembly could have had both intelligibility and an

orderly manner given the diversity and complexity of its membership and cultural milieu. The collapse of this "public"/"private"
dichotomy can be achieved only at the price of either chaotic
meetings or having only clone-like members who walk lockstep.

Those saints who are gifted in tongue speaking are strictly
regulated by Paul. The apostle has a threefold regulation which, I
imagine, would appear quite restrictive to the abusing tongue
speakers. The first of the three criteria of acceptability is the numerical ceiling — no more than three tongue speakers. Second,
Paul limits aspects of spontaneity by insisting that the tongue
speakers speak sequentially and not simultaneously. The third
criterion, and the only one directly related to intelligibility, was
that an interpreter of tongue speaking had to be present to make
the tongues intelligible.

**14:28 If there is no interpreter, the speaker should keep quiet in
the church and speak to himself and God.**
Paul did not view the church of God as a society of free
speech, nor did he believe its corporate meetings should be con-
ducted with disregard for the needs of the group and the larger
goals of its assemblies. Accordingly, Paul enforces his first "keep
quiet" (*sigatō*). It is lamentable that the NIV translation masks the
fact that in all three instances (14:28, 30, 34) the apostle uses the
same verb (*sigatō*) to command quietness from those threatening
orderliness. This verb is once rendered "keep quiet" (14:28), once
"should stop" (14:30), and once "remain silent" (14:34). Notwithstanding the peculiar slant of the NIV, the intent of Paul's imperative is to have the tongue speakers cease speaking in tongues until
they can do it in an acceptable manner (i.e., no more than three;
sequentially, intelligibly).

It is important to note that Paul's concern for the need for
"quietness" is not because he shares the Roman magical view
about the potential for offending deities. The Roman author Pliny
the Elder reflects the Roman mindset in these words,

> It apparently does no good to offer a sacrifice or to consult
> the gods with due ceremony unless you also speak words of
> prayer. In addition, some words are appropriate for seeking
> favorable omens, others for warding off evil, and still others

for securing help. We notice, for example, that our highest magistrates make appeals to the gods with specific and set prayers. And in order that no word be omitted or spoken out of turn, one attendant reads the prayer from a book, another is assigned to check it closely, a third is appointed to enforce silence. In addition, a flutist plays to block out any extraneous sounds. There are recorded remarkable cases where either ill-omened noises have interrupted and ruined the ritual or an error has been made in the strict wording of the prayer. [20]

The apostle's agenda here arises from a concern for edification of one's neighbor and not from a pagan preoccupation with some incidental offense of a deity.

The phrase "in the church" (see notes on 14:27) means the "worship service." The tongue speaker's confinement to quietness is not a total ban on this spiritual gift. Paul tells him to continue his exercise of this gift, but it must be inaudible.[21] Fee disagrees and takes the phrase "speak to himself" as in contrast to "in the church" and concludes that the tongue speaker should pray this way to God in private.[22] In either case, the ideas of "himself" and "speaking to God" take one back to the wording of vv. 2-4.

14:29 Two or three prophets should speak, and the others should weigh carefully what is said.

The reason that Paul puts the same numerical ceiling on prophets as he did on tongue speaking that was interpreted (no more than three) is that in certain ways prophecy's edge and superiority over tongue speaking (14:5) is diminished if tongues are accompanied by interpretation (14:5).

Unlike pagan prophecy, which required interpretation, Paul never speaks of prophecy in the church needing interpretation. Rather, the prophecy spoken through believers required careful weighing. The concern and need to evaluate prophecies and thereby the prophet who gives them is a well established scrip-

---

[20]Pliny the Elder, *Natural History* 28.2(3).10, 11. Translation taken from *As the Romans Did*, no. 364, p. 373.

[21]Witherington, *Conflict and Community in Corinth*, p. 286.

[22]Fee, *First Epistle*, p. 693.

tural perspective. A classic, but certainly not unique, Scripture in this regard is Deut 13:1-5 (cf. Deut 18:20-22). The prophecies of Jeremiah reveal a concern about this issue since he knew of numerous examples of false prophecies and false prophets. This phenomenon of false prophecy reached such epidemic proportions that Zechariah equates prophesying with falsehood (Zech 13:1-6) and by the Word of the Lord (Zech 1:1) proclaimed, "And if anyone still prophesies, his father and mother, to whom he was born, will say to him, 'You must die, because you have told lies in the Lord's name.' When he prophesies, his own parents will stab him" (Zech 13:3).

The Lord Jesus himself warned of false prophets, who were destined for eternal punishment, even though they were influential in the community of disciples and specialized in prophesying, in performing exorcisms, and in miracle working activities (Matt 7:15-23). Jesus exhorts the disciples to carefully evaluate prophetic claims (Matt 7:18-20), as do Paul (1 Thess 5:19-22) and John (1 John 4:1-3).

Paul's imperative to weigh carefully what these two or three prophets spoke is certainly no indication that these prophecies were just pious insights granted to particular believers. Neither Luke nor Paul believed that Paul's gospel was merely the result of spiritual insight. Rather both Luke and Paul affirmed that Paul's message was a result of direct revelation and had the *imprimatur* of God himself, yet both acknowledged that Paul's preaching should be evaluated (Acts 17:11; Gal 1:8-9). John Calvin addressed this theological and exegetical issue by noting "that the teaching of God is not subjected to the judgment of men, but their [i.e., the others] task is simply to judge, by the Spirit of God, whether it is His Word, which is declared or whether, using this as a pretext, men are wrongly parading what they themselves have made up."[23]

There are two main schools of thought in the matter of identifying "the others" (οἱ ἄλλοι, *hoi alloi*). Some scholars identify these as the other prophets or saints with the gift of the discernment of spirits (1 Cor 12:10). The other school of interpretation concludes,

---

[23]Calvin, *First Epistle*, p. 302.

in my opinion, correctly, that "the others" refers to the collective congregation.

14:30 And if a revelation comes to someone who is sitting down, the first speaker should stop.

The point of 14:30 is to regulate the issue of the orderliness of the prophetic gift. These believers must also manifest their spiritual gift of prophecy sequentially and not simultaneously (cf. 14:27). The picture he paints is of a second prophet receiving a revelation while the first prophet is still speaking. Paul directs the first one to stop speaking (σιγάτω, *sigatō*) and defer to the second prophet so he also can deliver his divine revelation. The reference to the fact that the second prophet is sitting down may point to the fact that these speakers were seated when listening, but arose to speak (cf. Jesus in Luke 4:16, 20).

14:31 For you can all prophesy in turn so that everyone may be instructed and encouraged.

In order to reassure (in the midst of correction) the Corinthian prophets, Paul confirms that each of the three prophets will have his turn. As a consequence, all those in the assembly will be instructed and encouraged (see notes on vv. 3-4).

14:32 The spirits of prophets are subject to the control of prophets.

The function of this verse is to respond to Corinthian prophets who would take the position, as a way to circumvent Paul's commandment in 14:30, that they cannot control the timing and duration of their prophetic revelations. The apostle's pointed remarks make it clear that as far as he is concerned each Corinthian prophet should exercise control over his own inner personal spirit. The necessity for such an emphasis from Paul is best located in the pagan matrix of these converts. Part and parcel of pagan theology and practice of prophetic inspiration was the concept of the loss of control. That was true in many examples of both Greek and Roman prophetic and oracular piety. Fee's analysis is correct when he concludes that Paul teaches a viewpoint here that is a radically different thing from the mania of the pagan cults. "There is no seizure here, no loss of control; the speaker is neither frenzied nor a babbler."[24]

14:33 For God is not a God of disorder but of peace. As in all the congregations of the saints,

If Paul's first argument against aberrant prophetic practices and theology was based upon an anthropology in which spirits of prophets are in submission to prophets (14:32), then his second argument is based upon the nature of God who inspires prophets. Unlike several pagan deities who engendered chaotic activities in worship and group meetings, the God of the Christian church in Corinth was no such deity. Responsibility for such disorderly and aberrant behavior could not, in Paul's theology, be laid at the feet of God. Peace, and not disorder, characterized the true God and his distribution of gifts in the assembled church.

Moreover, he continues, this peaceful attribute of God was uniformly revealed and (supposedly) evident in all the worship assemblies of believers everywhere. It is unfortunate that the NIV, along with several other 20th century English translations, divides 14:33 into two sentences, and erroneously makes 14:33b the beginning of a sentence continued into 14:34. Witherington is of the judgment that 33b goes with the instruction about women,[25] but Fee is certainly correct (though not for the right reasons in every case) when he concludes that 14:33b should be regarded "as the concluding word to these instructions [in the preceding verses] on order."[26]

2. Submission of Women (14:34-35)

[34]**women should remain silent in the churches. They are not allowed to speak, but must be in submission, as the Law says.** [35]**If they want to inquire about something, they should ask their own**

---

[24]Fee, *First Epistle*, p. 696.
[25]Witherington, *Conflict and Community in Corinth*, p. 287.
[26]Fee, *First Epistle*, p. 697.

husbands at home; for it is disgraceful for a woman to speak in the church.

14:34 women should remain silent in the churches. They are not allowed to speak, but must be in submission, as the Law says.

As one begins to investigate the unit of thought expressed in 14:34-35 in light of current studies, it is clear that not all interpreters believe that Paul authored these verses. While over the decades certain classically liberal scholars have doubted the genuineness of these verses, it is only recently that this perspective of doubt has been more widely accepted. At the present time it is not difficult to find modern feminist scholars who affirm that these verses were not written by Paul and apparently assume that most scholars now accept this view. More recently a group of evangelical authors have likewise concluded that these verses were not written by Paul and, in fact, are contradictory to Paul's beliefs. A clarion voice in this regard is the Pentecostal-evangelical author Gordon Fee. There are at least three issues which have led Fee to this flawed conclusion. These are: (1) it makes no sense for Paul to discuss the role of women in a chapter focused on problems with tongues and prophecy, and (2) there are some disagreements in the ancient Greek manuscripts regarding the location of these two verses in chapter 14, and (3) the treatment of women in these verses is in contradiction to 1 Cor 11:5 and Paul's views about women expressed elsewhere.[27]

In regard to point one, any interpreter of Paul knows the dangers of making an ancient author, Paul or someone else, fit into our preconceived ideas of how he should write on topics and treat issues. It is tragic to impose our own expectations and preferences onto Paul's works and force his material into a Procrustean bed. Moreover, since Paul's strategy toward the end of ch. 14 has shifted from demanding intelligibility to demanding an orderly demeanor, his critique of certain women on this basis is not so out of step with the surrounding context. Moreover, if the unacceptable speech of these women was part of the weighing and

---

[27]In addition to Fee's comments on 14:34-35, *First Epistle*, pp. 705-708, one should consult his *God's Empowering Presence*, pp. 272-281.

evaluation of prophecy (v. 29), then Paul's words to them are closely tied to his contextual treatment of the use of spiritual gifts.

Regarding the second issue, Fee well knows and acknowledges that there is no "direct manuscript evidence"[28] for his theory of interpolation and that "these two verses are found in all known manuscripts, either here [following 14:33] or at the end of the chapter."[29] One must wonder if Carroll Osburn is not right when he judges that Fee's attempts "look suspiciously like attempts to liberate Paul in terms of modern agendas."[30]

Even though Fee finds none of the exegetical efforts satisfactory, numerous exegetes have made reasonable proposals to demonstrate how 1 Cor 14:34-35 can co-exist with 1 Cor 11:4-5 and other pertinent Pauline texts (these scholars include D.A. Carson, Wayne Grudem, R. Martin, Witherington).

Until further and more substantive evidence and reasoning are forthcoming, Fee's conclusion that "this passage (1 Cor 14:34-35) is almost certainly not by Paul"[31] remains illfounded and uncogent.

Paul's injunction to "silence" (σιγάτωσαν, sigatōsan) must surely be interpreted with the same principles as those principles used in the interpretation of the two previous injunctions to "silence" in this context (14:28, 30 sigatō). In particular one ought to remember that all three imperatives for "silence" were in the setting of a correction of aberrant behavior, and therefore the silence desired was only in relationship to the point of abuse. For example, the "silence" placed upon the first prophet of 1 Cor 14:30 was in force only so long as he was in violation of the principle that God is the author of peace and of the regulation that prophecies were to be done sequentially.

In the same manner, the conditions of "silence" and "not allowed to speak" can only contextually and consistently mean that the ban against the speech of these women (γυναῖκες, gynaikes) is in force only so long as they are in violation of the principles and regulations of 1 Cor 14:34-35. The principle that these particular

---

[28]Fee, "Excursus: On the Text of I Corinthians 14:34-35" p. 278.

[29]Fee, *First Epistle*, p. 699.

[30]C.D. Osburn, "The Interpretation of 1 Cor 14:34-35," *Essays on Women in Earliest Christianity*, Vol. I (Joplin: College Press, 1994), p. 223.

[31]Fee, "Excursus: On the Text of I Corinthians 14:34-35," p. 281.

women were violating is that of submission (from ὑποτάσσω, *hypotassō*; cf. usage of this verb in 14:32 "are subject to the control").

The apostle's reference to "the Law" (ὁ νόμος, *ho nomos*) is not as enigmatic as many scholars have suggested. This type of use of the Old Testament is generally in line with Paul's technique at other places in 1 Corinthians. In particular, Paul felt quite comfortable in employing Scripture texts from the Old Testament to prescribe and interpret aspects of assembly activities. In 1 Cor 5:4 the church is assembled to censure a sinful fellow believer. The expulsion of wayward believers is authorized on the basis of a frequently found command ("Expel the wicked man from among you") from Deuteronomy (e.g., 17:7; 19:19; 22:21, 24; 24:7). First Corinthians 11 provides a singular example of the use of Genesis material from the Creation and Fall Narratives to insure propriety regarding liturgical head coverings in the worship assembly of believers. More to the setting and context of 1 Cor 14, Paul refers to the Law (though the quotation is principally from the Prophets) to interpret the phenomenon of tongue speaking in a worship service in the Roman colony of Corinth. The same apostle Paul who so naturally curbed unacceptable male and female head coverings practices during prophecy and prayer on the basis of principles from Genesis and challenged aberrant tongue speakers at Corinth with a theme from Isaiah, could with equal facility curb aberrant women's speech with a theme from Genesis.

It should be obvious that Genesis 1-3 does not any more explicitly mention liturgical head coverings than its says that women cannot speak in the assembly of believers! Moreover, Paul does not even imply or say that the text of Genesis says either of these. The authorizing phrase, "as the Law says" refers *not* to silence and speech, but to submission of certain Corinthian women whose comportment was in violation of the principle of submission.

One may or may not agree with Paul's teaching about the submission of women and his views about Genesis, but it seems to be blatant special pleading to attempt to discredit or to diminish the point of 14:34 by claiming it is unpauline, either in its view toward women or in its method of appropriation of Scriptural themes from the Old Testament.

The specific nature and extent of submission cannot be determined without an examination of the further information given in 14:35.

14:35 If they want to inquire about something, they should ask their own husbands at home; for it is disgraceful for a woman to speak in the church.

Based upon Paul's comments in 14:35a in the context of his general censure of disorderliness, it seems that he is disturbed by the fact that the questions and inquiries from certain women manifest an attitude and behavior that violates the precepts and principles given in 14:34. The translation of the NIV is not as consistent as it could be in some of the details of 14:35. Keeping in mind that the Greek word ἄνδρες (*andres*) can mean either "men" or "husbands" and that the Greek word γυναῖκες (*gunaikes*) can mean either "women" or "wives," one ought to translate these in a way that is contextually consistent. Accordingly, if the males mentioned in 14:35 are "husbands at home," then it only makes sense that the females mentioned in 14:34 are "wives" and not just women. If, on the other hand, one wishes to translate *gunaikes* in 14:34 as "women," then perhaps *andres* in 14:35 should be translated "men." If these two terms *gunaikes* and *andres* are kept away from marriage, then the *gunaikes* of 14:34 could include daughters (regardless of age) who were still in the home of a male (father, brother, or Roman guardian).

Regardless of how one translates and interprets *gunaikes* and *andres* in 14:34-35a, an important principle is stated in 14:35b, namely it is a disgrace for a woman to speak in an unsubmissive way in the assembly of the saints. By use of the connecting word "for" (γάρ, *gar*), the apostle conceptually connects his imperatives in 14:35a with the principles in 14:35b behind his imperatives. This is the fourth time Paul has appealed to the concept of disgraceful or shameful behavior (1 Cor 11:4, 5, 6; 14:35, αἰσχρός, *aischros*, and cognates) in 1 Corinthians. Based upon his use of this concept in this Corinthian correspondence, both believing men and women can be guilty of participating in behavior that is "shameful" to their gender.

If one can move beyond an interpretive method that only looks at verses in isolation and then interprets them only after having ripped them from the soil of their historical and rhetorical context, then one can more accurately visualize what the apostle is attempting to do. In light of a more holistic and historically sensitive interpretation several things become apparent:

1. Paul's statement of 1 Cor 14:35b "it is disgraceful . . ." should be kept in the immediate and particular context of the aberration of disorderliness that Paul is addressing.

2. The interpreter of Paul should acknowledge the apostle's explicit scriptural foundation of submissiveness as reflected in the Law.

3. Attempts to read Paul as either a feminist who violates cultural norms of the Greco-Roman world or a traditionalist who cannot get beyond his own cultural patriarchy usually arise from an ill-informed picture of Greco-Roman antiquity. The Roman world was anything but homogeneous in regard to its attitudes toward women. Not only were there differing attitudes among individuals toward women in the Greco-Roman setting, but the views vary depending whether women were being characterized from the perspectives of Roman law, ancient medicine and gynecology, Greco-Roman religious mores, ancient social institutions, etc.

The complexity of this situation is heightened by the fact that Greek culture and Roman culture did not always express the same views on these matters. The Roman author Cornelius Nepos, for example, observed that, "not all peoples look upon the same acts as honourable or base, but that they judge them all in light of the usage of their forefathers." One of the illustrations given of this by Cornelius Nepos deals with perceptions of acceptable behavior of women in certain public activities. "Many actions are seemly according to our [i.e., Roman] code which the Greeks look upon as shameful," reports this Roman author. In particular, "what Roman would blush to take his wife to a dinner-party? What matron does not frequent the front rooms of her dwelling and show herself in public?" inquires Cornelius. Matters are "very different in Greece," the reader learns, "for there a woman is not admitted to a dinner-party, unless relatives only are present." As a consequence, in Greece "she keeps to the more retired part of the house called 'the women's apartment,' to which no man has access who is not near of kin."[32]

3. Everything Fitting and Orderly (14:36-40)

[36]Did the word of God originate with you? Or are you the only people it has reached? [37]If anybody thinks he is a prophet or spiritually gifted, let him acknowledge that what I am writing to you is the Lord's command. [38]If he ignores this, he himself will be ignored.[a]

[39]Therefore, my brothers, be eager to prophesy, and do not forbid speaking in tongues. [40]But everything should be done in a fitting and orderly way.

[a]*38* Some manuscripts *If he is ignorant of this, let him be ignorant*

14:36 Did the word of God originate with you? Or are you the only people it has reached?

Verses 36-38 form one coherent unit of thought. In this section Paul gives his terse response to anticipated opposition to the views he has just expressed in this chapter. The point of 14:36 is probably related to the concept found in the fourfold reference to the fact that what he teaches to the Corinthians is in harmony with the same ideas that are found in all the churches (see notes on 14:33b). Robertson and Plummer correctly interpret Paul's point to the Corinthians in these words, "Were you the starting-point of the Gospel? or were you its only destination? Do you mean to contend that you have the right to maintain these irregularities?"[33]

---

[32]Cornelius Nepos, *Great General of Foreign Nations*, Preface 3-7. Translation taken from Loeb Classical Library (Cambridge: Harvard University Perss, 1960), pp. 369-371.

[33]Robertson and Plummer, *First Epistle of St. Paul*, p. 326.

14:37 If anybody thinks he is a prophet or spiritually gifted, let him acknowledge that what I am writing to you is the Lord's command.

Paul begins this verse by picking up the two words "prophet" and "spiritual" from the historical setting at the Corinthian church and the previous verses in chapter 14 to depict some of his antagonists. Even though Paul has preferred prophecy over tongues throughout 1 Cor 14, he knows that those with prophetic gifts are not without their own problems. The problematic prophets might include prophets who did not agree with Paul's restrictions of their practices (14:29-33), women prophets who did not agree with Paul's possible restrictions placed upon them (14:34-35), or prophets who thought Paul was too protective of tongue speakers (14:39). Paul's requirement that prophecy be weighed (14:29) surely implies that a Corinthian prophet's message could be contrary to Paul's own instruction (see notes on 14:29).

The Greek text of 14:37 has the term for "spiritual" (πνευματικός, *pneumatikos;* cf. 12:1; 14:1) and not "spiritually gifted." In a way analogous to the litmus test of 12:3 (see notes there), Paul sets forth his epistolary instruction as the litmus test of spiritual orthodoxy and orthopraxy. The phrase "what I am writing to you" patently refers to at least 1 Cor 12-14 and demonstrates thereby that Paul intends the Corinthians to understand that it is prescriptive and regulatory for their faith and practice. As the apostle states it, this instruction "is the Lord's commandment" (see 4:15, 16, 20-21).

14:38 If he ignores this, he himself will be ignored.

Scholars differ in their interpretation of the severity implied in Paul's teaching here. Barrett, for example, understands this to mean that the apostle "does not recognize the man in question as inspired in his opinion, not that he does not recognize him as a Christian."[34] Other scholars such as Kistemaker[35] and Fee[36] interpret Paul's words to mean that any who oppose his teaching, and

---

[34]Barrett, *First Epistle,* p. 334.
[35]Kistemaker, *First Corinthians,* p. 516.
[36]Fee, *First Epistle,* p. 712.

thereby the commandment of the Lord (14:37b), will be ignored (=not recognized) by God.

14:39 Therefore, my brothers, be eager to prophesy, and do not forbid speaking in tongues.

Paul's instruction here summarizes a strategy that was implicit throughout chapter 14. When they are done God's way, Paul has no interest in curtailing prophecy and tongue speaking. However, in light of the *practices* of certain Corinthian believers, Paul's goal was to radically alter the Corinthians' use of these two gifts. The apostle's encouragement of prophecy and his protection of tongue speaking at this juncture can only fit into the rest of this chapter with any kind of consistency if one realizes that Paul means prophecy and tongue speaking which take place as he taught it should! Otherwise this verse would negate both the doctrine and regulations spelled out in the prior verses (14:1-38).

Commenting on this verse from the tradition and perspectives of a Pentecostal, Fee[37] asks how it is that some 20th century believers "spend so much energy getting around the plain sense of vv. 39-40."[38] It is hoped that in Fee's question the idea of "plain sense" includes the exegetical and rhetorical integrity of this verse with the remainder of Paul's teaching in this chapter. Only a dogmatic kind of prooftexting would interpret 14:39 as giving Corinthian believers a Scripture loophole with which to obviate or neutralize the command of the Lord expressed in the restrictions on tongue speaking, and to a lesser extent prophecy, which permeate chapter 14.

It should be pointed out that any unrepentant and non-compliant Corinthian tongue speaker would have regarded Paul's theology and regulations in 1 Cor 14 as the height of prohibition. To those Corinthian saints who were non-Pauline in their loyalties or to a prophet or tongue speaker who was number four (cf. 1 Cor 14:27, 29), Paul's injunction at 14:39 would have appeared to have been theological "double-speak" at its worst and completely inconsistent with the tenor and instruction of the preceding verses in this chapter.

---

[37]Ibid., p. xi.
[38]Ibid., p. 713.

14:40 But everything should be done in a fitting and orderly way.

The apostle ends both this chapter as well as the three chapter unit 12-14 with an appeal to guiding principles. Pauline letters typically contain both the theological principles from which he works and specific applications he makes from these. Chapter 14 has been a clear combination of theological perspectives and specific commandments based upon these perspectives.

The apostle's commitment to a "fitting and orderly way" in the assembly arises not from a high-church liturgical orientation. Rather, Paul's commitment to this perspective stands on two spiritual pillars. The first pillar is the proper honor and appropriate reflection of the one triune God (12:4-11) who does not distribute gifts in a disorderly way (14:33). The second pillar is the loving (*agapē*) concern for others and their needs demonstrated concretely in choices made in the style and conduct of the assembly. On these two pillars rests Paul's theology of corporate worship in 1 Corinthians.

1 CORINTHIANS 15

VIII. MISUNDERSTANDING OF BELIEVERS' RESURRECTION (15:1-58)

A. THE GOSPEL PAUL PREACHED (15:1-11)

1. Relation of the Corinthians to the Gospel (15:1-2)

[1]Now, brothers, I want to remind you of the gospel I preached to you, which you received and on which you have taken your stand. [2]By this gospel you are saved, if you hold firmly to the word I preached to you. Otherwise, you have believed in vain.

15:1 Now, brothers, I want to remind you of the gospel I preached to you, which you received and on which you have taken your stand.

It is universally recognized by scholars that this lengthy chapter, the longest in 1 Corinthians, deals with misconceptions related to the resurrection of believers. There are, however, related scholarly questions about which there is not a consensus. How, for example, does this material follow upon the themes of the preceding chapters? Since Paul did not use the "now about" formula that often sets off new materials (see Introduction and notes on 7:1), some interpreters are convinced that this chapter is closely related to the closing ideas of ch. 14. T. Gillespie argues that the doctrinal misconception that provoked Paul's argument in ch. 15 would be an exclamatory slogan something like "there is no resurrection" (15:12). This slogan, he asserts, is an example of Christian prophecy which would require weighing and refutation.[1]

---

[1]Thomas W. Gillespie, *The First Theologians. A Study in Early Christian Prophecy* (Grand Rapids: Eerdmans, 1994), pp. 199-236.

Chapter 15, given this outlook, would be the apostle's critique of this false prophecy. There are at least two major flaws with this approach. First, there are other examples in 1 Corinthians where Paul introduces new topics and does not begin with the literary marker "Now about" (e.g., 1 Cor 11:2), a marker which only points to issues the Corinthians themselves wrote about. Second, there are none of the verbal links between the vocabulary at the end of chapter 14 and the arguments of chapter 15 which one would expect to find if the hypothesis of Gillespie were correct.

Another distinctive issue that scholars discuss is what exactly is the nature of "some" (15:12, ἐν ὑμῖν τινες, *en hymin tines*) of the Corinthians' disbelief. Some have asserted that the problem is not that these saints deny the resurrection (as Paul believes they do), but that they only affirm that the resurrection had already occurred. While it is the case that we do know of this aberrant belief based upon information from the Pastoral Epistles (2 Tim 2:8), such an argument about 1 Corinthians is very problematic. The very evidence that informs one about the nature and details of this misconception referred to in the Pastoral Epistles, is exactly what is lacking in ch. 15. Paul does not say there that they think the resurrection is already past or, conversely, that the resurrection has not yet occurred. Rather than grasping at the straws of speculative reconstructions, it is a much more reliable historical method to assume Paul knew what some of these believers were saying, particularly since his summary, unlike the other hypotheses, makes abundant sense in the context of the well known pagan worldview which ridiculed the concept of resurrection (Acts 17:32). The traditional reconstruction which sees some of the believers still being controlled by residual paganism fits comfortably with the Greco-Roman matrix of other aberrant views and practices discovered so far in the church of God at Corinth (see notes on 1 Cor 15:12).

The apostle moves into this doctrinal exposition by attaching the term gospel (εὐαγγέλιον, *euangelion*) to his discussion. The Greek term *euangelion* and its cognates are important to the apostle throughout his writings, especially in the Corinthian letters. This is demonstrated by phrases from 1 Corinthians such as "Christ did not send me to baptize, but to preach the gospel"

(1:17), "in Christ Jesus I became your father through the gospel" (4:15), "we put up with anything rather than hinder the gospel of Christ" (9:12), "Woe to me if I do not preach the gospel!" (9:16), and "I do all this for the sake of the gospel" (9:23).

The expressions "which you received" and "on which you have taken your stand" function to remind the readers of their previous loyalty to and reliance upon the gospel. This is Paul's way of accentuating their past acknowledgment of the gospel and its importance for them. There seems, however, to be little contextual justification for believing, as Kistemaker does, that the apostle writes these words to demonstrate that "He expects them not only to accept his gospel but also to proclaim it in Corinth and elsewhere."[2]

15:2 By this gospel you are saved, if you hold firmly to the word I preached to you. Otherwise, you have believed in vain.
These are some of the apostle's strongest words in this chapter. Here he sets forth the inextricable connection between the gospel he preached to them and their own salvation (σώζεσθε, *sōzesthe*). The continuance of their salvation is related by Paul to their own decision to "hold firmly to the word," which in this case must surely be the gospel of Jesus' death, burial, and resurrection (see 15:3-4). Admittedly there are some doctrines about Christ (e.g., the virgin birth) found other places in the New Testament which Paul never explicitly makes part of his preaching and instruction. The resurrection of Jesus, however, is not one of those. The doctrine of faith in Jesus' resurrection is too central in Paul's gospel for the interpreter to diminish the sense of a statement such as "you have believed in vain." Fee is quite accurate when he observes, "To deny the objective reality of Christ's resurrection is to have a faith considerably different from Paul's"[3] or again,

> There seems to be little hope of getting around Paul's argument, that to deny Christ's resurrection is tantamount to a denial of Christian existence altogether. . . . Nothing else is the Christian faith, and those who reject the actuality of the resurrection of Christ need to face the consequences of

---

[2]Kistemaker, *First Corinthians*, pp. 526-27.
[3]Fee, *First Epistle*, p. 737.

such rejection, that they are bearing false witness against God himself. Like the Corinthians they will have believed in vain since the faith is finally predicated on whether or not Paul is right on this issue.[4]

2. Basic Issues of the Gospel (15:3-4)

[3]For what I received I passed on to you as of first importance[a]: that Christ died for our sins according to the Scriptures, [4]that he was buried, that he was raised on the third day according to the Scriptures,

[a]*3 Or you at the first*

15:3 For what I received I passed on to you as of first importance: that Christ died for our sins according to the Scriptures,

Statements such as "I received" (παραλαμβάνω, *paralambanō*) and "I passed on" (παραδίδωμι, *paradidōmi*) point to the place of the living tradition in the early church. There are striking verbal similarities between 15:3 and the language the apostle uses about the transmission of the words of the Lord's Supper in 11:23 (I *received* from the Lord what I also *passed on* to you).

The words "of first importance" most likely point to the quintessence of the gospel which Paul preached. That is, while Paul's preaching and teaching touched upon many themes, not all of these themes were of equal weight and centrality to his saving message. Though the imagery has shifted, this concept is the same as that which he employed with architectural metaphors earlier in this letter. In 1 Cor 3 the apostle affirmed that the teaching ministry of others was based upon the one and only foundation stone, namely Jesus Christ (1 Cor 3:10-12). The entire structure of the church is important, but of first importance is the foundation stone, Jesus Christ.

Naturally there are many facets of God's work in Christ that Paul both preached and taught about, but he wants here, in 15:3-

---

[4]Fee, *First Epistle*, p. 745.

5, to emphasize the centrality of four of these major points. In the Greek text each of these is introduced by the term "that" (ὅτι, *hoti*). The first theological doctrine in the cluster of things of "first importance" is the death of Jesus. There are two aspects of this death which are especially important to Paul's gospel: the vicarious nature ("for our," ὑπὲρ ἡμῶν, *hyper hemōn*) of Jesus' atoning death and the scriptural attestation to this ("according to the Scriptures," κατὰ τὰς γραφάς, *kata tas graphas*).

Neither of these is surprising in light of what has already been encountered within 1 Corinthians. The statement that, "Christ, our Passover lamb, has been sacrificed" (1 Cor 5:7) patently reveals the Pauline use of blood-sacrifice language with reference to Christ's death and its vicarious benefit for believers. With the apostle's abiding conviction that the (Old Testament) Scriptures are "for us" (see notes on 1 Cor 10:11ff), it would be astounding had he not known and made use of scriptural attestation to the death of Jesus.

15:4 that he was buried, that he was raised on the third day according to the Scriptures,

Reference to the burial of Jesus is complemented by the burial narratives preserved in the Gospels. The burial, in turn, lies behind the testimony of the empty tomb accounts. This brief reference to the burial, and by implication the later empty tomb, militates against an interpretation that somehow believes in a "Risen Lord," while Jesus is still decaying in an unknown tomb.[5]

As Paul will emphatically state later in this chapter, the resurrection of Jesus by the hand of God is the *sine qua non* of the Christian faith. Even though Paul's letters are filled with information about the spiritual and doctrinal significance of Jesus' resurrection, much of that is missing in this chapter. In this argumentative setting Paul must keep his thoughts to the point of the actuality of Christ's resurrection.

---

[5]Craig L. Blomberg, *The Historical Reliability of the Gospels*, p. 110, observes, "Since no one saw Jesus leave the tomb, why did his followers claim that this happened on Sunday morning unless something objective had convinced them that only at this time was the tomb really empty?"

Much effort has been expended to find a scriptural citation to "the third day" in the Old Testament. Some have wearied of this and have concluded that the Scriptures referred to here must be New Testament (=Gospels). This view has not found many sympathizers since it creates more problems than it solves. From those who hold to the traditional view that the word Scriptures means Old Testament, some suggest that the prepositional phrase according to the Scriptures goes with the words he was raised, rather than the phrase on the third day,[6] while others believe that a text such as Hosea 6:2 seems a likely candidate to reflect a third day concept.[7]

3. Appearances and Apostleship (15:5-11)

[5]and that he appeared to Peter,[a] and then to the Twelve. [6]After that, he appeared to more than five hundred of the brothers at the same time, most of whom are still living, though some have fallen asleep. [7]Then he appeared to James, then to all the apostles, [8]and last of all he appeared to me also, as to one abnormally born.

[9]For I am the least of the apostles and do not even deserve to be called an apostle, because I persecuted the church of God. [10]But by the grace of God I am what I am, and his grace to me was not without effect. No, I worked harder than all of them — yet not I, but the grace of God that was with me. [11]Whether, then, it was I or they, this is what we preach, and this is what you believed.

[a]5 Greek Cephas

15:5 and that he appeared to Peter, and then to the Twelve.

The fourth and final "that" (ὅτι, hoti) clause mentions the importance of the post-resurrection appearances to Peter and then to the rest of the Twelve. That Jesus appeared (ὤφθη, ōphthē) to the

---

[6]See notes in C.K. Barrett, *First Epistle*, p. 340.

[7]Fee, *First Epistle*, p. 727 for this and other suggestions.

Twelve was widely known in the relevant documents of the early church, namely in the Gospels and the Acts of the Apostles. Paul explicitly states that his earlier preaching and teaching to the Corinthians included the facts about the Lord's appearance to the Twelve and their resurrection belief. Paul's personal eyewitness of the vision on the road to Damascus would hardly have had the same force for authentication of the resurrection as the eyewitness testimony of the Twelve.

This is the sole occurrence of this term "the Twelve" (τοῖς δώδεκα, *tois dōdeka*) in Paul's letters, and he uses it here in reference to the Twelve Apostles (cf. Matt 10:2; Mark 3:16; Acts 6:2; Rev 21:14). Peter (=Cephas) is singled out by Paul as the only member of the Twelve to name, a fact that possibly reflects Peter's own special leadership among the Twelve. Peter is clearly the only one of the Twelve mentioned by name as having a following among some of the Corinthians (1:12; 3:22; cf. 9:5). As was made clear in Luke's presentation of the criteria for replacing Judas (Acts 1), Paul himself could never be one of the Twelve. This group held a special place in this history of the church and, in the words of Luke's Gospel, fulfilled a unique kingdom ministry of sitting on thrones and judging the twelve tribes of Israel (Luke 22:30).

15:6 After that, he appeared to more than five hundred of the brothers at the same time, most of whom are still living, though some have fallen asleep.

In addition to the post-resurrection appearances to the Twelve, the Lord also appeared to a large group that numbered more than 500. The accounts in the Gospels reveal that Jesus was seen by many disciples, both men and women, following his resurrection. These accounts do not, however, depict scenes where the Lord appeared to this many disciples at the same time. In light of this fact, it seems prudent not to attempt to identify Paul's testimony here with any particular Gospel account.

Paul's reference to the availability (still living) of this eyewitness corroboration is an apologetic emphasis designed to give evidentiary support to the historical reliability of his own post-resurrection encounter. The phrase "fallen asleep" is a euphemistic reference to death (cf. 1 Cor 11:30; 15:6, 18, 20, 51; 1 Thess 4:13-15), and is an acknowledgment that some of these 500 are no longer alive.

15:7 Then he appeared to James, then to all the apostles,

It is quite likely that the James referred to here is James the brother of the Lord. Though he held an especially important role in the Jerusalem church according to Acts (Acts 15 and 21), he was not regarded as one of the Twelve. Paul's wording here could be taken to imply that James the brother of Jesus was in some sense an "apostle." A similar understanding of the apostolic ministry of James the brother of the Lord (not James who was one of the Twelve apostles) is revealed in Gal 1:19-2:12. There is surprisingly little information in the New Testament about the role of Jesus' earthly family in the early church.

15:8 and last of all he appeared to me also, as to one abnormally born.

Paul was clearly an apostle (see 1 Cor 1:1), but there is no evidence that he, or Luke in the Acts of the Apostles, regarded him as a member of the Twelve. Paul's encounter with the risen Lord, this defining experience of the apostolate, occurred abnormally, long after Jesus' ascension to the right hand of God the Father. The Greek phrase (τῷ ἐκτρώματι, tō ektrōmati) behind the English wording "abnormally born" is both unusual and negative as a term to describe Paul's apostolic calling. One interpretation of this birth imagery is that Paul's birth into apostleship was anything but normal. This view is suggested by Calvin when he comments,

> For just as babies do not come forth from the womb until they have been in it for the proper period of time and been fully formed, so our Lord followed a suitable time-table in creating, fostering and shaping the apostles. Paul, on the other hand, had been pushed out of the womb, before the

living spirit had scarcely had time to be properly conceived in him.[8]

Paul probably had more in mind, however, than the fact that he became an apostle in an out-of-the-ordinary fashion. Based upon philological considerations of the Greek phrase Paul used and upon the somewhat defensive rhetoric about his apostleship found in 15:9-11, "it seems hardly possible to understand this usage except as a term that describes him vis-a-vis the Corinthians' own view of apostleship."[9] That is, some of the Corinthians held pejorative views about Paul's calling and ministry, and he responds in part to that by this acknowledgment.

15:9 For I am the least of the apostles and do not even deserve to be called an apostle, because I persecuted the church of God.

Rather than conceding to the criticism of his detractors, which was based upon worldly wisdom and human strife, Paul goes a step farther and uses self-criticism. Paul's self-criticism, unlike his detractors, is predicated upon the wisdom of God. This is why Paul can so readily embrace the fact that he is the least of the apostles and is unworthy (οὐκ εἰμὶ ἱκανός, *ouk eimi hikanos*) of this calling. Paul understood the gravity of his prior animosity to God. Both the Pauline letters and the Acts of the Apostles are in agreement that before Paul's encounter with the risen Lord he was involved in the persecution of believers.

15:10 But by the grace of God I am what I am, and his grace to me was not without effect. No, I worked harder than all of them — yet not I, but the grace of God that was with me.

Since Paul did nothing to earn or deserve his apostolic ministry, he can only accept it on the basis of the grace of God. When Paul proclaims that he is what he is by the grace of God, "The Corinthians could not gainsay his status unless they wanted to quibble with God."[10] Paul's use of the term and concept of grace in this verse has two dimensions to it. The first two of the three

---

[8]Fee, *First Epistle*, p. 315.
[9]Ibid., p. 733.
[10]Witherington, *Conflict and Community in Corinth*, p. 301.

occurrences point to the saving grace which Paul experienced at the time of his obedience to the gospel (cf. Eph 2:8-10). His final use of grace in this verse points in the direction of grace which is ministry and gift empowering. According to the apostle, all Christian ministries and gifts (see ch. 12) are a manifestation of the gracious will of God. Consequently, Paul understands grace not only as saving grace, but also as equipping and empowering grace, with the latter clearly stemming from the former.

Paul surely believed that God's grace could be received in vain or without effect (εἰς ἐμὲ οὐ κενή, *eis eme ou kenē*). This phenomenon, in the words of the 20th century scholar Dietrich Bonhoeffer, was "cheap grace," a grace which bore no fruit. While the history of Christianity has been plagued by the curse of "grace without effect," Paul's own ministerial strategy is "hard work." Paul's harmonization of grace and hard work should not represent a spiritual or doctrinal problem as long as it is understood that the hard work is a manifestation of the empowering grace.

The apostle's closing ideas in this verse significantly address the issue of this divine empowerment in ministry among believers. The crucial phrase "yet not I" means that the apostle disowns not only meritorious effort in his own justification and salvation, but also in his ministerial activities. All credit goes to the everpresent and empowering grace of God in his life (ἡ χάρις τοῦ θεοῦ σὺν ἐμοί, *hē charis tou theou sun emoi*). This means, then, that Paul's heroic and sacrificial life, his stupendous zeal, and his Herculean accomplishments (cf. 1 Cor 4; 2 Cor 11; Rom 15; Acts 13-28) were, to adapt later language to the Corinthians, the work of God through a cracked clay pot (2 Cor 4:7ff). An illustration which has attempted to capture the paradox in Paul's words about hard work and the work of grace is given by Robertson and Plummer, "from a human point of view [it] is as the joy of a child who gives his father a birthday present out of his father's own money."[11]

---

[11]Robertson and Plummer, *First Epistle of St. Paul*, p. 342, quoting an earlier work by Weinel, p. 178.

15:11 Whether, then, it was I or they, this is what we preach, and this is what you believed.

The dual reference to "I or they" surely hints at some of the congregational disaffection for Paul and some preferences for other leaders, and perhaps other apostles. Paul's concern here is not to demand that they prefer him. On the contrary, Paul's point is to emphasize the fact that they and he all preached the same message. This verse is clearly a transitional verse into the main issue of confidence in the teaching of the resurrection of believers which follows in 15:11ff. In particular, the two terms "preach" (κηρύσσω, *kērussō* and its cognates) and "believe" (πιστεύω, *pisteuō* and its cognates) are introduced here in anticipation of their appearance in the following section (1 Cor 15:12, 14, 17).

Paul does not have in mind just any point that the apostles have preached or any doctrine which the readers have believed. He is vitally concerned to affirm that all the preaching they had experienced and the message which they had already confidently believed presupposed the resurrection of Jesus and the future resurrection of believers. "On the basis of this common faith," Fee rightly argues, "Paul will next turn to a direct confrontation with the Corinthians over their denial of the resurrection of the dead."[12]

B. CHRIST'S RESURRECTION AND THE RESURRECTION OF THE DEAD (15:12-34)

1. Consequences of Denying the Resurrection (15:12-19)

[12]**But if it is preached that Christ has been raised from the dead, how can some of you say that there is no resurrection of the dead? [13]If there is no resurrection of the dead, then not even Christ has been raised. [14]And if Christ has not been raised, our preaching is useless and so is your faith. [15]More than that, we are then found to be false witnesses about God, for we have testified about God that he raised Christ from the dead. But he did not**

---

[12]Fee, *First Epistle*, p. 737.

raise him if in fact the dead are not raised. [16]For if the dead are not raised, then Christ has not been raised either. [17]And if Christ has not been raised, your faith is futile; you are still in your sins. [18]Then those also who have fallen asleep in Christ are lost. [19]If only for this life we have hope in Christ, we are to be pitied more than all men.

15:12 But if it is preached that Christ has been raised from the dead, how can some of you say that there is no resurrection of the dead?

In the apostle's response to those believers who denied the future resurrection, he employed a particular type of rhetoric. The next several verses are constructed on the basis of logical argumentation, characterized by the particular use of the term "if." Witherington underscores the significance of this type of rhetoric in its historical setting with these words.

> It was a regular practice for a rhetor to try to refute an argument by showing that its logical consequences were unacceptable and thus that the logic must be flawed. Paul offers a kind of syllogism to correct their view. . . . This is one of the most rhetorically powerful and detailed arguments in the letter.[13]

With the words "some of you say" Paul makes it clear that this erroneous belief is coming from certain individuals within the church of God at Corinth. Since the readers have heard and accepted the resurrection of Christ, it is totally illogical, Paul reasons, for them to now accept the belief that the dead are not raised.

The specific doctrinal aberration to which Paul refers is that which denies that the dead are raised bodily. By denying the resurrection from the dead, the Corinthians were apparently still under the sway of their former pagan religious and philosophical views. Most, but certainly not all, of the Greco-Roman world at Paul's time believed in some form of post-mortem consciousness, either in a state of bliss or in a state of punishment. This is abun-

---

[13]Witherington, *Conflict and Community in Corinth*, p. 303.

dantly evident whether one looks at major philosophical and religious writers of the ancient world or at the archaeological evidence of tombstone epitaphs. Accordingly, the conflict between Paul and these erring believers was not over the idea of the immortality of the soul. Rather, they disagreed over whether the body, in any form, was raised from the dead. The fact that the nature of this resurrection body was an essential part of the stumbling block for the Corinthians is demonstrated by the fact that Paul later has to treat extensively the question "With what kind of body will they come?" (1 Cor 15:35-55).

In this regard, one can only speculate about what these believers actually thought about the resurrection of Christ and the nature of his resurrected body. Paul clearly assumes that they did believe in Jesus' resurrection. But what were their beliefs about the nature of Christ's raised body? Did they hold to the Pauline view about the nature of the resurrection of Christ's body and therefore only need to have Paul point out the illogical nature of their reasoning? Or, would they have been shocked when reading the accounts of the Lord's post-resurrection bodily appearances (esp. Luke 24)? There are no clear answers to these questions, but it is a point which may have contributed to the Corinthians' confusion.

15:13 If there is no resurrection of the dead, then not even Christ has been raised.

Paul turns the argument to demonstrate the logical consequences of the position of these Corinthians if they, rather than Paul, are correct. Since the apostle's argument rests upon the premise of an inextricable link between the believers' and Jesus' resurrection, he reasons that disbelief in the general resurrection of believers logically leads to disbelief in Christ's resurrection.

15:14 And if Christ has not been raised, our preaching is useless and so is your faith.

It is the erroneous conclusion of these saints, whether they recognize its error or not, that even Christ had not been raised (15:13). Consequently, if Christ had not been raised, then the early church's proclamation was empty and useless (κενόν, *kenon*), since

his resurrection was the centerpiece of the early church's proclamation. Moreover, not only is the message of the apostle futile,
the faith of the Corinthians is likewise useless (κενή, *kenē*), since
their belief was predicated upon the reality of Jesus' resurrection.

**15:15 More than that, we are then found to be false witnesses
about God, for we have testified about God that he raised Christ
from the dead. But he did not raise him if in fact the dead are
not raised.**

Furthermore (the list of the consequences of the Corinthians'
error continues), in addition to the falsity of the content of the
apostolic proclamation, the falsity of the character of the apostles
is now self-evident, if Christ had not been raised. Paul and the
others must, logically speaking, be regarded as "false witnesses
about God" (ψευδομάρτυρες τοῦ θεοῦ, *pseudomartyres tou theou*). The
basis of this charge of deceit and falsity is that Paul and the others
as mountebanks had inveigled the credulous Corinthians into believing a lie, namely that God had raised Jesus of Nazareth from
the dead.

While this charge is serious and damning if true, Paul argues
that it is the only logical conclusion one can reach about the
character of the apostles if the false doctrine of the Corinthians is
correct. If the dead are not raised, then God did not raise Jesus.

**15:16 For if the dead are not raised, then Christ has not been
raised either.**

Conversely, if the Corinthian position is accurate, then Christ
lies in an unknown Judean tomb, strangely enough never ex-
humed and put on display by the authorities — even after these
almost twenty years — to quash the belief of the Jesus movement
in their risen Lord.

**15:17 And if Christ has not been raised, your faith is futile; you
are still in your sins.**

Another dramatic revelation from Paul is that the faith of the
Corinthian believers is futile (ματαία, *mataia*). A second startling
consequence of this error is that the proclamation of the forgiveness of sins is a baldfaced lie. Interpreters of the New Testament

are more accustomed to associate forgiveness of sins with the death of Christ rather than his resurrection. The writers of the New Testament can obviously focus on distinct facets of God's work in Christ (e.g., birth, miracles, human suffering, death, resurrection, and ascension), and the same can be said of Paul. While Paul can focus separately on the significance of Christ's incarnation, his death, his ascension, his life of service, and his resurrection, it would be a distortion for interpreters to imagine that any one of these could stand alone in Paul's theology. All of these were held together in the person of Christ because it was in him that God was pleased to accomplish his work on behalf of mankind. Without the culminating work of God in the resurrection of Jesus, then all of his prior acts would be without consummation and validity.

15:18 Then those also who have fallen asleep in Christ are lost.

Having referred to numerous logical consequences of the errorists' position on the resurrection, he now turns to one that surely had a strong cultural and, therefore, emotional appeal since it related to the fate of the dead. Because of the concern ancient people had for their dead and the conditions of their dead friends and loved ones in the underworld, this consequence would have affected them strongly. Ironically, it is just because of their pagan presuppositions about proper concern for the dead that they might better listen to Paul's argument.

If there is no resurrection, then those fellow believers who have died in the few intervening years between the arrival of the gospel in Corinth (Acts 18) and the writing of 1 Corinthians are lost (ἀπώλοντο, *apōlonto*). There is no evidence for knowing how many of those there would have been who had fallen asleep in Christ. Whether the number was five, fifty, or five hundred, the apostle's argument is cogent. Regarding the dead saints, "Paul means that there is for them no future of any kind. Because they would thus have died in their sins, they perish along with rest of fallen humanity."[14]

---

[14]Fee, *First Epistle*, p.744.

15:19 If only for this life we have hope in Christ, we are to be pitied more than all men.

Paul has already revealed his own eschatological piety and confidence at several locations in the letter of 1 Corinthians. This verse makes it clear that for the apostle this earthly life is not the ultimate good. Paul's gospel assuredly contained the expectations of benefits for the believer in "this life" (ζωῇ ταύτῃ, *zōē tautē*). Irrespective, however, of all of the promised good in this present age, the substance of the believer's hope is anchored in the future. Given the paucity of the material and earthly blessings promised to the one who trusted in Christ, and given the relatively little that Paul says about the material significance and benefits of his doctrines, e.g., his Christology, one can better understand the emphasis of this verse.

Since the apostle's affirmation of the love of God and the justification of the sinner did not convert into specific material benefits similar to those ostensibly given by other ancient religions, Paul kept his central theological hopes focused upon a future created anew by God, rather than upon ephemeral things. Offers of good health, stellar performance in life's everyday transactions, victory in the vicissitudes of business and trade dealings, successful romantic relationships, and salvation from untimely disasters to family and farm were peculiarly, but significantly, absent from Paul's message.

2. The Fact of Christ's Resurrection (15:20-28)

[20]But Christ has indeed been raised from the dead, the firstfruits of those who have fallen asleep. [21]For since death came through a man, the resurrection of the dead comes also through a man. [22]For as in Adam all die, so in Christ all will be made alive. [23]But each in his own turn: Christ, the firstfruits; then, when he comes, those who belong to him. [24]Then the end will come, when he hands over the kingdom to God the Father after he has destroyed all dominion, authority and power. [25]For he must reign until he has put all his enemies under his feet. [26]The last enemy to be destroyed is death. [27]For he "has put everything under his

feet."ᵃ Now when it says that "everything" has been put under him, it is clear that this does not include God himself, who put everything under Christ. ²⁸When he has done this, then the Son himself will be made subject to him who put everything under him, so that God may be all in all.

ᵃ*27 Psalm 8:6*

15:20 But Christ has indeed been raised from the dead, the firstfruits of those who have fallen asleep.

Having spent the several preceding verses highlighting the damnable consequences that eventuate if the erring Corinthians were correct, he now turns his attention "to a positive testimony on Christ raised from the dead."[15] Not only does he wish to reaffirm the resurrection of Christ, but especially to emphasize the positive consequences of that fact for believers. For Paul the resurrection of Jesus was no mere artifact of ancient Palestinian piety that the later saints were to reverence from a historical distance. That fact of history had direct and immediate impact and significance on the lives of believers.

The term Paul uses to explicate the significance of Jesus' resurrection is firstfruits (ἀπαρχή, *aparchē*), an agricultural metaphor which has a rich eschatological application in Paul's writings (cf. Rom 8:23). Since Paul had mentioned in 15:18 the issue of the fate of those believers who had fallen asleep, he now stresses how his gospel understands the benefit of Christ's resurrection for them. Christ is the firstfruits for dead believers. In particular this metaphor means that in Jesus' resurrection the certainty of the resurrection of the saints is guaranteed. Jesus' resurrection is the firstfruit not because he was the first individual in human history to be raised, but because his was the only one which decisively overthrew death itself. All others who either before or after Jesus were raised from the dead died again, making it painfully clear that their resurrections had done nothing to eliminate death itself.

Consequently, there is never a question for believers of whether but only of when death will be permanently destroyed

---

[15]Kistemaker, *First Corinthians*, p. 546.

and their own bodies will be raised. The sovereign will of God
that will bring this to fruition at the Second Coming has, in Fee's
words, "been set inexorably in motion."[16] Using the frequent harvest metaphor for the end of the age (see Jesus' use in Matt 13),
Paul emphasizes that the initial stage of the final harvest has already occurred in the raising of Jesus of Nazareth. The presence
of the firstfruits, Jesus' resurrection, is proof of the future culmination of the entire harvesting process (see notes on 15:23).

**15:21 For since death came through a man, the resurrection of
the dead comes also through a man.**
At this point the apostle predictably drinks from the well of
Old Testament theological materials to undergird his point to
these mistaken (Gentile) members of the Corinthian church of
God. Specifically, he returns to narrative material from the opening chapters of Genesis, narratives which have served him so well
to this point, and utilizes concepts in the Adamic narratives. By
the parallelism of the two phrases "through a man," Paul set up a
typology of sorts to explain the work of Christ as firstfruits. The
two realities before mankind are death (θάνατος, *thanatos*) and resurrection from the dead (ἀνάστασις νεκρῶν, *anastasis nekrōn*), both
of which were realities triggered by the actions of individuals.

15:22 For as in Adam all die, so in Christ all will be made alive.
Paul designates the one man to be Adam and the other to be
Christ. Even though there are of course general similarities between the Adam-Christ illustration here and in Rom 5, there are
also some significant distinctions. As Calvin,[17] among others,
noted, the primary function of this Adam-Christ illustration in ch.
15 is to address the issue of physical death and the expectation of
a bodily resurrection, while the function of that illustration in
Rom 5 is to deal with the issue of spiritual death and the nature of
reconciliation.
In this verse Paul traces the origin of physical death back to
Adam, at a time when God promised Adam that because of his
disobedience he would die (Gen 2:17; 3:3). According to Paul "in

---

[16]Fee, *First Epistle*, p. 746.
[17]Calvin, *First Epistle*, p. 323.

Adam" all died. This concept of the activity of one person impact-
ing the lives of others has sometimes been called "corporate personality." Anyone familiar with human history could hardly deny
the fact that the decisions of one individual often has profound
and longlasting consequences upon others, sometimes upon innocent others. But Paul is doing more than making an observation about human history. His concern is the divine economy of
God. For Paul, the very principle which allows the decision of
Adam to affect others, likewise allows the decision of Christ to
affect others also. Without this concept of vicarious (on behalf of
others) effects, then no one could benefit from God's work in
Christ on our behalf.

Interpreters quite naturally disagree over whether Paul means
the same thing in both occurrences of the term "all" (πάντες, *pantes*) in 15:22. The point of disagreement is not so much whether
the first use of the term "all" (in Adam) means every human who
has or will ever live, but whether the second use of this term "all"
(in Christ) means the same. Specifically, will everyone be made
alive in Christ? The apostle certainly believed that both the right-
eous and the unrighteous would have to stand before God's
throne of judgment (2 Cor 5:10; cf. esp. John 5:29; Dan 12:2), but
is not Paul's contextual emphasis in 15:20-23 upon the benefits
that believers receive from Christ as the firstfruits of those who
have fallen asleep? If so, then at least Paul's immediate concern is
that all (who belong to him, 15:23) will be made alive. Kistemaker
makes the following observation:

> The adjective all should not be interpreted to mean that
> Paul teaches universal salvation. Far from it. . . . Whereas
> all people face death because of Adam's sin, only those
> who are in Christ receive life because of his resurrection.
> The New Testament teaches that the verb to give life refers
> only to believers and not to unbelievers. Paul elucidates the
> rising from the dead of Christ and his people but not that of
> pagans.[18]

---

[18]Kistemaker, *First Corinthians*, at 15:22.

15:23 But each in his own turn: Christ, the firstfruits; then, when he comes, those who belong to him.

He next elaborates on the imagery of the concept of Christ as firstfruits and the attendant question of the sequence of the harvest. Many theories, some more speculative than others, have been offered about what particular Corinthian misunderstanding Paul was responding to here. Calvin's suggestion seems worthwhile when he imagines one of the misinformed Corinthians might contest Paul's previous affirmations with the observation, "Although Christ has risen from the tomb, we rot in it."[19] This would necessitate, given Calvin's reconstruction, that Paul address the issue of "each in his own turn" (ἐν τῷ ἰδίῳ τάγματι, *en tō idiō tagmati*).

Paul's view of the order (*tagma*) seems to include three steps, though in these three the apostle clearly does not answer all the questions that have been put to him throughout the centuries by various interpreters. The three-step schematization generally follows this pattern:

1. Resurrection of Jesus as firstfruit   15:23
2. Resurrection of believers at Christ's return   15:23
3. The End   15:24
   a. when Christ gives the kingdom to God the Father
   b. when Christ destroys all dominion, authority, and power
   c. when all things are subjected to him (Christ) by God the Father

This pattern has no explicit reference to the resurrection of non-believers and in C.K. Barrett's opinion, "with this silence we must be content."[20] Although Paul does not use here the term "Second Coming," there can be no doubt in light of his other writings that this is what he has in mind by the Greek term *parousia* ("when he comes," ἐν τῇ παρουσίᾳ αὐτοῦ, *en tē parousia autou*).

---

[19]Calvin, *First Epistle*, p. 323.
[20]Barrett, *First Epistle*, p. 355.

15:24 Then the end will come, when he hands over the kingdom to God the Father after he has destroyed all dominion, authority and power.

By his use of this eschatological schema with its three stages Paul reveals the fact that his own doctrine of the resurrection of believers was closely tied to his view of the Second Coming of Christ. This is noteworthy since in the course of Christian history many have slowly moved away from Paul's inextricable link between the benefits of Jesus' resurrection for immortality and the End (cf. 15:53) and have moved toward attaching the benefits of Jesus' resurrection to the time of one's personal death.

Rather than Paul's model in 1 Cor 15 with its clear focus on the victory over death coming to the believer at his eschatological resurrection, some have thought more in terms of being immediately in the presence of God at the point of one's physical death, with little attention given to the imagery of describing dead believers as "those who have fallen asleep" (15:6, 18, 20, 51 and 7:39) until the coming of Christ and the End.

Since the kingdom of God can never come without the destruction of opponents, it is natural for him to link the eschatological possession and transfer of the kingdom to God the Father, its rightful owner, with destruction. While those who impugn the punitive picture of God in the New Testament usually look to the Apocalypse of John for their examples, this verse patently reflects the fact that the apostle Paul firmly believed in the punitive behavior of Christ and God the Father (cf. 2 Thess 1:3-12).

Paul has already made comments about the Roman political system, both in its execution of Jesus (see notes on 2:8) and its unrighteous judicial system (6:1-6), and his reference here to dominion, authority, and power would surely have included the dominant cultural, political, and religious forces of his time who stood in opposition to the kingdom of God. Nevertheless, Paul does not regard the Roman empire as the greatest opponents to God's monarchy. For the apostle Paul (a Roman citizen) the evil empire against which he fights is Adamic (see 15:21-22) and not a secular eschatology infatuated with the imperial cult and games.[21]

---

[21]See opposing view in Witherington, *Community and Conflict in Corinth*, pp. 295-305.

Rather, as Paul's argumentation and Scripture quotation through-out this entire chapter presupposes, death (15:26) and sin (15:54-57) are the major antagonists to the kingdom of God. There is no statement in this chapter or in other Pauline texts where such terminology occurs (e.g., Eph 1:21; 6:12; Col 1:16; Rom 8:38) to the effect that Christ came explicitly and intentionally to over-throw demonic forces associated with various human cultures and dictatorships.

15:25 For he must reign until he has put all his enemies under his feet.

With the introductory term "for" (γάρ, *gar*) he makes it clear that this verse is an expansion and explanation of 15:24. There is a verbal and conceptual link between these two verses which is lost in English translation. The concept of handing over the "kingdom" (βασιλεία, *basileia*) mentioned in 15:24 is further ad-dressed by the phrase he must "reign" (βασιλεύω, *basileuō*) in 15:25. Since 15:24 pictures the risen Lord in possession of the kingdom to give to God, 15:25 comments on Christ's current rule in this kingdom.

There is divine necessity (δεῖ, *dei*) that supports Christ's current lordship. He must rule until which time (i.e., the End) he (i.e., Christ) subjugates all enemies under his (i.e., Christ's) feet. Even though the notion of "enemies under his feet" was a widespread political idiom in antiquity, found in visual form in Roman coin-age and statuary, the presence of these words here must be traced back to the Old Testament. The verbal parallels between this wording in 15:25 and Psalm 110:1 ("until I make your enemies a footstool for your feet") and the Scripture citation from Ps 8:6 ("You made him ruler over the works of your hands; you put eve-rything under his feet") in 1 Cor 15:27 moves this beyond the realm of conjecture.

While there is partial subjugation of the enemies of God with the reign of Christ during human history, the final destruction and irreversible overthrow of these occurs only at the End. This verse also explains Paul's view of the current reign of Christ; it is necessary for the very reason that it is the means, the necessary means, through which God the Father is recapturing his rightful kingdom.

15:26 The last enemy to be destroyed is death.

Throughout the high, ebb, and low tides of human history and achievements not a single advancement has been made against death (θάνατος, *thanatos*) as Paul understood it. It stands there, as a defiant equalizer and voracious vortex that drains the life from every one of God's creatures. The apostle's evaluation about the inimical nature (ἐχθρός, *echthros*) of death is unaltered by the extension of life expectancy or an occasional resurrection from the dead as testified to by Scripture. In these circumstances death is only momentarily put into check, but never into checkmate. The certain victory over this last enemy was secured and guaranteed by Jesus' own resurrection, but will only come to full manifestation and fruition at the time of Christ's return, when all who have died are loosened from the embrace of death and its power. The destruction of death is when the general resurrection takes place (cf. Rev 20:13-14).

15:27 For he "has put everything under his feet." Now when it says that "everything" has been put under him, it is clear that this does not include God himself, who put everything under Christ.

These thoughts are added by Paul to clarify any possible misunderstandings about the extent of Christ's kingdom and, thereby, the relationship between Christ and God the Father. In his comments on these verses C.K. Barrett suggests that Paul wrote this to make it clear that "so far from its being true that God is subjected to Christ, Christ is subjected to God" and to dispel any possible Corinthian misconceptions that "at his exaltation Christ became the one supreme God. Obedience was and would through eternity continue to be part of the divine virtue of the Son."[22]

He wants to make it clear that Christ's subjugation of everything which is attested by Ps 8:6 (see notes on 1 Cor 15:25) does not include God the Father. This misconception appears ludicrous to Paul since to speak of the subjugation of God the Father

---

[22]Barrett, *First Epistle*, p. 360.

would be blasphemy. In addition, it would certainly call into question the logical character of the affirmations of the preceding verses. Since it was not an arbitrary fact that it was God the Father who was the one who put everything into submission to Christ (on the basis of the Father's divine monarchy; see notes on 3:23 and 11:3), then it would be illogical for the Father to now be in submission to one who was formally under his monarchy.

15:28 When he has done this, then the Son himself will be made subject to him who put everything under him, so that God may be all in all.

This verse completes the train of thought begun in 15:24 when the events of the End are discussed. Furthermore, the apostle makes explicit that the Son himself will enter a submission (ὑποταγήσεται, *hypotagēsetai*) throughout eternity, a submission to God that has for its purpose (*hina*) the unqualified omnipotence ("all in all," πάντα ἐν πᾶσιν, *panta en pasin*) and monarchy of the Father. That the goal of history and the foundation of the believer's future resurrection is the eschatological monarchy of the God of Abraham, Isaac and Jacob probably had little appeal to urbane Corinthians. But Paul's gospel of the resurrection of Christ (and hence of believers) was formulated within the world-view of Judaism and, in particular, Jewish apocalyptic thought. As J.C. Beker noted,

> It is curious that Paul, so conscious of his universal call to be 'the apostle to the Gentiles' (Rom 11:13), insists on a particularistic Jewish apocalyptic ideology to communicate the truth of the gospel in 1 Corinthians 15. . . . First Corinthians 15 provides us with an impressive example that the coherent center of the gospel is, for Paul, not simply an experiential reality of the heart or a Word beyond words that permits translation into a multitude of world views. . . . However applicable the gospel must be to a Gentile in his contingent situation, it does not tolerate a world view that cannot express those elements inherent in the apocalyptic world view and that to Paul seem inherent in the truth of the gospel. . . . Indeed, according to Paul, the gospel is integrally connected with his apocalyptic world view: he cannot conceive of the resurrection of Christ — which the Cor-

inthians affirm (1 Cor 15:1, 2, 11) – apart from the apocalyptic general resurrection of the dead. Both stand or fall together. [23]

Calvin refuted those who twisted this idea of "be all in all" to support a kind of universalism in which "the devil and the disobedient will be saved" with the following words, "So we see how impudent madmen of that sort are, when they twist this saying of Paul's to support their own blasphemies."[24]

3. Baptism, Suffering, and the Resurrection (15:29-34)

[29]Now if there is no resurrection, what will those do who are baptized for the dead? If the dead are not raised at all, why are people baptized for them? [30]And as for us, why do we endanger ourselves every hour? [31]I die every day – I mean that, brothers – just as surely as I glory over you in Christ Jesus our Lord. [32]If I fought wild beasts in Ephesus for merely human reasons, what have I gained? If the dead are not raised,

"Let us eat and drink, for tomorrow we die." [a]
[33]Do not be misled: "Bad company corrupts good character." [34]Come back to your senses as you ought, and stop sinning; for there are some who are ignorant of God – I say this to your shame.

[a] 32 Isaiah 22:13

15:29 Now if there is no resurrection, what will those do who are baptized for the dead? If the dead are not raised at all, why are people baptized for them?
Having completed a lengthy section in which he interpreted the meaning of Christ as firstfruits, Paul now turns to a different form of argumentation and rhetoric. Rather than using the more formal logical approach of 15:12-19, he now employs what most

---

[23] J.C. Beker, *Paul the Apostle*, pp. 170-171.
[24] Calvin, *First Epistle*, p. 328.

interpreters recognize as a form of reasoning which relies more heavily upon *ad hominem* appeals. The first response he gives to the "if there is no resurrection" questions has baffled interpreters for centuries. Scores of theories have been given to explain the meaning of the apostle's reference to the idea of baptism "on behalf of them [the dead]" (ὑπέρ αὐτῶν, *hyper autōn*). In Fee's judgment there are four important questions one must answer about this "genuinely idiosyncratic historical phenomenon."[25] These are: (1) Who was being baptized; (2) On whose behalf were they being baptized; (3) Why were they engaging in this practice; and (4) What difference did they think this practice would make? Without repeating all of the proposed solutions and the finely nuanced history of the interpretation of this somewhat enigmatic appeal (available in Fee's treatment) I would give the following tentative solution, though the textual and historical evidence is not available to answer Fee's four questions. Since Paul's question is stated in the third person rather than the second person, there is no need to believe that he is referring to a practice that his readership is participating in. That is, he did not ask "why are *you* baptized?" but "why are people baptized?" In light of the fact that there are a higher than usual number of allusions to and quotations from patently pagan materials in this *ad hominem* section (15:29-34), there is no intrinsic reason to doubt that Paul could be referring to a pagan practice to support his argument. This reference to a pagan practice would also make sense since paganism is the matrix of this particular misunderstanding among some of the Corinthians.

The particular reference to the act of water immersion rites presents no problem for this current interpretation. The ancient world was replete with non-Christian religions, both Jewish and pagan, who practiced some form of water immersions as a part of their religious beliefs. Since water immersion rites were sometimes characteristic of pagan cults which offered, among other things, hope of a post-mortem existence, the apostle perhaps has referred to a practice, known by the Corinthians, in which pagan individuals hope to secure some eternal blessing. Since Paul men-

---

[25]Fee, *First Epistle*, pp. 764-767.

tions the vicarious nature ("on behalf," ὑπέρ, *hyper*) of this baptism, this must have been a part of the pagan understanding which he has in mind.

Even if this were a current practice among some of the Corinthian believers (since there are allusions already in 1 Corinthians to their profound misunderstandings about water baptism: 1:13-17; 10:1-5), Paul mentions this not to endorse it, but to use this practice as an *ad hominem* argument to highlight the inconsistency of their beliefs.

15:30 And as for us, why do we endanger ourselves every hour?

If there is no eternal reward, no imperishable crown, Paul asks, "why do we endanger ourselves" at all times? This thought rests in part on his previous statement about the pitiful character of life if there is no resurrection. If one cannot interpret the voluntary misfortunes, dangers and painful experiences of this life with regard to the future, why undergo them? Since Paul's catalogues of sufferings (cf. 1 Cor 4:10-13; 2 Cor 11:23-29) point to many hardships that were voluntarily assumed, one can only reason that he could have lived without many of them. If there is no resurrection, he appeals, why constantly endure self-inflicted danger?

15:31 I die every day — I mean that, brothers — just as surely as I glory over you in Christ Jesus our Lord.

The apostle's statement about his daily death is a way to restate, though more emphatically, the idea given in 15:30. This autobiographical reference to daily death is not some notion of dying daily by "following Jesus." Based upon all the evidence from the Corinthian letters as well as Acts 19-20, Paul was often in danger of death at this juncture of his ministry. Especially noteworthy are his comments to this effect in 2 Cor 1:8-10, which contain the statements, "we despaired even of life," "we felt the sentence of death," "we might not rely on ourselves but on God who raises the dead," and "He has delivered us from such a deadly peril."

Paul connects the veracity of his statement about his daily death to the reality of his glory and boasting over the Corinthian saints. "The fact that they [the Corinthian saints] have been won to Christ out of the heathen world," Barrett writes, "is worth many deaths."[26]

15:32 If I fought wild beasts in Ephesus for merely human reasons, what have I gained? If the dead are not raised, "Let us eat and drink, for tomorrow we die."

Most modern interpreters, unlike Calvin,[27] rightly understand Paul's words about wild beasts in Ephesus to have a metaphorical sense rather than a literal one. Arguments in favor of a metaphorical sense include the improbability of local officials throwing a Roman citizen into the arena and the rhetorical and metaphorical use of wild beast imagery among philosophers and rhetoricians of Paul's day;[28] the apostle is probably referring to hardships and opposition he has faced in Ephesus.

The Greek phrase κατά ἄνθρωπον (*kata anthrōpon*) translated "for merely human reasons" in the NIV conveys Paul's sense of doing things with only a human perspective (cf. the use of this prepositional phrase in 1 Cor 3:3; 9:8; Rom 3:5; Gal 3:15) and in this rhetorical setting without the eternal perspective of the resurrection life in view. That is, if he had only a secular viewpoint and fought with wild beasts, what would be gained? The answer, of course, is nothing.

Paul next raises the nihilistic implications of the denial of the resurrection. If there is no resurrection, Paul reasons, why not just turn to base hedonism and focus only on what this life provides? If there is no eternity in prospect, he asks, why not let this life be consumed with consumption and satisfaction of human appetites? The wording of Paul's statement is taken from the LXX rendering of Isa 22:13, though the sentiments were well known in antiquity outside of Jewish circles.

The apostle hardly believes that he is describing the lifestyle of every person who does not accept the resurrection. His point, which is also affirmed by some pagan authors, is that if there is no

---

[26]Barrett, *First Epistle*, p. 365.

[27]Calvin, *First Epistle*, pp. 332-333.

[28]Robertson and Plummer, *First Epistle of St. Paul*, p. 362; Kistemaker, *First Corinthians*, p. 561; Fee, *First Epistle*, p. 770.

future life, then one should find all meaning in the joys and satisfaction of earthly appetites.[29]

15:33 Do not be misled: "Bad company corrupts good character."

The introduction of the hedonistic theme in conjunction with the denial of the resurrection (see notes on 6:14) is continued in this verse. Both the imperative ("do not be misled," μὴ πλανᾶσθε, *mē planasthe*) and the content of the quotation demonstrate that Paul is still focused on the fact that denial of the resurrection promotes moral dissipation. 1 Cor 15:33 contains a statement found in a work of the pagan author Menander,[30] though it is not at all clear that one should understand this as a quotation since this statement may well have already passed into common use as a moral aphorism long before Paul's time. In any case, the apostle clearly means for it to be understood as an adage which awakens the Corinthians to the imminent spiritual danger they are in, a danger which arises from misconceptions about the resurrection and is manifested in moral laxity.

15:34 Come back to your senses as you ought, and stop sinning; for there are some who are ignorant of God — I say this to your shame.

The forceful imperatives of this verse reveal that Paul believes that some of his readers are involved in sinful behavior (ἁμαρτάνετε, *hamartanete*). Moreover, because of his shame-based rhetoric about the ignorance of God among others, he is making a contrast between believers who are not ignorant, but act like they are. In this rhetorical context of a discussion of the resurrection, he is probably alluding to the ignorance some have of the resurrection.

The intended outcome of Paul's argument is that the erring Corinthians should experience shame (πρὸς ἐντροπὴν ὑμῖν, *pros entropēn hymin*). The rhetorical force is that they are sinning in ways that could only be explained on the basis of a fundamental ignorance of God, an ignorance which they cannot rightfully claim.

---

[29]See evidence in Robertson and Plummer, *First Epistle of St. Paul*, p. 363.

[30]Menander, *Thais* 218.

C. ANSWERS TO SOME QUESTIONS
ABOUT THE RESURRECTION (15:35-58)

1. A Twofold Question (15:35-41)

[35]But someone may ask, "How are the dead raised? With what kind of body will they come?" [36]How foolish! What you sow does not come to life unless it dies. [37]When you sow, you do not plant the body that will be, but just a seed, perhaps of wheat or of something else. [38]But God gives it a body as he has determined, and to each kind of seed he gives its own body. [39]All flesh is not the same: Men have one kind of flesh, animals have another, birds another and fish another. [40]There are also heavenly bodies and there are earthly bodies; but the splendor of the heavenly bodies is one kind, and the splendor of the earthly bodies is another. [41]The sun has one kind of splendor, the moon another and the stars another; and star differs from star in splendor.

15:35 But someone may ask, "How are the dead raised? With what kind of body will they come?"

Paul here enters a new section of his argumentation. It is clear that he is offering a response to two resurrection related questions. These inquiries focus on how the dead are raised and what kind of bodies they will have after they are raised. The fact that he has to give such an extended answer to these issues demonstrates, in my judgment, that these details about the "mechanics" of the resurrection may have been the very stumbling block which kept Corinthian believers from belief. This perspective makes complete sense in light of the pagan skepticism about this issue and the metaphysical assumptions they lacked which would be required to believe in the bodily resurrection.

To be sure, pagan mythology and legends preserved select accounts of resurrections, but these were often resuscitations of a corpse which eventually died again. In no instances were these resurrections viewed as the firstfruits of a general future resurrection at which time death would be destroyed.

15:36 How foolish! What you sow does not come to life unless it dies.

Paul expresses in strong language his criticism for a believer who would ask such a question. "The implication is not simply that such questions suggest one to have taken leave of his senses, but that one stands as the 'fool' in the OT sense — as the person who has failed to take God into account."[31] This harsh criticism from the apostle is not directed against a person in whom faith is seeking a better understanding, but rather against doubt used in the service of aberrant disbelief and (probably) sins of immorality (15:32-34).

Paul introduces here an agricultural illustration of seed and sowing to answer the specific question mentioned in 15:35 about the body (σῶμα, *sōma*). The Christ-based work of "making alive" (15:22; from ζῳοποιέω, *zōopoieō*) is reintroduced here by the phrase "come to life" (also from *zōopoieō*) and teaches that this is not going to happen before the death of the body. The expression "what you sow" (ὅ σπείρεις, *ho speireis*) is Paul's euphemistic way to interpret the death and burial of an individual's body (cf. esp. the language of John 12:24). The specific point of the illustration is that, "Only by dissolution of the material particles in the seed is the germ of life . . . made to operate. . . . Dissolution and continuity are not incompatible."[32]

15:37 When you sow, you do not plant the body that will be, but just a seed, perhaps of wheat or of something else.

This verse begins with the identical expression found in 15:36 "what you sow" (*ho speireis*; obscured by the NIV translation). The body (*sōma*) placed in the ground at the time of burial is not merely resuscitated at the resurrection. It certainly is not the body that will be in the resurrection. If the body placed in the ground is not the body to be raised, just what is an appropriate illustration for this interred body? Paul compares the interred body to a

---

[31]Fee, *First Epistle*, p. 780.
[32]Robertson and Plummer, *First Epistle of St. Paul*, p. 369.

naked seed (γυμνὸν κόκκον, *gymnon kokkon*; NIV, just "a seed"), with the adjective "naked" (*gymnon*) perhaps anticipating its use in 2 Cor 5:3-4 ("because when we are clothed, we will not be found naked . . . because we do not wish to be unclothed but to be clothed with our heavenly dwelling").

His point is to affirm the basic truth of a continuity between the seed that is planted and the plant that comes up from the ground. Since all must acknowledge "that corruption is the origin and cause of reproduction . . . ," Calvin argues, "It follows, therefore, that our appraisal of the power of God is far too spiteful and ungrateful, if we do not ascribe to Him, which is already plain before our eyes."[33]

15:38 But God gives it a body as he has determined, and to each kind of seed he gives its own body.

This verse is in many ways the apostle's answer to the question of 15:35 ("with what kind of body will they come?"). The resurrection body will be what God has determined it to be. Retaining the use of the seed-body illustration, he reasons that just as God determines what the emerging plant will look like, so also God will give to the human body (=seed) the form and nature which he determines. Paul intentionally makes the description somewhat vague, though his points about: (1) life arising from decay and corruption; (2) continuity between the seed planted and the plant that arises from the ground; and (3) the role of divine determination in the process are straightforward.

15:39 All flesh is not the same: Men have one kind of flesh, animals have another, birds another and fish another.

Here Paul shifts in his illustration, but he has not significantly altered his point, a point that is aimed at answering the questions of 15:35 by means of illustrations from the natural world. While the term flesh (σάρξ, *sarx*) is not normally used as a synonym for body (*sōma*) in Paul's anthropology, these two terms are employed in the same way in the illustrations given in 15:35-41. His concern is to furnish additional illustrative material to undergird the fact

---

[33]Calvin, *First Epistle*, p. 336.

that a rigid naturalistic worldview which does not recognize that there could be more than one kind of flesh does not acknowledge the variety in nature itself. Since nature, in Paul's illustration, points toward the fact that "all flesh is not the same," these misguided Corinthian believers need to acknowledge that there might just be a kind of resurrection reality in which their bodies will not have to be the same as they are during the present.

Another perspective that is inherent in Paul's use of these varying kinds of flesh (e.g., human, animal, birds, and fish) is that each has a flesh that is appropriate to its own environment. Birds, for example, are given a body that is appropriate for the conditions in which God made them to live, but the flesh appropriate for birds should not be evaluated on the basis of the appropriateness of the flesh given to humans.

15:40 There are also heavenly bodies and there are earthly bodies; but the splendor of the heavenly bodies is one kind, and the splendor of the earthly bodies is another.

Having now given illustrations from the world of plant life and then animal life, Paul now turns to another dimension of nature to buttress his perspectives. Celestial objects are now the focus of his illustrations. He once again wants to emphasize the fact that the observable universe teaches against the idea of the necessity of the uniformity of bodies. Since there are both heavenly bodies (σώματα ἐπουράνια, *sōmata epourania*) and there are earthly bodies (σώματα ἐπίγεια, *sōmata epigeia*) that differ (ἑτέρα, *hetera*) from one another, it should not be hard to accept, Paul implies, that a believer's worldview should not be confined to a narrow view of only one type of human body. In light of "these myriads of differences in one and the same universe," would it not be unimaginable for Paul, Robertson and Plummer remark, "to place any limit to God's power with regard either to the difference between our present and our future body, or to the relations between them"?[34]

Paul's particular use of the term "splendor" (*doxa*) reveals that he is doing more than giving a mere illustration. This term *doxa* is such a significant eschatological term for the apostle (see esp.

---

[34]Robertson and Plummer, *First Epistle of St. Paul*, p. 371.

Rom 5:1; 8:18-30; 2 Cor 16-5:10) that there can be little doubt that he chose this term because of the splendor associated with the resurrection body, as he states in 1 Cor 15:43 (raised in *doxa*; this verbal link is destroyed in the NIV when it renders the word "splendor" in 15:40-41 and "glory" in 15:43).

This dichotomy between heavenly and earthly also anticipates a similar dichotomy given in 15:47-49.

15:41 The sun has one kind of splendor, the moon another and the stars another; and star differs from star in splendor.

Just as Paul gave specific examples of the variety within the animal kingdom (e.g., birds, fish), so here he gives specific examples from among the types of heavenly bodies. One of the most obvious differences to ancient mankind regarding the sun, the moon, and the stars was the differing degrees of their brightness, mentioned here with the term "splendor" (*doxa*). Even though this illustration is used to advance Paul's eschatological point, he did not intend to teach, thereby, that the raised saints themselves had various degrees of splendor, a notion concerning which Calvin rightly remarked, "it has nothing to do with what Paul has in mind here."[35]

2. An Explanation of the Resurrection of the Dead (15:42-50)

[42]**So will it be with the resurrection of the dead. The body that is sown is perishable, it is raised imperishable;** [43]**it is sown in dishonor, it is raised in glory; it is sown in weakness, it is raised in power;** [44]**it is sown a natural body, it is raised a spiritual body.**

If there is a natural body, there is also a spiritual body. [45]**So it is written: "The first man Adam became a living being"[e]; the last Adam, a life-giving spirit.** [46]**The spiritual did not come first, but the natural, and after that the spiritual.** [47]**The first man was of the dust of the earth, the second man from heaven.** [48]**As was the earthly man, so are those who are of the earth; and as is the man from heaven, so also are those who are of heaven.** [49]**And just as**

---

[35]Calvin, *First Epistle*, p. 337.

we have borne the likeness of the earthly man, so shall we^a bear the likeness of the man from heaven.

15:42 So will it be with the resurrection of the dead. The body that is sown is perishable, it is raised imperishable;

With the opening words "so will it be" (οὕτως, *houtōs*) Paul brings the preceding points to bear upon the misconceptions and doubts of certain of the Corinthians regarding the resurrection of the dead. The imagery of sowing and seed is picked up from the previous use of those metaphors in 15:36-38. The term "perishable" (φθορά, *phthora*) is found in other well known eschatological sections within Paul's letters (e.g., Rom 8:21; 1 Cor 15:50) and characterizes the decaying nature of the creation because of Adam's transgression. The counterpoint to being covered over by the soil in order to rot and decay is the resurrection into an imperishable state (ἀφθαρσία, *aphtharsia*). This concept of imperishability has already appeared in this letter with reference to the crown the believer receives (9:25; cf. 15:50, 52, 53, 54)

15:43 it is sown in dishonor, it is raised in glory; it is sown in weakness, it is raised in power;

The apostle here continues to utilize a series of antitheses to dramatically accentuate the radical transformation which occurs at the End. Concepts such as "dishonor" (ἀτιμία, *atimia*) and "weakness" (ἀσθένεια, *astheneia*) point in the direction of the concept of bondage and enslavement (Rom 8:21) which Paul associated with the decaying and terminal character of human existence. This was a form of human existence which could only be ameliorated by the vanquishing of God's last enemy (15:26).

The eschatological doctrine of the resurrection of the body "in glory" (ἐν δόξῃ, *en doxē*) taught here is also taught by Paul in Phil 3:21, "We eagerly await a Savior from there [i.e., heaven], the Lord Jesus Christ, who, by the power that enables him to bring everything under his control, will transform our lowly bodies so that they will be like his glorious body." The pregnant doctrine of "power" (δύναμις, *dynamis*) is used with great versatility by Paul in the Corinthian letters. The usage that one finds here is similar to the thoughts of 2 Cor 13:4, "To be sure, he was crucified in weakness (ἐξ ἀσθενείας, *ex astheneias*), yet he lives by God's power (ἐκ δυνάμεως, *ek dynameōs*)."

15:44 it is sown a natural body, it is raised a spiritual body. If there is a natural body, there is also a spiritual body.

There are two noteworthy points about Paul's wording in this section. First, Paul emphasizes the continuity between man's earthly and heavenly existence by the common use of the term "body" (σῶμα, *sōma*) in the phrases "natural body" (σῶμα ψυχικόν, *sōma psychikon*) and "spiritual body" (σῶμα πνευματικόν, *sōma pneumatikon*). Secondly, after affirming continuity on the basis of the common term *sōma*, he then accents the discontinuity by the antithetical terminology "natural" and "spiritual." The word "natural" summarizes all the concepts associated with the preceding words (15:42-43) such as perishable, dishonor, and weakness, while "spiritual" is aligned with ideas such as imperishable, glory, and power.

Since Paul uses the adjective "spiritual" (*pneumatikos*) to correct misconceptions in chapter 15 as well as in chapters 12-14, some interpreters have hastily concluded that the two problems are substantially connected. This hardly seems to be the case, viewed historically. The reason for the accentuated emphasis upon "spirit" and "spiritual" in the discussion of gifts in chapters 12-14 (as opposed to Paul's discussion of gifts in Rom 12 and Eph 4) is best explained by Paul's need to combat the abiding influence of Greco-Roman polytheism and animism among his neophyte converts.

In light of what we understand about Pauline theology, the obvious reason he would use the term "spiritual" in 1 Cor 15 is because of his widespread and abiding conviction that the Spirit was the personality of the triune Godhead which effected the resurrection of Jesus. The frequent Pauline preference (in occasions distinct from the one we find in Corinth) is to explain the resurrection of Jesus and its religious implications for believers, both present and eschatological, in terms of the Holy Spirit. It should not, therefore, strike the modern interpreter as so out of the ordinary when Paul describes the resurrection body as a spiritual body. The vocabulary and perspectives necessary for Paul to discuss the spiritual body are indigenous within Paul's own experiences and thoughts and do not require a Corinthian matrix to explain their place in the rhetoric and arguments of 1 Cor 15.

In the last part of 15:44 the apostle appeals to self-evident experience to begin an argument for the resurrection of the body. That is, the Corinthians would grant his premise that there is a natural body. Paul begins a deductive argument which will finally be rooted (15:45-48) in the authority of Scripture.

15:45 So it is written: "The first man Adam became a living being"; the last Adam, a life-giving spirit.

Paul offers here scriptural attestation for the proof of the preceding verse, that if there is a natural body, there is also a spiritual body. Gen 2, in particular the narrative of Adam's creation, supplies the text and vocabulary for Paul's interpretation of the resurrection body. Using the Adam-Christ illustration (some would call it typology), Paul aligns Adam with the natural body and Christ with the spiritual body. Paul's argumentation is based, in part, on word plays which cannot be adequately represented in an English translation. The Greek word rendered "natural" in 15:44 is ψυχικός (*psychikos*), which is an adjectival cognate of the noun ψυχή (*psychē*). This noun *psychē* is translated "being" in the phrase "became a living being" in 15:45. Accordingly, Paul constructs a parallelism between the natural body of 15:44 and the Adamic living being of Gen 2:7.

Christ's role in this illustration is brought under the heading of "the last Adam," with Paul focusing on the life-giving (see notes on *zōopoieō* at 1 Cor 15:36) work of Christ. To describe Christ's work with the phrase "life-giving spirit" is precisely what Paul is compelled to do since he is focused upon an argument about the spiritual (*pneumatikos*) nature of the resurrection body.

It is a smaller part of the apostle's exposition to point out the fact that Adam was the first man while Christ — the life-giving spirit — is the last Adam. This Adam/Christ paradigm functions in this argument as a model for the chronological aspect (first . . . last; πρῶτος . . . ἔσχατος, *prōtos* . . . *eschatos*) of the natural body/ spiritual body.

When Paul treats eschatological issues in his letters it is not unusual for him to interact with this chronological aspect. He frequently shapes his discussions of eschatology with references to the "already" character of what believers now possess as well as with references to the "not yet" character of what believers will only possess at the End. Those who know the apostle's writings encounter this Pauline concern in words and phrase such as fruit-fruits of the Spirit (Rom 8:23), the Spirit as a deposit that guarantees what is to come (2 Cor 1:22), the Spirit has been given to us to serve as a deposit to guarantee what is to come (2 Cor 5:5; Eph 1:13-14).

15:46 The spiritual did not come first, but the natural, and after that the spiritual.

Here Paul sees a need to draw upon the chronological arrangement outlined in the previous verse and reiterate the implication of the sequence of the first and last Adam. The NIV translation has omitted the initial Greek adversative word ἀλλά (*alla*), which should have been translated "but" and would have given a good sense of Paul's intent to oppose possible misconceptions among his readers. While most interpreters would agree with C.K. Barrett's assessment that here "Paul's eye is still on the main run of the argument,"[36] there is no such consensus when it comes to the details of the function of Paul's argument. Some, like C.K. Barrett,[37] have been attracted to the idea that Paul is countering a view of the Adamic creation maintained by certain Hellenized Jews of the period, exemplified by the Jewish author Philo of Alexandria. Others believe that the apostle is giving a counter argument against some form of Gnostic theology with its creation myths about the Primal Man. Kistemaker[38] follows Gordon Fee's lead when Fee writes,

> Against the Corinthians, who assumed that they had already entered into the totality of pneumatic existence while they were still in their *psychikos* body, Paul insists that the latter

---

[36]Barrett, *First Epistle*, p. 374.
[37]Ibid.
[38]Kistemaker, *First Corinthians*, p. 577.

come first, that is, that they must reckon with the physical side of their of their present life in the Spirit.[39]

Much of Fee's understanding of the church of God at Corinth is of a church replete with pneumatics (*pneumatikoi*) who have a misinformed eschatology.[40] Fee's reconstruction at this point is both ill-founded exegetically (e.g., 1 Cor 4:8) and seriously flawed historically (e.g., eschatological women) and one should not hastily consent to an interpretation based upon such shaky foundations.

There is an alternative interpretation which takes into account the Pauline emphasis upon first and last in 15:45-46, but is not so entwined with the problematic reconstructions that characterize the Hellenistic Jewish, the Gnostic, and the pneumatic interpretations. This alternate view takes its cue from the contextual issue of those believers, from a Gentile heritage, who deny the general resurrection (15:12), especially in terms of their questions that Paul raises in 15:35.

In the opening words of 15:42-49 Paul describes (by illustration) the resurrection ("So will it be," οὕτως, *houtōs*). It should be kept in mind that the point of contention between the apostle and the erring Corinthians (as it is represented in this chapter of the letter) is not over whether there is a post-mortem consciousness, but when will it begin to occur. To state it in words of pointed contrast, Paul's misinformed readers believed in "life after death," while Paul (specifically in this chapter) believed in life after the resurrection! When he writes about the resurrection, he can only be speaking about the resurrection that occurs at the End, at one time, for everyone who has died. This means then that for these misinformed Corinthians, their own eschatological hopes were actually impeded by Paul. In this particular argument he offers no words about the felicitous condition of the dead saints — they only sleep. When Paul puts such emphasis on the occurrence of the resurrection of the spiritual body at, and only at, the End, this would understandably engender some adverse feelings and disbe-

---

[39]Fee, *First Epistle*, p. 791.

[40]Ibid., pp. 10-14 and p. 711 where he identifies this as "the central issue" at Corinth).

lief among those Corinthians who hoped for and believed in a widely held post-mortem eschatology.

Turning again to the wording of 15:46, it should be remembered that for Paul the phrase "the natural body" does not just refer to the body's existence from the time of birth to the time of death. For Paul, in light of Adamic influence, the natural body remains natural (ψυχικόν, *psychikon*) until the Adamic influence is annihilated at the return of Christ and the End. The spiritual body, on the other hand, does not refer to the condition and state of the believer following his personal death, but rather to the body at, and only at, the time of Christ's return and the End.

It is in the light of this reconstruction that Paul would rightfully need to argue for the fact that the natural body must precede the spiritual. To the Corinthian believer whose belief in immediate and personal post-mortem bliss either negated or diminished the Pauline doctrine of the general resurrection at the End, Paul writes that the natural body (which extends to the End) must precede the spiritual body (which begins only at the general resurrection). This reconstruction of the historical setting fits well with the beliefs and hopes one could rightly expect from new believers in an urban Roman colony like Corinth. It also takes seriously the fact, not always understood by interpreters in the "Christian West," that denial of the resurrection is not at all the same as denial of the afterlife and an afterlife consisting of rewards and punishments.[41]

15:47 The first man was of the dust of the earth, the second man from heaven.

Paul continues here to expand his understanding on the basis of scriptural authority and allusion, taking his imagery and concepts from the idea of the creation of man "from the dust of the

---

[41]J.C. Beker, *Paul the Apostle*, p. 152, rightly observed that, "Resurrection language is end-time language and unintelligible apart from the apocalyptic thought world to which resurrection language belongs. Resurrection language properly belongs to the domain of the new age to come and is an inherent part of the transformation and the recreation of all reality in the apocalyptic age. Thus, the resurrection of Christ, the coming reign of God, and the future resurrection of the dead belong together."

ground" in Gen 2:7. He mentions the "first man" (πρῶτος ἄνθρωπος, *prōtos anthrōpos*) and with his description symbolically points to the natural state of the body. That is, Adam's creation from the earth depicts his perishability and his weakness since concerning Adam God spoke, "for dust you are, and to dust you will return" (Gen 3:19).

The second man Christ has an origin radically different from Adam's. Since Christ came from the divine and eternal realms rather than the transient and seen world (cf. 2 Cor 4:18), he vouchsafes splendor, power, and imperishability (cf. 15:42-43). As numerous orthodox commentators have pointed out, Paul is not teaching, as early heretics inferred, that Christ's body was not a human body. It is the farthest thing from Paul's mind and theology to teach that Christ arrived on earth in the womb of the blessed Mary with a heavenly and supernatural body.

15:48 As was the earthly man, so are those who are of the earth; and as is the man from heaven, so also are those who are of heaven.

Paul here begins his explicit correlation between the two Adams, the first man and the second man, and their human counterparts or clones. The twice used phrase "so are those who" links these two images with earthly descendants. Since Paul believed that the general resurrection included both the saved and unsaved, it will hardly do to interpret the Adam/Christ illustration here as though it provided nomenclature for the saved and unsaved. Presumably he still writes about the resurrection of bodies here. Unlike the Adam/Christ typology of Rom 5 where these two are more alternatives, the illustration of 1 Cor 15 is not given to provide a choice. Unless Paul has quickly leapt from the subject under discussion and jettisoned his consistent use of the Adam/Christ illustration in chapter 15, then these two figures point to the two modes of bodily existence. That is, in this world every believer's body is Adamic while at the resurrection every believer's body is the Second Adam's. This interpretation not only conforms to the flow of Paul's argument in this chapter, but also makes sense in light of the interpretation of Genesis drawn in 15:46 and the historical situation sketched above.

15:49 And just as we have borne the likeness of the earthly man, so shall we bear the likeness of the man from heaven.

In this verse Paul brings to an end the section of 15:42-49. He acknowledges here that mankind has borne the likeness of Adam and so is subject in this life to a body that is terminal. The limitations of the first man, mortality, naturalness and dust, are the hallmarks of bearing the first man's likeness (εἰκόνα, *eikona*). Paul then shifts to the future tense in the latter part of the verse.[42] By use of the future tense of the Greek verb Paul points to the future End when the believers will be "like Christ" and bear the image (*eikona*) of one who is the life-giving spirit (15:45). With this statement of future realities Paul brings to an end his eschatological plea and instruction based upon the image and message of the Adamic story and the Adam-Christ illustration. With his opening words of this verse "and just as" (καὶ καθώς, *kai kathōs*) Paul made it plain to his readers at Corinth that he was just as certain about his future existence in the spiritual body as he was certain about his past lifelong existence in the natural body, a body whose course had been set, though only temporarily, by Adam.

15:50 I declare to you, brothers, that flesh and blood cannot inherit the kingdom of God, nor does the perishable inherit the imperishable.

Regarding this verse Herman Ridderbos noted that Paul "brings to the fore the heart of the matter that is at stake in I Corinthians 15 with great force and with a final, conclusive ar-

---

[42]There is an important textual variant in the Greek manuscripts at this verse. The Greek manuscripts followed by, among others, the NIV translation read in the latter half of the verse "shall we bear," which is based upon the Greek word φορέσομεν (*phoresomen*). Other manuscripts and interpreters prefer the Greek word φορέσωμεν (*phoresōmen*), a word whose only difference in spelling is that the second "o" is long (an omega) rather than short (an omicron). This ostensibly minor difference in spelling changes the verb from the future tense of the indicative mood into the aorist tense of the subjunctive mood, which in turn, changes the translation from "we shall bear" into "Let us bear." This commentary follows the future indicative translation given in the NIV. A strong and erudite defense of the other view is given by Fee, *First Epistle*, pp. 794-795.

gument, i.e., that of its necessity and indispensability."[43] Paul organizes the thought in this verse on the basis of a parallelism in which flesh and blood in 15:50a is parallel with perishable in 15:50b and kingdom of God in 15:50a is parallel with the imperishable in 15:50b.

In the doctrinal context of Paul's argument in chapter 15 he is not referring to mankind's carnal nature or sinful character when he mentions flesh and blood. The expression "flesh and blood" (σὰρξ καὶ αἷμα, *sarx kai haima*) is found other places in Scripture (e.g., Gal 1:16; Matt 16:17; and in reversed order in Eph 6:12; Heb 2:14) and is usually understood to refer to the idea of human beings, especially as distinct from God. Kistemaker observed in this regard that, "The expression as such is a figure of speech for the physical body. It is a Semitic phrase that occurs repeatedly in rabbinic sources to denote the utter frailty and mortality for a human being."[44]

The phrase the kingdom of God is used at other locations by the apostle in 1 Corinthians, once in reference to the operation of ecclesiastical matters (4:20) and four times to refer to God's eschatological kingdom (6:9, 10; 15:24, 50). Just as God's eschatological rule will not brook either the immoral (6:9-10) or any unsubjugated powers and authority (15:24), neither will it abide the presence of humanity still tethered to Adamic corruption and mortality.

Now using the term "perishable" (φθορά, *phthora*) to describe mankind's situation and "imperishable" (ἀφθαρσίαν, *aphtharsian*) for the condition of eternal life and heaven, Paul teaches that the perishable cannot inherit the imperishable.

---

[43]Ridderbos, *Paul. An Outline of his Theology*, p. 546; Fee, *First Epistle*, p. 797, introduces the unit of 15:50-58 by describing it as "this magnificent crescendo" with which "Paul brings to a conclusion the argument that began in v. 35."

[44]Kistemaker, *First Corinthians*, p. 580.

3. The Secret Revealed (15:51-58)

[50]I declare to you, brothers, that flesh and blood cannot inherit the kingdom of God, nor does the perishable inherit the imperishable. [51]Listen, I tell you a mystery: We will not all sleep, but we will all be changed — [52]in a flash, in the twinkling of an eye, at the last trumpet. For the trumpet will sound, the dead will be raised imperishable, and we will be changed. [53]For the perishable must clothe itself with the imperishable, and the mortal with immortality. [54]When the perishable has been clothed with the imperishable, and the mortal with immortality, then the saying that is written will come true: "Death has been swallowed up in victory."[a]

[55]"Where, O death, is your victory?

Where, O death, is your sting?" [b]

[56]The sting of death is sin, and the power of sin is the law. [57]But thanks be to God! He gives us the victory through our Lord Jesus Christ.

[58]Therefore, my dear brothers, stand firm. Let nothing move you. Always give yourselves fully to the work of the Lord, because you know that your labor in the Lord is not in vain.

[a]*54* Isaiah 25:8   [b]*55* Hosea 13:14

15:51 Listen, I tell you a mystery: We will not all sleep, but we will all be changed —

Paul's command to the readers to "listen" (ἰδού, *idou*, other versions "behold" or "look") is an "emphatic introduction of information of great moment."[45] He is going to share with them divine revelation concerning the metamorphosis of living saints at the time of the return of Christ.

At this juncture Paul elaborates on the question of the fate of those still alive at the End. There has been a long scholarly debate on whether in the preceding verse Paul was referring to both those who would be alive (i.e., flesh and blood) as well as those

---

[45]Robertson and Plummer, *First Epistle of St. Paul*, p. 376.

who would be dead (the perishable). Regardless of the outcome of that debate, it is clear in this verse that Paul does address the question about the fate of those alive at the time of the Lord's return.

Whether or not the Corinthians had specifically asked Paul about the issue of the "rapture" of the living saints as mentioned in 1 Thess 4:13-18 is unclear. In any case, he obviously wanted the readers to understand the significance of his doctrines about the spiritual body and the return of Christ for those believers who were still alive. While Paul obviously longs for the return of Christ in his own lifetime (1 Cor 16:22; cf. 1:7-8), one is hard pressed to demonstrate that a "this generation timetable" is required by Paul's use of the first person plural ("*We* will not all sleep") or that such a timetable had become part of Paul's eschatological doctrine.[46] Calvin was of the opinion that,

> When he says *we shall be changed*, he counts himself among those who will be alive at the coming of Christ. Since it was already the last times, the saints were to expect that day every single hour. Although in his letter to the Thessalonians he makes that remarkable prophecy about the scattering of the Church that would occur before the coming of Christ, that does not prevent him from confronting the Corinthians with the event here and now, as it were, and being able to put himself and them alongside those who would be alive when the day came.[47]

Paul teaches that the transformation about which he has been writing will happen both for the dead and the living. Those who are alive at Christ's return will be changed (from ἀλλάσσω, *allassō*).

15:52 in a flash, in the twinkling of an eye, at the last trumpet. For the trumpet will sound, the dead will be raised imperishable, and we will be changed.

The succession of illustrations is used here for the sudden and cataclysmic nature of the End and the attendant change that will take place in the bodily nature of those raised. In the phrase "at

---

[46]Cf. Fee, *First Epistle,* p. 800.
[47]Calvin, *First Epistle*, p. 344.

the last trumpet" the concept of last should not be interpreted as the last in a series of endtime events, as some interpret the seven angels with seven trumpets in Rev 8:6-11:15, but last in the sense that Christ was the last Adam (cf. 1 Cor 15:45). The imagery of the divine trumpet was well known in Jewish materials, both in canonical and extracanonical literature. The sound of the trumpet was explicitly associated with, among other things, the theophany at Mt. Sinai (Exod 19:13, 16, 19; 20:18; cf. Ps 47:5; Zech 9:14), with the victory of Holy War (Josh 6:5; Judg 7:18), with enthronement of kings (2 Sam 15:10; 1 Kgs 1:34, 39; 2 Kgs 9:13), with periods of consecrated worship (Lev 23:24; 25:9; Ps 81:3; Joel 2:15; cf. Isa 27:13) and with the sound of preparation for battle (Judg 3:27; Neh 4:20; Job 39:25; Jer 4:19-21; 51:27; Joel 2:1; Zeph 1:16).

With the rich use of this imagery in Jewish writings, it is no wonder that it is found in the teaching of Jesus, "And he [i.e., the Son of Man] will send his angels with a loud trumpet call, and they will gather his elect from the four winds" (Matt 24:31) and in other Pauline eschatological texts, "For the Lord himself will come down from heaven, with a loud command, with the voice of the archangel, and with the trumpet call of God, and the dead in Christ will rise first" (1 Thess 4:16).

It would be unwise to try to be too narrow in defining Paul's emphasis with the trumpet imagery here. In all probability Paul's use included elements of theophany, military victory and enthronement (cf. 15:24-28), and "summoning the dead from their graves."[48] Although it is not germane to the apostle's point in chapter 15, the reader should not forget that Paul had previously taught the Corinthians that the saints will participate in the eschatological judgment of the world (1 Cor 6:2).

Paul mentions the destiny of all saints in the closing words of this verse. Those who have died prior to the End will be raised up in a spiritual body, while those who are alive at the End will undergo a transformation. This verse makes it certain that Paul linked this resurrection of the saints to the return of Christ at the End, when the trumpet sounds.

---

[48]Fee, *First Epistle*, p. 802.

15:53 For the perishable must clothe itself with the imperishable, and the mortal with immortality.

Paul employs here a form of parallelism of thought. The terms "perishable" (φθαρτόν, *phtharton*) and "mortal" (θνητόν, *thnēton*) form one of the parallel groups, while the terms "imperishable" (ἀφθαρσίαν, *aphtharsian*) and "immortality" (ἀθανασίαν, *athanasian*) form the other. The NIV omits the translation of the Greek term δεῖ (*dei*) which means "it is necessary"; this term was used by Paul to affirm the fact that it was the divine decree of God (according to 15:54-55 prophesied in Scripture) that this process must happen.

The imagery of being clothed or clothing oneself (e.g., put off; put on) is utilized by Paul in portions of his letters when he deals with salvation (Gal 3:28), sanctification (Rom 13:12, 14; Eph 4:24; 6:11, 14; Col 3:10, 12; 1 Thess 5:8) and eschatology (1 Cor 15:53, 54; 2 Cor 5:3).

15:54 When the perishable has been clothed with the imperishable, and the mortal with immortality, then the saying that is written will come true: "Death has been swallowed up in victory."

Paul repeats the affirmations given in the preceding verse and grounds them in the truth and attestation of Scripture. Witherington observes that this is "the only place in his letters where Paul cites an OT text as a prophecy yet to be fulfilled."[49] This Scripture given in 15:54 is found in Isa 25:8, which is taken from a larger four chapter section of Isaiah (24-27) that is replete with eschatological vocabulary and themes. Paul points to a time when death itself is destroyed and only God's victory survives.

15:55 "Where, O death, is your victory? Where, O death, is your sting?"

Paul continues his quotation from Scripture but moves now to Hosea 13:14. A comparison of 1 Cor 15:55 with Hosea 13:14 reveals that Paul is not giving a direct quotation. The wording of Paul's citation is so different from the Hebrew and Greek Old Testament texts in Hosea 13:14 that Calvin was not certain that the

---

[49]Witherington, *Conflict and Community in Corinth*, p. 310.

apostle was even attempting to quote the Hosea text. He comments,

> I am quite clear in my own mind that he did not really intend to use the prophet's testimony here, so as to take advantage of his authority, but, in passing, simply adapted to his own purpose a saying which had passed into common currency. . . ."[50]

In this quotation death personified is taunted. Picking up on the term "victory" (νῖκος, *nikos*) in 15:54, Paul here points out that death's current victory is only apparent and temporary. In light of the coming End, death is stripped of its ostensible victory over mankind.

Next he mentions the sting (κέντρον, *kentron*) which death has temporarily used against mankind, but does not really describe this sting until the following verse.

15:56 The sting of death is sin, and the power of sin is the law.

Both the exact meaning of certain ideas in this verse and the rhetorical function of this sentence in the Corinthian setting have puzzled interpreters. Fee mentions "the dissonance these words seem to bring to the argument."[51] Holladay understands the general sense of Paul's words in the following way,

> The sting which death brings is the result of sin; prior to the first resurrection, the world still lived under the force and power of sin (Satan), and the continuance of death documents its continued power. But sin exhibits its power through the law. . . . These three things — sin, law, and death — represented to Paul the three essential ingredients of the world order whose doom was sealed when God raised Christ from the dead.[52]

---

[50]Calvin, *First Epistle*, p. 346.

[51]Fee, *First Epistle*, p. 805; at footnote 41 he notes interpreters who have thought that these words were a later gloss.

[52]Holladay, *First Letter*, pp. 211-12.

While it will be several months after this letter when Paul pens his famous letter to the Romans and develops, for contextual reasons, this relationship between law, death, and sin (especially chapters 5-8), he states it plainly here that physical death is inextricably tied (fundamentally in Adam, 15:21, 45ff) to the spiritual problem of sin and mankind's failure to relate to God's law properly.

15:57 But thanks be to God! He gives us the victory through our Lord Jesus Christ.

Picking up on the theme of eschatological victory over death that was introduced in 15:54-55, Paul affirms that victory has been ripped from death through Jesus Christ and given to believers. He locates the sources of this victory in God himself, since he was the one who gave the victory to believers through his work in the Lord Jesus Christ.

15:58 Therefore, my dear brothers, stand firm. Let nothing move you. Always give yourselves fully to the work of the Lord, because you know that your labor in the Lord is not in vain.

C.K. Barrett observed,

> It calls for no great effort of the imagination to hear Paul's vehement preaching in the climax of this paragraph, but he is not the kind of preacher to finish his discourse . . . in pure rhetoric. His apocalypse, and the enthusiasm with which he expounds it, are directed to a practical goal.[53]

Anyone familiar with Paul's use of the doctrine of the resurrection in letters such as Romans or Ephesians knows that "For Paul resurrection, both Christ's and the Christian's, is the basis for a new moral order."[54] His use of the term "therefore" (ὥστε, hōste) is a grammatical indication of this connection between the lengthy preceding doctrinal arguments and the imperatives of this verse about the believer's *life* and *attitudes*. Consequently, one would expect Paul to end this section, just as at 15:32-34, with admoni-

---

[53]Barrett, *First Epistle*, p. 384.
[54]Witherington, *Conflict and Community in Corinth*, p. 311.

tions about the believer's life and his participation in the work of the Lord.[55]

The admonitions of standing firm and being unmoved probably refer to Corinthian attitudes and loyalties toward the gospel "on which you have taken your stand" (15:1) and by which "you are saved, if you hold firmly to the word I preached to you" (15:2). Since the phrase "in the work of the Lord" is in a sentence beginning with "my dearest brothers" (even though they doubt the general resurrection and are foolish, cf. notes at 15:36), the work of the Lord must be a concept that includes all that is incumbent upon the life and lifestyle of every believer. Paul's point is made clearer by his later reference to their "labor in the Lord." We can only conclude that even though Paul disdains all efforts at self-righteousness and justification by human effort (Rom 1-4; Eph 2; Phil 3), work and labor were incumbent not only on the apostolic lifestyle (cf. 1 Cor 15:10), but also upon all believers who have received the victory of God mediated through the Lord Jesus Christ (15:57). Full abandonment to the work of the Lord is the normal believer's life for the apostle and "doing nothing is *not* a Pauline option."[56]

Paul began this chapter with a reference to the vanity of the believer's life without the gospel of the resurrection (15:1-2, 14) and appropriately ends it with the reverse implication that their years of labor and loyalty in response to the message of the resurrection will not be in vain. According to Paul's gospel this is the only implication that one could draw in light of God's victory (νῖκος, *nikos*) that had already been been awarded to believers (15:57), a victory attested by Scripture (15:3-4, 25-27, 32, 44-49, 53-56) and rooted in the resurrection of Jesus of Nazareth from the dead.

---

[55]Fee is of the opinion that, "The surprising feature of this exhortation is that, unlike vv. 33-34, it is not directed toward ethical behavior as such, but toward the work of the gospel," *First Epistle*, p. 807.

[56]J.P. Sampley, *Walking Between the Times. Paul's Moral Reasoning*, p. 101.

1 CORINTHIANS 16

IX. INSTRUCTION FOR THE COLLECTION (16:1-11)

A. THE COLLECTION FOR GOD'S PEOPLE (16:1-4)

[1]Now about the collection for God's people: Do what I told the Galatian churches to do. [2]On the first day of every week, each one of you should set aside a sum of money in keeping with his income, saving it up, so that when I come no collections will have to be made. [3]Then, when I arrive, I will give letters of introduction to the men you approve and send them with your gift to Jerusalem. [4]If it seems advisable for me to go also, they will accompany me.

16:1 Now about the collection for God's people: Do what I told the Galatian churches to do.

In verses 1-4 we find the apostle Paul treating the issue of a specific collection for the saints in Judea. He introduces this subject with the phrase "now about," (περὶ δέ, *peri de*) a phrase which he first used in 7:1. It is often thought that he employs this when he brings up issues that the Corinthians wrote to him about. It is plain in this section that this is a one-time special collection for the churches in Judea. There is no evidence from this text that Paul is attempting to establish a prescriptive pattern or practice for a weekly Christian contribution.[1]

In 16:1b Paul does indicate that the directions he is giving to the Corinthians are the same directions that he had given earlier

---

[1]On financial matters in Paul's letters see J.M. Everts, "Financial Support," *DPL*, pp. 295-300.

to the churches of Galatia. This is also the same collection that will be addressed at greater length in 2 Cor 8-9. Accordingly, we can tell from this evidence that the same instruction about this special collection had been given to the churches of Galatia, the churches of Achaia, and the churches of Macedonia.

16:2 On the first day of every week, each one of you should set aside a sum of money in keeping with his income, saving it up so that when I come no collections will have to be made.

While there are many questions about this collection that Paul does not answer for us, there are a few things that he makes clear. First of all, the instruction about giving is addressed to each of those in the Corinthian congregation. Secondly, he wishes them to collect these funds, or perhaps to reserve and put aside these funds, on a weekly basis. The wisdom of collecting funds on the first day of every week is obvious since that is when early Christians typically assembled. Interestingly, this weekly contribution is not for any ministries, overhead costs, or salaries arising from Christian activities in Corinth. These Sunday "collections" were only for an ad hoc need related to congregations in one small region of the Eastern Mediterranean. It is also clear that Paul wants them to set aside an amount that is appropriate to their own financial resources. Neither Paul nor any other writer in the New Testament addresses the practice of soliciting a tithe from Christians. And finally he makes it clear that he wants this done prior to his arrival so that once he is there, there is no longer a need for the money to be collected. It is important to keep in mind that this concern about not taking up money once Paul himself arrives needs to be seen in the context of Paul's hesitancy to accept money from the Corinthians.

In 1 Cor 9 Paul makes it clear that he wants to be financially independent from the Corinthians, and that he is concerned that his ministry not be viewed in terms of one that is based solely on the remuneration given to him by the Corinthians. This theme is continued in 2 Corinthians where Paul makes it clear again that when he worked among the Corinthians he was supported by Christians in other cities, so that his integrity with them would not be compromised (see 2 Cor 10-13). In this regard Paul is concerned that he not be viewed as some Greek sophist who merely speaks because of the money he receives in return for it. It is not at all clear what antecedent practices in Judaism would provide the appropriate background for Paul's instruction here concerning the contribution. We do know from intertestamental Jewish writings that the Jews who lived outside Jerusalem continued to collect money in the synagogues and send that money to Jerusalem to pay their temple tax in support of the Jerusalem temple service of the priests. In the instance of 1 Corinthians, the particular goal of this contribution was to offer benevolence to those believers who were in Jerusalem and Judea.[2]

16:3 Then, when I arrive, I will give letters of introduction to the men you approve and send them with your gift to Jerusalem.

Paul makes it clear that he wants the money to actually be carried to Jerusalem by individuals from the churches who have given the money. Consequently, he tells the Corinthians in 16:3 that he will give letters of introduction to the people who have been selected by the Corinthian church, and these letters of introduction will accompany these individuals with the money to Jerusalem. It is clear that Paul himself has no personal investment in the decision about whether he accompanies these believers to Jerusalem. We do know from later developments in his life (revealed in Romans and Acts) though that he did in fact accompany these funds to Jerusalem.[3]

16:4 If it seems advisable for me to go also, they will accompany me.

Paul does not indicate what criteria would be used to decide whether it was advisable for him to go. The suggestion has been made that this group of individuals who accompany Paul are referred to in passing in Acts 20. One can make an interesting correlation between Paul's letter and the narrative in Acts 20 when Paul departs from Ephesus, which is at the approximate time he pens the Corinthian letters. In reading the first six verses of Acts 20 one finds the names of individual Christian men who in fact come

---

[2]In general S. McKnight, "Collection for the Saints," *DPL*, pp. 143-147.
[3]R.H. Stein, "Jerusalem," *DPL*, pp. 472-473.

from some of the very regions which have made contributions to this collection mentioned in 1 Cor 16. Specifically, in Acts 20:4 there are references to those accompanying Paul at this point in his life, who come from the regions of Macedonia and Asia Minor. Even though in Acts Luke refers to the cities in these provinces and not to the particular provincial names, the following chart shows the points of probable correlation between the two:

1 Corinthians	Acts 20:4
Donations From	Accompanied By
1. Galatia (1 Cor 16:1)	1. Gaius of Derbe (Galatia)
2. Macedonia (2 Cor 8-9)	2. Aristarchus and Secundus of Thessalonica (Macedonia) Sopater of Beroea (Macedonia)

Apparently Paul's instructions given in this section of 1 Cor 16 were not followed, or at least not followed in the right way. One discovers later in 2 Cor 8-9 that Paul has to spend considerable time instructing the Corinthians about this contribution. He gently reminds them of their tardiness in coming up with these funds which they had promised to give.

B. PAUL'S TRAVEL PLANS (16:5-9)

[5]After I go through Macedonia, I will come to you — for I will be going through Macedonia. [6]Perhaps I will stay with you awhile, or even spend the winter, so that you can help me on my journey, wherever I go. [7]I do not want to see you now and make only a passing visit; I hope to spend some time with you, if the Lord permits. [8]But I will stay on at Ephesus until Pentecost, [9]because a great door for effective work has opened to me, and there are many who oppose me.

16:5 After I go through Macedonia, I will come to you — for I will be going through Macedonia.

Paul acknowledges in this verse that when he leaves Ephesus he will make his way to Achaia, to the city of Corinth, via Macedonia. This itinerary is confirmed in Acts 20:1-2, though Luke prefers the term Greece over Achaia in this instance.[4]

16:6 Perhaps I will stay with you awhile, or even spend the winter, so that you can help me on my journey, wherever I go.

Paul acknowledges in this verse that he intends to spend a few months with the Corinthians so that he can reestablish ties with them and that they may become supportive of his future ministerial work. Verse 6 also makes it clear that Paul is not certain at that point where he will be going when he leaves the city of Corinth. Having left a tumultuous and dangerous work in Ephesus, the Apostle knows the vicissitudes of his ministry and plans for travel (cf. Acts 20:19; 2 Cor 1:3-2:4).

16:7 I do not want to see you now and make only a passing visit; I hope to spend some time with you, if the Lord permits.

In this verse Paul justifies his delay in coming to them by saying that if he comes now it can only be for a short visit, but if he can wait and come later he will be able to stay longer with them. By use of the phrase "if the Lord permits," Paul reveals his conviction about the presence of God in his activities and itinerary. The book of Acts is filled with vignettes and statements pointing in the same direction (Acts 16:6-10; 18:21; 19:21; 22:17-21; 27:23-26).

16:8 But I will stay on at Ephesus until Pentecost,

By this statement Paul indicates both that he is writing the letter of 1 Corinthians from Ephesus and that he plans to remain there until the day of Pentecost. The reference to Pentecost indicates that Paul still thinks very much in terms of the Jewish liturgical feasts.[5] There is no indication that believers at this time were celebrating Pentecost from a Christian point of view. It is far too early in church history for people to think of Pentecost as the "birthday of the church." It is most natural to understand this reference to Pentecost as a reference to the Jewish holiday which

---

[4]On Paul's travels see P. Trebilco, "Itineraries, Travel Plans, Journeys, Apostolic Parousia," *DPL*, pp. 446-456.

[5]D.R. de Lacey, "Holy Days," *DPL*, pp. 402-404.

Paul himself would have honored as a Pharisee (cf. Acts 21:24; 23:6).

16:9 because a great door for effective work has opened to me, and there are many who oppose me.

In this verse the apostle gives the reason why he hopes to stay on longer in Ephesus. He acknowledges in verse 9a that there is a great door that has been opened for him by the Lord (cf. notes on 16:7) to be involved in an effective work. In the latter part of the verse he acknowledges, though, that this work will only be accomplished in spite of the great opposition against him and his ministry there.

There has been discussion about the relationship between the statements of 1 Cor 16:9 and the narrative presented in Acts 19. Both points found in 1 Cor 16:9, namely the great opportunities there and the great opposition to the gospel are also mentioned in the narrative in Acts. If one looks at the total evidence from the Acts of the Apostles concerning Paul's ministry in Ephesus, it is clear that ministry was characterized both by great opportunity for success and the reality of great adversity. While Acts 19 focuses more on the Pauline successes in Ephesus, chapter 20, when Paul speaks to the Ephesian elders, is clearly about the great adversities that he experienced during his ministry there (Acts 20:17-38). Paul's own references in 2 Cor 1 to the traumatic experiences he had in Asia must certainly include his extended ministry in Ephesus.

C. ASSISTING TIMOTHY (16:10-11)

[10]**If Timothy comes, see to it that he has nothing to fear while he is with you, for he is carrying on the work of the Lord, just as I am.** [11]**No one, then, should refuse to accept him. Send him on his way in peace so that he may return to me. I am expecting him along with the brothers.**

16:10 If Timothy comes, see to it that he has nothing to fear while he is with you, for he is carrying on the work of the Lord, just as I am.

This is the second time in 1 Corinthians that Paul mentions his co-worker Timothy. In 4:17 Paul had already mentioned Timothy as his son in the faith and as a faithful co-worker in the Lord.[6] When one reads in this verse that Paul is remaining in Asia and sending Timothy over into Greece, one is reminded of the corresponding text in Acts 19:21-22 which narrates Paul's stay in Ephesus. Acts 19:21 records Paul's decision to head to Jerusalem via Macedonia and Achaia as well as the fact that he would send ahead of him Timothy and Erastus to Macedonia. In 1 Cor 16:10 Paul is expressing to the Corinthians his hope that they will express solidarity with Timothy and the ministry that he is involved in.

16:11 No one, then, should refuse to accept him. Send him on his way in peace so that he may return to me. I am expecting him along with the brothers.

Paul indicates in this verse not only his desire that the Corinthians should participate with the work of Timothy, but also that Paul expects Timothy to return to him in Asia after he has completed his work in Greece. We do not know with certainty who the other brothers are who are mentioned in 16:11, but it would have been obvious to the Corinthians whom Paul had in mind.

X. CONCLUSION (16:12-24)

A. PERSONAL REQUESTS (16:12-18)

[12]Now about our brother Apollos: I strongly urged him to go to you with the brothers. He was quite unwilling to go now, but he will go when he has the opportunity.

---

[6]On Paul and his co-workers consult E.E. Ellis, "Coworkers, Paul and His," *DPL*, pp. 183-189.

¹³**Be on your guard; stand firm in the faith; be men of courage; be strong. ¹⁴Do everything in love.**

¹⁵**You know that the household of Stephanas were the first converts in Achaia, and they have devoted themselves to the service of the saints. I urge you, brothers, ¹⁶to submit to such as these and to everyone who joins in the work, and labors at it. ¹⁷I was glad when Stephanas, Fortunatus and Achaicus arrived, because they have supplied what was lacking from you. ¹⁸For they refreshed my spirit and yours also. Such men deserve recognition.**

16:12 Now about our brother Apollos: I strongly urged him to go to you with the brothers. He was quite unwilling to go now, but he will go when he has the opportunity.

One's interpretation of Paul's comments about Apollos in 16:12 must be interpreted in light of the other comments about Apollos found in chapters 1, 3, and 4.[7] The earlier references to Apollos are in the context of the fragmentation in the Corinthian community. It is clear in Paul's references to Apollos in those early chapters that he does not see himself at odds with Apollos. Rather, he and Apollos both work to spread the same gospel. Paul had apparently urged Apollos to make a trip to Corinth along with Timothy and other Christian brothers. It is equally clear that Apollos declined this request and decided he was not ready to go at that time. Even though Paul acknowledges that Apollos disregarded his apostolic wishes, he does not regard this as grounds for questioning Apollos' orthodoxy or the important role he has in the Christian mission. Paul concludes by stating that Apollos will go when he has the opportunity.

16:13 Be on your guard; stand firm in the faith; be men of courage; be strong.

Most commentators correctly see 16:13 as the beginning of the final section of 1 Corinthians. All four of the imperatives in this verse are clearly designed to serve a hortatory function and to express the seriousness of Paul's appeal to the Corinthians. The occurrence of the prepositional phrase "in the faith" indicates that

---

[7]In general see B.B. Blue, "Apollos," *DPL*, pp. 37-39.

Paul can use the term "faith" (πίστις, *pistis*) to refer not only to trusting God, but also to the content of his Christian message (cf. Jude 3).[8] In general the imagery of 16:13 is similar to that which will be found later in Eph 6:10ff, where Paul gives hortatory imperatives using the illustration of God's armor.

16:14 Do everything in love.

In the final imperative in this section, Paul reiterates the importance of love (see notes on 13:4-7).

16:15 You know that the household of Stephanas were the first converts in Achaia, and they have devoted themselves to the service of the saints. I urge you, brothers,

It has often been noted that in 1 Corinthians Paul does not refer to church leaders in the conventional vocabulary that he uses in other epistles (e.g., Phil 1:1).[9] For example, there are no references to elders or shepherds in 1 Corinthians, and there is certainly no attention given to the role of any leaders in helping to administer Paul's theology in the Christian community there. Interestingly, Paul introduces in 16:15 the household of Stephanas in the context of those to whom the Corinthians are to submit themselves. This household of Stephanas is singled out as the first converts in Achaia, and by the fact that they are devoted in Christian service to the saints.

16:16 to submit to such as these and to everyone who joins in the work, and labors at it.

Paul finishes the line of thought started in 16:15 with an object clause (ἵνα, *hina*). The urging that Paul mentions at the last part of 16:15 is completed in 16:16 when he says that he urges the Corinthians to submit themselves to those of the house of Stephanas. Furthermore, Paul says that the Corinthians should not only submit to those of the house of Stephanas, but also to those who are joined in the Christian work and activities in Corinth.

---

[8]L. Morris, "Faith," *DPL*, pp. 290-291.

[9]This complex issue is discussed by R. Banks, "Church Order and Government," *DPL*, pp. 131-137.

There are historical facts that provide part of the landscape for Paul's comments about leaders. It is true, for example, that synagogues contemporary with the Second Temple had formally designated leadership, both male and female, and that Paul himself referred to leaders as holding gifted offices. Even early on Paul included these leaders among the addressees in a Macedonian church (Phil 1:1). What remains yet a thorny problem for the modern interpreter is why the Corinthian church had no bishops and deacons like, for example, the Philippian church only 250 miles to the north (Phil 1:1) or the Ephesian church (Acts 20:17, 28) which was less than a week's journey to the east and of which the Corinthians had firsthand knowledge. Part of the answer may lie in evidence found in the pages of Scripture. Stretching from Genesis to the Gospels, the Scriptures are replete with the conviction that there are qualifications and requirements imposed upon those who would lead in God's economy of leadership. In light of the raucous demeanor, childish theology and neophyte status of so many of the Corinthians in the church of God, Paul may well have decided that none were qualified to be formal leaders.

16:17 I was glad when Stephanas, Fortunatus and Achaicus arrived, because they have supplied what was lacking from you.

Paul continues his discussion of Stephanas by also including a reference to Fortunatus and Achaicus and their arrival in Ephesus. 1 Cor 16:17b indicates that these three men are part of a delegation that had been sent by the Corinthians in their ongoing relationship with the apostle Paul. Gordon Fee is quite right in his commentary when he notes that "the three together would become a kind of official delegation from the church" at Corinth.[10] Although we cannot be certain, it is clearly possible that Fortunatus and Achaicus could be members of the household of Stephanas referred to earlier in 16:15. Paul also acknowledges in this verse that the arrival of these three men compensated for what was not supplied by the Corinthians themselves. Paul's reference here to the inadequacy of the Corinthians being supplied by these three men is probably designed to heighten the Corinthi-

---

[10]Fee, *First Epistle*, p. 832.

ans' appreciation for and loyalty to this family. This understanding would surely fit within the context of Paul's previous comments about the need for the Corinthians to submit to this household.

16:18 For they refreshed my spirit and yours also. Such men deserve recognition.

Paul mentions specifically that what was lacking on the part of the Corinthians that the household of Stephanas satisfied was the refreshment of Paul's spirit. That is made clear by the use of the word "for" at the beginning of 16:18. The presence of these men was able to refresh Paul's spirit in a way that could not be done by the entire Corinthian church since they had not come to see Paul in Ephesus. Paul also acknowledges that these three men in the household of Stephanas provide encouragement and refreshment to the spirit of the Corinthians also. The verse concludes by pointing out the relationship between this service provided and the authority that this household is to have among the Corinthians.

Verse 18b in the Greek text contains the inferential particle "therefore" (οὖν, *oun*) which has been left out of the NIV. With the occurrence of this word "therefore," Paul makes it clear that this is the reason the authority of this household should be recognized, namely because of their participation in service to Paul and, in general, to the saints in Achaia.

B. FINAL GREETINGS (16:19-24)

[19]**The churches in the province of Asia send you greetings. Aquila and Priscilla[a] greet you warmly in the Lord, and so does the church that meets at their house. [20]All the brothers here send you greetings. Greet one another with a holy kiss.**

[21]**I, Paul, write this greeting in my own hand.**

[22]**If anyone does not love the Lord — a curse be on him. Come, O Lord[b]!**

²³**The grace of the Lord Jesus be with you.**
²⁴**My love to all of you in Christ Jesus. Amen.** ᶜ

ᵃ*19* Greek *Prisca*, a variant of *Priscilla*　　ᵇ*22* In Aramaic the expression *Come, O Lord* is *Marana tha.*　　ᶜ*24* Some early manuscripts do not have *Amen.*

16:19 The churches in the province of Asia send you greetings. Aquila and Priscilla greet you warmly in the Lord, and so does the church that meets at their house.

As the apostle does at the ending of other letters he wrote, he concludes this letter with greetings from other congregations and saints in his part of the world to those to whom he is writing. In particular he sends the greetings from the churches in the province of Asia. One must keep in mind that Ephesus, the city in which Paul is located, is the cultural and political capital of the Roman province of Asia referred to here. Paul also mentions Aquila and Priscilla who had been his associates and co-workers since the time of his second missionary journey (Acts 18). Paul not only passes on greetings from this couple, but also acknowledges that Christian greetings come from the house church associated with Aquila and Priscilla. This is one of the several references throughout the Pauline letters to the phenomenon of churches meeting in the homes of individual Christians.

16:20 All the brothers here send you greetings. Greet one another with a holy kiss.

In this verse Paul passes on a general greeting from all the brethren with whom he is in contact. He admonishes the Christians in Corinth to greet one another with the holy kiss. This is one of several references in the letters of Paul and 1 Peter which make clear how widespread the practice of the holy kiss was in the early church. A quick tabulation of the Roman provinces in which this practice was commanded shows that this was not merely a peculiar regional practice within certain Pauline churches.

Geographical Dissemination of the Holy Kiss

Achaia	1 Cor 16:20
	2 Cor 13:12
Macedonia	1 Thess 5:26
Italy	Rom 16:16
Pontus	1 Pet 5:14
Galatia	1 Pet 5:14
Cappadocia	1 Pet 5:14
Asia	1 Pet 5:14 (cf. Ephesus
	as origin of 1 & 2 Cor)
Bithynia	1 Pet 5:14

16:21 I, Paul, write this greeting in my own hand.

Paul's acknowledgment that he writes this verse with his own hand indicates that the prior part of the letter was written by a scribe. Secondly, this reference to his own hand serves as a form of authentication to indicate that the letter comes from Paul himself, not someone merely claiming to represent Paul's views (cf. 2 Thess 2:2).

16:22 If anyone does not love the Lord — a curse be on him. Come, O Lord!

Paul has very terse comments in this verse for those who do not love the Lord. Paul consigns them to condemnation and coming under the wrath of God (ἀνάθεμα, *anathema*). The verse ends with Paul's citation of two Aramaic words (מרנא אתה, Greek μαράνα θά, *marana tha*) which were merely transliterated rather than translated in Paul's Greek letter to the Corinthians. Paul's petition is for the Lord to come. This indicates not only Paul's eschatological piety in his desire for the Lord to return, but also points to the eschatological condemnation that will come upon those who do not love the Lord. It would be at the risk of modernizing and distorting Paul's own theology if one minimized the close connection in this verse between eschatological piety and the damnation of nonbelievers. That is, Paul's desire for the Lord's (quick) return is to bring to fruition and consummation the anathema he has just pronounced upon those who do not love the Lord. [11] In the Corinthian setting the phrase "anyone who does not love the Lord" would refer to nonbelievers.

16:23 The grace of the Lord Jesus be with you.

The sentiments of this closing comment is similar to those located at the end of other Pauline letters. Unlike those upon whom Paul denounces a condemnation if they do not love God, Paul pronounces a blessing upon the Christians. In this verse Paul pronounces the grace of the Lord Jesus Christ upon the recipients of the letter.

16:24 My love to all of you in Christ Jesus. Amen.

Paul concludes the letter appropriately with a reference to his own love for those in Corinth who are in Christ Jesus. It is indicative of Paul's graciousness that his love is for all of those who are in Christ Jesus in Corinth and not merely those who happen to agree with his own theology. It has been clear throughout the book that the Corinthian church had its share of those who were detractors from Paul. The apostle, nevertheless, shares with them the love that he has for all of them.

---

[11]On other views see R.Y.K. Fung, "Curse, Accursed, Anathema," *DPL*, pp. 199-200.